Canal Zone Richard Prince YES
RASTA: Selected Court Documents
from Cariou v. Prince et al, including
The Videotaped Deposition of
Richard Prince, the Affidavit of
Richard Prince, Competing
Memoranda of Law in Support of
Summary Judgment, Exhibits
pertaining to Paintings and
Collages of Richard Prince and The
Use of Reproductions of Patrick
Cariou's Yes Rasta Photographs
Therein, And The Summary Ass
Whooping Dealt Prince By The
Hon. Judge Deborah A. Batts,
as compiled and revised by
Greg Allen for greg.org, April 2011

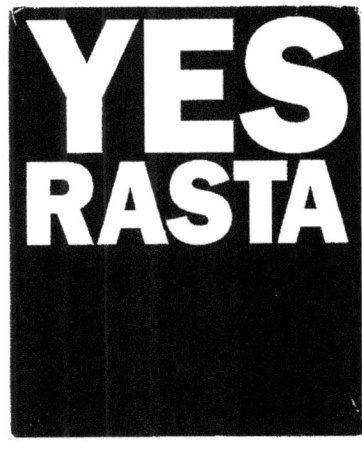

CONTENTS

Cariou v. Prince; SDNY Docket No. 08-11327

RICHARD PRINCE DEPOSITION ON OCT. 6, 2009 – BREAKDOWN OF EXAMINATION

Time	Pages	Topic
10:15 am	6	Deposition of Richard Prince begins.
	8-20, 32-83, 88-142, 144	Prince's early childhood, education, employment history, prior collections and early shows are addressed. Also touches upon Richard Prince's philosophy as an artist, his assets, and press.
	21-25	Prince's Answer to plaintiff's amended complaint.
	25, 72-73	Other lawsuits are discussed; Prince confirms he has never been sued before.
	26-27	Preparation for deposition.
	32	Prince's other collections.
11:46 am	81	[Videographer changes from tape one to tape two.]
	142-43	Profits from *Canal Zone* exhibition.
	150-84, 236	Richard Prince's creation of *Canal Zone*.
1:05 pm	163	[Recess taken. Videographer's tape two ends.]
1:53 pm	163	[Deposition resumes. Videographer begins tape 3.]
	178-84	Discussion about Prince's creation of *Canal Zone, 2007*
	185-98	Questions about Guns & Ammo series.
	195	Guns & Ammo series was about survival.
3:17 pm	234	Tape three ends.
3:29 pm	234	[Videographer begins tape four.]
3:29 pm	199-204; 219-235	Frey Essay/the pitch.
	237-241	Prince's purchase of *Yes Rasta*.
	242-44, 257-81	Glenn O'Brien interview.
4:25 pm	281	[Videographer's Tape four ends.]
4:29 pm	281	[Videographer begins tape five.]
	287-88	Sending images for interview.
	245-57	Titles of specific paintings are discussed.
4:29 pm	281	Questioned about commenting on *Yes Rasta*.

Cariou v. Prince; SDNY Docket No. 08-11327

RICHARD PRINCE DEPOSITION ON OCT. 6, 2009 – BREAKDOWN OF EXAMINATION

Time	Pages	Topic
	282-92	Use of other photos/stock photos
	292-301	Gagosian Gallery Press Release
	301-09	Schematic of show/paintings in exhibition
	309-10	Paintings are in storage.
	310-16	Prince negotiates agreement with plaintiff's counsel to end deposition at 6:15
	310, 317	Cease & desist letter.
	317-22	Guest list for *Canal Zone* 11/08/08 dinner.
	322-25	Gagosian Gallery accountings of Paintings sold.
	328	*Canal Zone* book copyright notice.
	330-43	Richard Prince describes process of creating *Back to the Garden*.
	344-51	Questions regarding image of Richard Prince's studio which shows an Image that appears in *Inquisition*.
5:51 pm	353	[Videographer Tape five ends.]
5:55 pm	353	[Videographer begins tape six.]
5:55 pm	351-54	Specific questioning about *Canal Zone, 2008*.
	355-61	Specific questioning on *Djuna Barnes, Natalie Barney, Renee Vivien and Romaine Brooks take over the Guanahani*.
	362-63	Specific questioning about *Graduation*.
	363-66	Specific questioning about *Tales of Brave Ulysses*.
	367-75	Pages from *Yes Rasta* and other materials onto which Richard Prince drew figures/notes.
6:20 pm	376-77	[Deposition ends.]

UNITED STATES DISTRICT COURT
SOUTHERN DISTRICT OF NEW YORK

PATRICK CARIOU,

   Plaintiff,

 vs.

RICHARD PRINCE, GAGOSIAN
GALLERY, INC., LAWRENCE
GAGOSIAN, and RIZZOLI
INTERNATIONAL PUBLICATIONS,
INC.,

   Defendants.

Index No.:
08 CIV 11327 (DAB)

~~~~~~~~~~~~~~~~~~~~~~~~~~~~~~~~~~~~~~

VIDEOTAPED DEPOSITION OF

RICHARD PRINCE

October 6, 2009
10:00 a.m.

140 Broadway
New York, New York

Reported By:
Bryan Nilsen, RPR

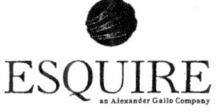

ESQUIRE
an Alexander Gallo Company

Toll Free: 800.944.9454
Facsimile: 212.557.5972

Suite 4715
One Penn Plaza
New York, NY 10119
www.esquiresolutions.com

	1		3
	Prince	1	Prince
	UNITED STATES DISTRICT COURT	2	APPEARANCES:
	SOUTHERN DISTRICT OF NEW YORK	3	
	------------------------------x	4	SCHNADER HARRISON SEGAL & LEWIS LLP
	PATRICK CARIOU,	5	Attorneys for Plaintiff
	Plaintiff, Index No.:	6	140 Broadway, Suite 3100
	vs. 08 CIV 11327 (DAB)	7	New York, New York 10005-1101
	RICHARD PRINCE, GAGOSIAN	8	BY: DANIEL J. BROOKS, ESQ.
	GALLERY, INC., LAWRENCE	9	BY: ERIC A. BODEN, ESQ.
	GAGOSIAN, and RIZZOLI	10	PHONE: (212)973-8000
	INTERNATIONAL PUBLICATIONS,	11	EMAIL: dbrooks@schnader.com
	INC.,	12	
	Defendants.	13	WITHERS BERGMAN LLP
	------------------------------x	14	Attorneys for Defendants Gagosian Gallery, Inc.,
		15	and Lawrence Gagosian
	VIDEOTAPED DEPOSITION OF RICHARD PRINCE	16	430 Park Avenue, 10th Floor
	New York, New York	17	New York, New York 10022-3505
	Tuesday, October 6, 2009	18	BY: HOLLIS GONERKA BART, ESQ.
		19	PHONE: (212)848-9800
		20	EMAIL: hollis.bart@withers.us.com
	Reported by:	21	
	Bryan Nilsen, RPR	22	
	JOB NO. 304040	23	
		24	
		25	

	2		4
1	Prince	1	Prince
2		2	APPEARANCES (Cont'd.)
3		3	
4		4	HANLY CONROY BIERSTEIN SHERIDAN FISHER & HAYES LLP
5		5	Attorneys for Defendant Richard Prince
6	October 6, 2009	6	112 Madison Avenue
7	10:00 a.m.	7	New York, New York 10016-7416
8		8	BY: STEVEN M. HAYES, ESQ.
9		9	PHONE: (212)784-6400
10	Deposition of RICHARD PRINCE,	10	EMAIL: shayes@hanlyconroy.com
11	held at the offices of Schnader Harrison	11	
12	Segal & Lewis LLP, 140 Broadway, New York,	12	WEISMANN CELLER SPETT & MODLIN P.C.
13	New York, pursuant to Notice, before	13	Attorneys for Defendant Rizzoli International
14	Bryan Nilsen, RPR, a Notary Public of	14	Publications, Inc.,
15	the State of New York.	15	445 Park Avenue, No. 1500
16		16	New York, New York 10022
17		17	BY: JOHN B. SHERMAN, ESQ.
18		18	PHONE: (212)371-5400
19		19	EMAIL: jsherman@wcsm445.com
20		20	
21		21	
22		22	ALSO PRESENT:
23		23	PETER LEDWITH - Videographer
24		24	Esquire Video Solutions
25		25	PATRICK CARIOU

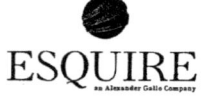

<table>
<tr><td colspan="2">5</td></tr>
</table>

	5
1	Prince
2	
3	
4	IT IS HEREBY STIPULATED AND AGREED,
5	by and among the attorneys for the
6	respective parties herein, that filing and
7	sealing be and the same are hereby waived.
8	
9	IT IS FURTHER STIPULATED AND AGREED
10	that all objections, except as to the form
11	of the question, shall be reserved to the
12	time of the trial.
13	
14	IT IS FURTHER STIPULATED AND AGREED
15	that the within deposition may be sworn to
16	and signed before any officer authorized
17	to administer an oath, with the same force
18	and effect as if signed and sworn to
19	before the Court.

5

1　Prince
4　IT IS HEREBY STIPULATED AND AGREED,
5　by and among the attorneys for the
6　respective parties herein, that filing and
7　sealing be and the same are hereby waived.
9　IT IS FURTHER STIPULATED AND AGREED
10　that all objections, except as to the form
11　of the question, shall be reserved to the
12　time of the trial.
14　IT IS FURTHER STIPULATED AND AGREED
15　that the within deposition may be sworn to
16　and signed before any officer authorized
17　to administer an oath, with the same force
18　and effect as if signed and sworn to
19　before the Court.

7

1　Prince
2　THE VIDEOGRAPHER: Will the court
3　reporter please swear in the witness.
5　RICHARD PRINCE, called as a
6　witness, having been duly sworn by a
7　Notary Public, was examined and testified
8　as follows:
9　　THE COURT REPORTER: Please state
10　your name and address for the record.
11　　THE WITNESS: Richard Prince,
12　151 Righter Road, Rensselaerville,
13　New York 12147.
15　EXAMINATION BY
16　MR. BROOKS:
17　Q. Good morning, Mr. Prince. My name
18　is Daniel Brooks. I represent Patrick Cariou
19　the plaintiff in this case.
20　　Can you tell us what your occupation
21　is?
22　A. I'm an artist.
23　Q. I understand you were born in the
24　Canal Zone --
25　A. Yes.

6

1　Prince
2　THE VIDEOGRAPHER: This is tape
3　number 1 in the videotaped deposition of
4　Richard Prince, in the matter of Cariou
5　versus Richard Prince, being heard before
6　the U.S. District Court, Southern District
7　of New York.
8　This deposition is being held at
9　Schnader Harrison Segal, 140 Broadway,
10　New York, New York, on October 6, 2009.
11　The time is 10:15 a.m.
12　My name is Peter Ledwith. I'm the
13　videographer. The court reporter is Bryan
14　Nilsen.
15　Counsel, will you please introduce
16　yourselves and who you represent.
17　MR. HAYES: Steven Hayes, counsel
18　for Richard Prince.
19　MS. BART: Hollis Gonerka Bart,
20　counsel for Larry Gagosian and Gagosian
21　Gallery.
22　MR. SHERMAN: John Sherman, counsel
23　for Rizzoli International Publications.
24　MR. BROOKS: Dan Brooks and Eric
25　Boden for the plaintiff.

8

1　Prince
2　Q. -- is that correct?
3　In 1949?
4　A. Yes.
5　Q. Did you attend school there?
6　A. No, I didn't.
7　Q. Where did you attend primary school?
8　A. Outside of Boston, a town called
9　Braintree, Massachusetts.
10　Q. Was it a boarding school or did you
11　live there?
12　A. What age are you talking about?
13　Q. Okay, let me back up.
14　How long did you live in the Canal
15　Zone?
16　A. We moved when I was about six years
17　old.
18　Q. To Massachusetts?
19　A. Yes.
20　Q. Did the six years you spent in the
21　Canal Zone affect your later work in any way?
22　MR. HAYES: As an artist you're
23　talking about?
24　MR. BROOKS: Yes.
25　A. Recently, yes.

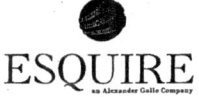

9

1	Prince
2	Q. How so?
3	A. I paid a visit to what is now called
4	Panama about three years ago, three or four
5	years ago. I'm not sure. And I started to
6	think about -- I started to think about the
7	place that I was born in.
8	Q. We'll get to this later obviously,
9	but did some of that thinking enter into your
10	creation of the works of art that are in the
11	Canal Zone book?
12	A. Yes, in the form of a pitch or a
13	screenplay that I wrote, and then I subsequently
14	sort of made up a story that I felt that could
15	be described with the title Canal Zone. I very
16	much liked the idea that the name of the place
17	that I was born had disappeared, that they no
18	longer call it the Canal Zone, they call it
19	Panama.
20	Q. The pitch -- and again, we'll get to
21	this later, but the pitch that you say you
22	wrote, was it originally called Eden Rock?
23	A. I think one of the working titles
24	was Eden Rock, yes.
25	Q. And that is a hotel in St. Barth's?

10

1	Prince
2	A. Yes, I believe so, yes.
3	MR. BROOKS: S-T, period, B-A-R-T-H,
4	apostrophe S, that's how we'll spell it
5	from now on.
6	BY MR. BROOKS:
7	Q. Do you have any education after high
8	school?
9	A. You mean college education?
10	Q. Yes.
11	A. Yes, I did attend college.
12	Q. What was the name of the college?
13	A. Nasson, N-A-S-S-O-N, College.
14	Q. In Maine?
15	A. Yes.
16	Q. Was that a small liberal arts
17	college?
18	A. Yes.
19	Q. Did you take any art courses at
20	Nasson College?
21	A. Yes.
22	Q. Did you take any photography
23	courses?
24	A. No.
25	Q. Briefly, can you describe the art

11

1	Prince
2	course or courses that you took at that college?
3	A. Mostly it was figure studies. I
4	studied the figure. I went to classes where
5	they had models.
6	Q. And what medium were you working in
7	in these courses?
8	A. Pencil, watercolor, collage, pen and
9	ink.
10	Q. How many years did you attend Nasson
11	College?
12	A. Four years.
13	Q. Did you graduate?
14	A. Yes.
15	Q. With a degree in what?
16	A. I guess liberal arts.
17	Q. A BA?
18	A. Yes.
19	Q. After college did there come a time
20	when you started working in New York City for
21	Time Life Magazines?
22	A. Yes.
23	Q. When was that, approximately?
24	A. 1975.
25	Q. And when did you finish college?

12

1	Prince
2	A. '71.
3	Q. What was the nature of your job or
4	jobs at Time Life?
5	A. I worked for a number of jobs.
6	First one was I worked in what they called the
7	employee bookstore. That was my main job. And
8	I worked -- I believe the title is called copy
9	process, which was tearing up the various
10	magazines that they published.
11	In those days, pretty primitive,
12	precomputer, we would tear up the magazine and
13	hand the editorial -- they were called hard
14	copies -- to the people who wrote those stories.
15	Q. Tear sheets?
16	A. Tear sheets.
17	Q. And was this advertising or actual
18	editorial -- non-advertising content?
19	A. What they wanted, what we would put
20	in these tubes and send, what they wanted was
21	the editorial copy.
22	Q. Articles?
23	A. Articles, yes, for the various --
24	I believe at the time they published seven
25	magazines.

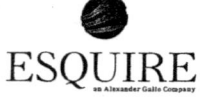

ESQUIRE
an Alexander Gallo Company

Toll Free: 800.944.9454
Facsimile: 212.557.5972

Suite 4715
One Penn Plaza
New York, NY 10119
www.esquiresolutions.com

13

1   Prince
2   Q.   While you were employed by Time Life
3   did you begin a practice of rephotographing
4   images --
5   A.   Yes.
6   Q.   -- that you encountered there?
7   A.   1977 I made a breakthrough in terms
8   of what I considered a breakthrough, and I
9   started to rephotograph images that were
10 essentially from magazines that Time Life
11 published and also the New York Times magazine.
12   Q.   Were the images advertisements?
13   A.   Strictly advertisements, yes.
14   Q.   In 1977 did you rephotograph four
15 photos from the New York Times magazine section?
16   A.   Yes.
17   Q.   What was the nature of those photos?
18   A.   They were images of living rooms,
19 advertisements. I don't recall who was the
20 advertiser, but -- and I believe they appeared
21 sequentially once -- once a week for four weeks
22 I believe.
23   Q.   And when you rephotographed those
24 four images what, if anything, did you do with
25 them? Did you exhibit them anywhere?

14

1   Prince
2   A.   No, I didn't.
3   Q.   Did some controversy arise from your
4   rephotographing those four images?
5   A.   Not at the time, no.
6   Q.   At a later time?
7   A.   A controversy? I think -- no, I
8   would more describe it as just people were very
9   perplexed and didn't particularly know what they
10 were looking at, because of the nature of the
11 transformation. It was a real photograph that I
12 was showing, not an image that I had torn out of
13 the magazine. Which is essentially when I first
14 tore it, it was a collage. I collaged it onto
15 paper. That's the very first way I showed the
16 images.
17   But I decided -- I mean that was
18 the breakthrough, was taking the apparatus, the
19 camera, and making a real photograph.
20   Q.   A photograph of a photograph?
21   A.   Well, it was a photograph of -- no,
22 it wasn't a photograph. It was a photograph of
23 a page --
24   Q.   From the magazine?
25   A.   -- in the magazine.

15

1   Prince
2   Q.   Did you have a solo exhibition at
3   the Ellen Sragow Gallery?
4   A.   Sragow, I believe.
5   Q.   Sragow?
6   A.   Yes.
7   Q.   When was that?
8   A.   It was a long time ago.
9   MR. HAYES: If you recall. If you
10 don't recall, say so.
11   A.   Well, '76 maybe.
12   Q.   And what was the content of the
13 exhibition?
14   A.   I guess you could describe the --
15 it's hard -- I believe they were images with
16 text. They would refer to it at the time as
17 narrative art.
18   Q.   Were the --
19   A.   They were stories that I had made up
20 about various locations in which I had visited.
21   Q.   And what medium were the images?
22   A.   I think they were drawing. I think
23 on one piece of paper it was drawing, and I
24 believe the -- photographs -- text that was put
25 out with a typewriter, and a lot of what was

16

1   Prince
2   then called white-out, which was a kind of
3   liquid paint that you used to correct a typo.
4   Q.   At some point did you begin
5   rephotographing ads for Marlboro cigarettes?
6   A.   I started that I believe in 1980 was
7   the first one.
8   Q.   And this has been known as the
9   Marlboro Cowboy photographs?
10   A.   I referred to them -- yes. I
11 started titling them Untitled, parentheses,
12 Cowboys.
13   Q.   And you say you started in 1980?
14   A.   Yes.
15   Q.   How long did you continue engaging
16 in that practice?
17   A.   Until -- I believe the last ones
18 were done in 1999.
19   Q.   How did you obtain the images of the
20 Marlboro cowboys?
21   A.   They used to come out -- when I was
22 working at Time Life they would come out -- we'd
23 get the magazines on Monday, and they would
24 appear in the magazine -- in the various
25 magazines.

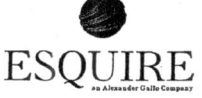

ESQUIRE
an Alexander Gallo Company

Toll Free: 800.944.9454
Facsimile: 212.557.5972

Suite 4715
One Penn Plaza
New York, NY 10119
www.esquiresolutions.com

	17
1	Prince
2	Q. Tobacco companies were still
3	permitted to advertise at that time?
4	A. Yeah. Before the Marlboro I had
5	made collages. I hadn't yet rephotographed, but
6	I believe I made collages when I was visiting
7	Cologne of Camel cigarette ads, which I still
8	have. But I pasted those -- I cut them out with
9	an exacto knife and I pasted them on paper.
10	About two years later, when I was
11	working at Time Life, I started to see the
12	cowboys, and I started to -- I had already been
13	rephotographing images for about three years, so
14	I sort of knew how I could appropriate and
15	sample these cowboys.
16	I could shoot around the actual
17	advertising copy and -- I mean do you want me to
18	go on or?
19	Q. Sure.
20	MR. HAYES: Do you want to read back
21	the question so the witness can determine
22	whether he's finished.
23	(Record read.)
24	BY MR. BROOKS:
25	Q. One thing is you said Cologne. Is

	18
1	Prince
2	that in Germany?
3	A. Yes.
4	Q. Do you know how to spell that?
5	MR. HAYES: C-O-L --
6	A. K-O-L-N.
7	Q. K-O-L --
8	A. Or C-O --
9	MR. HAYES: C-O-L-O-G-N-E.
10	A. I believe it's the same.
11	Q. In 1983 did you rephotograph a photo
12	by a photographer named Garry, G-A-R-R-Y, Gross?
13	A. I didn't rephotograph a photo by
14	him. I rephotographed an image that appeared in
15	a little advertising booklet that he had
16	self-published.
17	MR. BROOKS: Can I hear that again?
18	(Record read.)
19	BY MR. BROOKS:
20	Q. What was the nature of the image?
21	A. He apparently had taken an image of
22	Brooke Shields that I believe when she was
23	around 12 or -- years old. I don't exactly know
24	what the age was, but -- he was I believe
25	wanting to publish those images.

	19
1	Prince
2	I mean this was ten years later and
3	she had already grown up. I guess he wanted --
4	he wanted to publish posters of the original
5	shoot that he made that day.
6	Q. But getting back to my question, the
7	image that you saw in his materials was a
8	reproduction of that photo?
9	A. The image that I saw that day, that
10	evening when I received the little booklet, I
11	felt that my reaction to it is, oh, that's what
12	they're talking about. Because these images
13	were in the press at the time.
14	Q. But the image, was it a photograph,
15	that's all I'm asking?
16	A. In the booklet?
17	Q. Yes.
18	A. I didn't know what the image was.
19	All I saw was the reproduction.
20	Q. What was Brooke Shields wearing in
21	the picture?
22	A. She wasn't wearing anything at all.
23	Q. Did you make a photograph of that
24	image?
25	A. I rephotographed the image, yes.

	20
1	Prince
2	Q. And did you give it a title?
3	A. Yes, I did.
4	Q. What was the title?
5	A. Spiritual America.
6	Q. And you say you obtained the image
7	that you rephotographed in the mail in some kind
8	of advertising publication?
9	MR. HAYES: Objection. I don't
10	think he said that.
11	MR. BROOKS: Okay. I could be
12	wrong.
13	BY MR. BROOKS:
14	Q. Tell us again how you --
15	A. I received the image because someone
16	gave me the little pamphlet or --
17	Q. Okay. You didn't get it in the
18	mail?
19	A. I didn't get it in the mail.
20	Q. So you didn't purchase the pamphlet,
21	somebody gave it to you?
22	A. Someone gave it to me, yes.
23	Q. Did you obtain Mr. Gross's
24	permission to rephotograph the image?
25	A. No.

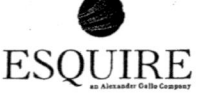

ESQUIRE
an Alexander Gallo Company

Toll Free: 800.944.9454
Facsimile: 212.557.5972

Suite 4715
One Penn Plaza
New York, NY 10119
www.esquiresolutions.com

21

1   Prince
2   Q.   Did you obtain his permission to
3   sell your photograph of the image?
4   A.   It wasn't for sale.
5   Q.   I'm going to hand you what I'd like
6   marked as Plaintiff's Exhibit 1, which is simply
7   a copy of the amended complaint in this lawsuit.
8   (Plaintiff's Exhibit 1, amended
9   complaint, was marked for identification,
10   as of this date.)
11   Q.   Mr. Prince, what I've placed in
12   front of you is a copy of the amended complaint
13   in this lawsuit. Have you ever seen it before?
14   A.   No.
15   Q.   I'm going to ask you to turn to
16   page 4, please. And I'm going to read you what
17   paragraph 13 states.
18   Quote, None of the defendants was
19   ever authorized by Plaintiff to appropriate the
20   photographs, comma, or to reproduce, comma,
21   distribute or display the photographs, comma, or
22   to adapt the photographs in order to create the
23   paintings or any other derivative work based on
24   the photographs, period. Defendant's conduct
25   was and continues to be a willful disregard of

22

1   Prince
2   Plaintiff's rights under the copyright act,
3   unquote.
4   Just for your information,
5   photographs are capitalized, initial capitalized
6   in that paragraph, and the photographs that are
7   being referred to are the photographs in this
8   book in my hand Yes Rasta, which we'll talk
9   about. You've seen this book before, right?
10   A.   Yes.
11   MR. BROOKS: Let's mark as
12   Plaintiff's Exhibit 2 Mr. Prince's answer
13   to the amended complaint.
14   (Plaintiff's Exhibit 2, answer to
15   amended complaint, was marked for
16   identification, as of this date.)
17   Q.   Mr. Prince, you'll recall just a
18   minute ago I read you an allegation in the
19   complaint, paragraph 13. Now, I'd like you to
20   turn to page 3 of the answer, which is
21   Exhibit 2, and I will read page 3.
22   MR. HAYES: Page 2.
23   MR. BROOKS: Page 3.
24   MR. HAYES: Page 3, sorry. And he's
25   asking you to look at --

23

1   Prince
2   Q.   Paragraph 13, which appears to be
3   the answer to the allegation I read before.
4   And this is what it states.
5   Prince denies the allegations in
6   paragraph of 13 of the complaint, comma, except
7   admits that any use of Plaintiff's photographs
8   by Prince was not specifically authorized by
9   Plaintiff, comma, and states that such
10   authorization was not required as Prince's use
11   of portions of the photographs in his art works
12   is proper artistic practice and appropriate
13   under applicable law.
14   First, I should ask you, have you
15   ever seen this answer to the amended complaint,
16   this document that you're looking at now,
17   before?
18   MR. HAYES: If you recall.
19   A.   No. No, I don't.
20   Q.   You don't?
21   A.   No.
22   Q.   Are you sure you never saw it or you
23   just don't remember?
24   A.   No.
25   Q.   No which?

24

1   Prince
2   A.   No, I've never -- no, I've never
3   seen this, no.
4   Q.   Did you discuss -- without going
5   getting into what you said, did you discuss the
6   preparation of this answer with anyone?
7   A.   No.
8   Q.   All right. If you look at
9   paragraph 13, which I just read to you, did you
10   play any role in preparing that answer to
11   paragraph 13?
12   A.   No.
13   Q.   I've read it into the record and
14   you've read it yourself. Do you agree with this
15   answer in paragraph 13?
16   MR. HAYES: Objection, calls for a
17   legal conclusion.
18   Q.   You can answer.
19   A.   To tell you the truth, I don't
20   really understand it.
21   Q.   Do you believe it to be true and
22   accurate?
23   MR. HAYES: Objection, calls for a
24   legal conclusion.
25   Q.   You can answer.

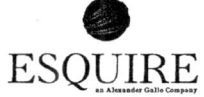

ESQUIRE
an Alexander Gallo Company

Toll Free: 800.944.9454
Facsimile: 212.557.5972

Suite 4715
One Penn Plaza
New York, NY 10119
www.esquiresolutions.com

25	27
1 Prince	1 Prince
2 MR. HAYES: Also, it seems to be	2 BY MR. BROOKS:
3 attempting to turn him into some kind of	3 Q. So just tell us what, if anything,
4 expert, but primarily calls for a legal	4 you reviewed before coming here today to prepare
5 conclusion.	5 for this deposition?
6 A. I mean, you know, this type of	6 A. I didn't really do anything. I
7 language I -- you know, is not something that I	7 just -- I wasn't even sure what I was supposed
8 feel comfortable commenting on.	8 to do today.
9 Q. Very well.	9 Q. Did you meet with any lawyers --
10 Let me just back up.	10 without getting into what you said to them or
11 Have you ever been sued before this	11 they said to you, did you meet with any lawyers
12 lawsuit in any court?	12 to prepare for this deposition?
13 A. No, I've never been sued.	13 A. I met with -- yeah, I met with
14 Q. Not by Garry Gross?	14 Steven.
15 A. No.	15 Q. Mr. Hayes?
16 Q. Have you ever been a party to any	16 A. Yes.
17 lawsuit or arbitration?	17 Q. Just the two of you?
18 A. Not that I believe, no.	18 A. Yes.
19 Q. Have you ever sued anyone?	19 Q. No one else was present during the
20 A. No, I've never sued anybody.	20 meeting?
21 Q. Have you ever had your deposition	21 A. No.
22 taken before today?	22 Q. Okay. Let me go back to this answer
23 A. No.	23 to paragraph 13 on page 3 of Exhibit 2. And
24 Q. What, if anything, did you do to	24 perhaps we can break this down so it's more
25 prepare for this deposition?	25 digestible.

26	28
1 Prince	1 Prince
2 A. I went over --	2 The answer says that you were not
3 MR. HAYES: I'll caution the witness	3 specifically authorized to use Plaintiff's
4 not to talk about any conversations with	4 photographs, do you see that?
5 counsel.	5 A. I wasn't specifically authorized?
6 THE WITNESS: I'm sorry?	6 Q. That's what this says.
7 MR. HAYES: Don't talk about the	7 A. Okay.
8 substance of any conversations with	8 Q. Is that true?
9 counsel as protected by attorney/client	9 MR. HAYES: Object to the form
10 privilege.	10 of the question, calls for a legal
11 A. I didn't really do much.	11 conclusion.
12 Q. Tell us what you did, even if it was	12 You can answer if you understand it.
13 very little, without divulging conversations	13 Q. You can answer.
14 with your lawyer.	14 A. I still don't understand why I'm --
15 A. I talked to my wife about it.	15 I wasn't specifically authorized.
16 Q. Did you review any documents?	16 Q. Did you ever ask Mr. Cariou, who is
17 A. Documents -- what type of documents?	17 sitting here, the plaintiff, for permission to
18 Q. Well, for instance, books, your	18 use his photographs from the Yes Rasta book?
19 book, the Canal Zone book?	19 A. I didn't really use his photographs.
20 MR. HAYES: Objection. Objection.	20 Q. Okay. Did you make use of them in
21 I understand that that's not a proper	21 any way?
22 question. That's work product.	22 A. I made use of them, yes.
23 MR. BROOKS: Are you directing him	23 Q. Did you ask for his permission to
24 not to answer?	24 make use of them?
25 MR. HAYES: No, I'll let him answer.	25 A. No.

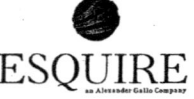

29

1   Prince
2   Q.   Did he specifically give you
3   permission to use --
4   A.   No.
5   Q.   Did he generally give you permission
6   to use the photographs?
7   A.   No.
8   Q.   Now, you say that the use you made
9   of the portions of the photographs -- withdrawn.
10   This answer says that the use you
11 made of portions of the photographs in your
12 artworks was a proper artistic practice. Do you
13 agree with that?
14   MR. HAYES: Again, object to the
15   form of the question on the grounds it
16   asks for a legal conclusion and attempts
17   to make the witness an expert.
18   But you can answer the question if
19   you understand it.
20   A.   I did use, in fact, portions of
21 photographs that appear in his book. Whether
22 they were for proper artistic practice, that's
23 a -- that's something I can't really -- I would
24 have to define proper. And I'm not sure if
25 there's any type of definition for proper

30

1   Prince
2   artistic practice.
3   But I did, in fact, use portions of
4   images that appear in his books. Eventually,
5   for paintings that I made into this -- they
6   were sort of ingredient -- part of a recipe
7   ingredients that were eventually made into this
8   show that I titled Canal Zone.
9   Q.   Were his photographs the subject of
10 your --
11   A.   No.
12   Q.   -- artworks?
13   A.   No.
14   Q.   The subject was some
15 post-apocalyptic vision of what would happen
16 after a nuclear war on a remote island?
17   A.   No, that was -- that's a subtext of
18 the whole Canal Zone type of pitch. It first
19 appeared when I was thinking about this project.
20   Q.   Okay. You know what, we'll get to
21 that. I've got -- your lawyers produced all the
22 documents. We'll go through them.
23   A.   Okay.
24   Q.   And I'm pretty sure what your answer
25 is going to be, but when you say -- when the

31

1   Prince
2   answer says here this was proper under -- it was
3   appropriate under applicable law, do you have
4   any idea what that refers to?
5   MR. HAYES: Again, same objections,
6   calls for an expert conclusion --
7   A.   No.
8   MR. HAYES: -- and is not a proper
9   question.
10   MR. BROOKS: Right. But it's in his
11   answer so I just want to see if he knows
12   what that means.
13   A.   No.
14   Q.   You have no idea?
15   A.   No.
16   Q.   I'd like to discuss with you your
17 artistic practice, quote/unquote, artistic
18 practice, a term used in the answer, which I
19 understand you've never seen the answer before.
20   You are an artist, so I assume you
21 have an artistic practice?
22   A.   I'd like to think so, yes.
23   Q.   Okay.
24   MR. BROOKS: Let's mark as
25   Plaintiff's Exhibit 3 two pages which have

32

1   Prince
2   been Bates stamped by us C57 and 58 when
3   they were produced in discovery.
4   MS. BART: Yesterday, correct?
5   MR. BROOKS: No, about six months
6   ago.
7   MS. BART: The original production.
8   MR. BROOKS: The initial disclosure
9   I should say.
10   (Plaintiff's Exhibit 3, two-page
11   printout from website, was marked for
12   identification, as of this date.)
13   Q.   Mr. Prince, you have a website?
14   A.   Yes, I do. Yes.
15   Q.   And is it www.RichardPrinceArt.com?
16   A.   Yes.
17   Q.   The first page of Exhibit 3 is a
18 photograph of somebody. Is that you?
19   A.   Yes.
20   Q.   And on the table in the photograph
21 there seems to be a book with some -- it looks
22 like a cowboy on a horse?
23   A.   Yes.
24   Q.   Is that a book with some of these
25 Marlboro cowboys we were talking about before?

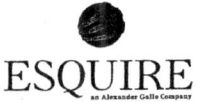

ESQUIRE
an Alexander Gallo Company

Toll Free: 800.944.9454
Facsimile: 212.557.5972

Suite 4715
One Penn Plaza
New York, NY 10119
www.esquiresolutions.com

	33
1	Prince
2	A. I think that book is a book called
3	Blasted Allegories that was published by the
4	New Museum. I think they used a cowboy image of
5	mine.
6	Q. But that's not your book?
7	A. It's not my book, no.
8	Q. Now, if you could turn to the second
9	page. There's a reference to -- it looks like
10	an essay called Practicing Without a License
11	1977, and beneath that there's a reference to
12	what looks like an essay called Appropriation
13	1978. Do you see those two?
14	A. Yes.
15	Q. Are those essays that you wrote?
16	MR. HAYES: Object to form.
17	THE WITNESS: I'm sorry?
18	MR. HAYES: Object to form. He's
19	calling them essays without establishing
20	what they are. So I'm objecting to form.
21	You can answer if you understand it.
22	MR. BROOKS: No, no, I'll withdraw.
23	BY MR. BROOKS:
24	Q. What are they?
25	A. I think they were sort of -- I was

	35
1	Prince
2	managing, with quotes around managing, rather
3	than quoting them, reproducing their effect and
4	look as naturally as they had been produced when
5	they first appeared.
6	Was this a description by you in
7	1977 of a practice that you were experimenting
8	with at that time?
9	A. Yes.
10	Q. Let's look at the second -- I'm
11	calling it an essay. Please don't be offended.
12	Just these words.
13	A. It's okay.
14	MR. HAYES: Just as long as you're
15	adopting that as a term of art for this
16	purpose, that's fine.
17	Q. Appropriation 1978 states --
18	MR. HAYES: So do you want to read
19	the rest of the --
20	MR. BROOKS: Not at this time, no.
21	MR. HAYES: Okay.
22	BY MR. BROOKS:
23	Q. Appropriation 1978 states -- and for
24	the record, I have not read the entire piece
25	that was written in 1977.

	34
1	Prince
2	trying to figure out what I was doing in 1977.
3	And since I was the one who was doing it, and it
4	was brand new, I felt that I was probably in the
5	position of trying to explain what the
6	experiment was in 1977.
7	Q. Now, when you were -- let's just
8	talk about the first one first in 1977. When
9	you were explaining the experiment who was your
10	anticipated audience for the explanation?
11	A. I didn't have any expectation of an
12	audience. Aside from a few other artist friends
13	I was totally in the dark. I was just basically
14	alone in my studio.
15	Q. Let me just ask a different
16	question. These are your words that you wrote
17	in or about 1977?
18	A. Yes.
19	Q. Okay.
20	A. I believe they are.
21	Q. The first sentence I will read into
22	the record says rephotography is a technique
23	for stealing, parenthesis, pirating, close
24	parenthesis, already existing images, comma,
25	simulating rather than copying them, comma,

	36
1	Prince
2	Appropriation 1978. I think
3	appropriation has to do with the inability of
4	the author slash artist to like his or her own
5	work, period. Especially if the work is all
6	theirs, period. I think it's a lot more
7	satisfying to appropriate, comma, especially if
8	you are attempting to produce work with a
9	certain believability, comma, an official
10	fiction let's say. If you take someone else's
11	work and call it your own, comma, you don't have
12	to ask an audience, quote, to take my word for
13	it, unquote, period. It's not like it started
14	with you and ended up being guessed at. The
15	effect you want to produce is not that different
16	from what an audience sometimes experiences when
17	viewing a good movie. And that's what -- and
18	then in quotes -- somebody named Christian Metz
19	called a general lowering of wakefulness.
20	MR. HAYES: I think what might have
21	been an inadvertent misstatement is the
22	sentence next to last is and what's that
23	as opposed to that's what.
24	Q. Oh, sorry. And what's that what
25	Christian Metz called a general lowering of

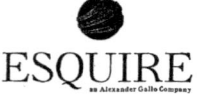

37

1   Prince
2 wakefulness, unquote.
3   (Clarification by reporter.)
4   Q.   Again, those were your words in
5 1978?
6   A.   Yes.
7   Q.   When you would -- now, I'm asking
8 about the first series of sentences. Okay?
9   A.   Mm-hmm.
10   Q.   Practicing without a license.
11   When you would rephotograph would
12 you actually use a camera?
13   A.   Yes.
14   Q.   So you would take an analog
15 photograph of some image, is that right?
16   A.   I would take a slide. I was using
17 slide film.
18   Q.   And then develop it?
19   A.   I would send it to a commercial lab
20 and have it developed.
21   Q.   Now, in this digital age that we're
22 in now are you able to appropriate images
23 without actually using a camera?
24   MR. HAYES: Objection to the form of
25   the question. Without actually using a

38

1   Prince
2 camera?
3   Q.   Well, for instance, like if you see
4 a photograph somewhere you can -- is it possible
5 to scan it and enlarge it?
6   A.   I suppose so.
7   Q.   And do a high-definition copy of it
8 without using a camera?
9   MR. HAYES: If you know.
10   A.   I guess so.
11   MS. BART: Excuse me, I'd like to
12 hear the question back, please.
13   (Record read.)
14   MR. HAYES: I attempted to interpose
15 an objection that the question calls for
16 speculation, and I'll do that now.
17   MR. BROOKS: Okay.
18 BY MR. BROOKS:
19   Q.   But you can answer.
20   A.   I guess so.
21   Q.   Well, you guess so?
22   MR. HAYES: Don't guess. If you
23 know, say so. If you don't, say so.
24   A.   Yes, I believe you can. Yes.
25   Q.   In creating the works that were in

39

1   Prince
2 the Canal Zone show isn't is a fact that you
3 scanned some of Plaintiff's images directly onto
4 the canvas?
5   A.   No.
6   MR. HAYES: Objection.
7   MS. BART: Objection, form.
8   A.   No.
9   Q.   Did somebody do that at your
10 request?
11   MS. BART: Same objection.
12   A.   What I would do is send -- after I
13 tore the image out of the book --
14   Q.   You're talking about Plaintiff's
15 book?
16   A.   Yes.
17   I would send it off to a commercial
18 lab. And I believe it's called inkjet process.
19   Q.   Right.
20   A.   Now, I don't know too much about it
21 except that it -- you're able to reproduce in
22 almost any scale onto different surfaces. The
23 surface which I chose was canvas.
24   Q.   Right. And the name of the lab that
25 you used?

40

1   Prince
2   A.   NancyScans.
3   Q.   Where are they located?
4   A.   Chatham, New York.
5   Q.   Chatham, New York.
6   Near where you live Upstate?
7   A.   It's about an hour, yes.
8   Q.   And that's why -- we'll get to this
9 again later --
10   A.   Okay.
11   Q.   -- but in the book, the Canal Zone
12 book, it says the images -- some of your
13 paintings rather, are inkjet and acrylic on
14 canvas, correct?
15   A.   Yes.
16   Q.   And other material?
17   A.   And other mediums, yeah.
18   Q.   Have you ever heard of an inkjet
19 printer?
20   MR. HAYES: Objection.
21   Meaning other than in this context
22 or?
23   MR. BROOKS: No, just in general.
24   A.   I don't understand -- heard of an
25 inkjet printer?

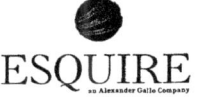

ESQUIRE
an Alexander Gallo Company

Toll Free: 800.944.9454
Facsimile: 212.557.5972

Suite 4715
One Penn Plaza
New York, NY 10119
www.esquiresolutions.com

Richard Prince   October 6, 2009

41
1   Prince
2   Q.   Have you ever gone into like a
3   Kinko's and asked them to make a copy for you?
4   A.   No.
5   Q.   Do you have a printer at home?
6   A.   No, I don't.
7   Q.   In your studio?
8   A.   No.
9   Q.   Do you have a computer?
10   A.   I have a computer.
11   Q.   Let me ask you a few questions about
12   the 1978 -- I'm going to call it an essay.
13   MR. HAYES: That's fine.
14   MR. BROOKS: I understand it's not
15   an essay.
16   MR. HAYES: Yeah, he adopted the
17   term. As long as we're clear it's an
18   adopted term, that's fine. No problem.
19   BY MR. BROOKS:
20   Q.   Was it ever published anywhere,
21   Appropriation 1978, other than on your website?
22   A.   The Appropriation 1978?
23   Q.   Right.
24   A.   I think a form of it or another --
25   maybe another edit of it was probably -- some of

42
1   Prince
2   the sentence structure was probably used.
3   I know the general lowering of
4   wakefulness was used in a book that I wrote
5   called Why I Go to the Movies Alone.
6   Q.   That was the name of your book?
7   A.   Yes.
8   Q.   And do you know when that book came
9   out?
10   A.   1983.
11   Q.   With respect to the essay, it states
12   appropriation has to do with the inability of
13   the author slash artist to like his or her own
14   work.
15   Do you feel that you have an
16   inability to like your own work?
17   A.   I think at the time I wrote
18   it I was -- I was very interested in
19   anti-expressionism. I was very interested in
20   works or artworks that did not have to do with
21   personal dreams. I was very interested in
22   making things up and fiction and turning the
23   fiction into something that you can believe in.
24   Again, I have to say also that in
25   this year, especially '77 to '78, I was also

43
1   Prince
2   interested in reflecting about what was going on
3   at the time. I believe I was, what, twenty --
4   MR. HAYES: Nine.
5   A.   Twenty-nine.
6   I had only been in New York for four
7   or five years. I was also very interested in
8   the whole punk rock movement and felt very much
9   a part of that attitude.
10   And the idea of not liking your own
11   work I thought was a kind of avant-garde,
12   revolutionary, very poetic position to take at
13   the time. Because most artists you meet have
14   these large egos and love what they do. So I
15   took the opposite point of view.
16   Q.   And why did you feel that it was,
17   quote, more satisfying to appropriate?
18   A.   I felt that, you know, again, I like
19   the idea of having a bit or a part or a share of
20   a public image, much like the pop artists who I
21   very much grew up with. And I was especially
22   enamored of Andy Warhol at the time.
23   And I felt that I wanted to
24   contribute to something that already existed in
25   the world.

44
1   Prince
2   Q.   You're speaking in the past tense,
3   fair enough, because I'm asking you about --
4   A.   Yeah, this is what I'm -- I'm trying
5   to approximate what I was feeling thirty years
6   ago.
7   Q.   Let's talk about now. Do you still
8   find it more satisfying to appropriate than to
9   create your own work?
10   A.   Yeah, I do. I feel that I like to
11   get as much fact into my work and reduce the
12   amount of speculation. I believe there's too
13   much -- I like an artwork where that when you
14   see something, like a cowboy or a girlfriend, I
15   mean these are, in fact, true.
16   Q.   Or a nurse?
17   A.   Or a nurse, or a hood.
18   Q.   And you feel, if it's not yours --
19   MR. HAYES: Let him finish.
20   MR. BROOKS: I'm sorry.
21   MR. HAYES: Have you finished your
22   answer?
23   THE WITNESS: I'm sorry. Yes.
24   Q.   And you feel if it's not yours it's
25   more believable to the audience?

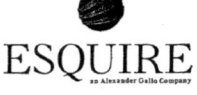

ESQUIRE
an Alexander Gallo Company

Toll Free: 800.944.9454
Facsimile: 212.557.5972

Suite 4715
One Penn Plaza
New York, NY 10119
www.esquiresolutions.com

45

1   Prince
2   MR. HAYES: Objection,
3   mischaracterizes what he said.
4   But if you want -- you can respond
5   to that if you want, but the statement --
6   A.   I feel it's totally mine.
7   Q.   Okay. But in the essay you said you
8   find appropriating satisfying especially if you
9   are attempting to produce work with a certain
10   believability?
11   A.   Yes.
12   Q.   So there's something about
13   appropriating images from other people that
14   helps you make a work of art that's more
15   believable, is that right?
16   A.   I guess you can say that, yes.
17   Q.   Do you still feel that way?
18   A.   Probably not as much as I did in
19   1978.
20   Q.   But to some extent?
21   A.   I think you could say that.
22   Q.   Is it part of your message now that
23   your artwork is more believable because it was
24   taken from someone else?
25   A.   I don't have a -- I don't really

46

1   Prince
2   have a message.
3   Q.   Okay. Is appropriating images from
4   other people, does that also make your job
5   easier in creating a new image?
6   A.   No. Not really, no.
7   Q.   Does it make it harder?
8   A.   No, it's just something that --
9   something that I do and I love to do, and I've
10   always -- you know, I've been doing this for
11   quite a while.
12   Q.   Right.
13   When you began to engage in the
14   practice of rephotographing the work of others
15   did you consider yourself at that time to be a
16   skilled photographer?
17   A.   No.
18   MR. BROOKS: Let's mark as
19   Plaintiff's Exhibit 4 an article, or
20   actually an interview with Bates stamp
21   pages C226 through 228.
22   And this was I believe produced in
23   response to your discovery requests on
24   Friday.
25   MS. BART: We got them actually on

47

1   Prince
2   Monday.
3   MR. BROOKS: Well, I can't help
4   that.
5   (Plaintiff's Exhibit 4, interview,
6   was marked for identification, as of this
7   date.)
8   Q.   Mr. Prince, you've been handed
9   what's been marked as Plaintiff's Exhibit 4.
10   Do you recall being interviewed in
11   ArtForum Magazine in 2003?
12   A.   Boy. I don't really recall being
13   interviewed, no.
14   Q.   Do you know who Steve Lafreniere is?
15   A.   No, I don't.
16   Q.   Let's look at the second page of
17   this exhibit. And there's a question up at the
18   top where the interviewer is asking, I'd always
19   assumed that you purposely made your early
20   photos have an amateur look and that you'd done
21   them quickly, but looking at them today would
22   suggest otherwise. How worked on were pictures
23   like Untitled, three women looking in the same
24   direction, 1980.
25   Before I read the answer, did you

48

1   Prince
2   have a work Untitled with three women looking in
3   the same direction in 1980, if you recall?
4   A.   Yes.
5   Q.   And here's what appears to be your
6   answer. RP, I had limited technical skills
7   regarding the camera. Actually, I had no
8   skills. I played the camera. I used a cheap
9   commercial lab to blow up the pictures. I made
10   editions of two. I never went into a darkroom.
11   And yes, I really worked hard on Women, capital
12   W, period. I mean that piece still looks like
13   it was purposely made.
14   Do you recall making this statement?
15   A.   Yes.
16   Q.   And was it a true statement?
17   A.   Yes, it was. It's absolutely true.
18   Q.   The next question says, So you sort
19   of fell into photography, and the answer is, In
20   the early '80s I didn't have the subject matter
21   for painting, I didn't have the, quote, jokes,
22   initial cap J, unquote, until 1986. What I did
23   have was magazines. I was working at Time Life
24   and was surrounded by magazines. I wanted to
25   present the images I saw in these magazines as

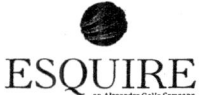

49

	Prince
1	Prince
2	naturally as when they first appeared. Making a
3	photograph of them seemed the best way to do it.
4	I didn't exactly, quote, fall, unquote, as much
5	as steal, period.
6	Did you make that statement?
7	A. Yes, I did.
8	Q. Was that a true statement?
9	A. Yes, it is.
10	Q. When you said you had no skills,
11	I mean what did you mean?
12	A. I didn't have any skills. I had
13	never really -- I liked the idea of not knowing
14	how to use a mechanical apparatus at the time.
15	I didn't know anything about the medium.
16	Q. Right.
17	Do you remember saying in a
18	subsequent interview that you destroyed
19	photography?
20	A. Yes, I shot the sheriff or something
21	like that. Yeah, I did.
22	Q. What did you mean by that?
23	A. I changed it. I revolutionized it.
24	Q. How?
25	A. I changed it completely.

50

	Prince
1	Prince
2	Q. How?
3	A. Well, rephotography actually you
4	could -- thirty years later people download.
5	You could actually substitute the word download
6	for rephotography. I mean I did it.
7	Q. Download an image on your computer?
8	A. It's the same thing really.
9	Q. And scan it --
10	A. I mean I'm talking poetically here,
11	philosophically. Again, it's all an
12	experimentation. But I did destroy and change
13	the whole -- the whole medium actually.
14	And that's what I was trying to
15	do at the time was revolutionize an artistic
16	practice that up to that time was pretty boring,
17	really.
18	Q. In the essays we looked at in the
19	previous exhibit, Exhibit 3.
20	A. Mm-hmm.
21	Q. 1977 and 1978 essays, and in this
22	interview in 2003, were you trying to depict
23	yourself as an outlaw or a rebel?
24	MR. HAYES: Object to the form.
25	A. I think I was playing a part, yes.

51

	Prince
1	Prince
2	And the part was this idea of the artist as a
3	kind of cliche. And I was very much an
4	outsider. And I was interested in playing a
5	role. Again, fictionalizing myself.
6	Q. As an outlaw?
7	A. Yes.
8	Q. Kind of like Robin Hood stealing
9	from Philip Morris?
10	MR. HAYES: Objection to the form.
11	A. No.
12	MR. HAYES: Objection.
13	A. No. I was making things up.
14	Q. Right.
15	A. I was extremely -- to tell you the
16	truth, I was extremely conservative, on the
17	other hand, in terms of my artistic attitude.
18	And I knew that in order to maybe
19	discover something new I had to change a bit and
20	take on another persona. And I felt that by
21	playing, quote, as I said in the interview, the
22	camera, just like a punk rock guitarist who
23	picks up a guitar, seven days later he's playing
24	on stage. He doesn't know how to play the
25	guitar, but it's his inability which shines

52

	Prince
1	Prince
2	through, which is really exciting.
3	And the fact that he's not a
4	virtuoso -- it's the very limitations I think
5	that make -- can actually make great art. And
6	that's basically what all this, these two essays
7	and these two quotes in this particular
8	interview is about.
9	MR. BROOKS: Let's mark as
10	Plaintiff's Exhibit 5 two pages Bates
11	stamped C229 and 230.
12	It's a portion of -- or it is an
13	interview in French.
14	MS. BART: Do you have an English
15	translation for the witness and counsel?
16	MR. BROOKS: Later. That will be
17	Exhibit 6. I'm on Exhibit 5.
18	MS. BART: Well, I'd like to have
19	a copy of the translation so that I can
20	determine whether or not I need to object
21	to any of your questions with this
22	exhibit.
23	MR. BROOKS: Okay. All right.
24	Fine.
25	MS. BART: Excuse me, I'd like to

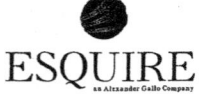

ESQUIRE
an Alexander Gallo Company

53	55
1 Prince	1 Prince
2 have it before you question --	2 trying to ask him.
3 MR. BROOKS: I'm going to give	3 MS. BART: Do it.
4 that to you after I ask him a couple of	4 MR. BROOKS: You know, your
5 questions about this document.	5 objections are supposed to be succinct,
6 MS. BART: I object to this line of	6 non-argumentative --
7 questioning.	7 MS. BART: They are succinct.
8 MR. BROOKS: Fine. That's fine.	8 MR. BROOKS: -- and non-suggestive.
9 BY MR. BROOKS:	9 MS. BART: I'm not engaging.
10 Q. Mr. Prince, take a look at --	10 Continue.
11 (Interruption by reporter.)	11 MR. BROOKS: Fine. Neither am I.
12 (Plaintiff's Exhibit 5, interview in	12 BY MR. BROOKS:
13 French, was marked for identification, as	13 Q. Mr. Prince, were you interviewed by
14 of this date.)	14 a publication called Liberacion Next?
15 MR. BROOKS: I object to counsel	15 A. I'm sorry, what --
16 conferring --	16 MR. HAYES: Read the question back.
17 MS. BART: There's no question	17 A. No, no, no, no. What was the --
18 pending.	18 Q. Liberacion Next.
19 MR. HAYES: There's no question	19 A. Next?
20 pending, is there?	20 Q. Yes.
21 Or read the question back that's	21 MR. HAYES: Is the question were you
22 pending.	22 interviewed by that publication?
23 MR. BROOKS: There was a question	23 A. I don't know.
24 pending. I started asking a question.	24 Q. Now, do you speak French?
25 MR. HAYES: What was the question?	25 A. No, I don't.

54	56
1 Prince	1 Prince
2 MR. BROOKS: I don't remember.	2 Q. At all?
3 MR. HAYES: Okay, well, read it	3 A. No, I don't.
4 back.	4 MR. BROOKS: Let's mark as
5 (Clarification by reporter.)	5 exhibit -- Plaintiff's Exhibit 6 an
6 BY MR. BROOKS:	6 English translation of a portion of the
7 Q. Mr. Prince, take a look at what's	7 French text in Exhibit 5.
8 been marked as Plaintiff's Exhibit 5, please.	8 (Plaintiff's Exhibit 6, English
9 It's two pages.	9 translation of portion of French
10 A. Mm-hmm.	10 interview, was marked for identification,
11 MR. HAYES: Just for the record, I	11 as of this date.)
12 am going to object to any questions about	12 Q. Mr. Prince, you've been handed
13 this document which is in French without	13 Plaintiff's Exhibit 6 --
14 having an English translation be provided.	14 MR. HAYES: Actually, have you been
15 MR. BROOKS: Fine. Your objection	15 handed six? I don't have a copy of it.
16 is noted.	16 Okay. Here's six. Got it.
17 MS. BART: Unless you can lay a	17 Q. Okay. The second page of
18 foundation --	18 Plaintiff's Exhibit 6 has a photo.
19 MR. BROOKS: Let me just ask the	19 Do you see that?
20 question.	20 A. This one?
21 MS. BART: I'm going to finish my	21 Q. Yes. The photo of the cowboy on a
22 objection, counsel.	22 horse?
23 Unless you can establish that this	23 A. Yes.
24 person reads and speaks French.	24 Q. Do you see it?
25 MR. BROOKS: Well, that's what I'm	25 A. Mm-hmm.

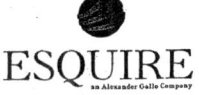

ESQUIRE
an Alexander Gallo Company

Toll Free: 800.944.9454
Facsimile: 212.557.5972

Suite 4715
One Penn Plaza
New York, NY 10119
www.esquiresolutions.com

Richard Prince   October 6, 2009

	57		59
1	Prince	1	Prince
2	Q. Do you recognize it?	2	limiting it to these two questions.
3	A. Yes.	3	MR. HAYES: I understand that, but I
4	Q. What is it?	4	want to be able to see --
5	A. It's an image of a cowboy.	5	MR. BROOKS: I don't have a
6	Q. Does it have any relationship to you	6	translation of the balance.
7	or your work?	7	MR. HAYES: But can I just finish
8	A. Yes.	8	why? I want to be able to see it in
9	Q. What?	9	context. That's a perfectly fair
10	A. It's an artwork that I did I believe	10	question. I want to see -- anything you
11	in 1989.	11	want to ask him about I want to see it in
12	Q. Is it a rephotograph of one --	12	context so if I have a follow-up question,
13	A. Yes.	13	for example, the opportunity to ask about
14	Q. -- of these Marlboro cowboys?	14	the entire article.
15	A. Yes.	15	If you are asking him about a
16	Q. The name of the interviewer on	16	portion of it and you're only translating
17	page 2 appears to be Olivier Wicker. Do you	17	a portion of it, I don't speak French,
18	know him?	18	unfortunately.
19	A. No, I don't know him. If it's --	19	MR. BROOKS: Well --
20	are you sure it's a him? I mean --	20	MR. HAYES: You're denying me the
21	Q. No, I'm not.	21	opportunity to review it and ask any
22	A. It's a him?	22	follow-up questions.
23	MR. HAYES: It could be a her.	23	MR. BROOKS: Okay.
24	Q. It could be.	24	MR. HAYES: So I object --
25	A. You know, I get interviewed so many	25	MR. BROOKS: I do speak French. The

	58		60
1	Prince	1	Prince
2	times that -- especially at this particular	2	rest of it has nothing to do with these
3	moment. I believe that was a woman. But I	3	two questions. You have my word.
4	can't be sure of that.	4	MR. HAYES: I'm not questioning --
5	Q. The date was an interesting date.	5	MR. BROOKS: And you're free to get
6	It's February 29th of last year on a leap --	6	your own translation obviously.
7	leap February 29th.	7	MR. HAYES: I'm not questioning your
8	A. Okay.	8	word, but I'm simply asking at this
9	Q. Do you remember if you were in	9	deposition it's appropriate to give me a
10	France then?	10	translation of the entire article.
11	A. I don't remember. The 29th -- no, I	11	MR. BROOKS: I don't have it.
12	can't answer that.	12	MR. HAYES: Therefore, I object.
13	Q. Okay. There are two questions and	13	BY MR. BROOKS:
14	answers that are reproduced in this interview.	14	Q. Now, getting back to what I said.
15	The first question says, You work essentially	15	When I started --
16	from existing images, what is your opinion on	16	MS. BART: Join.
17	copyright. The answer says, I have always	17	Q. You said, When I started out, no one
18	worked without authorization -- I'm going to get	18	was paying any -- no, I'm sorry. You said, I
19	to the rest later, but -- I've always worked	19	have always worked without authorization, is
20	without authorization, is that correct?	20	that true?
21	MR. HAYES: I would just like to	21	A. I'm not sure I said that. I mean
22	stop for one second.	22	I -- it sounds -- when I read that whole
23	Do you have a translation of the	23	paragraph it sounds like something that was
24	entire article?	24	translated.
25	MR. BROOKS: No, because I'm only	25	But, you know, I don't -- I don't --

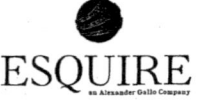

ESQUIRE
an Alexander Gallo Company

Toll Free: 800.944.9454
Facsimile: 212.557.5972

Suite 4715
One Penn Plaza
New York, NY 10119
www.esquiresolutions.com

61

1   Prince
2   it probably meant that I've always worked --
3   I don't really ask permission probably is what
4   I meant or -- I don't know. Authorization
5   doesn't sound like something I would say, but --
6   Q.   Right.
7   Do you recall giving the interview
8   with an interpreter?
9   A.   I don't -- I'm thinking that this
10   interview might have taken place in New York
11   alongside Mark.
12   Q.   Mark Jacobs?
13   A.   Yeah, but I don't recall Next.
14   I do recall giving an interview with
15   Mark for a French newspaper.
16   Q.   Okay. Let's go on to the balance of
17   the answer, and you can tell me whether or not
18   it accords with your recollection of what you
19   might have said.
20   Which does not mean that I do not
21   understand the reason why copyright exists. The
22   material I work on, I buy it, then I modify it,
23   and I know quite well from what moment an image
24   or object becomes mine. That is what I did for
25   the Marlboro cowboys. I bought an original

62

1   Prince
2   drawing that the brand had used as a medium for
3   an advertising campaign. I put it in a frame
4   alongside another photo of a cowboy. So you
5   understand that I do not pay more attention to
6   copyright than that.
7   Do you recall giving an answer --
8   A.   Yeah, but that last sentence does
9   sound like something that was translated because
10   that doesn't make any sense. But I was probably
11   referring to, yes.
12   I think in order to continue the
13   cowboy series, I started actually finding out --
14   I mean this gets back to the idea of discovering
15   and going into new territory, which was a
16   complete surprise to me that this is how organic
17   something can start.
18   I discovered you could buy original
19   drawings that the Marlboro company had
20   commissioned and used as advertisements before
21   they started making advertisements with
22   photographs. And I would go online and buy them
23   at auctions. And I liked very much that I could
24   buy these drawings.
25   And what I did was I juxtaposed them

63

1   Prince
2   in a new way, presented them in a new way.
3   Whether or not I was -- you know,
4   I've never really been aware that -- again, the
5   idea of -- as far as I know -- I mean I'm not --
6   I just really don't understand -- and I still
7   don't, copyright. However, I do believe at the
8   time there was no copyright for advertising
9   images.
10   Q.   I'm just trying to understand. I
11   understand this was probably translated from
12   French to English, so I understand that.
13   When you say you bought, and you
14   just testified that you bought drawings, did you
15   buy the drawing or the right to reproduce the
16   drawing, if you know?
17   A.   I bought the drawing.
18   Q.   And did you buy it from Philip
19   Morris or did you buy it in an auction --
20   A.   I bought it in auction.
21   Q.   -- or from some other person who
22   owned it?
23   A.   I bought it at auction.
24   Q.   And what do you mean -- again, it
25   may be because it was translated, what do you

64

1   Prince
2   mean that you put the image alongside another
3   photo of a cowboy? And I'm just looking at this
4   photo here, I only see one cowboy.
5   MR. HAYES: First of all, could you
6   ask him what he meant -- or did he say it
7   and what he meant, because he's pointed
8   out that this translation may not be
9   accurate --
10   MR. BROOKS: Right.
11   MR. HAYES: -- I'd just like to get
12   it down straight about what happened.
13   MR. BROOKS: Right.
14   BY MR. BROOKS:
15   Q.   What's your best recollection of
16   what you meant?
17   A.   What I meant was I was trying to
18   describe the work that I had made with the
19   original drawing that I bought of the Marlboro
20   ad.
21   Q.   But did you have a practice when you
22   did these Marlboro rephotographs of putting one
23   cowboy next to another within the same frame?
24   A.   Not at the -- not when I started
25   out, no. I mean what I'm describing here is a

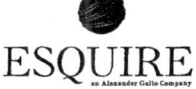

ESQUIRE
an Alexander Gallo Company

Toll Free: 800.944.9454
Facsimile: 212.557.5972

Suite 4715
One Penn Plaza
New York, NY 10119
www.esquiresolutions.com

Richard Prince   October 6, 2009

65
1 Prince
2 new body of work that I'm still working on to
3 this day, which is I'm buying original drawings
4 and watercolors that Marlboro used for their
5 advertising.
6 Q. You're still doing that?
7 A. I collect them. Yeah, they're part
8 of my collection. I don't sell them. I collect
9 them.
10 I put them into frames next to
11 photographs of cowboys. So there's a
12 juxtaposition between the two mediums. I kind
13 of like that. I think it's very creative.
14 Q. And this is for your personal
15 viewing?
16 A. This is for my personal mania for
17 collecting books and other artworks by other
18 artists.
19 Q. Now, let's look at the second
20 question. The question is, You never had any
21 problems, question mark. And the answer is,
22 When I started out, no one was paying any
23 attention to me. Who would have been concerned
24 by a guy who appropriated an image from an ad?
25 What purpose would it serve to sue me? I was

67
1 Prince
2 Q. And so the two of you put together a
3 spring collection for Louis Vuitton?
4 A. No, I -- I didn't put anything
5 together. I gave him ideas for -- my job, or --
6 you know, what I was supposed to do was to work
7 with the font, I guess you call it, the Louis
8 Vuitton, their logo. I was supposed to come up
9 with a variation that they then could put on
10 handbags.
11 Q. And was that done?
12 A. Yes, it was.
13 Q. Were you paid?
14 A. I was paid.
15 Q. Let's take a look at -- let me just
16 say something. I'm going to come back to that
17 so, just so --
18 MR. HAYES: We'll leave it right
19 here.
20 Q. -- it can be kept on top of the pile
21 because I am going to come back to it.
22 MR. HAYES: Sure. This is actually
23 the copy here, this is my copy.
24 MR. BROOKS: All right. Fine.
25 Let's mark as Plaintiff's Exhibit 7

66
1 Prince
2 living in an apartment in East Village -- in the
3 East Village, where the rent was $75 a month.
4 My job earned me $100. I had enough left to
5 eat, drink, and buy supplies to paint. But if,
6 unfortunately, I were to be sued today, I would
7 call upon a law firm. However, it would not
8 bother me in the slightest for someone to
9 appropriate my work. And it's rather funny for
10 me to work with a company Louis Vuitton whose
11 sales revenue depends in large part on defending
12 its copyright.
13 Do you recall giving an answer along
14 those lines?
15 A. That's pretty good. Yeah. That's a
16 pretty good translation.
17 Q. And did you work on the 2008 spring
18 collection for Louis Vuitton together with Mark
19 Jacobs?
20 A. Yes.
21 Q. Who is Mark Jacobs?
22 A. He's a friend.
23 Q. No, but what is his -- what is he
24 known for?
25 A. He's a fashion designer.

68
1 Prince
2 a two-page article which was produced with
3 Bates stamps C83 and 84.
4 (Plaintiff's Exhibit 7, two-page
5 article, was marked for identification, as
6 of this date.)
7 Q. Mr. Prince, please take a look at
8 Plaintiff's Exhibit 7. You'll see it was
9 written -- do you know Randy Kennedy, the
10 reporter who wrote this?
11 A. I know of him, yes.
12 Q. From the New York Times?
13 A. Yes.
14 Q. It looks like this article was
15 written December 6th, 2007, and that was on the
16 occasion of your mid-career retrospective at the
17 Guggenheim, is that right?
18 A. Yes.
19 Q. What was the name of that show?
20 A. Spiritual America.
21 Q. After the Brooke Shields photograph?
22 A. Yes.
23 Q. Now, that -- I should say
24 rephotograph, that Brooke Shields image.
25 The name, the title Spiritual

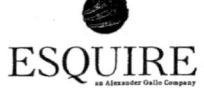

ESQUIRE
an Alexander Gallo Company

Toll Free: 800.944.9454
Facsimile: 212.557.5972

Suite 4715
One Penn Plaza
New York, NY 10119
www.esquiresolutions.com

69

1   Prince
2   America, where did you get that from?
3   A.   It was an Alfred Stieglitz image
4   that I saw at the Metropolitan Museum of Art.
5   (Discussion off the record.)
6   Q.   You saw it where, at the
7   Metropolitan Museum of Art? What did you say?
8   A.   Yes. Yes. That's where I saw the
9   image.
10   Q.   The Stieglitz image?
11   A.   The Stieglitz image was titled.
12   Q.   Right.
13   A.   Spiritual America.
14   Q.   If you go down to the fourth
15 paragraph do you see it starts with the words
16 when Mr. Prince started reshooting ads, do you
17 see that?
18   A.   Yes.
19   MR. HAYES: I caution the witness,
20 you can take your time to read the entire
21 document that's put in front of you.
22   Any documents put in front of you,
23 just you take the time to read the entire
24 document.
25   Just so he knows.

70

1   Prince
2   BY MR. BROOKS:
3   Q.   That goes for any document I show
4   you today.
5   Now, this paragraph states when
6   Mr. Prince started reshooting ads, first prosaic
7   ones of fountain pens and furniture sets and
8   then more traditionally striking ones like those
9   from Marlboro, he said he was trying to get at
10 something he could not get at by creating his
11 own images. He once compared the effect to the
12 funny way that, quote, certain records sound
13 better when someone on the radio station plays
14 them, than when we're home alone and play the
15 same records ourselves, unquote.
16   Do you recall making a statement to
17 that effect?
18   A.   Yeah, it's a great statement.
19   Q.   But it's your statement?
20   A.   The quote?
21   Q.   Yes.
22   A.   Yes, that's a statement. Whether I
23 made it to him, I don't recall.
24   Q.   And is it correct that before you
25 started rephotographing the Marlboro commercials

71

1   Prince
2   ads you did fountain pens and furniture sets?
3   A.   Yes.
4   Q.   The next paragraph it says,
5   referring to you, But he was not circumspect
6   about what it meant or how it would be viewed.
7   In the 1992 discussion at the Whitney Museum of
8   American Art he said of rustling the Marlboro
9   aesthetic, colon, quote, no one was looking,
10 this was a famous campaign, if you are going to
11 steal something, you know, you go to the bank.
12   Did you make a statement to that
13 effect?
14   A.   I really can't say that, but it
15 sounds like something I might have said at the
16 time, yes.
17   Q.   Have you ever compared yourself to
18 Willy Sutton?
19   A.   I believe that I was probably
20 riffing on the Willy Sutton comment, and I was
21 probably being a bit of a -- again, playing the
22 part of kind of a punk rock artist at the time.
23   Q.   And just for the record, who is
24 Willy Sutton, as far as you know?
25   A.   I believe he was a bank robber.

72

1   Prince
2   Q.   The next paragraph states people
3   might not have been looking at the time when his
4   art was not highly sought, but as his reputation
5   and prices for his work rose steeply, dash, one
6   of the Marlboro pictures set an auction record
7   for a photograph in 2005, comma, selling for
8   1.2 million dollars, dash, they began to look,
9   and Mr. Prince has spoken of receiving threats,
10 comma, some legal and some more physical in
11 nature, comma, from his unsuspecting lenders.
12 He is said to have made a small payment in an
13 out-of-court settlement with one photographer
14 Garry Gross who took the original shot for one
15 of Mr. Prince's most notorious early borrowings,
16 an image of a young unclothed Brooke Shields.
17 Mr. Prince declined to comment for this article,
18 comma, saying in an e-mail message only, quote,
19 I never associated advertisements with having an
20 author, unquote.
21   Now, is it true that you started
22 receiving legal threats at some point?
23   A.   No, that's probably something that I
24 just made up.
25   Q.   Did Garry Gross ever threaten to sue

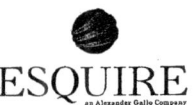

ESQUIRE
an Alexander Gallo Company

Toll Free: 800.944.9454
Facsimile: 212.557.5972

Suite 4715
One Penn Plaza
New York, NY 10119
www.esquiresolutions.com

	73			75	
1	Prince		1	Prince	
2	you?		2	in for context the following paragraph and	
3	A. No, he never did.		3	its reference to the fair use exceptions	
4	Q. Did you ever reach an out-of-court		4	to copyright law?	
5	settlement with Garry Gross?		5	BY MR. BROOKS:	
6	A. No.		6	Q. Did you send an e-mail to this	
7	Q. You're positive?		7	reporter saying, at the top of page 2 of the	
8	A. I'm positive.		8	exhibit, I never associated advertisements with	
9	As far as I can tell, I'm positive.		9	having an author?	
10	I actually -- in 1992 I guess that's what		10	A. It sounds like something I would	
11	they're talking about, your last quote here,		11	have said. Whether or not I sent an e-mail to	
12	you're talking about -- I mean Mr. Kennedy is		12	him, I don't know. I don't recall.	
13	talking about a 1992 discussion at the Whitney,		13	Q. And you -- that actually is	
14	and I believe at that time I bought the rights		14	something you believe, right?	
15	to the image for $2,000.		15	A. Yeah. Advertisements have no	
16	Q. From Gary Gross?		16	authors. They're art directed though, and I	
17	A. Yes.		17	believe -- I believe that sincerely. I believe	
18	Q. Because he threatened to sue you?		18	they're psychologically hopped-up images that	
19	A. No. I was told by the Whitney that		19	are too good to be true. They look like they	
20	I -- in order to exhibit that image I made a		20	have a life of their own, and they look like a	
21	concession, or they advised me that it would		21	film still.	
22	probably be best that -- and I believe I sort of		22	I don't believe I've ever seen	
23	reached out to him at the time.		23	an author or an artist's signature on an	
24	Because up until then, that image		24	advertisement.	
25	that I rephotographed from that pamphlet that he		25	What I believe -- they're associated	

	74			76	
1	Prince		1	Prince	
2	had produced in 1983, I made one copy, an 8 by		2	with products. And I believe I started taking	
3	10, and I gave it away. And it wasn't until		3	them, rephotographing them because of those	
4	1992 that it came back into the limelight, and I		4	qualities.	
5	think my attitude changed a bit and I was sort		5	Q. Do you see further down on the	
6	of willing to become more part of the process I		6	second page of Exhibit 7 -- withdrawn.	
7	suppose.		7	Have you ever heard of Jim Krantz,	
8	Q. And at that time you made ten copies		8	K-R-A-N-T-Z, before?	
9	plus an artist proof?		9	A. No.	
10	A. At the time there was ten copies and		10	Q. Well, he apparently was at least one	
11	I believe two artist proofs, none of which I		11	of the people who did the ads for Marlboro.	
12	own.		12	A. He did?	
13	MR. HAYES: By the way, do you want		13	Q. According to this article.	
14	to read into the record the following		14	And I'm just going to call your	
15	paragraph --		15	attention to what he is quoted as saying at the	
16	(Clarification by reporter.)		16	bottom of page 2. Fourth paragraph from the	
17	MR. HAYES: Do you want read into		17	bottom it says, Mr. Krantz said he considered	
18	the record the following paragraph --		18	his ad work distinctive, comma, not simply the	
19	MR. BROOKS: No, no, you can do that		19	kind of anonymous commercial imagery that he	
20	when you have redirect. I don't want to		20	feels Mr. Prince considers it to be.	
21	spend my time --		21	I take it you disagree with	
22	MR. HAYES: Okay. Just read back --		22	Mr. Krantz's statement?	
23	let me restate my statement because the		23	MR. HAYES: Well, objection on	
24	court reporter didn't get it.		24	several grounds. First of all, we don't	
25	The question is do you want to read		25	know that Mr. Krantz actually said this.	

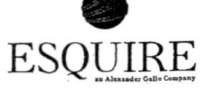

Toll Free: 800.944.9454
Facsimile: 212.557.5972

Suite 4715
One Penn Plaza
New York, NY 10119
www.esquiresolutions.com

77

```
1            Prince
2        MR. BROOKS: Right.
3        MR. HAYES: And what you're now
4    doing is you're taking this entirely out
5    of context without consenting, for
6    example, to read the paragraph above that
7    I asked you to read in to put the entire
8    article into context.
9        MS. BART: I think you should do
10   that now for the record --
11       MR. HAYES: That article -- that
12   paragraph says Mr. Krantz --
13       MR. BROOKS: Now, I -- listen, if
14   you're going to enforce the seven-hour
15   rule, I object to your saying anything
16   other than objection, or direct him not to
17   answer.
18       MR. HAYES: I object to the witness
19   being asked questions without it being put
20   in context by reading appropriate parts of
21   the rest of the article, which --
22       MR. BROOKS: Fine.
23       MR. HAYES: -- by the way, is two
24   sentences --
25       MR. BROOKS: Which you can read when
```

78

```
1            Prince
2    you do redirect, if you wish.
3        A.  No. Listen, I'll -- here's the
4    thing. You know, I don't know Mr. Krantz, and I
5    have no -- I'm sure he's a great guy and a great
6    photographer, you know, and I'm sure he took
7    great photographs for the Marlboro. I don't
8    know if he did or not.
9        But, you know, it had -- what he did
10   has nothing to do with what I do.
11       Q.  I understand.
12       There's a statement attributed to
13   him. He may or may not have made it. Let me
14   just ask you, do you disagree with the statement
15   that's attributed to him?
16       MS. BART: Objection, form, rule of
17   optional completeness.
18       Q.  The statement is Mr. Krantz said he
19   considered his ad work distinctive, not simply
20   the kind of anonymous commercial imagery that he
21   feels Mr. Prince considers it to be.
22       MR. HAYES: Objection, calls for
23   speculation, it's improper complete.
24       The quote -- the attributed quote,
25   it calls for speculation. That's
```

79

```
1            Prince
2    incorporated in the question. I think the
3    question is improper, and I join with
4    Ms. Bart's objection.
5        Q.  So now you can answer.
6        Do you disagree with that statement
7    attributed to --
8        A.  I'm sure he has -- I mean, you know,
9    I respect his feelings.
10       Q.  So you agree with what he's saying?
11       MR. HAYES: Well, what he's saying,
12   you're agreeing with his statement about
13   that Mr. Krantz considers his work
14   distinctive or imagery that he feels or
15   what Mr. Prince considers it to be.
16   You're asking for Mr. Prince's state of
17   mind about Mr. Krantz's artwork --
18       MR. BROOKS: Mr. Hayes, you're
19   starting to obstruct.
20       MR. HAYES: I'm not. There are two
21   statements in there. Which one are you
22   asking about?
23   BY MR. BROOKS:
24       Q.  Do you agree that the Marlboro ads
25   that you rephotographed are distinctive?
```

80

```
1            Prince
2        A.  Well, they're distinctive for me,
3    yes.
4        Q.  What does that mean?
5        A.  They're distinctive for me in many,
6    many ways. I mean I can talk about it for an
7    hour. You know, they're cowboys but they're not
8    cowboys. They seem to represent something about
9    America. They're political I suppose. With me
10   not really being a political artist. They're
11   great-looking images.
12       Again, you know, when I first took
13   them -- I mean had a show of cowboys in 1984.
14   No one paid any attention. There was nothing
15   ever written on them. And no one bought any.
16       I like them. I mean that's as
17   simple as I can say. I think they're great
18   images.
19       THE VIDEOGRAPHER: Two minutes.
20       A.  Sorry --
21       Q.  No, I appreciate that.
22       Now, if you would go back to
23   Exhibit 6, remember I said we were going to go
24   back --
25       MS. BART: I think he wants to --
```

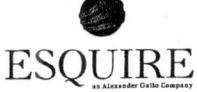

ESQUIRE
an Alexander Gallo Company

Toll Free: 800.944.9454
Facsimile: 212.557.5972

Suite 4715
One Penn Plaza
New York, NY 10119
www.esquiresolutions.com

	81		83

81

1   Prince
2   MR. BROOKS: Five minutes?
3   MS. BART: Two minutes.
4   MR. BROOKS: Shall we stop now?
5   THE VIDEOGRAPHER: Yes.
6   11:37. Off the record.
7   End of tape 1.
8   (Recess taken: 11:37 a.m.)
9   (Proceedings resumed: 11:46 a.m.)
10   THE VIDEOGRAPHER: 11:46.
11   On the record. Beginning of tape 2.
12   BY MR. BROOKS:
13   Q.   We were looking at Exhibit 7, and
14   there's a -- on the first page of it there's a
15   picture of one of those cowboys.
16   A.   Mm-hmm.
17   Q.   Is that one of your rephotographs
18   that you sold?
19   A.   No.
20   Q.   No? That's an original?
21   A.   I don't know.
22   Q.   Okay. It's not one of yours?
23   A.   It's not one of mine.
24   Q.   Now, could you go back to Exhibit 6,
25   please, and the second page of it?

82

1   Prince
2   A.   Which is Exhibit 6?
3   MR. HAYES: Exhibit 6 is this.
4   MR. BROOKS: That's the translation.
5   MR. HAYES: Translation of the
6   portion of the article.
7   MR. BROOKS: Right.
8   BY MR. BROOKS:
9   Q.   At the bottom you said it's -- and
10   it's rather funny for me to work with a company
11   Louis Vuitton whose sales revenue depends in
12   large part on defending its copyright.
13   That was a reference to the 2008
14   collection that you helped Mark Jacobs with?
15   A.   Yes.
16   Q.   And what was funny about that?
17   A.   I just felt that this was a
18   situation, a new situation for me, which I was
19   providing them with images, and they needed to
20   make sure that they had -- I believe I provided
21   them with very obscure images of cartoons.
22   And I just thought it was funny
23   because, you know, I'm -- they're a commercial
24   outfit, very big, and I'm just -- I was just an
25   artist. They needed to know -- you know, I

83

1   Prince
2   guess I felt that I was lucky that I didn't have
3   those kinds of concerns because I believe -- you
4   know, they operate in the real world, and I
5   don't.
6   Q.   You're aware that they spend a lot
7   of effort trying to prevent knock-offs, right?
8   A.   They made me aware of that, yes.
9   And I was glad of the fact that I didn't have to
10   be in their shoes.
11   Q.   Right.
12   A.   I felt it was kind of silly, to tell
13   you the truth.
14   Q.   Well, they spent a lot of money
15   designing that collection I assume, right?
16   A.   I believe they did, yes.
17   Q.   So somebody could knock it off in
18   China and they would lose sales, right?
19   MS. BART: Objection to form.
20   MR. HAYES: Objection.
21   Q.   Right?
22   A.   I guess so, yeah.
23   Q.   You, on the other hand, in Exhibit 6
24   said, However, it would not bother me in the
25   slightest for someone to appropriate my work.

84

1   Prince
2   Do you see that?
3   A.   Yes.
4   Q.   Do you copyright your work?
5   A.   No, I don't.
6   Q.   Do you realize that there's a
7   copyright notice in the Canal Zone book?
8 ·   A.   No, I didn't know. I didn't really
9   look at the Canal Zone book.
10   Q.   Ever?
11   A.   I've looked at it. I approved I
12   believe what they call the galleys.
13   Q.   Did you look at the inserts?
14   A.   You mean -- what do you mean
15   inserts?
16   Q.   Well, for one thing, the James Frey,
17   F-R-E-Y, story?
18   A.   Yes.
19   Q.   By insert I mean the pages are
20   smaller than the regular pages.
21   A.   Yes.
22   Q.   So you looked at that?
23   A.   Yes.
24   Q.   And there were some cartoon drawings
25   with the James Frey --

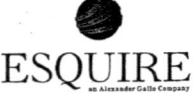

85

Prince

1
2   A.   Yes.
3   Q.   -- essay or story?
4   A.   Yes.
5   Q.   Do you know where those cartoons
6   came from?
7   A.   They came from my collecting cartoon
8   books.
9   Q.   But then there were little captions,
10   were those original into the cartoons?
11   A.   I don't recall if they were original
12   or not.
13   Q.   For instance, How do I know you
14   won't kiss and tell?
15   A.   Right. I don't know if they were --
16   I might have made up my own captions, I often
17   do, to mismatch. And I believe those cartoons
18   were collaged onto palm trees, which I -- it was
19   part of my contribution to the cartoon to make
20   it different and suggested again the jungles of
21   Panama.
22   MR. BROOKS: Okay. Just so my
23   outline doesn't get all screwed up, I'm
24   going to mark this as Exhibit 42.
25   MR. HAYES: 42?

86

Prince

1
2   MR. BROOKS: Out of order.
3   So this will be the exhibit I guess.
4   (Plaintiff's Exhibit 42, Canal Zone
5   book, was marked for identification, as of
6   this date.)
7   MR. BROOKS: These pages are Bates
8   stamped -- Mr. Hayes, could you help him
9   find the page Bates stamped 213? It's in
10   the very back.
11   MR. HAYES: You can find it faster
12   than me, but sure.
13   There we go.
14   BY MR. BROOKS:
15   Q.   Mr. Prince, this is the book I was
16   referring to before.
17   A.   Mm-hmm.
18   Q.   And it was published in connection
19   with an exhibition at the Gagosian Gallery in
20   November-December 2008, is that correct?
21   A.   Yes.
22   Q.   It says -- in the third paragraph
23   I guess it says publication copyright 2008,
24   Gagosian Gallery, Ding Dong the Witch is Dead,
25   copyright 2008, James Frey, and that's -- is

87

Prince

1
2   that a reference to his story?
3   MR. HAYES: If you know.
4   Q.   If you know.
5   A.   No, I don't know.
6   Q.   Everything is if you know.
7   A.   No, I don't know.
8   Q.   And it says all artworks copyright
9   2008 Richard Prince, insert images copyright
10   2008 Richard Prince. Do you see that?
11   A.   Yes.
12   Q.   Have you ever seen that before?
13   A.   If I did I never really paid
14   attention to it.
15   Q.   And then at the bottom of the page
16   it says all rights reserved, no part of this
17   publication may be used or reproduced in any
18   manner whatsoever without prior written
19   permission from the copyright holders.
20   Do you see that language?
21   A.   Yes.
22   Q.   So you created some artworks that
23   are depicted in this book Exhibit 42, correct?
24   A.   Yes.
25   Q.   And you spent some time and effort

88

Prince

1
2   doing it?
3   A.   Yes.
4   Q.   And you spent some money I assume,
5   right?
6   A.   Yes.
7   Q.   And you don't mind if somebody just
8   copies some of these images and sells them?
9   A.   No, I don't.
10   If they can make a contribution --
11   Q.   You answered.
12   A.   -- I'm all for it.
13   MR. BROOKS: Let's mark as
14   Plaintiff's Exhibit 8 an interview of
15   Mr. Prince. And those pages have been
16   Bates stamped in our initial disclosure
17   C59 to 64.
18   This is going to get very congested
19   there. Maybe you might just want to put
20   that -- because I'm not going to come back
21   to that book for a while, maybe just --
22   MR. HAYES: Sure.
23   MR. BROOKS: Plaintiff's Exhibit 8.
24   (Plaintiff's Exhibit 8, interview,
25   was marked for identification, as of this

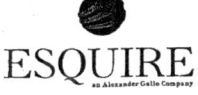

ESQUIRE
an Alexander Gallo Company

Toll Free: 800.944.9454
Facsimile: 212.557.5972

Suite 4715
One Penn Plaza
New York, NY 10119
www.esquiresolutions.com

89

	Prince
1	Prince
2	date.)
3	Q. Mr. Prince, you've been handed
4	what's been marked as Plaintiff's Exhibit 8.
5	Do you, first of all, know
6	Brian Appel, A-P-P-E-L?
7	A. I know who he is, yes.
8	Q. And do you recall being interviewed
9	by him sometime in 2007?
10	A. Yes, I do.
11	Q. Have you ever seen this I guess
12	publication of that interview before?
13	A. No, I've never seen it before.
14	Q. At the time you gave this interview
15	you were still being represented by the Barbara
16	Gladstone Gallery, is that right?
17	A. When was this, 2007?
18	Q. Yes. I'm not sure what month.
19	Let me help you. If you look at the
20	very top --
21	A. I was showing with her, yes, 2007 --
22	Q. If you just look at the very first
23	statement Mr. Appel made, he says hope you had a
24	chance to read my review of your last show at
25	Barbara Gladstone. Do you see that?

90

	Prince
1	Prince
2	A. Yes.
3	Q. Do you remember when you switched,
4	if you did, from Barbara Gladstone to Gagosian
5	Gallery as your representative?
6	A. I've never really switched.
7	Q. Does Barbara Gladstone Gallery still
8	represent you as well?
9	A. She represents some of my work, yes.
10	Q. Currently?
11	A. Currently.
12	Q. And does Gagosian Gallery represent
13	some of your work?
14	A. He has some of my work on
15	consignment, yes.
16	Q. Okay. But doesn't he do other --
17	render other services for you, for instance,
18	help sell your art?
19	A. That's what they're -- both of them
20	are supposed to do.
21	Q. Market it?
22	A. Yes.
23	Q. Do you have a written contract with
24	Gagosian Gallery?
25	A. I have no contracts.

91

	Prince
1	Prince
2	Q. It's just a handshake?
3	A. There's not even a handshake.
4	Q. When he sells -- withdrawn.
5	When Gagosian Gallery sells your art
6	for you do they keep a percentage and give you a
7	percentage?
8	A. Yes.
9	Q. And is it always 60 percent that you
10	get?
11	A. No.
12	Q. No?
13	A. It's different. It depends on what
14	work sells.
15	Q. Okay. And is it negotiated on a
16	work-by-work basis rather than in some
17	underlying agreement?
18	A. It's very fluid. It depends upon my
19	mood at the time that it sells. I can fluctuate
20	this, whatever you call it, a sliding scale. I
21	don't know.
22	Q. So whatever arrangement you have
23	with Gagosian Gallery, it's just a set of oral
24	understandings --
25	A. Yes.

92

	Prince
1	Prince
2	Q. -- is that right?
3	No written contract?
4	A. No written contract.
5	Q. Now, turning to Plaintiff's
6	Exhibit 8, the -- I guess the second question
7	Mr. Appel asked you. I'll read it. One of the
8	highlights of the summer for me was having the
9	pleasure of seeing two of your controversial
10	rephotography pieces from 1983 turning up in two
11	excellent survey shows, semicolon, the
12	subversively seductive, quote, Untitled
13	Girlfriend on Motorbike, unquote, a
14	44-by-64-inch ectocolor print of a scrawny nude
15	biker girl awkwardly splayed on top of a Harley
16	Davidson motorcycle in the Christine Bell
17	curated, quote, Girls on Film, unquote, exhibit
18	at Zwimmer, Z-W-I-M --
19	MR. HAYES: Zwirner I believe it is.
20	Q. -- Zwirner, Zwirner, Zwimer,
21	Z-W-I-R-N-E-R, and Wirth, W-I-R-T-H, and the
22	notorious, quote/unquote, Spiritual America, a
23	24-by-20-inch ectocolor print after an original
24	by Garry Gross of a prepubescent Brooke Shields
25	emerging nude from a steamy bathtub in the

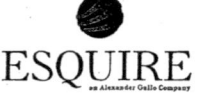

ESQUIRE
an Alexander Gallo Company

93

1 Prince
2 Donna-De-Salvo-curated, quote/unquote, landscape
3 exhibit from the permanent collection at the
4 Whitney Museum of Art.
5   That was a mouthful, but --
6   MR. HAYES: And it goes on more. Do
7 you want to read it?
8   MR. BROOKS: It does go on. It goes
9 on for six pages. I'm not going to read
10 it all.
11   MR. HAYES: No, I mean that question
12 went on or that statement went on more.
13   MR. BROOKS: Yeah, I know. But this
14 is the part I'm focusing on.
15 BY MR. BROOKS:
16   Q. The scrawny nude biker girl, is that
17 the photo to the right of the text?
18   There appears to be a photo called
19 Untitled Girlfriend 1993?
20   A. I don't know.
21   Q. Okay. Fair enough.
22   You don't remember rephotographing
23 that image?
24   Do you see the girl on the
25 motorcycle?

94

1 Prince
2   A. Yes.
3   Q. Okay. You don't -- that's not your
4 work?
5   A. That's my work.
6   Q. Oh, okay.
7   A. I don't know if that's what he's
8 referring to though.
9   Q. Okay. Forget about him. Let's just
10 ask you. Is that your work?
11   A. Yes, it is.
12   Q. Okay. And where did you -- did you
13 take that photo yourself or rephotograph it?
14   A. No. No, I didn't. I rephotographed
15 that image from an image that appeared in a
16 motorcycle magazine.
17   Q. Without authorization?
18   MS. BART: Objection, form.
19   MR. HAYES: Objection to form.
20   A. No, I --
21   Q. Without asking for permission?
22   A. I gave myself permission.
23   Q. Yes. But did you ask the magazine
24 or the person who took the picture?
25   A. No, I didn't.

95

1 Prince
2   MS. BART: Objection, form.
3   Q. Now, why is Spiritual America, if
4 you -- I don't know if you agree with this or
5 not, but he calls it notorious, do you agree
6 with that characterization?
7   A. No.
8   Q. Do you realize the police in London
9 just seized it in the Tate Gallery the other
10 day?
11   A. I was informed of that fact I
12 believe while I was breaking down on the
13 Palisades Parkway on Thursday afternoon.
14   Q. And were you told why the police in
15 London confiscated it?
16   A. No. I didn't.
17   Q. Obscenity laws?
18   A. I have been told nothing at all why.
19 I don't -- to tell you the truth, I don't know
20 if the police seized it. If you're telling me
21 this, it's news to me.
22   Q. I don't know.
23   Well, you say it's news to you but
24 somebody told you --
25   A. Well, the police --

96

1 Prince
2   (Interruption by court reporter.)
3 BY MR. BROOKS:
4   Q. Let's just withdraw it.
5   Somebody told you the police had
6 seized it?
7   A. Yes.
8   Q. Could you turn to the second page of
9 what's been marked as Exhibit 8. There's a
10 picture there in the upper right-hand corner?
11   A. Yes.
12   Q. Is that Spiritual America?
13   A. Yes, it is.
14   Q. And it says after an original by
15 commercial photographer Garry Gross, edition of
16 ten plus one AP -- what does AP mean?
17   A. Artist proof.
18   There's actually two. It should --
19   Q. It should say two.
20   And this was done by you in 1983?
21   A. Not the edition of ten plus two APs,
22 no.
23   Q. Oh, he's testified about that. That
24 was done subsequently in connection with the
25 Whitney show?

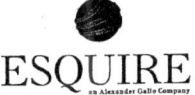

ESQUIRE
an Alexander Gallo Company

Toll Free: 800.944.9454
Facsimile: 212.557.5972

Suite 4715
One Penn Plaza
New York, NY 10119
www.esquiresolutions.com

97	99
Prince	Prince
1	1
2 A. Yes.	2 believe the last one was maybe $150,000.
3 Q. Okay, sorry.	3 Q. Now, if you could look back at
4 And the one you did in 1938 you say	4 page 1 of Exhibit 8, there's a quote there from
5 you gave away?	5 you beneath that question, a part of which I
6 A. Yes.	6 read where you said -- I'm going to just quote,
7 Q. The ten you did in 1992, did you	7 it's part of the question, I just want to ask
8 sell them?	8 you if that part of your statement -- the part
9 A. I believe the ten started to be	9 of the answer reflects your thinking.
10 editioned around 1987 through 1992 they were	10 I like to think about making it
11 sold.	11 again instead of making it new.
12 Q. Okay. And who is Donna De Salvo,	12 MR. HAYES: Can you just show me
13 what was she --	13 where you are? I'm sorry, I don't know
14 A. She's a curator --	14 where you are.
15 Q. -- can you explain what that --	15 MR. BROOKS: Yeah, I'm sorry. First
16 A. -- curator at the Whitney.	16 page, it says -- it's the second answer.
17 Q. Of a show called Landscape?	17 MR. HAYES: Oh, got it. The second
18 A. I don't know that.	18 sentence -- the third sentence in the
19 Q. Spiritual America was one of the	19 answer, right?
20 works -- you don't?	20 MR. BROOKS: I'll read the whole
21 A. I don't recall. A lot of times I	21 answer, but it's not necessary.
22 don't get that type of information.	22 BY MR. BROOKS:
23 Q. Have you exhibited Spiritual America	23 Q. The machinery of America,
24 at the Whitney?	24 quote/unquote, that's a pretty good way of
25 A. That's a good question. Did I	25 describing the way images get out there. I like

98	100
Prince	Prince
1	1
2 exhibit it in my show in nineteen -- that would	2 to think about making it again instead of making
3 have been 1992?	3 it new. Making it new was an Ezra Pound way of
4 Q. I guess.	4 thinking, paren, industrial, close paren, and,
5 A. I believe I did.	5 quote, making it again, unquote, is a more
6 Q. Do you know how much that	6 R. Prince way of doing it, paren, technological,
7 rephotography -- withdrawn -- that work sells	7 close paren. Advertising images aren't really
8 for now?	8 associated with an author, more with a product
9 A. No, I don't.	9 slash company, and for the most part put out or,
10 Q. Do you know what the most one of	10 quote, art directed, unquote. They kind of end
11 them is sold for is? I'm talking about	11 up having a life of their own. It's not like
12 Spiritual America.	12 you're taking them from anyone.
13 A. Spiritual America?	13 I know the answer goes on, but that
14 I believe -- you mean the original	14 part that I quoted is similar to what you were
15 Spiritual America or the edition?	15 testifying to about half an hour ago, correct?
16 Q. The edition.	16 A. Yes.
17 A. The edition?	17 Q. That's your view, okay.
18 Q. I'm sorry, when you say edition are	18 A. Yes.
19 you saying A-D or E-D, because I'm not --	19 Q. Do you have a different standard or
20 MR. HAYES: E-D.	20 artistic practice for taking images when there
21 Q. E-D.	21 is a disclosed author and it's not an
22 A. E-D.	22 advertisement?
23 Q. Edition, okay.	23 A. No, not really. It's just a
24 A. The edition, I don't believe there's	24 question of whether I like the image.
25 been one up for sale for quite some time. But I	25 Q. If you like it then you'll consider

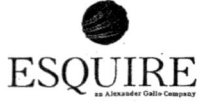

101	103
1 Prince	1 Prince
2 appropriating it?	2 it was auctioned at Christie's in 2007?
3 MR. HAYES: Object to the form.	3 A. I believe the top one is -- probably
4 You can answer.	4 the -- I was told in excess of two-million
5 THE WITNESS: I'm sorry?	5 dollars.
6 Q. You can answer.	6 Q. Right.
7 MR. HAYES: I objected to form, but	7 A. Is that true?
8 you can answer it.	8 Q. Let's look at page 2 of the article.
9 A. That's very difficult to answer	9 In the middle of the page in quotes
10 because it really depends on the --	10 Mr. Appel, speaking of number 1, dash, your,
11 Q. Okay.	11 quote/unquote, Untitled Cowboy from 2001 that
12 A. -- my mood of the day.	12 sold at Christie's this last May reset your
13 Q. I understand. But when you do take	13 world auction record for a photograph of
14 images, let's just say when you do, you don't,	14 2.8-million dollars. Does that sound right?
15 in your own mind, differentiate between	15 A. I wasn't aware it was that much, but
16 advertisements and things where you know who the	16 yes, it sounds right.
17 author is and it's not an advertisement, is that	17 Q. And beneath the Brooke Shields photo
18 what you're saying?	18 there's a nurse with a -- like a mask, right?
19 MS. BART: Objection, form.	19 A. Yes.
20 A. No, I -- I mean it's a good example	20 Q. And you've done a series of
21 right here because the girlfriend is editorial.	21 portraits of these nurses, right?
22 Q. Right.	22 A. Portraits --
23 A. And the cowboy is advertisement.	23 Q. Portraits is the wrong word?
24 Girlfriend came from a lifestyle	24 A. -- would be a good way to describe
25 magazine which was a whole new type of magazine	25 them, yes.

102	104
1 Prince	1 Prince
2 for me.	2 Q. Okay, fine.
3 Q. Right.	3 And these were taken from the covers
4 A. You're talking about after I left	4 of pulp novels?
5 Time Life.	5 A. Pulp paperbacks that I collect, yes.
6 Q. Right.	6 Q. And those sell in the range of five
7 A. Whole new subject matter was opened	7 to six-million dollars apiece, is that right,
8 to me.	8 the nurse paintings?
9 Q. But in both cases you felt you could	9 A. No.
10 give yourself permission, as you said --	10 Q. What range do they sell for, if you
11 A. Yes, I like --	11 know?
12 Q. -- to take both images, right?	12 A. Today?
13 A. You have the green light, yes.	13 Q. Yeah.
14 Q. For both?	14 A. Maybe two-million dollars.
15 A. Yes.	15 Q. How about a year and a half ago --
16 Q. And then you referred to this, but	16 A. Well, that was --
17 above the girlfriend, is that from a series, the	17 Q. -- before Lehman Brothers?
18 girlfriend, is that a series you did?	18 A. That's at auction. Are you talking
19 A. Yes.	19 about at auction price or primary price?
20 Q. Okay. Above that there's another of	20 Q. Either.
21 these Marlboro cowboys?	21 A. Secondary?
22 A. Yes.	22 Q. Either.
23 Q. Is that your work?	23 A. I don't have any idea what auction,
24 A. Yes.	24 but primary is --
25 Q. And how much was that one sold when	25 Q. From the dealer?

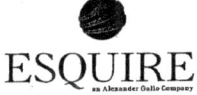

ESQUIRE
an Alexander Gallo Company

Toll Free: 800.944.9454
Facsimile: 212.557.5972

Suite 4715
One Penn Plaza
New York, NY 10119
www.esquiresolutions.com

105		107	

105

1   Prince
2   A.   From the dealer it's about -- it
3 depends on the size. A small one may be half a
4 million dollars. A large one, depends upon --
5 again, it depends upon what I think, how I feel
6 about it.
7   I mean I have one in my house you
8 could have today for -- I would, you know, if
9 you want to give me eight-million dollars I'll
10 sell it to you.
11   Q.   Okay. We'll talk about that after
12 the deposition.
13   A.   Okay.
14   Q.   Can you finance it?
15   MS. BART: For life.
16   Q.   You've said you collected -- I read
17 about some of your collections. You have On the
18 Road, Jack Kerouac, an original?
19   A.   Yes.
20   Q.   And you have the copy that was owned
21 by Cassady, right? Neal Cassady, the Neal
22 Cassady--
23   A.   Yes, we are quite certain that it
24 was owned by both Neal Cassady and his wife
25 Carolyn Cassady.

106

1   Prince
2   Q.   And then you collected photographs
3 of celebrities that you then autographed in
4 their names?
5   A.   I started to collect autographs --
6 no, I started to collect images of celebrities,
7 8-by-10 publicity pictures, which I then had the
8 stupid idea of signing them to myself. Which I
9 thought was --
10   Q.   Like Dear Richard, Love Madonna?
11   A.   Which I thought was a great idea at
12 the time.
13   Q.   Right. In this book there's a
14 picture of Madonna and another woman --
15   A.   Yes.
16   Q.   -- taken from her Sex book, correct?
17   A.   Yes.
18   Q.   Did you get permission from her to
19 do that?
20   A.   To reproduce it where?
21   In this book?
22   Q.   In this Canal Zone book?
23   A.   Can I see it?
24   MR. HAYES: Sure.
25   MS. BART: What page is it on?

107

1   Prince
2   A.   I think I know what you're talking
3 about.
4   MR. HAYES: Let's just get it so we
5 all know. 157?
6   MR. BROOKS: 157, yes.
7   A.   Okay.
8   Q.   So that image is from her Sex book,
9 Madonna's Sex book?
10   A.   No. That is not from her Sex book.
11 I believe it appeared -- that image I believe I
12 bought, that's a real signature --
13   Q.   Whose signature?
14   A.   I bought it. It's her signature.
15   Q.   Madonna's?
16   A.   Yes.
17   Q.   Okay. You bought the --
18   A.   I bought the image probably at some
19 kind of Glamourcon convention.
20   Q.   Right, okay.
21   There's also a photo in there from
22 Planet of the Apes?
23   A.   Yes.
24   Q.   The movie.
25   Did you get permission to use that?

108

1   Prince
2   A.   Permission to use it?
3   Q.   Yes, in this book.
4   A.   In the book?
5   Q.   Yes.
6   A.   No.
7   Q.   And there's one of Tarzan and Jane?
8   A.   Yeah.
9   Q.   Did you get permission to use it?
10   A.   No.
11   MR. BROOKS: All right. I'd like to
12 mark as Plaintiff's Exhibit 9 an article
13 Bates stamped C234 and 235.
14   (Plaintiff's Exhibit 9, article, was
15 marked for identification, as of this
16 date.)
17   Q.   Who is Sante D'Orazio?
18   A.   Who is he? Are you asking me?
19   Q.   Yes.
20   A.   He is a fashion photographer.
21   Q.   Is he friend of yours?
22   A.   Yes -- well, he was.
23   No, he's a friend.
24   Q.   Okay. This has a picture of an
25 image. It says Richard Prince Spiritual America

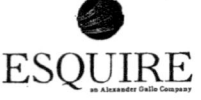

ESQUIRE
an Alexander Gallo Company

Toll Free: 800.944.9454
Facsimile: 212.557.5972

Suite 4715
One Penn Plaza
New York, NY 10119
www.esquiresolutions.com

	109		111

109

Prince

1   Prince
2 four, Roman four, 2005. Do you see that?
3   A.   Yes.
4   Q.   Do you recognize that photo?
5   A.   Yes.
6   Q.   Before I ask you about it, was there
7 a Spiritual America two and three?
8   A.   Yes.
9   Q.   Okay. What were those? What do
10 those depict?
11   A.   I believe they were collections of
12 memorabilia that were associated with the
13 gallery that I constructed in order to show the
14 original Spiritual America, like the invitation.
15   Q.   Right. Was that -- I'm sorry.
16   A.   The invitation and things of that
17 matter.
18   Q.   Was that down on the Lower East
19 Side?
20   A.   Yes.
21   Q.   On Rivington Street?
22   A.   Yes.
23   Q.   Is that right?
24   A.   Yes.
25   Q.   And what's the name of that gallery?

111

Prince

1   Prince
2   Q.   The photo --
3   A.   Yes.
4   Q.   -- that Mr. D'Orazio took?
5   A.   Yes. By not being there is a
6 transformative -- the absence of the author is
7 I believe a way to transform an image.
8   Q.   Okay.
9   A.   Especially from its original intent.
10   It's to do with the history of
11 portraiture. Usually traditional portraiture
12 usually you associate a man or a woman behind a
13 camera with the subject in front of them.
14   Q.   Right.
15   A.   My way of taking portraits is to be
16 nowhere near both the subject and the camera.
17 Completely revolutionary. Completely new. And
18 therefore, a way to transform what Sante was --
19 I made suggestions about let's put a motorcycle,
20 let's put some smoke in, have her put a bikini
21 on, and have her try to replicate the original
22 image.
23   Q.   I got that.
24   A.   Okay. Well, you asked me the
25 question and I'm just trying to answer it.

110

Prince

1   Prince
2   A.   It doesn't exist anymore. The name
3 of the gallery was Spiritual America.
4   Q.   So whose idea was it to take this
5 picture, photo, of Brooke Shields?
6   A.   Mine.
7   Q.   And why did you collaborate with a
8 photographer, comma, Sante D'Orazio?
9   A.   He told me he knew her.
10   Q.   So you did not?
11   A.   No, I've never met her.
12   Q.   Well, did you meet her when you took
13 this picture?
14   A.   No.
15   Q.   He took the picture?
16   A.   Yes.
17   Q.   You weren't there?
18   A.   No, I wasn't.
19   Q.   Are there some hard feelings --
20   A.   No. No.
21   Q.   You just weren't there?
22   A.   I just -- well, I wasn't there by
23 purpose.
24   Q.   Okay. What was the purpose?
25   A.   To transform the image.

112

Prince

1   Prince
2   Q.   But once he took the photo,
3 Mr. D'Orazio --
4   A.   Yes.
5   Q.   -- did you do anything physically to
6 change it?
7   A.   Yes.
8   Q.   Tell us what you did.
9   A.   I showed it --
10   Q.   Besides not being there?
11   A.   I showed it in the original -- I
12 mean, get this, the original gallery that
13 Spiritual America had originally been shown in
14 in 1983.
15   Q.   In the same frame?
16   A.   In the same -- no, differently. I
17 didn't show it in the frame.
18   Q.   But the same gallery?
19   A.   The same space.
20   Q.   The same space?
21   A.   Yes.
22   Q.   Because that wasn't the name of it
23 in 1983?
24   A.   No, the space in 1983 was Spiritual
25 America and the space in nineteen --

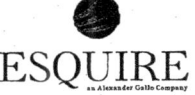

ESQUIRE
an Alexander Gallo Company

Toll Free: 800.944.9454
Facsimile: 212.557.5972

Suite 4715
One Penn Plaza
New York, NY 10119
www.esquiresolutions.com

Richard Prince   October, 2009

113

Prince

2. Q. 2005.
3. A. -- 2005 was, again, named -- for two
4. weeks I rented the same space and called it
5. Spiritual America.
6. Q. So that was your contribution, if
7. you will, to this?
8. A. Yes. My contribution was to also
9. edit the shoot.
10. Q. Can you explain that?
11. A. He gave me 300 images that he took
12. that day. And I said this is the one.
13. Q. And once you picked the one that you
14. wanted to use, did you do anything to change it
15. in any way?
16. A. I took it to a commercial lab and
17. told them to blow it up as big as they could.
18. Q. But keep it high definition?
19. A. We did a bit of retouching. And I
20. decided to pushpin it to the wall so that when
21. it hung, the bottom would curl up just above the
22. floor, which I thought was a pretty good idea.
23. Q. Right.
24. A. Very different from the original,
25. which was an 8 by 10, totally different scale,

114

Prince

2. in a gold frame.
3. Q. Did you -- withdrawn.
4. Somewhere in here I read that that
5. steam is actually liquid nitrogen, is that
6. right?
7. A. I don't know.
8. Q. Where did I read that?
9. Nitrogen fog. She's mired ankle
10. deep in a nitrogen fog. But you don't know?
11. A. No.
12. Q. In the original one, the one where
13. she was ten years old, there was actual steam
14. from the bathtub? You don't know?
15. A. I don't know that.
16. Q. Okay. All right.
17. So the idea here is it's evoking in
18. a humorous way the original Spiritual America
19. with the subject as a willing participant with a
20. bathing suit on?
21. MR. HAYES: Object to the form, but
22. you can answer.
23. A. I wouldn't say that. But if that's
24. your impression --
25. Q. Okay.

115

Prince

2. A. I mean every -- you know, it's what
3. the image imagines.
4. Q. But this photo, the appeal of this
5. photo assumes that one knows what Spiritual
6. America, the original Spiritual America --
7. A. No.
8. Q. No? Okay.
9. A. Not at all.
10. Q. It doesn't matter?
11. A. I did not tell anybody about the
12. show. I did not invite anybody to the show. No
13. one was privileged. There was no press release
14. about the showing of this image.
15. Q. So people wandered in off the street
16. and saw it?
17. A. People were invited to dinner and
18. ended up at the gallery.
19. Q. And how long was it showing there?
20. A. Two weeks.
21. Q. It also says there are two -- well,
22. how many copies of the originals of this were
23. there?
24. A. Of this particular photograph?
25. Q. Spiritual America.

116

Prince

2. A. Four. Maybe six in the edition.
3. Q. Did you sell them?
4. A. I believe Barbara Gladstone sold
5. some of them.
6. Q. For you?
7. A. For me.
8. Q. Do you notice here, this is in 2009,
9. it's stating that -- you know Phillips de Pury,
10. do you know that auction house?
11. A. Mm-hmm.
12. Q. They're offering this, apparently,
13. photo for sale for between 400,000 and 600,000
14. British pounds?
15. A. Mm-hmm.
16. Q. Does that strike you as the correct
17. price for this?
18. A. I don't know what the correct price
19. would be for that photograph.
20. Q. Do you know if it was sold in that
21. price range?
22. A. It was -- I don't believe it was
23. sold.
24. Q. Do you believe it's a valuable piece
25. that has some value?

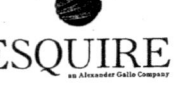

ESQUIRE
an Alexander Gallo Company

Toll Free: 800.944.9454
Facsimile: 212.557.5972

Suite 4715
One Penn Plaza
New York, NY 10119
www.esquiresolutions.com

117

Prince

1
2   MR. HAYES: Object to the form.
3   Q.   Some market value?
4   A.   I never get involved in the market
5 value. I have no interest in the market.
6   Q.   When Barbara Gladstone sold some of
7 your copies of that original or some of the
8 originals from the edition, you received money,
9 right?
10   A.   From the original which, this or --
11   Q.   Spiritual America Four?
12   A.   Four?
13   Q.   Yes.
14   A.   Yes.
15   Q.   Okay. So it has some value?
16 Somebody bought it and you got some
17 of the money, right?
18   A.   If that's what you mean by value,
19 yes. I received money from the sale of
20 Spiritual America Four, yes.
21   Q.   Any recollection of about how much
22 you received for the ones that Barbara Gladstone
23 sold?
24   A.   No, I really don't know.
25   Q.   Do you know if Spiritual America

118

Prince

1
2 Four is copyrighted?
3   A.   No, I don't know.
4   Q.   Do you share the proceeds when it
5 was sold with Mr. D'Orazio?
6   A.   No. No, I don't.
7   Q.   You keep the proceeds?
8   A.   When there's a sale of this image,
9 yes, it's between myself and the dealer who
10 sells it.
11   He was -- I gave him a print.
12   I also gave Brooke Shields a print.
13   Q.   She must have been appreciative?
14   A.   I'm a, you know, agreeable guy.
15   Q.   So getting back to in Exhibit 6
16 where you said, However, it would not bother me
17 in the slightest -- excuse me -- for someone to
18 appropriate my work.
19   A.   Yes.
20   Q.   Would that extend to Spiritual
21 America Four?
22   A.   Yeah. I mean I don't -- I don't try
23 to control those kinds of things.
24   Q.   But I mean just you wouldn't mind if
25 somebody did exactly what you did --

119

Prince

1
2   A.   They already have.
3   Q.   You can scan it --
4   A.   I saw it on someone's screen --
5   MS. BART: Objection, form.
6   (Multiple speakers talking at once.)
7   (Interruption by reporter.)
8   (Discussion off the record.)
9   (Record read.)
10   MR. HAYES: Can I make a suggestion?
11 Withdraw both questions, restate the
12 first question.
13 BY MR. BROOKS:
14   Q.   You wouldn't mind if somebody sold
15 Spiritual America Four, somebody else?
16   A.   No.
17   Q.   Without your permission?
18   A.   They don't need my permission.
19   Q.   And you're saying it has been done?
20   A.   I don't know whether they've been
21 able to sell it. I haven't been able to sell
22 mine. Whether they've sold theirs, I don't
23 know.
24   Q.   Well, you sold some of yours, right?
25   A.   I sold some of mine, yes.

120

Prince

1
2   Q.   And how do you know somebody else is
3 trying to sell Spiritual America Four?
4   A.   I've seen it. That's the thing
5 about technology, it's what's new, it's what one
6 has to adjust to. I've seen it on the web.
7   Q.   And that's fine with you?
8   A.   It's fine with me, yeah. I have no
9 control over it. I mean it's their piece, not
10 mine.
11   Q.   It's their piece?
12   A.   They're putting their name on it.
13   Q.   Who is they?
14   A.   I don't recall. I don't know who
15 the person is.
16   Q.   Okay. So your view is if you create
17 a work of art -- do you consider this a work of
18 art?
19   A.   Yes, I do.
20   Q.   If you create a work of art anyone
21 else who wants to is free to copy it and sell
22 it?
23   A.   That's the optional or the operative
24 word you just said. Free.
25   Q.   Right.

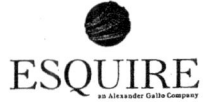

ESQUIRE
an Alexander Gallo Company

Toll Free: 800.944.9454
Facsimile: 212.557.5972

Suite 4715
One Penn Plaza
New York, NY 10119
www.esquiresolutions.com

121

Prince

2   A. And art is about freedom. It's not
3 about being restricted. If I was restricted
4 then I couldn't transform these images.
5   Q. So but as far as you're concerned,
6 somebody else can just copy Spiritual America
7 Four, make no changes to it, and sell it, and
8 that's fine with you?
9   A. Yes, that's fine with me.
10   Q. That's part of your artistic
11 philosophy?
12   A. I believe that, yes.
13   Q. Does it matter if the person copying
14 your work is known as an appropriation artist or
15 does it not matter, can anyone do it, as far as
16 you're concerned?
17   A. There have been people who are known
18 as appropriation artists who have done what I've
19 done because of what I did.
20   Q. Right. But let me ask you this.
21 Do you feel that because you are known for
22 appropriating the work of others your reputation
23 itself entitles you to engage in that artistic
24 practice?
25   MS. BART: Objection to form.

122

Prince

2   MR. HAYES: Objection.
3   A. Reputation is a tricky word.
4   Q. Well, you have a reputation for
5 borrowing, appropriating things from other
6 people, right?
7   MS. BART: Objection, form.
8   MR. HAYES: Objection also.
9   A. My intentions were never to make
10 myself a reputation. It was always -- my
11 intentions were always to make great art.
12   Q. Okay. But are you aware that you
13 are known as somebody -- prominently known as
14 somebody who appropriates work of others?
15   MR. HAYES: Objection.
16   MS. BART: Same.
17   A. I am told that, yes. I don't
18 necessarily acknowledge it.
19   Q. And whether you are or not, you
20 don't feel that your reputation for that
21 practice has anything to do with your right to
22 do it, your freedom to do it, right?
23   MR. HAYES: Objection.
24   MS. BART: Objection to form.
25   A. I don't understand the question.

123

Prince

2   Q. I know. It was badly worded.
3 You said before, you think people
4 are free to take the work of others, copy it,
5 and sell it, right?
6   MR. HAYES: Objection.
7   A. I believe artists --
8   Q. Artists?
9   A. -- should be as free as possible,
10 yes, in their studios.
11   Q. And does it matter if those artists
12 are known for the practice of appropriating or
13 not?
14   MR. HAYES: Objection, form.
15   A. It could be an art student. I would
16 encourage it.
17   Q. Okay. I understand.
18   MR. BROOKS: Let's mark as
19 Plaintiff's Exhibit 10 a two-page article
20 in something called the Copyright
21 Litigation Blog, Bates stamps C55 and 56.
22   (Plaintiff's Exhibit 10, Copyright
23 Litigation Blog, was marked for
24 identification, as of this date.)
25   Q. Mr. Prince, the person who wrote

124

Prince

2 this blog, again, states that the occasion is
3 your one-man show at the Guggenheim, do you see
4 that, entitled Spiritual America?
5   A. Yes. You're referring to this man
6 Ray Dowd?
7   Q. Yes, he's an attorney I believe.
8 You don't know him I take it?
9   A. No. Is he an art critic or -- you
10 say he's an attorney?
11   Q. Yes. I think he does copyright law.
12 I don't really know.
13   A. And this is a blog?
14   Q. It looks like -- it's the Copyright
15 Litigation Blog. And he also has written a
16 textbook on that.
17   MR. HAYES: That's what the title of
18 the document is --
19   Q. Anyway, I'm not going to ask you
20 about any legal questions.
21   A. No, I just want to make sure I know
22 what I'm looking at.
23   Q. I think he's an attorney and he's
24 written -- it tells you in the lower right-hand
25 corner the name of the book he wrote.

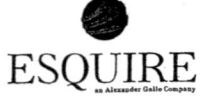

125

Prince

1
2 A. Okay.
3 Q. On the second page of this -- and
4 take your time, if you want to read the first
5 page --
6 A. No, I was just going over this
7 eight-track photograph little -- I wonder where
8 he got that. That's kind of cool.
9   Anyway -- I'm sorry.
10 Q. He didn't get that from you?
11 A. Yeah, he got that from me. That's
12 very early.
13 Q. Well, now, for the record, we better
14 have you explain what you're referring to about
15 the Eight-Track. I wasn't going to ask you, but
16 since you mentioned it --
17 A. Oh. No, no --
18 Q. -- you should explain what you're
19 talking about.
20 A. The Eight-Track photograph, I think
21 I was -- again, I was talking about -- I think I
22 was talking about hip-hop, and sampling was
23 coming in at the time.
24   Pirating was the term that was being
25 used by rappers in the late '70s. This is very

126

Prince

1
2 early, when that practice of sampling -- and I
3 was always trying to hook my art up with musical
4 terms. That's all.
5   So the Eight-Track photograph was
6 eight different ways in which you could make a
7 photograph.
8 Q. So it's an analogy, is that what --
9 A. I think it was just a description.
10 Q. But you're analogizing your
11 practices in the visual arts with what --
12 A. I just -- I probably was just trying
13 to talk about what was possible to do with the
14 mechanism, the apparatus. It's kind of esoteric
15 mumbo jumbo to tell you the truth.
16 Q. Got it.
17   On the second page there's a
18 statement --
19 A. Sorry.
20 Q. There's a statement which says --
21 I'll read it -- as we move into a world where
22 digital photography and sophisticated
23 consumer-level photo-retouching software is
24 available, appropriating and manipulating images
25 has become a widespread phenomenon.

127

Prince

1
2   And then it refers to you.
3   His -- that means you. His
4 appropriation may foreshadow the copyright
5 battles of the future and a weakening of the
6 visual artist's copyright.
7   With reference to the first sentence
8 that I read, do you agree with that?
9   MR. HAYES: Objection.
10   MS. BART: I'm going to object to
11 form, especially using this blog as
12 evidence.
13   MR. BROOKS: Okay.
14   MR. HAYES: It also calls for a
15 legal conclusion, and I join in her
16 objections.
17   MR. BROOKS: Well, the first
18 sentence has nothing to do with any legal
19 conclusions.
20   I asked him if he agrees that
21 appropriating is becoming -- has become a
22 widespread phenomenon, thanks to advances
23 in technology.
24 A. I don't believe I'm -- have the
25 knowledge to answer that question properly.

128

Prince

1
2 Q. Fine, okay.
3 A. I don't know whether it's become
4 widespread.
5 Q. How about the second sentence, do
6 you agree that your artistic practices are
7 weakening visual artists' copyright?
8   MR. HAYES: Objection. That calls
9 for a legal conclusion.
10 A. Again, I would have no idea.
11 Q. Now, when you had the retrospective
12 at the Guggenheim -- and we all know what the
13 Guggenheim looks like, it spirals up from the
14 bottom to the top -- was the entire museum
15 dedicated to exhibiting your works, or was it
16 just a part of the museum?
17   When you had your --
18 A. The majority of the museum.
19 Q. Starting at the bottom or the middle
20 or where?
21 A. Starting in what they call the
22 rotunda.
23 Q. When you walk in?
24 A. Yes.
25 Q. But it didn't go all the way up to

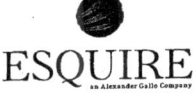

129

1	Prince
2	the top?
3	A. Yes, it did.
4	Q. It did? Oh, so it was the entire
5	spiral?
6	A. Oh, you're talking about the spiral?
7	Q. Yes.
8	A. Yes.
9	MR. BROOKS: Okay, fine.
10	MR. HAYES: Just for clarity, there
11	are other exhibit spaces at the
12	Guggenheim.
13	MR. BROOKS: I'm aware of that.
14	MR. HAYES: Gotcha.
15	BY MR. BROOKS:
16	Q. And did you exhibit the most recent
17	works -- withdrawn.
18	As you walked up -- as one walked up
19	the spiral was there a chronological sequence to
20	the works being exhibited?
21	A. Not really.
22	Q. No? Okay.
23	A. No. We tried to -- can I say deejay
24	the show. I mean for lack of a better -- I mean
25	that's actually how I saw --

130

1	Prince
2	Q. Right.
3	A. Because I had a large hand in
4	curating the show.
5	Q. Let me just read you what he said
6	and then you can tell me whether he's correct in
7	your view or incorrect.
8	MR. HAYES: This is back in
9	Exhibit 10?
10	MR. BROOKS: It is.
11	A. Sorry.
12	Q. He says, But as you go up the
13	Guggenheim spiral, comma, you will note less
14	wholesale appropriation, comma, and more
15	borrowing of bits and pieces, period. Once an
16	artist is successful and no longer judgment
17	proof, dot dot dot, remaining an outlaw becomes
18	problematic. His latest series consists of
19	scanning faces from the works of De Kooning and
20	sticking pornographic cutouts onto their bodies.
21	Do you see what I just read?
22	A. Yes.
23	Q. Is there any -- do you agree with
24	his observation or disagree?
25	MR. HAYES: Object to the form of

131

1	Prince
2	question. It calls for speculation and it
3	calls for a legal conclusion.
4	MR. BROOKS: It doesn't --
5	MS. BART: And continuing objection
6	on the use of a blog as, quote, evidence.
7	BY MR. BROOKS:
8	Q. Okay. You can tell us whether you
9	agree with what he wrote that I just read.
10	A. I disagree.
11	Q. You don't behave more cautiously now
12	because you have more assets than you did in the
13	1970s?
14	MS. BART: Objection, form.
15	MR. HAYES: Objection.
16	Q. You can answer.
17	A. No.
18	Q. And so those things you wrote in
19	those essays in your early career still describe
20	your artistic practice?
21	MR. HAYES: Objection, form.
22	A. Part of my -- part of the -- I mean
23	I'm into all kinds of things these days.
24	Q. Okay. But you still find it
25	satisfying to appropriate?

132

1	Prince
2	MR. HAYES: Objection,
3	mischaracterizes the testimony and it
4	calls for speculation.
5	MR. BROOKS: I'm not referring to
6	his testimony. I'm referring to the
7	exhibit.
8	BY MR. BROOKS:
9	Q. Do you still find it more satisfying
10	to appropriate --
11	MR. HAYES: What exhibit are you
12	referring to? Is it Exhibit 10?
13	MR. BROOKS: No, I'm referring to
14	his own website Exhibit 3.
15	A. Website?
16	Q. Yeah, where you said in the essay --
17	MR. HAYES: Oh, I see.
18	A. I have nothing to do with my
19	website.
20	Q. No, no, no.
21	A. I'm sorry.
22	Q. In the website there's a quote from
23	an essay you wrote in 1978.
24	A. Okay.
25	Q. Which you already testified to.

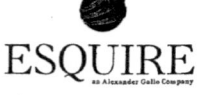

Richard Prince   October 6, 2009

	133
1	Prince
2	A. Yes.
3	Q. Where you said it was more
4	satisfying to appropriate?
5	A. Is it -- are you asking is it still
6	satisfying?
7	Q. Yes, right, because it makes it more
8	believable. Is that still your impression --
9	A. It's still exciting, yes.
10	Q. Now, you certainly are very
11	successful now, wouldn't you agree?
12	A. Compared to?
13	Q. Okay. Well, let me give you
14	some examples. Instead of living in a
15	75-dollar-a-month apartment in the East Village,
16	you have a house in the Hamptons, right?
17	A. Yes.
18	Q. Where in the Hamptons?
19	A. Wainscott.
20	Q. Near East Hampton?
21	A. Yes. I mean, yes, if you want to
22	make a long story -- yes, I guess.
23	Q. All right.
24	A. By standard measurements I am
25	successful in terms of -- are you talking about

	135
1	Prince
2	Q. -- for 11-and-a-half-million
3	dollars?
4	MR. HAYES: Object to the form of
5	the question.
6	A. Townhouse.
7	Q. Townhouse.
8	For 11-and-a-half-million dollars?
9	A. Yes.
10	Q. Which was less than Jeff Koons spent
11	for his nearby townhouse, right?
12	A. I don't know what Jeff did.
13	MR. BROOKS: All right. Let's mark
14	as Plaintiff's Exhibit 11 an article from
15	Art Info --
16	THE WITNESS: Am I being punished
17	for --
18	MR. HAYES: No. Just wait for the
19	next question.
20	THE WITNESS: I'm just kidding.
21	It was a joke.
22	(Plaintiff's Exhibit 11, article,
23	was marked for identification, as of this
24	date.)
25	Q. This exhibit Plaintiff's 11 has been

	134
1	Prince
2	money?
3	Q. Yes.
4	A. I guess so. I don't know what
5	other -- you know, I don't really compare myself
6	to --
7	Q. You belong to a country club in
8	Bridgehampton?
9	A. I'm an honorary member. I play
10	golf.
11	Q. Do you curate their shows?
12	A. No, I don't.
13	Q. Did you ever?
14	A. No.
15	Q. You have a house and studio in
16	Rensselaerville, New York?
17	A. Yes, I do.
18	Q. And the Guggenheim built -- you have
19	a museum there or --
20	A. No. I built a museum, which burned
21	down.
22	Q. I understand that.
23	And you recently bought a six-story
24	mansion at 57 East 78th Street --
25	MR. HAYES: Objection.

	136
1	Prince
2	Bates stamped C236 to 238.
3	You're familiar with the New York
4	Observer?
5	A. Yes.
6	Q. And do you have the article in front
7	of you, the exhibit?
8	A. Yes, I have it in front of me.
9	Q. Fine. And is this correct that as
10	described in this exhibit you bought this
11	11-and-a-half-million-dollar house?
12	A. That's what I paid for the house.
13	Q. Okay. Cash?
14	MR. HAYES: Objection. What's the
15	relevance of what he paid for the house
16	and whether he paid cash in this lawsuit?
17	You can answer it if you want to
18	answer it, but I think --
19	A. I'm not going to answer that. It's
20	no one's -- well.
21	Q. What does that mean, there's a
22	humidification system and a backup generator?
23	Is that true?
24	MR. HAYES: Objection to the form of
25	the question.

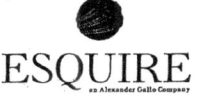

ESQUIRE
an Alexander Gallo Company

Toll Free: 800.944.9454
Facsimile: 212.557.5972

Suite 4715
One Penn Plaza
New York, NY 10119
www.esquiresolutions.com

137

1	Prince
2	A. I'm not going to answer these
3	questions.
4	Q. Do you live there?
5	A. I live there, yes.
6	I mean seriously.
7	Q. All right. Let's move on.
8	Do you have your own airplane?
9	A. No.
10	Q. You're taking flying lessons though,
11	right?
12	A. No, I made that up.
13	Q. Okay. All right, you said --
14	A. I make -- I say a lot of things --
15	Q. That aren't true?
16	A. That aren't -- well, no. It's more
17	about -- it depends upon the interviewer. I try
18	to be creative, let's put it that way.
19	Q. Okay. So when you said you were
20	taking flying lessons in your own airplane, that
21	was not true?
22	A. I was being creative.
23	Q. Which means it wasn't true?
24	MR. HAYES: Objection to the form
25	of the question. It's been asked and

138

1	Prince
2	answered.
3	A. I would leave that up to the
4	audience. I mean I don't want to tell -- I
5	don't want to say whether or not -- I might --
6	I might be flying, taking flying lessons. I
7	don't see the relevance of that.
8	Q. That's fine. But you understand
9	you're under oath right now?
10	A. Oh.
11	Q. Do you understand that?
12	A. Yes.
13	Q. Did anyone tell you that?
14	A. Yes.
15	Q. So do you understand it's important
16	in this deposition to tell the actual truth?
17	A. Yes, I do. But I'm trying to
18	explain what I meant when you asked me --
19	Q. I asked you if you owned an
20	airplane.
21	A. And I said no.
22	MR. HAYES: Well, no, you asked him
23	several questions. Do you want to read
24	them back --
25	A. And then you said --

139

1	Prince
2	MR. HAYES: Wait a second.
3	You asked him questions about --
4	MR. BROOKS: All right. Let's not
5	argue about what I asked him.
6	BY MR. BROOKS:
7	Q. Go on.
8	MR. HAYES: No, wait. Wait.
9	You asked him about --
10	MR. BROOKS: I asked him if he owned
11	an airplane and if he took flying lessons
12	in his airplane.
13	MR. HAYES: Okay. So are you asking
14	him that question again?
15	Do you own an airplane?
16	A. No, I don't.
17	Q. Have you ever taken flying lessons?
18	A. No, I have not.
19	Q. But you understand the difference
20	between taking flying lessons and never having
21	taken flying lessons?
22	A. Yes.
23	MR. HAYES: Object to the form.
24	Q. One is -- I mean those are two
25	different things, right?

140

1	Prince
2	A. Yes.
3	Q. And one could be true and the
4	other -- I mean one is true and the other can't
5	be true?
6	MR. HAYES: Objection.
7	Q. You either have taken flying lessons
8	or you haven't.
9	MR. HAYES: Objection to the form of
10	the question.
11	A. I understand that.
12	Q. So in this deposition I will ask you
13	to do your best to give us the actual truth
14	instead of like what somebody might imagine the
15	truth could be.
16	A. But you asked me about that
17	interview.
18	MR. HAYES: That's the point.
19	A. When I said did I -- you said, you
20	quoted --
21	Q. I asked you if you had taken flying
22	lessons in your own plane. I didn't mention an
23	interview. You did.
24	MR. HAYES: Well, wait a second now.
25	MS. BART: That's not true.

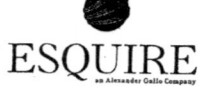

ESQUIRE
an Alexander Gallo Company

Toll Free: 800.944.9454
Facsimile: 212.557.5972

Suite 4715
One Penn Plaza
New York, NY 10119
www.esquiresolutions.com

141

1   Prince
2   MR. HAYES: Let's go back and read
3   that back.
4   MR. BROOKS: No, we're not going to
5   read it back.
6   MR. HAYES: It's not true.
7   MR. BROOKS: All right, fine. It is
8   what it is. All right?
9   MR. HAYES: I know. But you just
10   said --
11   MR. BROOKS: No, I don't want to
12   waste --
13   MR. HAYES: But you did talk about
14   the interview. That's not a truthful
15   statement.
16   MR. BROOKS: He said I might have
17   said that in an interview when I wasn't
18   telling the truth.
19   I didn't say there was an
20   interview -- I didn't know there was an
21   interview, okay, until he said it.
22   MR. HAYES: Then read it back.
23   MR. BROOKS: We'll read it back
24   later.
25   MS. BART: He certainly was sworn in

142

1   Prince
2   at the beginning to tell the truth --
3   MR. BROOKS: I understand.
4   MS. BART: -- and he agreed to do
5   that.
6   MR. BROOKS: Hopefully that's what
7   we'll get.
8   MR. HAYES: Why don't you give us
9   some other questions so we can move along?
10   MR. BROOKS: I'm going to move
11   along. I would try to move along faster
12   if there were not constant interruptions
13   that violate Rule 30(c)(2) --
14   MR. HAYES: There has been violation
15   of the rule.
16   MR. BROOKS: -- of the federal
17   rules.
18   MR. HAYES: Ask a question.
19   MR. BROOKS: Constantly.
20   MR. HAYES: Not true.
21   Ask a question.
22   BY MR. BROOKS:
23   Q.   Do you know how much you made on
24   selling the paintings that were part of the
25   Canal Zone exhibit and Canal Zone book?

143

1   Prince
2   A.   No, I don't.
3   Q.   Do you have any rough idea?
4   A.   Ballpark figure -- that I made?
5   Q.   Yes.
6   A.   Maybe two-million dollars, three,
7   two-point-five.
8   MR. HAYES: Don't guess. If you
9   know, say so.
10   A.   I don't know.
11   Q.   Do you know how many of those
12   paintings were sold?
13   A.   No, I don't.
14   Q.   Do you know if any of them were
15   sold?
16   A.   Yes, I believe some were sold.
17   Q.   How do you know that?
18   A.   I know that because I get
19   statements.
20   Q.   From?
21   A.   Gagosian Gallery.
22   MR. BROOKS: Let's mark as
23   Plaintiff's Exhibit 12 -- I'm just
24   anticipating an objection.
25   This is a French interview in

144

1   Prince
2   Le Figaro Magazine, which you've had since
3   whenever we made our initial disclosure in
4   April of this year.
5   It's Bates stamped C78 through C82.
6   And you were free to make a
7   translation of it if you wanted to. I
8   made a translation of the part I want to
9   ask him about.
10   So let's mark as Exhibit 12 the
11   French interview and Le Figaro as
12   Exhibit 13.
13   MR. HAYES: But since you now made a
14   statement about position I can now make a
15   statement, correct?
16   Which is, I have no idea when you
17   produced documents you were going to ask
18   about certain documents at the deposition.
19   MR. BROOKS: We made our initial
20   disclosure in April of this year. This is
21   Bates stamped C78 --
22   MR. HAYES: Yes, sir.
23   MR. BROOKS: -- through 82. That
24   was part of our initial disclosure.
25   MS. BART: Mr. Brooks --

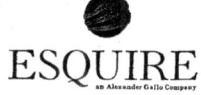

ESQUIRE
an Alexander Gallo Company

Toll Free: 800.944.9454
Facsimile: 212.557.5972

Suite 4715
One Penn Plaza
New York, NY 10119
www.esquiresolutions.com

145

Prince

1
2   MR. BROOKS: Excuse me, I'm not
3   finished. I'm not finished.
4   MS. BART: I'm trying to cut --
5   MR. BROOKS: I'm not finished.
6   MS. BART: Fine. Let him make his
7   speech.
8   MR. BROOKS: It's an interview in
9   French. Given the consternation I
10   witnessed last time, I'm going to mark the
11   English translation as Exhibit 13 at the
12   same time and hand him 12 and 13.
13   I'm simply telling you that 13 does
14   not purport to translate the entire French
15   article.
16   MR. HAYES: That's all you do.
17   MR. BROOKS: It translates the part
18   I'm interested in.
19   If you want to translate the other
20   parts, you could have done that at any
21   time since April to now.
22   MR. HAYES: And of course I had no
23   idea you were going to be asking questions
24   about it because you never said you were
25   going to ask questions about it --

146

Prince

1
2   MR. BROOKS: It was produced, so --
3   MR. HAYES: But go ahead and mark it
4   and ask what you want to ask --
5   MR. BROOKS: You don't have to look
6   at it. If it's produced --
7   MR. HAYES: You just finished making
8   a speech that took up a certain amount of
9   time. I want to respond to it.
10   You never said you were going to ask
11   questions about it. Mark it. I have an
12   objection. Move forward.
13   MR. BROOKS: Of course I never said
14   I was going to ask questions on it.
15   MR. HAYES: Then I would have no
16   idea you were going to.
17   But just mark it, I have an
18   objection, and we'll move forward.
19   MR. BROOKS: Okay. So 12 is an
20   interview in Le Figaro Bates stamped C78
21   through 82.
22   And 13 is a translation of a portion
23   of that article Bates stamped C239 through
24   241.
25   (Plaintiff's Exhibit 12, Le Figaro

147

Prince

1
2   interview in French, was marked for
3   identification, as of this date.)
4   (Plaintiff's Exhibit 13, portion of
5   Le Figaro interview translated, was marked
6   for identification, as of this date.)
7   MR. HAYES: For clarity, Exhibit 12
8   is the full article in French?
9   MR. BROOKS: Correct.
10   MR. HAYES: And Exhibit 13 is what
11   we're told is a translation of a portion
12   of the article into English?
13   MR. BROOKS: Correct. Correct.
14   BY MR. BROOKS:
15   Q.   And so if you look at 12,
16   Mr. Prince, which is the one with the
17   photograph. It's in French.
18   A.   Yes.
19   Q.   The one there in French.
20   No, you're looking at 13.
21   The one there --
22   A.   In French. You want me to look --
23   Q.   No, no. Do you remember being
24   interviewed by Le Figaro on or about
25   November 3rd, 2008?

148

Prince

1
2   A.   I don't remember, no.
3   Q.   But if you were, it was not in
4   French, it was you were speaking in English,
5   correct?
6   A.   I was speaking in English, yes.
7   Q.   Fine. So that's 12.
8   Now, 13 is a translation that we
9   obtained of a portion of the interview.
10   So I'm looking at the page stamped
11   C240. Do you see that, Mr. Prince?
12   A.   Yes.
13   Q.   Is that a picture of you?
14   A.   Yes.
15   Q.   Working on one of the nurse --
16   A.   Yes.
17   Q.   -- artworks?
18   A.   Yes.
19   Q.   Okay. And the question was, When
20   will we see your next series on Rastafarians,
21   and your answer was, I will be showing them at
22   the Larry Gagosian Gallery in New York on
23   November 8th.
24   That was correct, right, that's when
25   the showing was at the Gagosian Gallery?

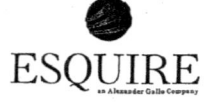

149

1   Prince
2   A. November 8th, yes.
3   Q. And was this interview in -- do you
4   know if the occasion for this interview was that
5   the show was about to open, if you remember?
6   A. I believe -- this doesn't make any
7   sense.
8   Q. Because?
9   A. It says here -- this interview I
10 believe was published at the Patrick Saguin
11 Gallery.
12   Oh, wait a minute. I did this
13 interview for the Patrick Seguin Gallery that
14 opened in November 29th with Le Figaro.
15   Q. Of 2008?
16   A. With -- I believe with this person
17 from Le Figaro.
18   Q. Valerie Duponchelle?
19   A. No, with Patrick Seguin.
20   Q. It just says -- I'm just telling
21 you what it says in English -- interviewed by
22 Valerie Duponchelle. That's not your
23 recollection?
24   A. I don't remember who I was
25 interviewed by. But I believe this interview

150

1   Prince
2   was for the occasion of a show.
3   Q. A show of yours?
4   A. Of mine at the Patrick Seguin
5   Gallery.
6   Q. A show that has nothing to do with
7   the Canal Zone?
8   A. It had nothing to do with the Canal
9   Zone.
10   Q. All right. Well, for whatever
11 reason, they asked you some questions about the
12 Canal Zone --
13   A. Yes.
14   Q. -- probably because of the temporal
15 proximity. So I would like to have you look at
16 the second question.
17   Your series will be up at a time
18 when perhaps Barack Obama will be president.
19 It could become iconic if it coincides with a
20 pivotal moment in American history. And --
21   (Interruption.)
22   (Record read.)
23   Q. So then the answer apparently was,
24 That's possible. It is strange for a white man
25 like myself to start painting black people. I

151

1   Prince
2   found a black-and-white book on Rastafarians
3   when I was on vacation in St. Barth's. I
4   started drawing directly in the book like I had
5   done before in a book of De Kooning's work. For
6   two or three years I continued to be inspired by
7   three Rastafarians -- I'm sorry, I continued to
8   be inspired by these Rastafarians. I drew faces
9   on their faces using the shades of the book, the
10 different skin colors, the wild hair styles, all
11 dreadlocked, their poses and their looks. I was
12 listening to Rasta music at the time, one of my
13 son's tapes.
14   Was that a Bob Marley tape?
15   A. No, it wasn't. It was a group
16 called Radiodread. One word.
17   Q. Now, the black-and-white book on
18 Rastafarians that you found, was that this
19 Yes Rasta book by Patrick Cariou?
20   A. Yes.
21   Q. And you said you started drawing in
22 the book. You actually -- actually in the book,
23 you didn't copy, you just write in the book, you
24 were drawing things?
25   A. Yes.

152

1   Prince
2   Q. Which you had done with some
3   De Kooning works before?
4   MS. BART: Objection, form.
5   Q. Go ahead.
6   A. I had done the same thing to a
7   De Kooning book.
8   Q. Right. Now, you said -- I'm reading
9   what you said -- for two or three years I
10 continued to be inspired by these Rastafarians.
11   So, given --
12   A. That's the translation. This --
13   Q. Okay.
14   A. Can I just say that this is --
15   Q. Yes.
16   A. I've read this interview.
17   Q. Yes. In French?
18   A. Because it just came out in a book.
19   Q. Yes.
20   A. It's one of the worst translations
21 I've ever read. Anyway, I'm just -- I just
22 would like to get that on the record.
23   Q. Okay. But this translation was done
24 for my law firm, so you certainly haven't read
25 this translation. You may have read another bad

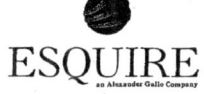

153

1   Prince
2 translation, but you haven't read this one.
3   A.   Oh. Well --
4   Q.   This was done for us recently.
5   A.   Okay. All right.
6   Q.   But -- fine. If it's incorrect, I
7 would like to know.
8   So is it correct that you were
9 drawing in the Yes Rasta book?
10   A.   Yes.
11   Q.   And is it correct that given that
12 this is 2008, this interview, that this drawing
13 in the book went on for two or three years?
14   A.   The drawing in the book -- no, I
15 believe it started when I bought the book.
16   Q.   In 2008?
17   A.   When I was on vacation. So 2005.
18 I bought the book and I started -- I was on
19 vacation, and I started to make drawings in the
20 book.
21   Q.   Okay.
22   A.   And --
23   Q.   You were on vacation?
24   MR. HAYES: Hold on. He hasn't
25 finished his answer.

154

1   Prince
2   A.   Because you had asked me if I had
3 been doing it for two or three years. I did it
4 for two weeks out of every year for two years.
5 So I was drawing in the book for maybe
6 approximately three to four weeks.
7   Q.   Total?
8   A.   I'm just trying to answer the
9 question.
10   Q.   Just so I'll understand.
11   A.   Okay.
12   Q.   You found this book in St. Barth's?
13   A.   I bought it at a bookstore.
14   Q.   In St. Barth's?
15   A.   Yes.
16   Q.   Where? In a hotel gift shop or --
17   A.   It was a regular bookstore.
18   Q.   A bookstore?
19   A.   Yes.
20   Q.   On St. Barth's?
21   A.   In St. Barth's, yes.
22   Q.   And you think around 2005?
23   A.   Yes. To the best of my
24 recollection, yes, 2005.
25   Q.   And then did you -- I understand it

155

1   Prince
2 wasn't continuous, but did you start writing in
3 the book right then or did you --
4   A.   I believe I did probably the next
5 day.
6   Q.   And then at some point you put it
7 aside?
8   A.   I started writing first. I used it
9 as a notebook. I started making notes because
10 of my Canal Zone idea.
11   Q.   For the pitch?
12   A.   Because I was -- yeah, I was writing
13 about the pitch because of -- yeah, there was
14 some blank pages.
15   Q.   In the book?
16   A.   In the book.
17   Q.   You wrote things like CIA, Jack
18 Ruby?
19   A.   Yes.
20   Q.   Lee Harvey Oswald, CIA?
21   A.   Yes.
22   Q.   Kennedy?
23   A.   Right.
24   Q.   Something about the Kennedy
25 assassination apparently?

156

1   Prince
2   A.   I was thinking out loud, yes.
3   Q.   Okay, good.
4   Then what was it -- and I realize
5 the translation may not be --
6   A.   That's okay.
7   Q.   And feel free to tell us it's wrong.
8 But it says for two or three years I continued
9 to be inspired by these Rastafarians. What, if
10 anything, inspired you about them?
11   MR. HAYES: Objection to the form.
12 You can answer.
13   A.   I believed at the time that I had
14 maybe made a connection to the De Kooning
15 paintings that I was painting. And I believe
16 I had found subject matter that I knew nothing
17 about, which is a position I like to put myself
18 in, in order to discover new things and be able
19 transform something that once existed over here
20 to over here.
21   Q.   Okay.
22   A.   So therefore, when I say perhaps I
23 was inspired, I decided with the De Kooning
24 women paintings my contribution would be a man.
25 And I felt -- I mean and this is, again, it's a

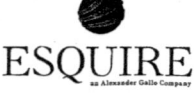

ESQUIRE
an Alexander Gallo Company

Toll Free: 800.944.9454
Facsimile: 212.557.5972

Suite 4715
One Penn Plaza
New York, NY 10119
www.esquiresolutions.com

Richard Prince   October 6, 2009

157

1	Prince
2	long time ago, but I believe I was thinking that
3	the man in the De Kooning paintings should be a
4	Rastafarian.
5	Q. Let me just back up.
6	You said something about this
7	brought back to you growing up in the Canal Zone
8	for six years?
9	MR. HAYES: In his prior answer?
10	Q. No, earlier today.
11	Do you remember saying something
12	like that?
13	MS. BART: Can I hear the question
14	back, please?
15	A. Yes, I remember you, yeah, you
16	asking me a question about the Canal Zone.
17	Q. Right.
18	A. Yeah. I mean I remember the
19	question.
20	MR. HAYES: Could I have this
21	question read back, the last question?
22	(Record read.)
23	MR. HAYES: In this book?
24	MR. BROOKS: Yes.
25	THE WITNESS: I'm sorry, so can I

158

1	Prince
2	have --
3	BY MR. BROOKS:
4	Q. Did seeing this book Yes Rasta
5	somehow make a connection in your mind with the
6	Canal Zone?
7	A. Yes. I would -- yes, I'd say that.
8	Q. Now, have you been back to the Canal
9	Zone -- you said you went to Panama?
10	A. I had gone to Panama. And I had
11	just seen the jungles.
12	Q. Fairly recently?
13	A. Probably -- probably, yes.
14	In approximate to when I found the
15	book -- yes.
16	Q. In approximation to 2005?
17	A. Yes.
18	Q. Are there Rastafarians in the Canal
19	Zone now known as Panama, that part of the Canal
20	Zone?
21	A. No, there aren't.
22	Q. Are there any in St. Barth's?
23	A. No.
24	Q. Is the population of St. Barth's
25	primarily white, French white people?

159

1	Prince
2	Well, you've been going there 12
3	years, right?
4	A. Yes, I would agree with that.
5	Q. Now, the show that you were being
6	asked about that was going to be at the Gagosian
7	Gallery several days after the interview, was
8	that your first solo exhibition at the Gagosian
9	Gallery?
10	A. At that space or with Gagosian?
11	Q. Okay. Let's start with that space,
12	which is on West 24th Street.
13	A. 24th Street?
14	Q. Yes.
15	A. My first solo, yes.
16	Q. Okay. Now, you broadened the
17	question, which is fine. How about the other
18	Gagosian galleries of which there are a number,
19	right?
20	A. I've had shows at other galleries.
21	Q. But as of November 8th, 2008, had
22	you had any solo shows at the Gagosian Gallery
23	prior to November 8th, 2008, at any Gagosian
24	Gallery?
25	MR. HAYES: Any location he's asking

160

1	Prince
2	you about.
3	A. Any location?
4	Q. Any Gagosian Gallery location?
5	A. Prior to? Yes.
6	Q. Okay. But this was the first one at
7	that Chelsea gallery?
8	A. Yes.
9	Q. Did you believe that the photos in
10	the Yes Rasta book, did you believe they were
11	distinctive?
12	A. Well, I didn't really --
13	MS. BART: Objection, form --
14	A. -- look at them as --
15	MS. BART: Hold on one second,
16	please.
17	Objection, form, calls for a legal
18	conclusion. The witness is here as a fact
19	witness, not an expert.
20	MR. HAYES: I join in the objection.
21	Q. Did you believe they were
22	distinctive?
23	MS. BART: Same objections.
24	A. I didn't think I would describe my
25	reaction. Also, I didn't really look at them as

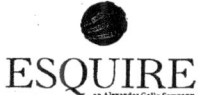

ESQUIRE
an Alexander Gallo Company

Toll Free: 800.944.9454
Facsimile: 212.557.5972

Suite 4715
One Penn Plaza
New York, NY 10119
www.esquiresolutions.com

161		163	
1	Prince	1	Prince
2	photographs.	2	THE VIDEOGRAPHER: 1:05 p.m.
3	Q. What did you look at them as?	3	Off the record. End of tape 2.
4	A. Images in a book.	4	(Recess taken: 1:05 p.m.)
5	Q. Do you have any reason to doubt that	5	(Proceedings resumed: 1:53 p.m.)
6	they're photographs?	6	THE VIDEOGRAPHER: 1:53. On the
7	A. I don't know if he made original --	7	record. Beginning of tape 3.
8	I mean I'm not in a position to say whether they	8	BY MR. BROOKS:
9	were original photographs to begin with. I	9	Q. Mr. Prince, we were looking before
10	don't know. I just saw them in -- I saw images,	10	we broke for lunch at Exhibit 13. And we had
11	reproductions of images in a book.	11	talked about the first question and answer that
12	I mean that's my -- that was my	12	you were asked and that you gave.
13	reaction. I believe my initial reaction was one	13	Then there's a second question which
14	of which I associated with the Canal Zone.	14	says, What will the format for this new series
15	Q. Did you like the pictures?	15	be, a large format like the nurse paintings,
16	A. Yes.	16	question mark. And then your answer, Larger,
17	Q. In the book?	17	there are several figures white or black female
18	A. I liked the pictures.	18	nudes beside clothed Rastafarians --
19	Q. You liked them a lot?	19	MR. HAYES: It's not the second
20	A. I liked them, yes.	20	question, actually it's the third, just
21	Q. You thought they were original?	21	for clarity.
22	MS. BART: Objection, form, calls	22	Go ahead.
23	for a legal conclusion.	23	A. Okay, I got it.
24	MR. HAYES: Objection.	24	MR. BROOKS: You're right, third
25	MR. BROOKS: No, it doesn't.	25	question.

162		164	
1	Prince	1	Prince
2	MS. BART: Please check 17 U.S.C.	2	BY MR. BROOKS:
3	A. I didn't have that reaction, no.	3	Q. Larger with several figures white or
4	I mean my reaction was they were documentary I	4	black female nudes beside clothed Rastafarians,
5	suppose.	5	a forest contrast like in the Luncheon on the
6	Q. Had you seen pictures like that	6	Grass by Manet from 1862-63 which still struck
7	before of Rastafarians?	7	me in the Picasso exhibition at the Musée
8	MR. HAYES: Objection.	8	d'Orsay. I combined the Rastafarians from the
9	A. Yes, I had had a book on Bob Marley	9	book with a series of hands playing the guitar
10	that I was also looking at the same time.	10	that I cut out and pasted. The nurses -- played
11	Q. Right.	11	on the uniform, the Rastafarians's uniform is
12	And did you consider incorporating a	12	merely a pair of shorts, almost nothing.
13	picture from the Bob Marley book into this Canal	13	Sometimes they are nude like the women painted
14	Zone exhibition?	14	from magazines or from photos of models in my
15	A. I did.	15	studio. In pictorial terms there is little
16	Q. And what made you decide not to do	16	difference between white and black. It is this
17	that?	17	kind of formal question that interests me. I've
18	A. I did do it.	18	already had a small Rastafarian exhibition in
19	Q. It's in the book?	19	St. Barth's. I called it Canal Zone as a
20	A. I believe there's an image --	20	reference to the Panama Canal of my childhood.
21	Q. Of Bob Marley?	21	I had put together a scene with gangs portrayed
22	A. Not of Bob Marley. It was an image	22	by the Rastafarians to music by Ziggy Marley,
23	that was in the Bob Marley book.	23	Bob Marley's oldest son, and the Wailers, his
24	Q. We'll get to that later because I	24	original group.
25	wouldn't begin to know where it is.	25	With respect to this Manet painting,

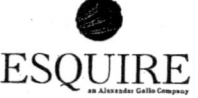

ESQUIRE
an Alexander Gallo Company

Toll Free: 800.944.9454
Facsimile: 212.557.5972

Suite 4715
One Penn Plaza
New York, NY 10119
www.esquiresolutions.com

165

1   Prince
2   Le déjeuner sur l'herbe --
3   A.   Right.
4   Q.   Le déjeuner sur l'herbe, do you know
5   it by that name?
6   A.   Yeah, the Luncheon on the Grass?
7   Q.   Yes.
8   A.   Yes.
9   Q.   There are men, clothed men and naked
10 women in that, as I recall, in that painting,
11 right?
12   A.   Yes.
13   Q.   And you had just seen it at the
14 Musée d'Orsay?
15   A.   Yes. At that time there were
16 several -- yes, I did.
17   Q.   Were you trying in the photos in the
18 Canal Zone book or some of the -- not photos.
19 Let me start again.
20   Was it your intention when you made,
21 created the paintings that are in the Canal Zone
22 book, to evoke the Luncheon on the Grass, Manet
23 painting?
24   A.   I was aware of Picasso's homage to
25 Manet. And I was also in the middle of making

166

1   Prince
2   an homage to De Kooning at the time.
3   I don't believe there was a direct
4   interest in making or pointing to that
5   particular painting. It was more about the fact
6   that I was interested in Picasso paying homage
7   to a previous artist.
8   And I think, point of fact, I would
9   cite Cézanne's bathers as a more -- interest in
10 mine of making the Canal Zone paintings.
11   Q.   Okay. Are you saying that one of
12 the points or one of the messages in the Canal
13 Zone paintings was to evoke Cézanne's bather
14 paintings?
15   A.   I think if in fact there was a
16 message, it was -- there was three people, yes,
17 specifically Cézanne's bathers because of the
18 composition, Picasso's hands and feet, and the
19 masks that were on the De Kooning women.
20   Q.   Did you put the masks on the
21 De Kooning women or were they there already?
22   A.   Sometimes yes, sometimes no.
23   Q.   And the feet, some of these
24 paintings -- and we'll look at them later --
25 have very large elephantine types of feet --

167

1   Prince
2   A.   Yes.
3   Q.   -- is that what you're referring to?
4   A.   Yeah. Feet that I would paint on
5   the paintings.
6   Q.   So correct me if I'm wrong, but are
7   you saying that these, some of these Canal Zone
8   paintings were a tribute -- I'll say tribute
9   instead of homage -- to Picasso, De Kooning, and
10 Cézanne?
11   MR. HAYES: Object to the form, but
12   you can answer.
13   A.   Well, I'm really interested in
14 making art that, you know, transforms something
15 that's already existed without getting involved
16 in the original intent of the image. I like
17 to -- I want to transform the existing image.
18   And by doing, by quoting, or in the
19 style of Picasso or in the style of De Kooning,
20 or even thinking about the composition of
21 Cézanne's bathers, it was a way in which I could
22 transform those images, yes.
23   Q.   Which images?
24   A.   The images that I first found in the
25 Yes Rasta book.

168

1   Prince
2   Q.   Where did you get the series of
3   hands playing the guitar?
4   A.   There are several magazines
5   published. I mean to be -- you know, what I
6   remember specifically is Guitar Magazine. But
7   there were other magazines. I don't recall the
8   names, but I do recall they were like -- there
9   are several that you can buy on the newsstand.
10   Q.   And did you cut those out as well?
11   A.   Cut them out with -- yes, I did.
12   Q.   And did you paste them onto the
13 other images?
14   A.   Yes.
15   Q.   And then you sent the whole thing to
16 that lab?
17   A.   NancyScans.
18   Q.   NancyScans. So they can be scanned
19 onto the canvas?
20   A.   I'm not sure I would word it like
21 that.
22   MR. HAYES: Object to the form.
23   Q.   So it could be transferred onto the
24 canvas?
25   A.   What I -- no, I'm not sure I would

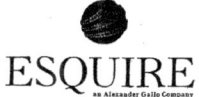

ESQUIRE
an Alexander Gallo Company

Toll Free: 800.944.9454
Facsimile: 212.557.5972

Suite 4715
One Penn Plaza
New York, NY 10119
www.esquiresolutions.com

169		171	
1	Prince	1	Prince
2	word what I would -- that I sent to NancyScans.	2	Q. And what kind of magazine is that?
3	Q. What did you send to NancyScans?	3	A. It's a publishing. They publish
4	A. I sent a collage.	4	books.
5	Q. What does that mean?	5	Q. When you said men's magazines --
6	A. A collage.	6	A. They published a book on men's
7	Q. Well, in this case what do you mean	7	magazines.
8	by collage?	8	Q. And that's where you got the --
9	A. It means I ripped out a reproduction	9	A. That's where I got some of the
10	from a book or a magazine and cut it up, pasted	10	images.
11	it, scotch taped, and then mounted it on a piece	11	Q. Did you get some from -- I'll use
12	of white paper and drew some dimensions,	12	the term loosely -- porno magazines?
13	60 inches wide and --	13	A. Porno?
14	Q. So it could be enlarged?	14	MR. HAYES: Objection to form.
15	A. So it could be enlarged -- yeah, I	15	How loosely?
16	mean I just say 60, yes, various sizes.	16	Q. Pornographic magazines.
17	Q. And then NancyScan would enlarge it	17	A. Pornographic?
18	to the size you told them?	18	Q. I'm only asking you that because
19	A. Yes.	19	I've read that in a number of the articles.
20	Q. And then they would send it back to	20	A. Yeah.
21	you?	21	Q. I don't know if it's true, so that's
22	A. They would send it back to me.	22	why I'm asking you.
23	Q. By electronically or physically?	23	A. I mean -- I suppose you're talking
24	A. Physically. They would send me --	24	about like something that's like triple X or --
25	Q. So in this process that you've	25	you know -- I'm trying to think here.

170		172	
1	Prince	1	Prince
2	described you never actually used a camera,	2	I mean Richard Kern and Eric Kroll's
3	correct, you personally?	3	images have been described -- I wouldn't
4	A. For this, for the Canal Zone series,	4	describe their images as pornographic, but they
5	no, I've never used a camera, no.	5	have been by other people.
6	Q. And where did you get the nude	6	Q. Were some of the nude females just
7	females that are in many of these paintings?	7	anonymous where you didn't know who the
8	A. Mostly from Taschen, a lot from --	8	photographer was who had taken the pictures?
9	they had published a series of books on men's	9	A. Especially the ones from the Taschen
10	magazines that was edited by a friend of mine,	10	publications they were -- even some of the
11	that she sent me the books. And also --	11	credits I suppose were anonymous where I didn't
12	(Interruption.)	12	know the models, I didn't know -- you know, I
13	A. Should I continue?	13	didn't really pay attention.
14	Q. Yes.	14	Q. And were some of them, some of the
15	A. I remember some of the women came	15	nude females in these paintings, models you had
16	out of two specific photographers' books,	16	hired for those paintings?
17	Richard Kern and Eric Kroll.	17	A. I hired a nude model, yes.
18	Q. With a K?	18	Q. The woman with the apron?
19	A. Kroll with a -- K-R-O-L-L.	19	A. Yes.
20	And Kern with a K.	20	Q. But she's not in the Canal Zone
21	Q. Now, you said Taschen, is that what	21	paintings, right? Or maybe she is. I don't
22	you said, T-A --	22	think she is --
23	A. Taschen Publishers. T-A-C-H --	23	A. She was in -- I know -- I recall one
24	MR. HAYES: T-A-S-C-H-E-N.	24	painting she's painted out, but there's a very
25	A. T-A-S-C-H-E-N.	25	thin -- there's a lot of ghosts in some of these

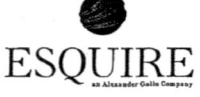

Richard Prince   October 6, 2009

<table>
<tr><td>

173

1   Prince
2   paintings. A lot of things got painted out.
3   That's part of the process. That's part of my
4   technique of how I transfer images and how I
5   make them different.
6   Q.   Right.
7   A.   So it's hard to say whether or not
8   she's in the painting. She's in the painting
9   physically in her representation, but it's very
10   difficult to see her. However, she is in the
11   catalog.
12   Q.   Right. And to the extent she's in
13   the painting did somebody take her photograph?
14   A.   I hired her and I took -- I spent an
15   afternoon taking her photograph, yes.
16   Q.   So the photograph of that --
17   photographs of that woman in the inserts are
18   photographs that you took?
19   A.   I took, yes, I took them.
20   Q.   Did you have any assistants helping
21   you with cutting out, pasting, sending things to
22   NancyScan or did you do it yourself?
23   A.   I did it myself.
24   Q.   You do have at least two assistants,
25   right, Betsy and -- Betsy Biscone and Eric

</td><td>

175

1   Prince
2   Q.   In your garage, okay.
3   And in the summer do you do some of
4   your artwork there rather than in
5   Rensselaerville?
6   A.   Yes.
7   Q.   And these Rasta paintings, that's
8   what they've been called in a lot of articles,
9   that were in the Canal Zone, were those done in
10   your Long Island studio?
11   A.   Well, the Canal Zone paintings were
12   mostly done by myself in the garage studio or
13   the studio in Long Island, yes.
14   Q.   In Wainscott?
15   A.   In Wainscott.
16   Q.   Okay. Now, in this interview in
17   Figaro you also said you had a small Rastafarian
18   exhibition in St. Barth's, correct?
19   A.   I don't believe -- is that what I
20   said?
21   Q.   That's what it says here.
22   MR. HAYES: That's what the
23   translation said.
24   Q.   I already had a small Rastafarian
25   exhibition in St. Barth's, and this is in

</td></tr>
<tr><td>

174

1   Prince
2   Brown?
3   A.   Yes.
4   Q.   Do you have other assistants as
5   well?
6   A.   Yes.
7   Q.   How many others?
8   A.   Do you want their names?
9   Q.   No.
10   A.   No, no. I have -- you mean
11   assistants that help me maybe in the studio
12   while I was doing these paintings?
13   Q.   Right.
14   A.   Two.
15   Q.   In addition to those two?
16   A.   Yes.
17   Q.   So that's a total of four?
18   A.   Yes.
19   Q.   And some of the e-mails and things
20   refer to a Long Island studio?
21   A.   Yes.
22   Q.   And where is that?
23   A.   It's in Wainscott.
24   Q.   In your house in Wainscott?
25   A.   I have a little studio in my garage.

</td><td>

176

1   Prince
2   November of 2008.
3   A.   Well, I was probably wrong in
4   describing the exhibition that way, although I
5   did probably -- if that's the translation, I did
6   call the exhibition Canal Zone.
7   I don't believe -- I don't
8   remember -- I don't think -- it was a fairly
9   casual exhibition, so I don't believe there was
10   an invitation card. So I don't know if there
11   was a title to the show. I doubt very much --
12   usually you make up a postcard and you put the
13   title, but I don't think we did that for that
14   show.
15   Q.   Let me just ask you this. This is
16   in late 2007, there was a show at the Eden Rock
17   Hotel in St. Barth's of some of your work,
18   correct?
19   A.   Yes.
20   Q.   And it was called the Eden Rock
21   show?
22   A.   I don't think we called it anything,
23   but I might be mistaken.
24   Q.   But it was about maybe 14 or 15
25   different works, right?

</td></tr>
</table>

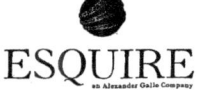

Toll Free: 800.944.9454
Facsimile: 212.557.5972

Suite 4715
One Penn Plaza
New York, NY 10119
www.esquiresolutions.com

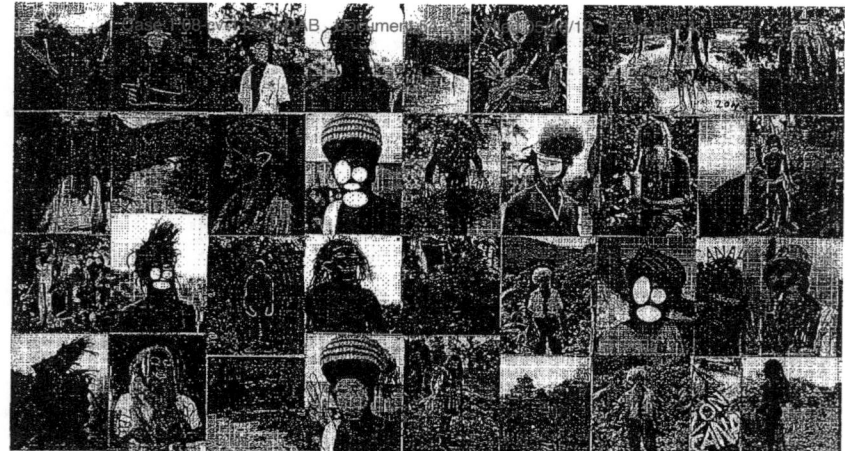

RICHARD PRINCE *The Canal Zone*, 2007 Mixed media on homosote, 48 x 82 3/4 inches, (121.9 x 210.2cm) PRINC 2007.0033

GAGOSIAN GALLERY

177

Prince

1
2   A.   Yes, I believe that would be about,
3   yes.
4   Q.   And were any of those works -- and
5   I'm not talking about the Canal Zone, I'm sorry,
6   I don't want to confuse you.
7   A.   That's okay.
8   Q.   I'm talking about the one the year
9   before in St. Barth's.
10   A.   Right.
11   Q.   Were any of those works --
12   withdrawn.
13   Did any of those works contain
14   materials, images appropriated from the
15   Yes Rasta book?
16   MS. BART: Objection to form.
17   MR. HAYES: Objection as to form.
18   A.   Yes.
19   Q.   How many of those 14 or 15
20   paintings?
21   A.   There was one collage.
22   Q.   Right. And that was called Canal
23   Zone, right?
24   A.   I believe it was, yes.
25   Q.   We're going to look at that in a

178

Prince

1
2   second, but of those paintings that were
3   exhibited at the Eden Rock Hotel, are any of
4   those in the Canal Zone book?
5   A.   There wasn't a painting that was
6   exhibited in that particular exhibition. It was
7   a collage.
8   Q.   Well, there are 14 or 15 works,
9   right?
10   A.   No, there were -- the 14 -- I
11   thought you were referring to -- the other 14 or
12   15 paintings in that show were different
13   paintings.
14   Q.   No, I understand that. I
15   understand. They don't have material images
16   taken from Yes Rasta?
17   A.   Right. Right.
18   Q.   I'm just asking you, those
19   paintings, were any of those in the Canal Zone
20   book or the Canal Zone show at Gagosian
21   Gallery --
22   A.   Oh, no. No.
23   Q.   -- in 2007?
24   Now, how about the one collage which
25   does have images from the Yes Rasta book, the

179

Prince

1
2   one you did in 2007, was that either in the
3   Canal Zone book or exhibited at the Canal Zone
4   show at the Gagosian Gallery?
5   A.   It was never exhibited at -- it
6   didn't get in the show at the Canal Zone exhibit
7   at Larry Gagosian's.
8   Q.   Okay. And it's not in the book?
9   A.   It's not in the book.
10   MR. BROOKS: Let's mark as
11   Plaintiff's Exhibit 14 a document produced
12   by Gagosian defendants Bates stamped
13   GGP003781.
14   (Plaintiff's Exhibit 14, GGP003781,
15   was marked for identification, as of this
16   date.)
17   Q.   Mr. Prince, does this refresh your
18   recollection that the title of that work of art
19   was The Canal Zone, comma, 2007?
20   A.   That's what it says here, yes.
21   Q.   And is this the work of art you've
22   been describing that was part of the show at the
23   Eden Rock?
24   A.   Yes.
25   Q.   And this is the only one on display

180

Prince

1
2   at that show that had images taken from the
3   Yes Rasta book, is that correct?
4   A.   Yes.
5   Q.   And all of these images in this --
6   what did you call it, a --
7   A.   Collage.
8   Q.   Collage. These were all taken from
9   the Yes Rasta book, correct?
10   A.   These images were what I would refer
11   to as -- it was sort of like, yes, they were
12   torn out, they were pages that were torn out of
13   the Yes Rasta book.
14   Q.   And does this relate back to what
15   you were saying before that over the course of a
16   couple years you intermittently wrote in the
17   book and looked at it?
18   A.   Yes, I think this probably was done
19   over the course of probably three seasons in
20   St. Barth.
21   Q.   Is that because you left the book
22   there when you --
23   A.   I left a number of, you know -- also
24   there was -- yes, I left a number of art-related
25   materials at the house.

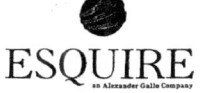

ESQUIRE
an Alexander Gallo Company

Toll Free: 800.944.9454
Facsimile: 212.557.5972

Suite 4715
One Penn Plaza
New York, NY 10119
www.esquiresolutions.com

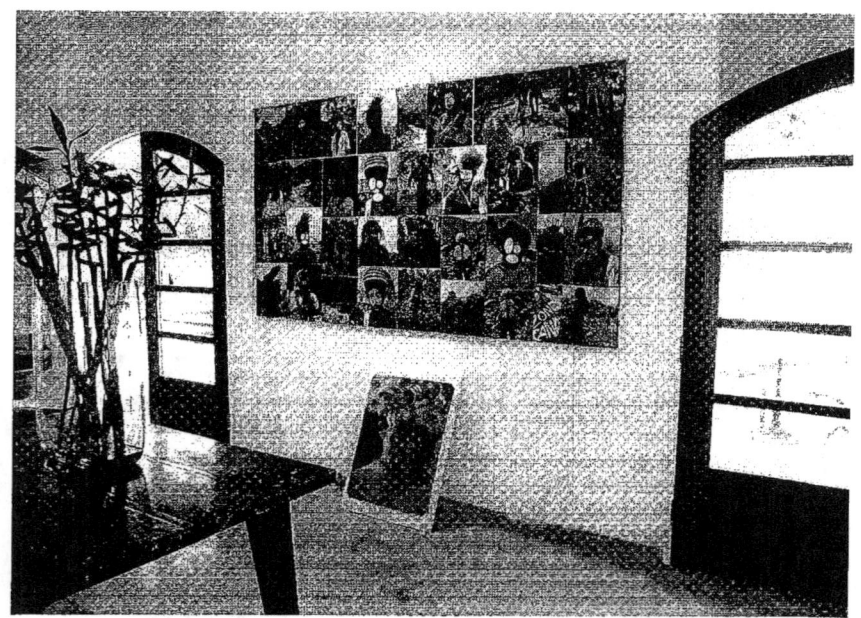

181

	Prince
1	Prince
2	Q. In St. Barth's?
3	A. In St. Barth.
4	Q. Including Yes Rasta?
5	A. Including the book.
6	Q. The one you bought?
7	A. Yes.
8	Q. I got it. Okay.
9	What does mixed media on homasote
10	mean, do you know?
11	A. It's a description of the different
12	mediums that I -- the fact that I did use
13	different mediums, meaning paint --
14	Q. That explains the mixed media part.
15	MS. BART: Let him finish, please.
16	MR. HAYES: He's asking about
17	homasote, what that means.
18	Q. Yes, what does that mean?
19	A. It's the material which the pages
20	were pushpinned on. It's approximately an
21	8-by-4 piece of, for lack of a better word,
22	plywood.
23	MR. HAYES: It's wood?
24	THE WITNESS: Yeah.
25	MR. HAYES: Like a masonite type of

182

	Prince
1	Prince
2	wood?
3	THE WITNESS: Yeah.
4	MR. BROOKS: I'm sorry?
5	MR. HAYES: It's like masonite, like
6	masonite manufactured wood.
7	MR. BROOKS: Okay.
8	BY MR. BROOKS:
9	Q. Now, did you have an assistant
10	helping you with the creation of Canal Zone 2007
11	or did you do it yourself?
12	A. I did it myself.
13	Q. And did you send it to a lab to be
14	completed?
15	A. No. This is a -- this is just what
16	I would refer to as an original collage.
17	Q. Okay. So you tore out these
18	pictures -- you nailed them to the piece of
19	plywood?
20	A. Yes.
21	Q. So it wasn't -- then it wasn't
22	enlarged?
23	A. This particular piece?
24	Q. Yes.
25	A. No.

183

	Prince
1	Prince
2	Q. And you did not obtain Mr. Cariou's
3	permission to create Canal Zone 2007, did you?
4	MS. BART: Objection, form.
5	MR. HAYES: Objection as to form.
6	Q. You can answer.
7	A. No.
8	MR. BROOKS: I'd like to mark as
9	Plaintiff's Exhibit 15 a one-page document
10	Bates stamped GGP004296.
11	(Plaintiff's Exhibit 15, GGP004296,
12	was marked for identification, as of this
13	date.)
14	(Discussion off the record.)
15	Q. Mr. Prince, Plaintiff's Exhibit 15
16	depicts the same work of art that we've been
17	looking at as Exhibit 14, is that correct?
18	A. Yes.
19	Q. Canal Zone 2007?
20	A. Yes.
21	Q. Where are we seeing this, is this at
22	the Eden Rock Hotel or somewhere else or what?
23	A. It's at the Eden Rock gallery.
24	Q. So this is actually a photo of that
25	show, that exhibition, a part of it?

184

	Prince
1	Prince
2	A. Part of it, yes.
3	Q. So are each of the pictures, the
4	photos in this collage, an entire -- represent
5	an entire page from Yes Rasta?
6	A. I think they're individual pages.
7	Q. Right. Because this was not
8	enlarged?
9	A. No.
10	Q. Do you remember when the show at the
11	Eden Rock was put together or planned?
12	A. Probably November of 2007.
13	You know, I -- that's a guess.
14	MR. BROOKS: Let's mark as
15	Exhibit Plaintiff's 16 a series of e-mails
16	Bates stamped GGP004309, 4317 and 4325.
17	(Plaintiff's Exhibit 16, series of
18	e-mails, was marked for identification, as
19	of this date.)
20	Q. If you could look at the first page
21	of Exhibit 16, it appears to be an e-mail to you
22	dated August 8th, 2007. Do you see that?
23	A. Mm-hmm.
24	Q. And Jazz Man 611, is that somebody
25	from the Eden Rock Hotel that you know?

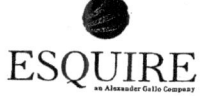

ESQUIRE
an Alexander Gallo Company

Toll Free: 800.944.9454
Facsimile: 212.557.5972

Suite 4715
One Penn Plaza
New York, NY 10119
www.esquiresolutions.com

185

1   Prince
2   A.   Yes.
3   Q.   And he was responding to an e-mail
4   from you dated August 3rd it looks like, saying
5   that Larry Gagosian was going to handle
6   everything. Do you see that?
7   A.   Yes.
8   Q.   And that right now he's previewing
9   three other works at his house out here on
10   Long Island. What did you mean by that, if you
11   remember?
12   A.   There were three works that were
13   going to be part of the show.
14   Q.   The Eden -- we're calling it the
15   Eden Rock show. I know that might not have been
16   the name.
17   A.   Okay.
18   Q.   And what do you mean -- what does
19   that mean to you, previewing? Was he showing
20   them to potential buyers, is that it?
21   A.   He -- I had given him -- we were
22   sort of -- I like to refer to Larry's house
23   as off-off-off-broadway, sort of a way of
24   previewing different works that have never
25   been shown before.

186

1   Prince
2   Q.   Okay. And his house is out in
3   East Hampton?
4   A.   Yes.
5   Q.   And what did you mean when you said
6   he'll be the one handling the percentages? What
7   did that mean?
8   A.   I believe at the time I didn't want
9   to do the show independently. I wanted someone
10   to represent my interests in the show.
11   Q.   Was this the first time you worked
12   with Mr. Gagosian?
13   A.   No.
14   Q.   You had worked with him before then?
15   A.   Yes.
16   Q.   Now, what did you mean when you said
17   at the bottom of this first page, it's
18   storyboards -- I-T, apostrophe S -- storyboards
19   for a screenplay called Eden Rock, everybody
20   loves it so far? What were you talking about?
21   A.   I was talking about the paintings.
22   Q.   Okay. But what is this -- maybe
23   this is my ignorance -- what is a storyboard for
24   a screenplay?
25   A.   It sort of looks like a comic book

187

1   Prince
2   where you're -- it's almost like a graphic
3   novel, where in instead of words you're drawing
4   pictures of different scenes.
5   Q.   Scenes of a potential movie?
6   A.   Yes, I suppose so, yes.
7   Q.   Now, if you look on the second page
8   of this Exhibit 16, there's an e-mail from
9   somebody named David Matthew. Is that -- that
10   is the person at the Eden Rock Hotel?
11   A.   I believe he's one of the owners.
12   Q.   But he's not the David Matthews
13   Band, right?
14   A.   No.
15   Q.   It's a different -- okay.
16   And he says the exhibition to open
17   December 18th and close end of February, that's
18   down about five paragraphs. Do you see that?
19   A.   Yes.
20   Q.   So in September 14th it was planned
21   that the show would be -- would run for
22   approximately two-and-a-half months, is that
23   right?
24   A.   I believe so, yes.
25   Q.   And is that your recollection of

188

1   Prince
2   when that show ran, December 18th, '07, to the
3   end of February '08?
4   A.   I didn't have any -- I didn't
5   particularly pay attention to when it was going
6   to close. So if it says it was going to close
7   here in February then I assume that that's what
8   it meant.
9   Q.   Were you there when it opened?
10   A.   I was there when it opened.
11   Q.   And then if you look at the third
12   page, it appears to indicate there would be
13   12 to 14 works for the show --
14   A.   Yes.
15   Q.   -- do you see that?
16   Does that seem right?
17   A.   Yes.
18   MR. BROOKS: I'd like to mark as
19   Plaintiff's Exhibit 17 an e-mail Bates
20   stamped GGP004326.
21   (Plaintiff's Exhibit 17, e-mail, was
22   marked for identification, as of this
23   date.)
24   Q.   Is Plaintiff's Exhibit 17 an e-mail
25   that you sent?

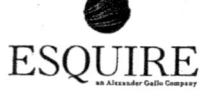

189

1   Prince
2   A.   Me?
3   Q.   Yes.
4   A.   Yes.
5   Q.   And you wanted a friend of yours
6   Lisa Evans to look at some of these Eden Rock
7   paintings?
8   A.   Yes.
9   Q.   Was that with a view to selling her
10 one or more paintings?
11   A.   I was probably thinking that her
12 husband might be interested in buying one.
13   Q.   Her husband is Michael Evans?
14   A.   Yes.
15   Q.   Is he a collector?
16   A.   He had just about started to be one
17 about that time.
18   Q.   What's his occupation?
19   A.   That's a good question. I believe
20 he works for a broker -- what's that -- one of
21 those --
22   Q.   Hedge funds?
23   A.   No, a -- you know, like Lehman
24 Brothers.
25   Q.   Brokerage firm?

190

1   Prince
2   A.   Yeah, you know --
3   MR. HAYES: Investment bank?
4   THE WITNESS: What?
5   MR. HAYES: An investment bank?
6   THE WITNESS: Yeah, an investment
7   bank.
8   Q.   In fact, he later bought one of your
9   paintings at the Canal Zone show, didn't he?
10   A.   Yes.
11   Q.   Which one?
12   A.   I believe it was -- I would have to
13 look. I mean I know the painting, I just don't
14 recall the title.
15   Q.   Okay. You can visualize it?
16   A.   I can visualize it, yes.
17   Q.   Can you visualize how much he paid
18 for it?
19   MR. HAYES: Objection to form.
20   MS. BART: Objection to form.
21   Q.   You can answer.
22   A.   I believe he paid around two-million
23 dollars, but I don't know that for sure because
24 of -- I'm not --
25   Q.   -- sure which painting it was?

191

1   Prince
2   A.   I know which painting it was, I just
3   don't know --
4   Q.   The title?
5   A.   -- the exact amount.
6   Q.   All right.
7   MR. BROOKS: Let's mark as
8   Plaintiff's Exhibit 18 an e-mail from
9   Mr. Prince dated July 26, 2007, Bates
10 stamped GGP004307.
11   (Plaintiff's Exhibit 18, e-mail
12 dated July 26, 2007, was marked for
13 identification, as of this date.)
14   Q.   Is this an e-mail that you sent to
15 Larry Gagosian?
16   A.   It looks -- yes, I believe it is.
17   Q.   And you said you had a couple of
18 thoughts about guns and ammo, what did you mean
19 about that? What did you mean by using that
20 phrase guns and ammo?
21   A.   I believe it was a way of trying to
22 describe the paintings that were going to be
23 shown at Eden Rock at that show.
24   Q.   So it says this is a storyboard for
25 a screenplay about some guy named Charles

192

1   Prince
2   Company?
3   A.   Mm-hmm.
4   Q.   For the record, you have to say yes
5   or no.
6   A.   Oh, I'm sorry. Yes.
7   Q.   All right. He arrives in
8   St. Barth's with his wife and children and finds
9   out when he gets to St. Barth's that something
10 horrible has happened?
11   A.   Yes.
12   Q.   A nuclear war consuming most of
13 civilization, is that right?
14   A.   Yes.
15   Q.   And then he becomes Charlie Company
16 instead of Charles Company by which you meant
17 what?
18   A.   I just thought it was an interesting
19 way to change his name. He becomes an action
20 hero.
21   Q.   Becomes weaponized?
22   A.   Yes.
23   Q.   So that --
24   A.   He can fight --
25   Q.   In the aftermath of nuclear war he

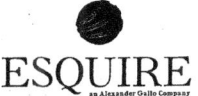

ESQUIRE
an Alexander Gallo Company

Toll Free: 800.944.9454
Facsimile: 212.557.5972

Suite 4715
One Penn Plaza
New York, NY 10119
www.esquiresolutions.com

193

Prince

2 has to fend for himself, is that the idea?
3   A. Yes.
4   Q. You compared him to Steven Segal?
5   A. Yes.
6   Q. And Under Siege?
7   A. Yes.
8   Q. Which is a movie where a submarine
9 is taken over?
10   A. Yes.
11   Q. And he kills everyone, right?
12   I think I saw that movie.
13   I agree with you, it was a good
14 movie.
15   MR. HAYES: A couple of Steven Segal
16 fans here.
17   MR. BROOKS: What?
18   MR. HAYES: We got a couple of
19 Steven Segal fans here.
20   MR. BROOKS: Yeah, I liked that
21 movie.
22   MS. BART: The only two.
23 BY MR. BROOKS:
24   Q. And then Jimi Hendrix is going to be
25 on the soundtrack, right? Is that right?

194

Prince

2   A. I believe in this version, yeah.
3 Yeah, that's what it says, yes.
4   Q. So anyway, at the end you say,
5 Anyway, this is what I'm thinking these
6 paintings are about. And then you say, In my
7 movie is the title of the whole set of paintings
8 at least for now, and Eden Rock is the title of
9 the screenplay. That was your thinking at the
10 time?
11   A. I believe I was writing a piece --
12   Q. Right.
13   A. -- for ArtForum that was called In
14 My Movie, or maybe I had already written -- it
15 was published. But these were some of the
16 things, yes, I was thinking about.
17   Q. And when you say you were writing an
18 article in Art -- what did you say?
19   A. Forum.
20   Q. This is separate from what you've
21 been calling the pitch, right?
22   A. Yes.
23   Q. That's a different thing?
24   A. Yes.
25   Q. Okay. Now, I just want to go back

195

Prince

2 to this phrase you wrote.
3   Anyway, this is what I'm thinking
4 these paintings are about. Do you see that
5 language?
6   A. Yes.
7   Q. So tell me what were they about,
8 these paintings?
9   A. The guns and ammo paintings?
10   Q. The paintings at the Eden Rock show.
11   A. Yeah, the ones that we referred to
12 as guns and ammo.
13   Q. Okay.
14   A. You want me to describe them or tell
15 you --
16   Q. Well, I think we have some images of
17 them that have been produced. But just what was
18 your thinking in making those paintings?
19   A. They reminded me of science fiction
20 paintings.
21   Q. And did they have anything to do
22 with the Canal Zone in your mind?
23   A. I believe they were about -- they
24 represented a way of how -- or the images in
25 these paintings represented survival.

196

Prince

2   Q. Now, how did the -- this Canal Zone
3 2007, which was Exhibit 14, how did that fit in
4 with these guns and ammo paintings, if it did?
5   A. It didn't.
6   Q. But it was in the same show?
7   A. In the same show.
8   Q. Okay.
9   MR. BROOKS: Let's mark as
10 Plaintiff's Exhibit 19 two pages Bates
11 stamped GGP004330 and 4332. Or is there a
12 third page? No.
13   (Plaintiff's Exhibit 19, GGP004330
14 and 4332, was marked for identification,
15 as of this date.)
16   Q. Exhibit 19 has two pages, the first
17 has smaller versions of some of these images,
18 and on the second page they're slightly larger.
19 Do you see that?
20   A. Yes.
21   Q. Now, one of these paintings is that
22 Canal Zone 2007 mixed media on wood, correct?
23   A. Yes.
24   Q. And the others are what you were
25 saying, referring to as guns and ammo?

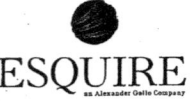

ESQUIRE
an Alexander Gallo Company

Toll Free: 800.944.9454
Facsimile: 212.557.5972

Suite 4715
One Penn Plaza
New York, NY 10119
www.esquiresolutions.com

197

1   Prince
2   A.   Yes.
3   Q.   Now, are these cut off or is that
4 all there was in the painting, a person's legs
5 and part of a gun, or was there actually a
6 face --
7   A.   That's the painting.
8   Q.   That's the painting?
9   So it's just kind of from the waist
10 down and you can kind of see a gun, a machine
11 gun I guess, or automatic weapon?
12   A.   In some of them, yes.
13   Q.   In some of them.
14   And a snake biting somebody or
15 something?
16   A.   Mm-hmm, yes.
17   Q.   All right. On the first page there
18 are names of people. Did they buy these
19 paintings as indicated?
20   A.   I believe so, yes.
21   Q.   Abby Rosen, best known for having
22 been my landlord about eight years on Park
23 Avenue, he owns all those buildings, right?
24   A.   Mm-hmm, yes.
25   Q.   The Seagrams Building and the Lever

198

1   Prince
2 House and all those, right?
3   A.   Mm-hmm.
4   Q.   And we all know who Ron Perelman is.
5 Okay. Donny Deutsch is an advertising person or
6 public relations person? Don't know him?
7   A.   I don't know him.
8   Q.   Did Larry Gagosian buy one of these
9 paintings? His name is listed here.
10   A.   I gave him --
11   Q.   You gave him.
12   A.   -- the painting.
13   MR. BROOKS: Let's mark as
14 Exhibit 20 an article from the Art
15 Newspaper Bates stamped C00242 and 243.
16   (Plaintiff's Exhibit 20, article
17 from Art Newspaper, was marked for
18 identification, as of this date.)
19   Q.   Have you ever seen this article
20 before in the Art Newspaper?
21   A.   Yes, I was aware of it.
22   Q.   Let me ask you this. There are some
23 photos at the top of the article, which, if you
24 will compare them with Exhibit 14, seem to
25 represent a part of that work, the Canal Zone

199

1   Prince
2 2007. Take Exhibit 14 if you want and compare
3 them. Don't take my word for it.
4   Or 15. Either one will do.
5   14 is probably better.
6   See --
7   A.   Yes.
8   Q.   -- there's a guy with a hat?
9   A.   Mm-hmm, yes.
10   Q.   There are like eight frames there,
11 right, or eight collaged pages. And so that
12 comes from --
13   A.   Yes.
14   Q.   -- the canal Zone 2007 painting
15 work --
16   A.   It seems like --
17   Q.   -- apparently?
18   A.   No, not apparently. It comes from
19 this section, the middle of the collage.
20   Q.   Correct. Indicating the middle of
21 Exhibit 14, right?
22   A.   Yes.
23   Q.   Do you have any idea of how either
24 the Art Newspaper or Andrew Goldstein who wrote
25 this piece got a part of Exhibit 14?

200

1   Prince
2   A.   No clue. I don't.
3   Q.   Okay. In the third paragraph he
4 states that, among other things, that Garry
5 Gross sued you over Spiritual America and that
6 the case was settled out of court. That's not
7 correct?
8   A.   That is not correct.
9   Q.   You also say that -- he also says
10 rather that the essay for the show's catalog,
11 for instance, was written by James Frey.
12   Is it pronounced fray or fry? How
13 do you pronounce F-R-E-Y?
14   A.   I believe it's fray.
15   Q.   Fray, okay.
16   The essay for the show's catalog,
17 for instance, was written by James Frey, the
18 controversial author who fabricated whole swaths
19 of his 2003, quote, memoir, unquote, A Million
20 Little Pieces.
21   Now, this is a reference to the
22 catalog for the Canal Zone show in 2008,
23 correct?
24   MS. BART: Objection, form.
25   A.   I -- I don't know. I'm --

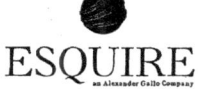
ESQUIRE
an Alexander Gallo Company

Toll Free: 800.944.9454
Facsimile: 212.557.5972

Suite 4715
One Penn Plaza
New York, NY 10119
www.esquiresolutions.com

	201		203
	Prince	1	Prince
1		2	MS. BART: Objection, form.
2	Q. Okay. Well, was there a catalog for	3	Q. Have you ever heard that he was on
3	the Canal Zone show that took place at the	4	the Oprah Winfrey Show talking about the book
4	Gagosian Gallery --	5	and then went back on the show and told her this
5	A. Yes.	6	was not an actual memoir, it was fiction?
6	Q. -- in November-December 2008?	7	A. Yes, I was aware of that.
7	A. Yes.	8	Q. When did you become aware of that?
8	Q. And was there a story in there by	9	A. That's hard to say.
9	James Frey?	10	Q. Let me ask you this. Was it before
10	A. Yes, there was.	11	you met and made his acquaintance or after?
11	Q. Did you ask him to write it?	12	A. It was before I made his
12	A. I did.	13	acquaintance.
13	Q. And did he write it?	14	Q. And how did you become acquainted
14	A. He did write it.	15	with him?
15	Q. And did he base it on your pitch?	16	A. He was -- I met him because he was a
16	A. He based it on my pitch.	17	collector of art, and an author.
17	Q. And additions to your pitch that you	18	Q. Yes. And after A Million Little
18	wrote in 2008?	19	Pieces he wrote a book Bright Shiny Morning?
19	MS. BART: I'm sorry, can I hear the	20	A. Yes.
20	question again?	21	Q. Did you design the cover for him?
21	(Record read.)	22	A. No, I did not design it.
22	A. I think I told him of the additions.	23	Q. What did you do?
23	I'm not positive but I think, yes.	24	A. I provided the images.
24	Q. And also had an opportunity to see	25	Q. For his cover?
25	some of the Canal Zone paintings in your		

	202		204
1	Prince	1	Prince
2	Long Island studio in the summer of 2008,	2	A. Yes.
3	correct?	3	Q. What images?
4	A. Yes.	4	A. They were images that I had
5	Q. You invited him there?	5	published in a previous book of mine.
6	A. Yes.	6	Q. What was the name of that book?
7	Q. And was his essay based, as far as	7	A. Adult Comedy Action Drama.
8	you know, on those paintings as well as your	8	Q. So you gave him those images and
9	pitch and the additions to your pitch?	9	then somebody else designed the cover for his
10	A. His essay was essentially based on	10	book?
11	my pitch.	11	A. Yes.
12	Q. Last question, was it also based on	12	Q. All right. We've been talking --
13	the so-called guns and ammo paintings that were	13	withdrawn.
14	part of the 2007 show at the Eden Rock, if you	14	Before we get to this pitch that
15	remember?	15	you wrote, I'd like you to go back and look at
16	A. I don't think so, no.	16	Exhibit 4 again, which is the interview of you
17	Q. Okay. Now, how long have you known	17	with Steve Lafreniere.
18	Mr. Frey?	18	Do you remember we were looking at
19	A. Three years.	19	this interview before?
20	Q. Did you know him when he wrote	20	A. Yes.
21	A Million Little Pieces?	21	Q. It was in 2003, correct?
22	A. No.	22	A. This was 2003.
23	Q. Are you aware that he misrepresented	23	Q. Well, that's what it says on the
24	that book as a memoir?	24	front page, ArtForum March 2003.
25	A. No.	25	A. Yes, that's what it says.

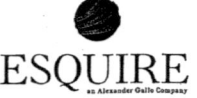

ESQUIRE
an Alexander Gallo Company

Toll Free: 800.944.9454
Facsimile: 212.557.5972

Suite 4715
One Penn Plaza
New York, NY 10119
www.esquiresolutions.com

205

1	Prince
2	Q. Okay. Now, at the bottom of the
3	second page -- I don't mean to rush you. If you
4	want to look at --
5	A. No.
6	Q. -- something on the first page, be
7	my guest.
8	The interviewer at the very bottom
9	is asking you, is naming three other well-known
10	contemporary artists, right?
11	A. Yes.
12	Q. Longo, Schnabel, and Sherman.
13	You know those people, right?
14	A. Yes, I do.
15	Q. And he says -- or she -- no, he says
16	that they've all made movies and I've wondered
17	why you haven't. Do you see that question?
18	A. Yes.
19	Q. And then, according to this, your
20	answer was I'm not very collaborative, I like
21	being alone, working alone, I hate actresses,
22	I don't like having to ask permission, a green
23	light is not something I would be happy waiting
24	for. Does that sound like an answer you gave in
25	2003?

206

1	Prince
2	A. It's the answer I gave, yes.
3	Q. And then the interviewer asks you
4	anyway, well, what movies do you like, just from
5	the '80s, and I see you mentioned Road Warrior
6	and Blade Runner, which I guess you would agree
7	those are both post-apocalyptic movies, is that
8	right?
9	A. Yes.
10	Q. And I'm not really familiar with
11	the others. Are any of the others also
12	post-apocalyptic movies?
13	A. Terminator.
14	Q. Okay, all right. That's an Arnold
15	Schwarzenegger movie?
16	A. Yes.
17	Q. And did that, did your appreciation
18	for that genre inform your writing of the pitch,
19	of your pitch?
20	A. I guess you could say that, yes.
21	MR. BROOKS: Let's mark as
22	Exhibit 22 -- just so you know, I skipped
23	21, I'm not going to -- it's not going to
24	be marked.
25	Exhibit 22 is the pitch, Bates

207

1	Prince
2	stamped PR79 and 80.
3	(Plaintiff's Exhibit 22, pitch, was
4	marked for identification, as of this
5	date.)
6	Q. Mr. Prince, is this the pitch you
7	wrote for a movie -- for a movie?
8	A. Yes.
9	Q. And do you remember we were looking
10	at an e-mail you sent to Mr. Gagosian, is this
11	the pitch that you were referring to in that
12	e-mail?
13	A. Probably, yes.
14	Q. Are there different versions of it?
15	A. Yes.
16	Q. Okay. Did you type it yourself on
17	the computer?
18	A. Yes, I did.
19	Q. Okay. So, again, it's this Charles
20	Company, which is a person and not a company,
21	and his family, they arrive in St. Barth's,
22	everyone is crying because there's a nuclear
23	war, correct?
24	A. Yes.
25	Q. And what are we supposed to do, most

208

1	Prince
2	of the world is destroyed, correct?
3	A. Yes.
4	Q. And you say you compare this to
5	On the Beach and Lord of the Flies?
6	A. Yes.
7	Q. For reasons that are probably
8	obvious?
9	A. Yes.
10	Q. And he's an architect in this
11	version, this person Charles Company?
12	A. Yes.
13	Q. And not somebody who's used to
14	shooting people or anything like that?
15	A. No, he's not used to.
16	Q. But he learns, he has to learn?
17	A. He adapts, yes.
18	Q. And they stay at the Eden Rock Hotel
19	with some other people?
20	A. I believe his relatives, yes.
21	Q. And, again, that's a hotel in
22	St. Barth's?
23	A. Yes.
24	Q. All right. Now, and then at the
25	very end it says his son is standing lookout.

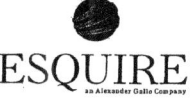

ESQUIRE
an Alexander Gallo Company

Toll Free: 800.944.9454
Facsimile: 212.557.5972

Suite 4715
One Penn Plaza
New York, NY 10119
www.esquiresolutions.com

209	211
Prince	Prince
1	1
2 Does that refer to these guns and ammo paintings	2 Q. A treatment -- oh, a book.
3 or not?	3 A. It's being published as a book
4 A. I think when it says cut to a year	4 called -- they did not want to use the original
5 later --	5 title, Eden Rock. It doesn't matter.
6 Q. Yes.	6 It's a book, or will be published as
7 A. Does it say that?	7 a book, I have no idea when.
8 Q. Yes, it does.	8 Q. I'm not going to even ask you who
9 A. Those paintings are the substitute	9 it is, just is the ghostwriter James Frey or
10 for what I would call the storyboard.	10 somebody different?
11 Q. In other words, the bottom half of	11 A. It's someone different. I --
12 somebody's body sometimes with a gun?	12 Q. I don't need to know.
13 A. Yes.	13 A. Okay.
14 Q. Did you ever submit this pitch or a	14 Q. Now, the pitch that I just showed
15 subsequent version of it to a movie studio or	15 you, Exhibit 22, was that at some point
16 production company?	16 displayed on the wall at the Eden Rock Hotel
17 A. Production company, I don't know if	17 during what we've been calling the Eden Rock
18 that's how you would describe it. So I can't	18 show?
19 say -- I would have to say no.	19 A. Yes.
20 Q. Who did you submit it to --	20 Q. And why?
21 withdrawn.	21 A. Why -- I felt that it would give a
22 Did you submit it to anyone with a	22 certain type of texture to the show and -- since
23 view to getting it made into a movie?	23 the show -- I believe at the time in 2007 I
24 A. Yes.	24 added on to that pitch, and --
25 Q. To getting a green light?	25 Q. Right. There's another document I'm

210	212
Prince	Prince
1	1
2 A. Yes.	2 going to show you in a minute.
3 Q. And can you tell us who you	3 A. And I felt that it would add a
4 submitted it to?	4 certain texture or another reading, it would
5 MR. HAYES: Is it okay if I consult	5 help perhaps with the interpretation perhaps,
6 with him for a second?	6 give it another interpretation of the
7 MR. BROOKS: Yes.	7 possibility of how one would walk into the
8 (Discussion off the record.)	8 gallery and get a feeling for the works that
9 A. Michael Ovitz.	9 were on the wall.
10 Q. The former talent agent?	10 Q. Right. Now, just look at Exhibit 15
11 A. Yes.	11 for a second, which showed that Eden Rock -- no,
12 Q. Do you know him, is he a friend of	12 that Canal Zone -- no, the one that shows it
13 yours?	13 actually on the wall.
14 A. Yes.	14 MS. BART: 16.
15 Q. Is he a collector?	15 MR. BROOKS: No, I think that was
16 A. Yes.	16 15.
17 Q. And what happened? Did it -- I	17 A. Yeah, I got it.
18 haven't seen it in the local movie theater.	18 MS. BART: 16.
19 MR. HAYES: Yet.	19 MR. BROOKS: 16, okay.
20 Q. Not yet.	20 BY MR. BROOKS:
21 A. Do you want to know?	21 Q. So is that -- so the pitch was
22 Q. Yes, please tell us.	22 posted somewhere in proximity near that Canal
23 A. His -- we hired a ghostwriter.	23 Zone 2007?
24 Q. For the screenplay?	24 A. Yes.
25 A. No, to write a book.	25 Q. Somewhere near there?

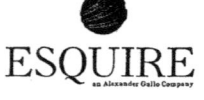

ESQUIRE
an Alexander Gallo Company

Toll Free: 800.944.9454
Facsimile: 212.557.5972

Suite 4715
One Penn Plaza
New York, NY 10119
www.esquiresolutions.com

14   Djuna Barnes, Natalie Barney, Renée Vivien, and Romaine Brooks Take Over the Guanahani

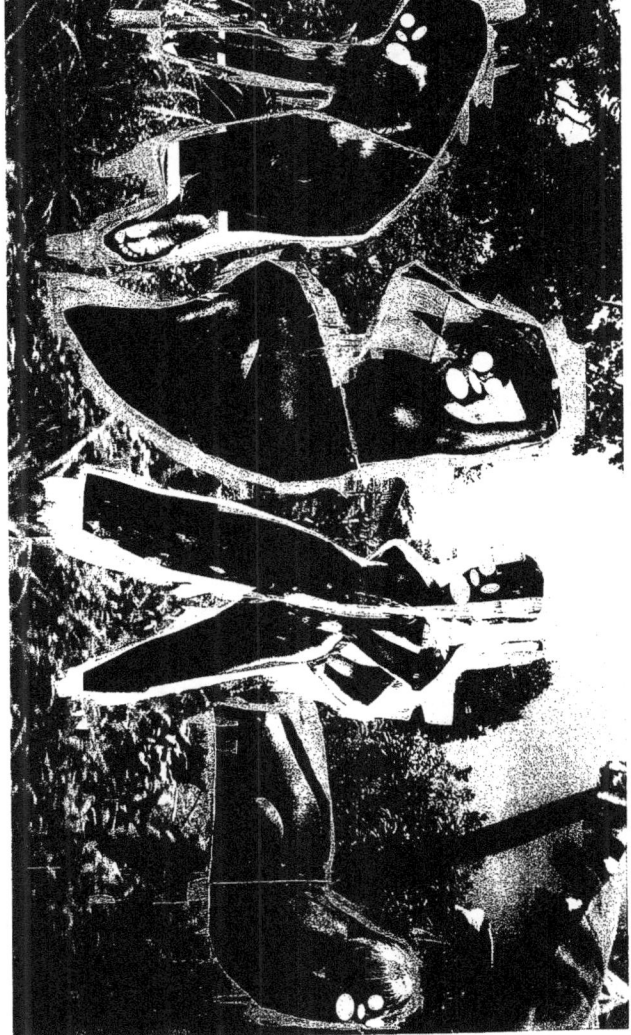

213

1	Prince
2	A. Somewhere.
3	Q. With those other works?
4	A. Yes.
5	Q. Okay. And, again, that show was
6	December 2007 to, according to the e-mail, the
7	end of February 2008, the show at the Eden Rock?
8	A. Yes.
9	MR. BROOKS: Now, let's mark as
10	Exhibit 23, Plaintiff's 23, pages Bates
11	stamped PR75 and 76.
12	(Plaintiff's Exhibit 23, e-mails,
13	was marked for identification, as of this
14	date.)
15	Q. This e-mail -- there are two
16	e-mails. One is -- they're both to Betsy
17	Biscone. Does she work for you?
18	A. Yes.
19	Q. It says she's the Prince studio
20	manager, is that her title?
21	A. Yes.
22	Q. And she's writing to somebody at
23	Gagosian, right, Louise Neri?
24	A. Yes.
25	Q. And she says, I hope -- I'm looking

214

1	Prince
2	at the second e-mail. She says, I hope this
3	finds you well. And it says, Per Richard's
4	request, please find attached the pitch which
5	was displayed on the wall at the Eden Rock Hotel
6	in St. Barth's the last December 2007 Eden Rock
7	show. And then she says, Also find below
8	additional writing Richard did this past spring
9	of '08. And then at the bottom there are some
10	additional Eden Rock slash pitch material
11	written March 2008.
12	Do you see that?
13	A. Mm-hmm, yes.
14	Q. Did you write those additional
15	points to the pitch?
16	A. Yes.
17	Q. So let's see. It says more on
18	Eden Rock. And you're saying there are Rastas
19	who escape from a cruise ship?
20	A. Yes.
21	Q. And they were a band?
22	A. Yes.
23	Q. Like a rock-and-roll band on the --
24	a reggae band on the cruise ship?
25	A. Yes.

215

1	Prince
2	Q. And they go to the Hotel Manapany?
3	A. Yes.
4	Q. Is that an actual hotel --
5	A. Yes.
6	Q. -- in St. Barth's?
7	And then there are --
8	MR. HAYES: You have to answer.
9	A. Yes.
10	Q. There are backpackers. So this is
11	another tribe, if you will?
12	A. Yes.
13	Q. And are there any backpackers in any
14	of the Canal Zone paintings?
15	MS. BART: Objection to form.
16	Q. As you used the term?
17	MR. HAYES: Objection to form.
18	A. No, there are no backpackers.
19	Q. Then the third group is the Amazons,
20	which you refer to as four lesbians who escape a
21	second cruise ship. Do they later take over a
22	hotel also?
23	A. Yes.
24	Q. The Guanahani?
25	A. Guanahani.

216

1	Prince
2	Q. And, again, like why did they take
3	over a hotel, because of the nuclear war?
4	A. They take it over because I wanted
5	them to take it over.
6	Q. And why -- I just look at these
7	pictures, why are those nude women lesbians?
8	I mean how do you know that?
9	A. I like lesbians.
10	Q. But how does the observer know
11	they're lesbians?
12	A. The title of the painting --
13	Q. Four names?
14	A. The four names were very famous
15	expatriate lesbians living in Paris.
16	Q. Iconic lesbian artists and writers?
17	A. Iconic.
18	Q. What are their names?
19	A. Renée Vivien, Djuna Barnes -- I have
20	to refer to the title.
21	Q. You don't remember?
22	MR. HAYES: Do you want to refer to
23	the title?
24	MR. BROOKS: No, I want to see if he
25	remembers.

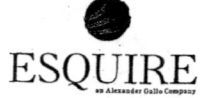

ESQUIRE
an Alexander Gallo Company

Toll Free: 800.944.9454
Facsimile: 212.557.5972

Suite 4715
One Penn Plaza
New York, NY 10119
www.esquiresolutions.com

Richard Prince   October 6, 2009

217

Prince

1
2   A.   Romaine Brooks, and the most famous
3   one, she was from the State of Maine and she was
4   the one who ran the salon that was the
5   alternative to Gertrude Stein.
6   Q.   In Maine?
7   A.   The name?
8   Q.   In Maine?
9   A.   No, in Paris.
10 Q.   Something Barnes?
11 A.   No, Djuna Barnes was a writer,
12 friend of --
13 Q.   All right. Well, when we look at
14 the painting it will probably come back.
15   So what are four lesbians from the
16 early 20th century doing on St. Barth's in --
17 now, when there's a nuclear war, like why are
18 they there?
19 A.   Your guess is as good as mine.
20 That's what I do, I make things up.
21 Q.   And when do you decide to do the --
22 A.   Natalie Barney.
23 Q.   That's it.
24   Barney or Barnes?
25 A.   Natalie Barney.

219

Prince

1
2   depictions of let's call them, to use your term,
3   the ultimate ones?
4   A.   No.
5   Q.   And are there any depictions of this
6   guy Charlie Company or his family?
7   A.   You could say his daughter got into
8   a couple of the pictures.
9   Q.   One of the nude women?
10 A.   Yes.
11 Q.   Is she a lesbian too?
12 A.   No.
13 Q.   So when we get to that painting
14 you'll --
15 A.   I don't think -- it's not -- well,
16 you probably have it. It's not in the catalog.
17 Q.   All right. I already asked you
18 about this, but let's mark as Plaintiff's 24
19 pages Bates stamped PR88 through 91.
20   (Plaintiff's Exhibit 24, PR88
21 through 91, was marked for identification,
22 as of this date.)
23 Q.   Mr. Prince, I've placed in front of
24 you Plaintiff's Exhibit 24. If you could look
25 at -- start out by looking at the second page,

218

Prince

1
2   Q.   When did you decide to do the Canal
3   Zone paintings, the ones that are in the Canal
4   Zone book?
5   A.   June of 2008, late June.
6   Q.   So after you wrote this let's call
7   it an addendum to your pitch?
8   A.   Yes.
9   Q.   By the way, in the paintings -- I
10 didn't finish, besides the Amazons there are
11 also the ultimate ones. Those are like masters
12 of the universe?
13 A.   Ultimate ones? That I don't -- I
14 don't -- to tell you the truth, I don't know
15 what I was referring to -- power.
16   Oh, maybe the people who owned
17 things.
18 Q.   Like the hedge fund people who go
19 there at Christmas time?
20 A.   Maybe, yeah.
21 Q.   And then also Charlie Company also
22 represents family, and that's also a tribe
23 according to this?
24 A.   Yes.
25 Q.   Now, in the paintings are there any

220

Prince

1
2   which appears to be an e-mail from Betsy Biscone
3   at Prince Studio to James Frey, do you see that?
4   At the top of the second page?
5   A.   Yes.
6   Q.   She says, Lovely speaking with you
7   just now, and she is attaching the pitch,
8   capital T, capital P, correct?
9   A.   Yes.
10 Q.   And then she says, And a few images
11 from last December's Eden Rock show. So those
12 are images of what you called before guns and
13 ammo, those paintings, from the Eden Rock show?
14 A.   Yes.
15 Q.   And then -- that was September 9th,
16 2008. And then on September 11th, 2008, the
17 same person Betsy writes to Melissa -- do you
18 know Melissa at Gagosian Gallery?
19 A.   Yes.
20 Q.   She says towards the bottom of that
21 e-mail, Lastly, we love James' draft, I just
22 sent Richard off to the city and ask that he
23 touch base with him today. Can you believe he
24 wrote all that in just one night?
25   Were you aware that he had taken

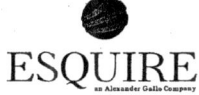

ESQUIRE
an Alexander Gallo Company

Toll Free: 800.944.9454
Facsimile: 212.557.5972

Suite 4715
One Penn Plaza
New York, NY 10119
www.esquiresolutions.com

Richard Prince   October 6, 2009

	221
1	Prince
2	your pitch and changed it quickly like that in
3	September?
4	MS. BART: Objection, form.
5	A. No.
6	Q. You can answer.
7	A. No, I wasn't aware of it.
8	Q. Well, you gave him the pitch, right?
9	I mean we agreed to that, right?
10	A. I believe I verbally gave him the
11	pitch, yes.
12	Q. And it looks like Betsy actually
13	emailed it to him?
14	A. If she did -- if she says she did,
15	I believe her.
16	Q. But then she said -- she also said
17	he did a draft. Okay, my question is did you
18	ever see that draft?
19	A. No.
20	Q. To this day?
21	A. A draft by James Frey?
22	Q. Yes.
23	A. No.
24	Q. You know he wrote an essay that's in
25	the Canal Zone book?

	223
1	Prince
2	Q. Okay.
3	A. -- bad for him.
4	Q. He was getting paid for this I
5	assume, right?
6	A. I don't know if he -- I doubt he got
7	paid --
8	Q. Not by you?
9	A. -- but I don't know.
10	Q. If he got paid it wasn't by you?
11	A. No, it wasn't by me.
12	MR. BROOKS: Let's mark as
13	Plaintiff's Exhibit 25 pages PR92 to 95.
14	(Plaintiff's Exhibit 25, PR92 to 95,
15	was marked for identification, as of this
16	date.)
17	Q. This is Exhibit 25. It's a --
18	I believe it's a draft of what later was
19	incorporated into the Canal Zone book by
20	James Frey.
21	Just take a look at it, and you may
22	have seen it, you may not have seen it, I just
23	want to know if you think you've seen this
24	before as opposed to the essay that's actually
25	in the book?

	222
1	Prince
2	A. Yes.
3	Q. Have you ever read it?
4	A. I've read it.
5	Q. When was the first time you read it?
6	A. I think just before he might have
7	submitted it. I don't know exactly the
8	sequence.
9	Q. When you say submitted it, you mean
10	submitted it for inclusion in the Canal Zone
11	book?
12	A. I think so.
13	Q. And when you read it before it was
14	submitted what was your reaction, if any?
15	A. To be honest with you, I was a
16	little disturbed by it.
17	Q. Because?
18	A. I thought it was misogynistic.
19	Q. Did you try to get him to change it
20	or get somebody to have him change it?
21	A. No.
22	Q. Was that because there wasn't enough
23	time or was there some other reason?
24	A. He had just lost a child, and I
25	felt --

	224
1	Prince
2	A. Yes. Are you -- yes.
3	Q. The question is have you seen this
4	before?
5	A. Yes. Yes.
6	Q. And when was that?
7	A. Early September of 2008.
8	Q. Besides being misogynistic did you
9	find this also to be racist?
10	MS. BART: Objection, form.
11	A. No.
12	Q. Did you find it to -- well, let me
13	ask you, if you look at the second page at the
14	top it says, You go to sleep on sheets that cost
15	more than most people on the island make in a
16	year, who cares fuck 'em, fuck them, let them
17	sleep in dirt. As long as the food is warm and
18	the drinks are cold and everything stays
19	perfect, you go to sleep.
20	Did you have a reaction to that
21	paragraph that I just read?
22	A. I felt he was probably closer to the
23	mark with that kind of paragraph in terms of
24	creating a very violent and trying to describe a
25	difficult situation that people found themselves

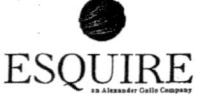

ESQUIRE
an Alexander Gallo Company

Toll Free: 800.944.9454
Facsimile: 212.557.5972

Suite 4715
One Penn Plaza
New York, NY 10119
www.esquiresolutions.com

	225			227	
1	Prince		1	Prince	
2	in trying to survive.		2	Q. But you before -- you said before, I	
3	Q. Now, this part where he goes to		3	mean I didn't ask you this, you said you found	
4	sleep, no one knows yet about the nuclear		4	some of it misogynistic, is that an example?	
5	exchange, right, this is before a difficult		5	MS. BART: Objection, form.	
6	situation arises, correct?		6	A. My interpretation of that, I could	
7	A. In his time line I believe, yes, it		7	say that that's misogynistic and I probably had	
8	seems like that was before people found out.		8	a little bit of a problem with it. But we were	
9	Q. Right. Because then he goes to		9	trying to make kind of realistic -- I wanted to	
10	sleep and then he's shaken awake and then he		10	make -- my idea for the movie was to make	
11	finds out, right?		11	something that was, again, like the Road	
12	Okay, so in that context you still		12	Warrior.	
13	have the same reaction to that paragraph I just		13	Q. Right.	
14	read about the sheets costing more than what		14	A. Like 28 Days Later.	
15	people on the island make in the year?		15	Q. Is that a movie?	
16	MR. HAYES: In the context of the		16	A. Yes.	
17	time line of it coming before?		17	Q. Oh. I never heard of it.	
18	MR. BROOKS: Well, and his reaction		18	A. It's a zombie -- very realistic --	
19	to it given that that was the timing of		19	Q. Okay. Let me ask you this.	
20	that paragraph.		20	Were you finished?	
21	MR. HAYES: I'm going to object as		21	A. Yes.	
22	to form.		22	Q. At the beginning it starts out you	
23	MS. BART: Join.		23	are 46 years old; you are married and have two	
24	A. It's an impression I have. I mean		24	children; teenage girls 13 and 15; they are	
25	I'm not really a literary critic. I mean I'm an		25	supple, budding, on the edge of becoming women;	

	226			228	
1	Prince		1	Prince	
2	artist and I kind of go with -- but, yes, I		2	you work in finance; you are a partner in your	
3	still believe that paragraph is probably --		3	company; you have 40-million dollars in the	
4	would hold up. I probably wouldn't edit it out		4	bank, a Fifth Avenue co-op, a house on the pond	
5	if I was his editor, which I'm not.		5	in Sagaponack; you belong to a club in the city	
6	Q. On the third page, under the third		6	and a club at the beach; you have a driver in	
7	set of asterisks, is this what you meant by some		7	the city, a Mercedes and a Range Rover out east;	
8	of the misogynistic material: The hotel is		8	your daughters both have horses; you never fly	
9	becoming encampments; water, food and bullets		9	commercial; you never buy off the rack; you	
10	become currency; women become slaves; some cook,		10	never cook or clean, you have people who do that	
11	some clean, some carry children, some take care		11	for you.	
12	of children, some care for the sick and the		12	Is that -- was that supposed to be,	
13	wounded, some care for prisoners; some of the		13	in your interpretation, a description of	
14	women become objects of pleasure and they are		14	somebody who's likeable, who you want to root	
15	defiled, they are defiled every day, they are		15	for him in this bad movie or --	
16	defiled in every way you can imagine; et cetera;		16	MS. BART: Objection, form.	
17	is that an example of the misogyny that troubled		17	MR. HAYES: Objection, form.	
18	you about the essay?		18	Q. You can answer.	
19	MS. BART: Objection, form.		19	MR. BROOKS: Can you read the	
20	MR. HAYES: Objection to form also.		20	question back, please?	
21	A. I think that's probably a reflection		21	A. Umm --	
22	about how he was feeling at the time that he was		22	Q. I just want to make sure you heard	
23	writing.		23	the question.	
24	Q. He being James Frey?		24	A. I heard the question.	
25	A. Yes.		25	Q. Okay.	

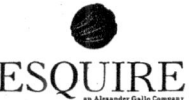

ESQUIRE
an Alexander Gallo Company

Toll Free: 800.944.9454
Facsimile: 212.557.5972

Suite 4715
One Penn Plaza
New York, NY 10119
www.esquiresolutions.com

229

1 Prince
2 A. It's a movie. I love -- I love
3 Gekko in Wall Street. He's not a character
4 that's very -- he's not a nice guy. I think
5 sometimes -- you know, you write -- in the
6 course of a screenplay or a pitch you write
7 about people that aren't very nice.
8 Q. Well, like in Road Warrior you're
9 supposed to root for the Mel Gibson character,
10 right?
11 A. I guess some people would. I don't
12 know.
13 Q. Do you know if in this case you're
14 supposed to root for this 46-year-old guy who
15 never flies commercial or not?
16 MR. HAYES: Objection to form.
17 MS. BART: Objection to form.
18 Q. I mean are you supposed to hope that
19 somebody kills him and takes over his house or
20 whatever, his hotel room?
21 MR. HAYES: Objection to form.
22 MS. BART: Same.
23 MR. HAYES: Objection.
24 A. I mean you're asking me to be a
25 movie critic. I --

230

1 Prince
2 Q. Well, it's your movie, right?
3 MR. HAYES: No.
4 MS. BART: But that's not his
5 script.
6 A. It's not my -- it's his essay based
7 on -- based.
8 Q. Right. On your pitch?
9 A. Really, I mean I think you would
10 have to ask him this question.
11 Q. I'm going to.
12 A. I think this would have to be more
13 fleshed out in order to answer that kind of
14 question, whether or not I would root for a guy
15 like that. I mean I don't know what that has to
16 do with anything --
17 MS. BART: Me neither.
18 A. -- that we're talking about, but --
19 Q. Well, let me ask you this. Does
20 this pitch or the essay that ended up in the
21 Canal Zone book, do either of them have anything
22 to do with the paintings, your paintings in the
23 Canal Zone book and show?
24 MS. BART: Objection to form.
25 MR. HAYES: Objection to form.

231

1 Prince
2 Q. You can answer.
3 A. You mean does his essay?
4 Q. Have any bearing on your paintings
5 in the Canal Zone show and book?
6 A. I think there are parts of his essay
7 that are fairly close to my original pitch,
8 not -- but I wouldn't say all of his essay.
9 Q. But are they also --
10 MS. BART: I had attempted to
11 interpose an objection before the witness
12 started speaking, and I will do that now.
13 Q. I think maybe you misunderstood my
14 question. My question was whether the pitch or
15 the essay had a bearing on your paintings that
16 are in the show and the book?
17 MS. BART: Objection to form.
18 MR. HAYES: Form also.
19 A. Does my pitch have anything to do --
20 is that the question?
21 Q. Let's start with your pitch.
22 A. I'm sorry, I'm getting just a little
23 confused here.
24 Q. There's a Canal Zone book and a
25 show, right, that was at the Gagosian Gallery at

232

1 Prince
2 the end of 2008, right?
3 A. Yes.
4 Q. Those were your paintings, right?
5 A. Yes.
6 Q. Okay, first, your pitch that you did
7 in 2007 and modified in March 2008 --
8 A. Yes.
9 Q. -- does that relate to your
10 paintings?
11 A. Yes.
12 Q. Does his modification of your pitch
13 relate to your paintings?
14 MR. HAYES: Objection to form.
15 MS. BART: Join.
16 A. Does his modification -- again, part
17 of his modification I would say, not all of it.
18 Q. Can you tell me which part?
19 A. Well, bear in mind that's not the
20 final draft.
21 MR. HAYES: So you -- what you want
22 him to do is compare the draft to the
23 painting --
24 MR. BROOKS: Well, I'm going to --
25 (Multiple speakers talking at once.)

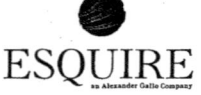

Toll Free: 800.944.9454
Facsimile: 212.557.5972

Suite 4715
One Penn Plaza
New York, NY 10119
www.esquiresolutions.com

233

Prince

1 (Interruption by reporter.)
2 MR. HAYES: You want him to compare
3 the draft or --
4 MR. BROOKS: Well, that's what we're
5 talking about now.
6 MR. HAYES: Let me just finish.
7 Or the essay?
8 MR. BROOKS: Right now the draft.
9 (Discussion off the record.)
10 MR. BROOKS: Let's get this answer
11 and then we'll take a break.
12 A. Yeah, I would say every year at
13 Christmas you and your family go to St. Barth.
14 That has to do with my original pitch.
15 You stay in Eden Rock --
16 (Clarification by reporter.)
17 A. You stay in Eden Rock.
18 Everything is gone. Everything
19 is gone.
20 Every major city in North America,
21 Russia, Europe, Middle East, that has to do with
22 my original pitch.
23 First day you're shocked, second day
24 you're scared, third day you're confused, fourth
25

234

Prince

1 day you're panicked, fall apart on the fifth,
2 sixth day it is a riot, seventh day is doom.
3 He could have written -- he could
4 have just submitted that and that would have
5 been enough for me, personally.
6 But, as I said, I'm not -- I'm not a
7 censor, and I'm not an editor. And I was the
8 one who asked him to write what he wanted to
9 write, you know. I wasn't about to change
10 anything that he had given me.
11 I mean these are his words.
12 Your money is worthless, your job
13 title, that's all --
14 Q. I think he's run out of film.
15 A. I'm sorry.
16 THE VIDEOGRAPHER: 3:17. Off the
17 record. End of tape 3.
18 (Recess taken: 3:17 p.m.)
19 (Proceedings resumed: 3:29 p.m.)
20 THE VIDEOGRAPHER: 3:29. On the
21 record. Beginning of tape 4.
22 BY MR. BROOKS:
23 Q. I think, Mr. Prince, you might have
24 been interrupted at the end of your answer. You
25

235

Prince

1 might not remember what the question was. It
2 was something about whether there were things in
3 the draft essay by Mr. Frey that related to the
4 paintings in the Canal Zone show, and I think
5 you mentioned a few. And if you have any others
6 you want to add, please do.
7 A. I don't really think that anything
8 that James ultimately wrote for the essay for
9 the Canal Zone publication had anything to do
10 with the paintings really.
11 I told him he could write anything
12 he wanted. I gave him carte blanche.
13 And ultimately he wrote, as far as
14 I can see, a variation, a very tiny -- again,
15 there's one paragraph of a pitch that I had made
16 to him and was continually updating at the time.
17 Whether he even got the updates, I really
18 can't -- I don't know.
19 But ultimately what I think he
20 turned in was something that had to do with his
21 own problems, which, as I said, he had just lost
22 a baby.
23 Q. Do you have anything else to add to
24 that answer?
25

236

Prince

1 A. No.
2 MS. BART: Objection, form.
3 Q. Now, you mentioned that you bought a
4 copy of Yes Rasta in a bookstore you think in
5 about 2005 in St. Barth's?
6 A. Yes.
7 Q. When you decided to make the
8 paintings did you then buy additional copies of
9 Yes Rasta?
10 A. I believe we were informed that the
11 book was out of print when I bought the -- I
12 don't actually know -- I believe we got them on
13 eBay. I really don't know where we got the
14 additional books.
15 Q. All right. But you did get
16 additional books?
17 A. Yes.
18 Q. How many?
19 A. I think we bought maybe four
20 additional books.
21 Q. In 2008?
22 A. Yes.
23 MR. BROOKS: Let's mark as
24 Plaintiff's Exhibit 27 a one-page document
25

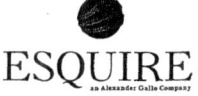

ESQUIRE
an Alexander Gallo Company

Toll Free: 800.944.9454
Facsimile: 212.557.5972

Suite 4715
One Penn Plaza
New York, NY 10119
www.esquiresolutions.com

237

```
1         Prince
2    Bates stamped PR38.
3         (Plaintiff's Exhibit 27, PR38, was
4    marked for identification, as of this
5    date.)
6         (Discussion off the record.)
7         MR. BROOKS: It's been pointed out
8    to me -- and, for the record, I skipped
9    Exhibit 26 as well.
10        MR. HAYES: So this is 27?
11        MR. BROOKS: This is 27. There will
12   not be an Exhibit Plaintiff's 26.
13   BY MR. BROOKS:
14        Q.  Mr. Prince, you say you bought the
15   three -- well, you said you bought four books.
16   Does this refresh your recollection that you
17   actually bought three additional books?
18        A.  As I said, I wasn't sure -- three or
19   four, I guess it says three here.
20        Q.  Right. And it also says you didn't
21   buy them from eBay, you bought them from a
22   company called Powerhouse Books. Do you see
23   that?
24        A.  Yes.
25        Q.  How did you know to order the books
```

238

```
1         Prince
2    from Powerhouse Books?
3         A.  I didn't. I think Betsy was the one
4    who took care of that.
5         Q.  Okay.
6         (Discussion off the record.)
7         MR. BROOKS: Okay. I have four
8    copies of this book, and I'm going to have
9    one of the copies deemed marked as
10   Exhibit 42.
11        MR. HAYES: Exhibit 42?
12        MR. BROOKS: I'm sorry, 41.
13   No, not that. 41.
14        And I'm going to distribute copies
15   of the book so counsel can follow along
16   with me, but I'm not proposing to give you
17   these books because these are the only
18   four we have.
19        However, at some point if you
20   desire, if you don't have the book already
21   yourselves, we'll make a copy of this. I
22   can tell you it's almost impossible to
23   make a good copy of this. So that's why
24   we're doing it this way.
25        MR. HAYES: Okay.
```

239

```
1         Prince
2         MR. BROOKS: But I will give you the
3    books for use during the deposition.
4    Actually, I only have two, you're going to
5    have to share.
6         MS. BART: I'm not sharing with him.
7         MR. HAYES: That's what a lot of
8    people say.
9         (Plaintiff's Exhibit 41, Yes Rasta
10   book, was marked for identification, as of
11   this date.)
12        Q.  So we've handed you what's been
13   marked as Plaintiff's 41. And is this the book
14   that you bought in about 2005?
15        A.  Yes.
16        Q.  And then you bought three more
17   copies in 2008 apparently?
18        A.  Apparently I did, yes.
19        Q.  From Powerhouse Books?
20        A.  Yes.
21        Q.  Can you turn to the last page of the
22   book?
23        MR. HAYES: The last page of
24   printing or the last page --
25        MR. BROOKS: The last page.
```

240

```
1         Prince
2         MR. HAYES: Okay.
3         MR. BROOKS: There's a word for that
4    but I am blanking on it. Colophon page or
5    something like that.
6    BY MR. BROOKS:
7         Q.  It says Yes Rasta, copyright 2000,
8    Powerhouse Cultural Entertainment Inc.;
9    photographs copyright 2000, Patrick Cariou;
10   essay copyright 2000, Perry Henzell.
11        And further down -- and then it says
12   all rights reserved, no part of this book may be
13   reproduced in any manner or transmitted by any
14   means whatsoever, electronic or mechanical
15   including photocopying, recording, and Internet
16   posting display and retrieval without the prior
17   written permission of the publisher.
18        And then it says it's published in
19   the United States by Powerhouse Books.
20        Did you see all that?
21        Do you see that now?
22        A.  I see it now, yes.
23        Q.  And did you notice that when you
24   bought the book in 2005?
25        A.  No, I didn't.
```

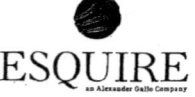

ESQUIRE
an Alexander Gallo Company

Toll Free: 800.944.9454
Facsimile: 212.557.5972

Suite 4715
One Penn Plaza
New York, NY 10119
www.esquiresolutions.com

241

Prince

1
2   Q.   Did you look to see who the
3   publisher was so you could order more books?
4   A.   I think probably by 2008 we --
5   that's probably how we got ahold of the
6   additional books.
7   Q.   Right.
8   MO   MS. BART: Objection. Move to
9   strike answer as speculative.
10   Q.   Did you personally ever notice that
11 there was a copyright notice in the Yes Rasta
12 book?
13   A.   No.
14   Q.   Do you know what I mean by copyright
15 notice?
16   MR. HAYES: Objection as to form.
17   A.   Do you mean the little C with the
18 circle on it?
19   Q.   Yes.
20   A.   Yes.
21   Q.   Now, in the -- withdrawn.
22   In your book do you know who the
23 copyright owner is of the essay?
24   A.   No, I don't.
25   MR. BROOKS: Let's mark as

242

Prince

1
2   Plaintiff's Exhibit 28 an interview in
3   Interview Magazine Bates stamped C65
4   through C77.
5   (Plaintiff's Exhibit 28, interview
6   in Interview Magazine, was marked for
7   identification, as of this date.)
8   Q.   Mr. Prince, do you recall being
9   interviewed in Interview Magazine by Glenn
10 O'Brien?
11   A.   Yes. Yes.
12   Q.   And that was when, do you remember?
13   A.   I believe it was early September,
14 the actual interview.
15   Q.   And part of the interview is about
16 the upcoming Canal Zone show?
17   A.   Yes.
18   Q.   Was that the reason the interview
19 was set up or one of the reasons?
20   A.   No.
21   Q.   Okay. But before the interview --
22 let me back up. Glenn O'Brien in the beginning
23 of the interview says that in the spirit of full
24 disclosure he is good friends with you, is that
25 true?

243

Prince

1
2   A.   Yes.
3   Q.   You've known him a long time, right?
4   A.   Yes.
5   Q.   You did some illustrations for a
6   book of poems that Glenn O'Brien wrote a long
7   time ago?
8   A.   Yes.
9   Q.   Lozenge eyes?
10   A.   Yes.
11   Q.   Is that a technique that you
12 borrowed from John Baldessari?
13   A.   No.
14   Q.   Did you borrow it from someone?
15   A.   No.
16   Q.   It's your own technique?
17   A.   What do you mean by technique?
18   Q.   Putting lozenge eyes on --
19   A.   It's my own. I came up with the
20 idea, yes.
21   Q.   And you did it for Glenn O'Brien's
22 book?
23   A.   Yes.
24   Q.   To illustrate his poetry?
25   A.   To illustrate his poetry, yes.

244

Prince

1
2   Q.   Now, before he interviewed you isn't
3   it true that he asked you if you could get him
4   images of the paintings that were going to be
5   displayed at the Canal Zone exhibition?
6   A.   He asked me that?
7   Q.   Yes.
8   A.   I don't recall.
9   Q.   Do you see on the very first page of
10 this interview beneath -- there's a photograph,
11 is that a photograph of you?
12   A.   Yes.
13   Q.   There are it looks like five images?
14   A.   Mm-hmm, yes.
15   Q.   And those, all five of those are
16 paintings of yours that were on display at the
17 Canal Zone exhibition at the Gagosian Gallery in
18 November-December 2008?
19   A.   Yes.
20   Q.   And do you know how he got them?
21   A.   No, I don't.
22   Q.   Or how Interview Magazine got them?
23   A.   No, I don't.
24   Q.   Can you tell me by looking at those,
25 at the first page of Exhibit 28, the name of the

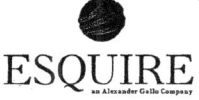

ESQUIRE
an Alexander Gallo Company

Toll Free: 800.944.9454
Facsimile: 212.557.5972

Suite 4715
One Penn Plaza
New York, NY 10119
www.esquiresolutions.com

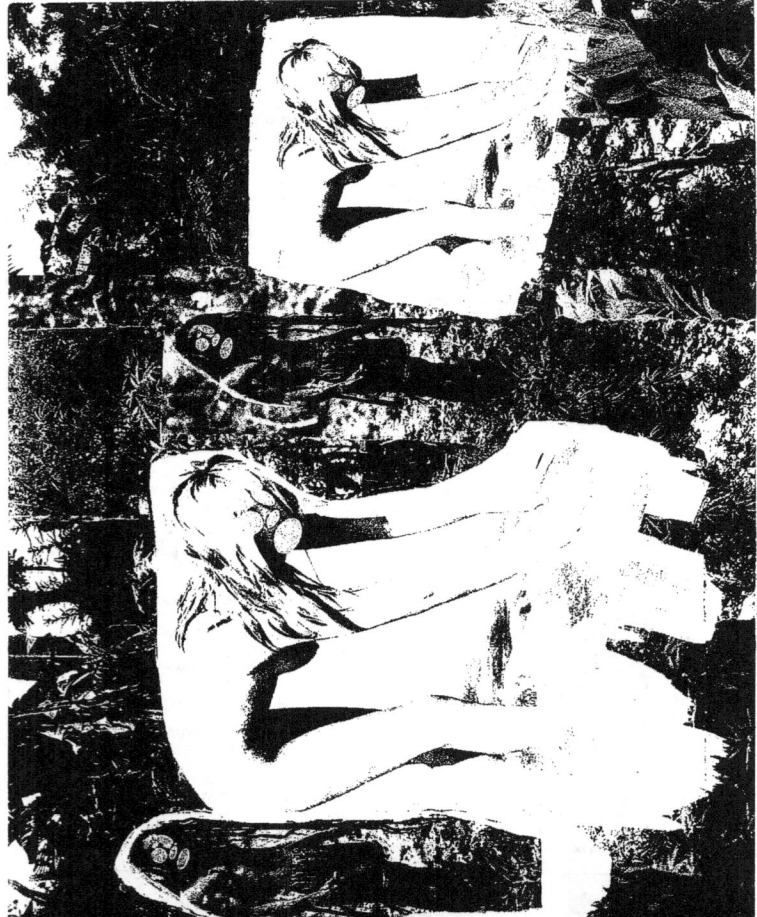

Richard Prince   October 6, 2009

245

Prince

1 first painting, the one beneath your image to
2 the left?
3
4   A.   That's a detail of the painting. Is
5 that -- it could be James Brown's Disco Ball
6 maybe.
7   Q.   Did you -- who came up with the
8 titles for these paintings?
9   A.   I did.
10   Q.   All by yourself?
11   A.   Yes.
12   Q.   The one to the right is a detail
13 from what painting, can you tell us?
14   A.   I can't recall that title.
15   Q.   And then the one -- I'm going
16 counter-clockwise. The one beneath that,
17 there's a woman, I don't know, it looks like
18 she's bending over, maybe in water. The one on
19 the lower right, that's a detail from which
20 painting?
21   A.   I think that's called On the Beach,
22 or On the Beach On the Beach, I'm not quite --
23 but it's something about on the beach.
24   Q.   Or it could be The Ocean Club,
25 right?

246

Prince

1
2   MS. BART: Objection, form.
3   MR. HAYES: Objection to form.
4   A.   Oh, The Ocean Club, yes, that's
5 true.
6   Q.   It is The Ocean Club, right.
7   And The Ocean Club is a hotel in
8 Paradise Island?
9   A.   Ocean Club was a club on Chambers
10 Street that was in operation approximately 1979,
11 1980.
12   Q.   Chambers Street in Manhattan?
13   A.   Yes.
14   Q.   And is that what you named it after?
15   A.   Yes.
16   Q.   The one to the left of that in the
17 middle lower -- the middle, the lower row, what
18 is that an image from?
19   A.   That's a detail of a painting I
20 believe is called Cheese and Crackers.
21   Q.   And finally the one to the left of
22 it?
23   A.   Detail of an image called Ding Dong
24 the Witch is Dead.
25   Q.   Do you know if any of those

247

Prince

1
2 paintings were sold?
3   A.   I believe -- I believe one of these
4 five paintings were sold. In fact, I'm pretty
5 sure.
6   Q.   Which one?
7   A.   If it's James Brown -- the one in
8 the upper left-hand corner.
9   Q.   And was that sold for 2.7-million
10 dollars?
11   A.   No. No. Actually, it wasn't sold,
12 it was traded -- I traded that for another
13 painting.
14   Q.   And who did you trade it to?
15   A.   Larry Gagosian.
16   Q.   For a Larry Rivers painting?
17   A.   Yes. Part -- I mean it was part of
18 a Larry Rivers trade, this painting.
19   Q.   The Larry Rivers painting is Dying
20 and Dead Veteran?
21   A.   Yes.
22   Q.   Do you know the value of it?
23   A.   I think -- I think he was talking
24 about around 2-million dollars at the time.
25   Q.   But Larry Rivers was dead then,

248

Prince

1
2 right?
3   A.   Yes.
4   Q.   So who was talking, Mr. Gagosian?
5   A.   I'm sorry?
6   Q.   Who was talking about 2-million
7 dollars? You said he.
8   A.   Oh, Larry. Larry Gagosian was
9 talking about it.
10   Q.   Are these titles that you came up
11 with an important component of these paintings?
12   MS. BART: Objection, form.
13   MR. HAYES: Objection as to form
14 too.
15   A.   I would like to think so, yes.
16 Again, it's speculative.
17   Q.   But you have trouble remembering the
18 names of the paintings?
19   A.   I think I just named them pretty
20 close. The Ocean Club I was off a little bit.
21 It did have something to do with a beach.
22   As I said, I would like to think
23 that they -- they're important. But they're
24 not -- I think they help in the transformation
25 of and they're part of the process in

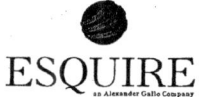

Toll Free: 800.944.9454
Facsimile: 212.557.5972

Suite 4715
One Penn Plaza
New York, NY 10119
www.esquiresolutions.com

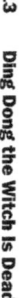

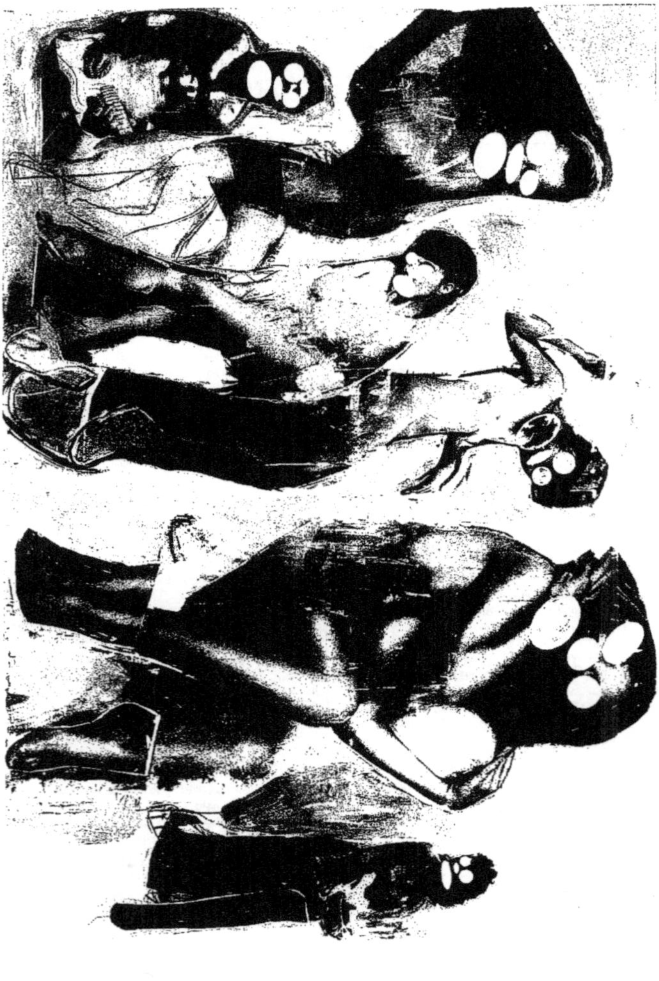

13   Ding Dong the Witch Is Dead

249

	Prince
1	Prince
2	recontextualizing the image.
3	Yeah, I would have to say giving
4	them -- I think titles for me are very
5	important. I guess I'm answering your question
6	because I don't know if they're important to
7	other people. But to me they are.
8	Q. And how do the titles inform us
9	about the subject and meaning of the paintings
10	in the Canal Zone exhibition?
11	A. I think they create a certain kind
12	of isolation and removal and set up a kind of
13	another type of story. It's -- it creates
14	another type of subtext that you can read into
15	the painting.
16	Like James Brown's Disco Ball, I
17	think it's poetry. It's a great way to describe
18	the painting. It removes the image from its
19	original intent totally.
20	I don't believe any of the images in
21	this particular book Yes Rasta had anything to
22	do with James Brown. However, my painting now
23	does. I think that's one way in which a title
24	helps makes my work different and it makes it
25	into another -- gives it another reading.

251

	Prince
1	Prince
2	A. In the painting. I believe -- I
3	believe those images, the bodies are kind of
4	moving to the type of music that maybe James
5	Brown created.
6	Q. Okay. And what about Cheese and
7	Crackers, what does that have to do with that
8	painting?
9	A. Cheese and Crackers is probably --
10	has to do with the middle image, which has
11	remnants of a De Kooning head. That's a --
12	that's what I would call a painting that's a
13	bridge painting between De Kooning paintings and
14	the Canal Zone paintings.
15	Q. Are you talking about the woman with
16	her legs spread?
17	A. Yes, the woman with her legs open
18	and she's waving. And I just felt like Cheese
19	and Crackers was a way to describe her
20	expression.
21	Q. How so?
22	A. As I said, it's a very light kind of
23	fun, hi-how-are-you type of expression. You
24	know, they're the sort of -- they represent a
25	kind of a band. Every painting basically

250

	Prince
1	Prince
2	Q. Okay. So what does this painting in
3	the left-hand corner of Exhibit 28 of the first
4	page, what does it have to do with James Brown?
5	A. I believe at the time I had just had
6	bought James Brown's disco ball at auction that
7	day that I named the painting.
8	Q. Okay.
9	A. And I believe I had just finished
10	the painting. And I think sometimes titles --
11	it's kind of like when worlds collide, you get
12	very lucky sometimes in terms of the
13	spontaneity, the happening. It's like a
14	performance.
15	Q. Well, is James Brown's disco ball
16	the subject of that particular painting?
17	A. I think so.
18	Q. Is there a disco ball in that
19	painting?
20	A. I think there are probably -- it's
21	only a detail, but I think there's probably --
22	to my way I would interpret it, there's probably
23	five disco balls in that painting.
24	Q. In this segment or in the other part
25	of this --

252

	Prince
1	Prince
2	represents a kind of a band. And --
3	Q. Do you mean a musical band?
4	A. Yeah, a musical band. I mean that's
5	one of the things that I was thinking of when I
6	was making these paintings.
7	Q. So are we still with the
8	post-apocalyptic theme but with bands?
9	A. We're with all those kinds of
10	things. And I think that my naming them Cheese
11	and Crackers, maybe that was the name of the
12	band rather than the name of the painting. And
13	I think that a lot of bands come up with crazy
14	names.
15	Q. Right.
16	A. I mean these are some of the things
17	that I'm thinking about.
18	Q. What about The Ocean Club, what's
19	the significance of that name, that title?
20	A. I think The Ocean Club was --
21	primarily had to do with the female figure, the
22	way that female figure got repeated in the
23	image. She was at the beach.
24	Q. Was that one of the lesbians?
25	A. No, that's not the lesbian painting.

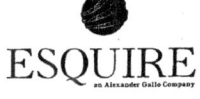

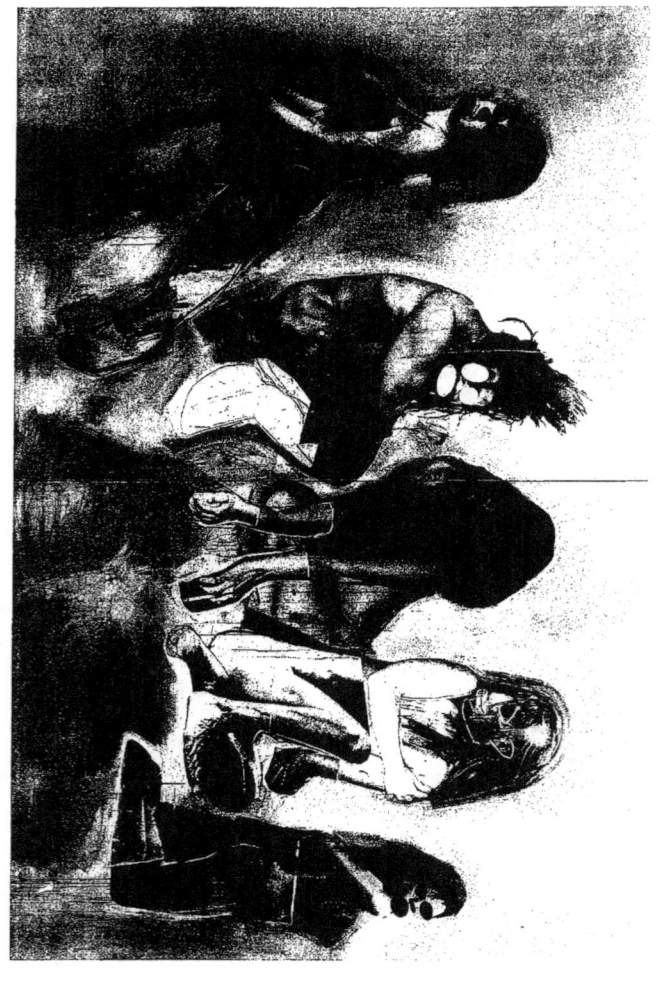

11   James Brown Disco Ball

253

```
1              Prince
2        Q.  So the only lesbians are in that one
3    painting?
4        A.  No.  One shows up in another
5    painting.  But primarily the -- the four -- the
6    lesbian painting -- that was in the show.
7        Q.  Yes.
8        A.  But I don't know if it's in the
9    catalog.  I would have to check.  I know that
10   another lesbian showed up in another painting.
11   I know that's not in the catalog.
12       Q.  How about -- I notice there's one
13   that was part of the show, even though I don't
14   think it's in the book, called Pumpsie Green?
15       A.  Pumpsie Green.
16       Q.  So he was the first African-American
17   player on the Boston Red Sox?
18       A.  My hero.
19       Q.  Which was the last team to
20   integrate?
21       A.  My hero.
22       Q.  Correct?
23       A.  Yes.  Second baseman I believe.
24       Q.  And what does that have to do with
25   this?
```

254

```
1              Prince
2        A.  I just love the name.
3        Q.  So it has nothing to do with it?
4        A.  I think it was just a way of giving
5    a nod to my boyhood hero.
6        Q.  Not to the fact that the Red Sox
7    were the last team to integrate?
8        A.  I didn't know that.
9        Q.  Then it wasn't.
10           MR. BROOKS:  You know what, I'm
11   going to go back, and let's as mark as
12   Exhibit 27, that was -- there was no
13   Exhibit 27 --
14           MS. BART:  Yeah, we have one.
15           (Clarification by reporter.)
16           MR. BROOKS:  Okay.  Let's go back
17   and mark as 26 -- it's a two-page document
18   Bates stamped GG --
19           THE WITNESS:  Do we have this
20   document?
21           MR. HAYES:  No, he's got to give it
22   to us.
23           (Discussion off the record.)
24           (Plaintiff's Exhibit 26, e-mail, was
25   marked for identification, as of this
```

255

```
1              Prince
2    date.)
3        Q.  This is now 26.
4            Do you have an assistant named Eric
5    Brown?
6        A.  Yes, I do.
7        Q.  Do you see he was asked about two of
8    these paintings, numbers 510 and 511, and he's
9    asking -- somebody was asking at Gagosian for a
10   list so he could match the numbers with the
11   titles.  And he wrote at the bottom of the first
12   page Anita attaches a list of the works she
13   received from the Long Island studio, can you
14   please double check that RPS510 and 511 match
15   what you have received.  Please check the title
16   on back painting.  Richard couldn't remember
17   which was which.
18           Do you recall that?
19           This relates to the painting called
20   Île-de-France?
21           MR. HAYES:  Objection as to form.
22       A.  No, I don't remember this.
23           I don't -- is Île-de-France on here?
24       Q.  That's 511.
25           No, it's not on --
```

256

```
1              Prince
2        A.  I know the painting Île-de-France,
3    I think.
4            (Discussion off the record.)
5    BY MR. BROOKS:
6        Q.  Getting back to this interview with
7    Glenn O'Brien.  So I'm showing you part of
8    Exhibit 42.  And it's page, Bates stamped at the
9    bottom, C00140.  Is that Île-de-France?
10       A.  Yes, it is.
11       Q.  And it was originally untitled?
12       A.  I don't know what originally it was.
13       Q.  And they asked you for the name and
14   you couldn't remember and told them to look on
15   the back of the painting, is that right?
16       A.  I don't remember that.  I do know
17   that if there was any -- if there was a question
18   about -- if there was a question about it, I
19   probably wasn't present and I probably said to
20   whoever was doing the shipping, look on the
21   back.
22       Q.  And you didn't say you couldn't
23   remember the title?
24       A.  I don't remember the exchange at
25   all.
```

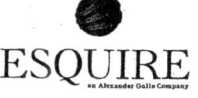

ESQUIRE
an Alexander Gallo Company

Toll Free: 800.944.9454
Facsimile: 212.557.5972

Suite 4715
One Penn Plaza
New York, NY 10119
www.esquiresolutions.com

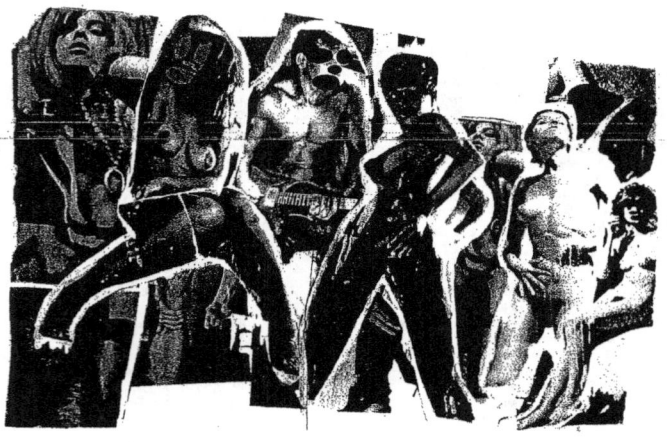

Richard Prince
Pumpsie Green, 2008
Ink jet, acrylic and collage on canvas
77 x 100 1/2 inches
195.6 x 255.3 cm
(Inv# RPS587)

257

	Prince
2	Q. Could you look back at -- back on
3	Exhibit 28, look on page, the page Bates
4	stamped --
5	MR. HAYES: 28 or 26?
6	MR. BROOKS: 28. The interview.
7	MR. HAYES: Okay.
8	MR. BROOKS: Interview Magazine.
9	BY MR. BROOKS:
10	Q. On page C0073 apparently Leonardo
11	DiCaprio walked in?
12	A. I'm sorry, where are we?
13	MR. HAYES: 73, right here.
14	Q. C73.
15	A. Okay.
16	Q. Do you see that?
17	A. Yes.
18	Q. Do you recall him walking in during
19	this interview?
20	A. Yes.
21	Q. And he said Tobey Maguire can't make
22	it until later?
23	A. Yes.
24	Q. Were they considering, to your
25	knowledge, buying one or more of your paintings

258

	Prince
2	from the Canal Zone show?
3	A. Yes.
4	Q. Jointly?
5	A. Yes.
6	Q. And did you hold some of the
7	paintings for them?
8	A. I didn't hold them, no.
9	Q. Did Gagosian?
10	A. I don't know if he held them.
11	Q. Did you ask them to?
12	A. No, I don't believe I did.
13	Q. Do you know if either of them bought
14	any of the paintings?
15	A. They did not buy any of the Canal
16	Zone paintings.
17	Q. Now turn to page C75, please, on
18	Exhibit 28.
19	A. 75?
20	Q. Yes. Just before we leave this
21	issue with Leonardo DiCaprio and Tobey Maguire,
22	do you recall that they wanted you to hold Color
23	Me Mine and Mr. Jones?
24	A. I believe they were interested in
25	those two paintings, yes.

259

	Prince
2	Q. All right. Now, we're on page 75,
3	and Mr. O'Brien is asking you, So how did you
4	get into these Rasta pieces that are you doing
5	now? I know a little bit about it.
6	Do you see where I'm reading from?
7	MR. HAYES: Right here.
8	A. Yes, I see.
9	Q. And then your answer was, That was
10	just from hanging out in St. Barth's for the
11	last 12 years?
12	A. I see that -- I see that that was my
13	response, yes.
14	Q. And had you been going to
15	St. Barth's for vacations for about 12 years
16	prior to 2008?
17	A. Seems like -- that seems the right
18	amount of years, yes.
19	Q. And then he said, And we all know
20	how many Rastas there are in St. Barth's. He
21	was being facetious you thought?
22	MS. BART: Objection to form.
23	MR. HAYES: Objection, form.
24	A. I don't know -- I would imagine he
25	was -- he's a bit of a jokester.

260

	Prince
2	Q. Right.
3	A. But I really can't speak to what he
4	was implying.
5	Q. Right. But you said there aren't
6	that many Rastas in St. Barth's, right?
7	A. There aren't that many.
8	Q. In fact, there aren't any, right?
9	MS. BART: Objection to form.
10	MR. HAYES: Objection.
11	A. I would disagree with that.
12	Q. Oh, I thought you said that before.
13	A. I've --
14	Q. There are some?
15	A. There are people -- let me put it
16	this way then. I don't know that much about
17	Rastafarians. However, I do believe I have seen
18	people who look like Rastafarians in St. Barth.
19	That's the best I can answer that question.
20	Q. Do you think Manny Ramirez looks
21	like a Rastafarian?
22	A. I don't know who Manny Ramirez is.
23	MS. BART: Objection to form.
24	I don't think -- that's just really not
25	relevant.

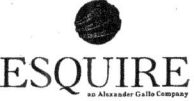

ESQUIRE
an Alexander Gallo Company

Toll Free: 800.944.9454
Facsimile: 212.557.5972

Suite 4715
One Penn Plaza
New York, NY 10119
www.esquiresolutions.com

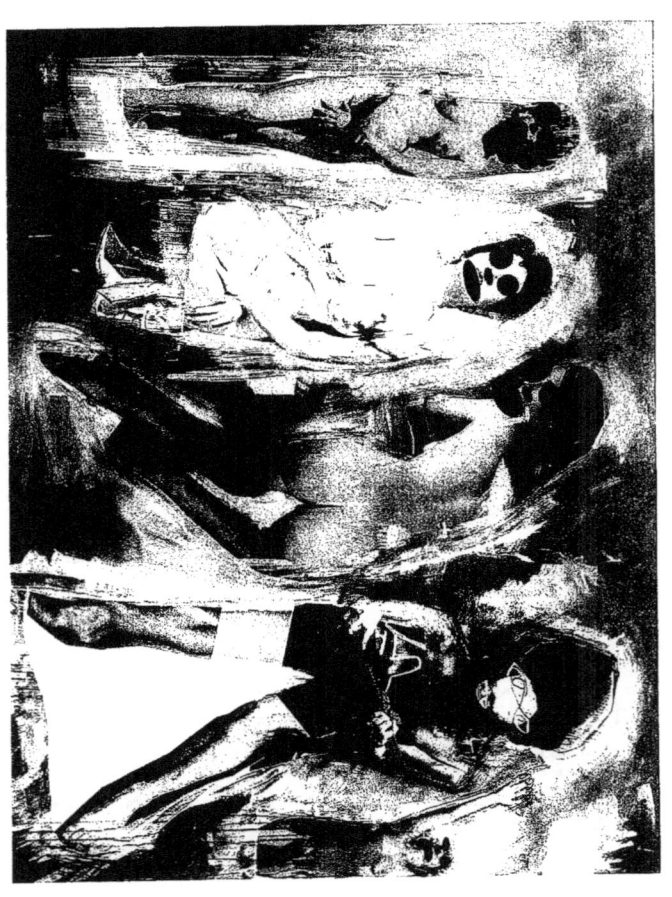

10   Color Me Mine

261

Prince

1
2   Q.   I thought you were a Red Sox fan?
3   A.   I never said I was a Red Sox fan.
4   Q.   You don't know who Manny Ramirez is?
5   A.   No, I don't.
6   MS. BART: What does this have to do
7   with this case?
8   Q.   All right. Now, you say you picked
9   up a book on them?
10 A.   In -- literally, yes, I picked up a
11 book.
12 Q.   Okay. And that's the Yes Rasta
13 book --
14 A.   Yes.
15 Q.   -- that we've been talking about,
16 that's in front of you? Okay.
17   Now, down a few lines you said, But
18 I love the look, comma, and I love the dreads.
19 What did you mean by that?
20 A.   What do you mean what do I mean by
21 that? I just said it. I love the look and I
22 love the dreads.
23 Q.   What did you love about the look?
24 A.   I love the way they looked.
25 Q.   How so?

262

Prince

1
2   A.   I don't know how to answer that
3   question, how so. I love the way they looked.
4   I mean that's usually I get -- that's how I
5   respond to images.
6   I think maybe I liked the way that
7   they were so different.
8   Q.   Than what?
9   A.   Than myself. I don't have dreads.
10 I wish I could. I mean I think that was some of
11 the thinking or some of the -- perhaps it goes
12 back to the girlfriends. The reason why I took
13 the girlfriends is I wanted to be a girlfriend.
14 I think some of the attraction that
15 I had to some of these people who looked like
16 Rastas in St. Barth, hanging out at the bars, I
17 said to myself, gee, I wish I could look like
18 that some day.
19   So if I can't look like that maybe
20 I should paint them. Maybe that's a way to
21 substitute that desire. I mean that's the only
22 way I can answer that love question.
23 Q.   All right. But had you ever seen --
24 I think you testified about this before lunch,
25 had you ever seen pictures of Rastas before?

263

Prince

1
2   A.   Had I ever seen pictures?
3   Q.   Yes.
4   MR. HAYES: Objection to the form.
5   A.   When?
6   Q.   Ever?
7   A.   I'm sure I had.
8   Q.   And didn't you say had you a book
9   about Bob Marley with Rastas in it?
10 A.   I think I went out and tried to buy
11 a book at the same time.
12 Q.   Right. So what was it about these
13 pictures that made you want to copy them?
14   MS. BART: Objection to form.
15   MR. HAYES: Objection, form.
16 A.   I think, again, it's that notion
17 about when worlds collide. I happened to be
18 listening to Radiodread. Do you know who
19 Radiodread is? It's a band that sampled and
20 replicated Radiohead's album, and did it in a
21 reggae manner. And my son, my stepson was
22 playing it on vacation in St. Barth.
23 Q.   When you found this book?
24 A.   And I was very much into that album.
25 I played it over and over. And then the next

264

Prince

1
2   day I walk into a bookstore and what do I pick
3   up, a book that had pictures of Rastas in them.
4   I said to myself, hmm, something is in the air.
5   And that's my -- that's how I
6   react -- that's how things happen. It was pure
7   chance.
8   Q.   Okay.
9   A.   And it's a great -- I thought that
10 was a great marriage, the fact that I was
11 listening to Radiodread, which I loved, and I
12 saw what I considered these really kind of
13 interesting documents.
14 Q.   When you say interesting documents,
15 are you talking about the photos in Yes Rasta?
16 A.   Yes.
17 Q.   What was interesting about them?
18 A.   I think I've already said that.
19 I'll say it again. I liked -- I was looking for
20 black-and-white images of figures.
21 Q.   Why?
22 A.   I wanted to put them next to my
23 De Kooning women.
24 Q.   Are there any De Kooning women in
25 the Canal Zone book?

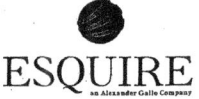

ESQUIRE
an Alexander Gallo Company

Toll Free: 800.944.9454
Facsimile: 212.557.5972

Suite 4715
One Penn Plaza
New York, NY 10119
www.esquiresolutions.com

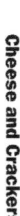

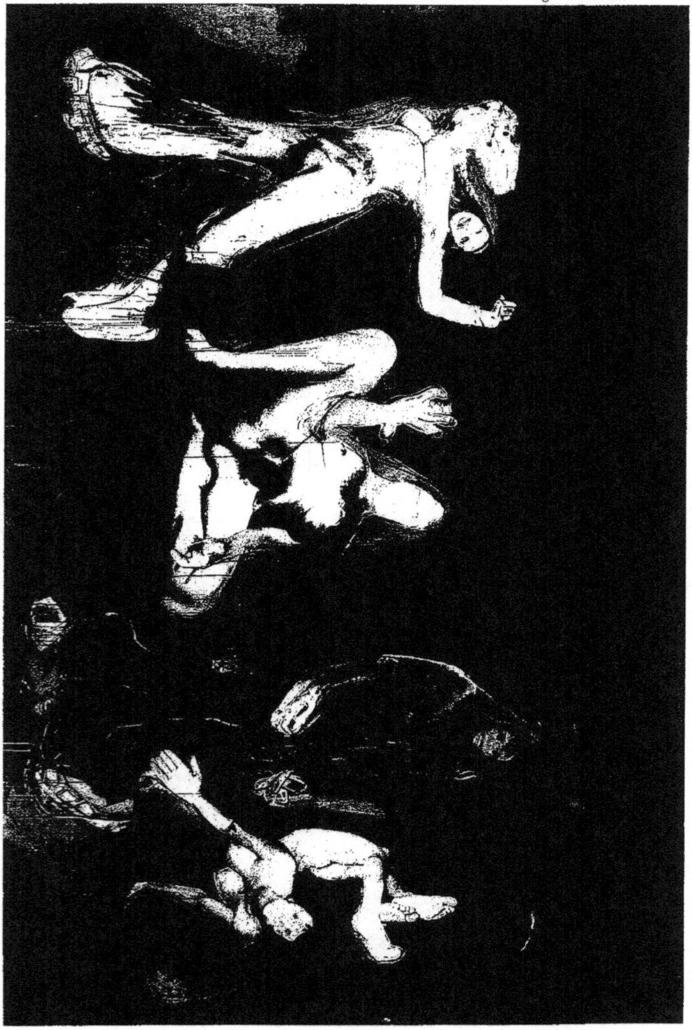

21   Cheese and Crackers

265	267
Prince	Prince
1	1
2 A. Yes, there's one right on the cover.	2 There's no -- there's no plan.
3 I think she's off to the right. And I think we	3 Q. Right. Is there a message?
4 just talked about the one in Interview Magazine.	4 A. There certainly is a message.
5 I think you were talking about Cheese and	5 Q. What is the message?
6 Crackers.	6 A. The message is to make great art
7 Q. Right. Right.	7 that makes people feel good. That's my message.
8 A. That's a De Kooning woman right	8 Now, I know it might not be someone else's, but
9 here.	9 I believe that's also the way I've always
10 Q. Okay.	10 defined art.
11 A. She has a face that was painted by	11 Q. Now, you're talking again about the
12 De Kooning. And that was one of the very --	12 guy who lands in St. Barth's. This is on the
13 that was painted in June of '08. As I said, it	13 next page. And it says so he and his relatives
14 was a bridge painting. I was trying to channel	14 take over a hotel, they take over Eden Rock. Do
15 my inner De Kooning in that painting.	15 you see that?
16 Q. In Cheese and Crackers?	16 A. Yes.
17 A. In Cheese and Crackers.	17 Q. Now, there actually are no pictures
18 Q. Now, getting back to the interview,	18 in the Canal Zone paintings of the guy who got
19 you said that you liked -- we just looked at	19 off the plane and his relatives, is that right
20 this. When you said I love the book, I love the	20 or not right?
21 dreads, so I just started fooling around with	21 MR. HAYES: Objection to the form.
22 this book, drawing it like I did with the	22 A. There are no pictures of Charlie
23 De Kooning paintings.	23 Company and --
24 You've already explained that, you	24 Q. Right.
25 wrote right in the first book, right?	25 A. There might be, there might not be.

266	268
Prince	Prince
1	1
2 A. Yes.	2 I believe there aren't of Mr. Company.
3 Q. And then it says, Then I wrote the	3 Q. He's supposed to be a white guy,
4 proposal, which I pitched to Hollywood, it was	4 right?
5 called Eden Rock. And then it goes through the	5 A. He's a white guy.
6 story about the guy who gets off the plane.	6 No, I believe his daughter -- I
7 A. Yes.	7 think only his daughter shows up in one of the
8 Q. And look at the next page.	8 paintings later.
9 So were you saying that the	9 Q. Then you say the Rastas escaped from
10 Yes Rasta book inspired your idea for the pitch?	10 their cruise ship and they take over their own
11 A. No.	11 hotel, the Manapany, right?
12 Q. No? Okay.	12 A. Yes.
13 A. What was inspiring was, again,	13 Q. And are there any pictures of them
14 another element in this kind of crazy marriage.	14 taking over the Manapany in the Canal Zone book?
15 The day before I went in and found this book I	15 A. No.
16 noticed these cruise -- these monumental cruise	16 Q. And then you said and then there's a
17 ships.	17 lesbian group of girls who escape and take over
18 Q. In St. Barth's?	18 their own hotel, the Guanahani?
19 A. In St. Barth. And I started looking	19 A. Yes.
20 at them and saying there's another thing that	20 Q. And those are those four literary
21 should be in my screenplay. And yes, who should	21 artistic women from the early 20th Century?
22 be on that boat is a reggae band. So I had that	22 A. Yes.
23 in my head.	23 Q. And there's a painting of them?
24 So I think what inspires what, it's	24 A. Yes.
25 all very organic here. It's all very fluid.	25 Q. And then you said -- this is to

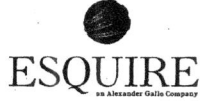

ESQUIRE
an Alexander Gallo Company

Toll Free: 800.944.9454
Facsimile: 212.557.5972

Suite 4715
One Penn Plaza
New York, NY 10119
www.esquiresolutions.com

269

1   Prince
2   Gerald O'Brien in the interview -- so everybody
3   has their own hotel, and that's where the video
4   game rights come into this pitch.
5   Where do the video game rights come
6   into this pitch?
7   A.   Is that -- are you asking me --
8   you're asking me?
9   Q.   These are your words in the
10   interview?
11   A.   Right.
12   Q.   What did you mean?
13   A.   I think I was thinking about the
14   fact that I know nothing about video games
15   and -- but my -- all my stepson's friends play
16   them. And I felt that there might be a
17   possibility to -- I had seen some of the
18   graphics involved in some of these games when
19   they play, and I felt that the different tribes
20   that take over the different hotels and they
21   kind of, you know, it was just a thought. And
22   I think I ran this by Michael Ovitz and he loved
23   the idea.
24   Q.   So you viewed this whole thing as an
25   extremely commercially successful potential

270

1   Prince
2   venture, paintings --
3   A.   The pitch?
4   MR. HAYES: Objection.
5   Q.   Paintings, movies, and video game
6   rights, right?
7   MR. HAYES: Objection as to form.
8   A.   No, I've never thought that what I
9   do or what I produce or what I put out will
10   ever, one, sell.
11   I've made art for 34, 35 years and
12   nothing sold. What I -- my experience in terms
13   of what I make, it seems that a lot of people
14   just couldn't dig it. And to tell you the
15   truth, it was not one -- when I put up the Canal
16   Zone show at Larry Gagosian's there was not one
17   review in any newspaper, in any magazine. And I
18   find that incredibly unsuccessful.
19   Q.   But weren't some of the paintings
20   sold before the show even opened?
21   A.   They were sold, yes.
22   Q.   For millions of dollars?
23   A.   I wouldn't characterize it for
24   millions. For a couple of million dollars,
25   there were two paintings I believe that were

271

1   Prince
2   sold before the Lehman Brothers meltdown, yes,
3   there were two paintings that were sold for
4   approximately 2-million dollars.
5   Q.   Then you say that we got a
6   ghostwriter to do the story. Is that James
7   Frey?
8   A.   No.
9   Q.   Oh, that's the ghostwriter Ovitz got
10   for you?
11   A.   That was -- I was referring to the
12   ghostwriter for Eden Rock.
13   Q.   Not James Frey?
14   A.   No. James Frey is not the
15   ghostwriter.
16   Q.   And it's being published, you say,
17   and eventually hopefully it will be totally
18   fucked by Hollywood, but I don't care because
19   it's all under a pseudonym, my name is not
20   attached to it.
21   What did you mean by that? Why
22   didn't you want your name attached to the
23   screenplay or the movie?
24   A.   They were never going to write what
25   I initially saw as something I would want to

272

1   Prince
2   have my name attached to.
3   I knew that -- I know or I am
4   imagining the mechanisms of Hollywood I know
5   enough to not get involved.
6   Q.   So why did you want to do the
7   screenplay and the video rights?
8   A.   I was very interested in the movie
9   The Player, which is all about a pitch, and I
10   was very interested in the fact that I could
11   maybe write a one-and-a-half-page outline and
12   see if it could turn into something.
13   Q.   Okay. Back to page C76 of this
14   interview. Are you there?
15   A.   Yes.
16   Q.   You say, So anyway, the Rastas and
17   the lesbians started starring in these pictures
18   and were kind of like bands, there are like five
19   people to a picture, and every picture has a
20   title to it.
21   A.   Okay.
22   MR. HAYES: Just wait one second
23   while he catches up to you.
24   A.   Where are we?
25   Q.   It's C76.

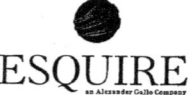

ESQUIRE
an Alexander Gallo Company

Toll Free: 800.944.9454
Facsimile: 212.557.5972

Suite 4715
One Penn Plaza
New York, NY 10119
www.esquiresolutions.com

273

	Prince
1	Prince
2	A. So anyway -- oh, okay, Fulton Ryder
3	is the pseudonym. So anyway? Yes.
4	Q. So anyway, the Rastas and the
5	lesbians started starring in these pictures and
6	were kind of like bands, there were like five
7	people to a picture and every picture has a
8	title to it. It sort of becomes an allegory.
9	It's just something I needed to get out of my
10	system. The pictures are very quickly done,
11	they're not really thought about, and there's a
12	collage element to them that's very primitive.
13	Paste up, cutting with scissors, and squeegeed
14	on with paint. It's something that I can do by
15	myself and I like that aspect of it. I don't
16	need assistants. I don't need anybody.
17	What did you mean by the pictures
18	are not really thought about? Did you mean by
19	you?
20	A. I like to paint a painting and
21	finish it within a day, day and a half tops. I
22	like instant paintings.
23	Q. In the case of these paintings what
24	did you mean that they're not really thought
25	about?

274

	Prince
1	Prince
2	A. That's --
3	MS. BART: Objection, form, and
4	asked and answered.
5	A. I'm trying to answer your question.
6	That's what I mean. I like -- I like when I do
7	things fast. I think they should be done very
8	quickly. I think when they drag on, you know,
9	you can overthink it. I don't like a painting
10	that's overcooked.
11	Q. Okay. I understand your answer, but
12	I was asking about these paintings, not what you
13	generally like.
14	A. No, I'm talking about these specific
15	paintings. They were done day, half a day, some
16	of them took two hours. That's what was so
17	satisfying about the process. You know,
18	Especially Around Midnight, a painting that you
19	had previously said that I didn't remember the
20	title to --
21	Q. No, that was Île-de-France.
22	A. You didn't say that. You pointed to
23	an e-mail from Eric Brown suggesting that Eric
24	thought that I didn't remember the title.
25	Q. Île-de-France.

275

	Prince
1	Prince
2	A. Well, it wasn't Île-de-France.
3	That's not the way I remember the question. It
4	was Round About Midnight.
5	Q. When you read the transcript you'll
6	see.
7	A. Fine. Okay.
8	Q. But let's get back to what you were
9	saying about doing them quickly. What is it
10	that you were saying, that you like to do them
11	quickly because?
12	MS. BART: Objection --
13	A. I don't like to --
14	(Multiple speakers talking at once.)
15	(Interruption by reporter.)
16	MS. BART: Objection to form and
17	asked and answered.
18	MR. HAYES: And I joined in it.
19	MS. BART: He just doesn't like the
20	answer.
21	A. It has to do with technique. I come
22	up with various techniques that are very new, no
23	one's ever done them before. Like the squeegee.
24	No one had ever painted a painting
25	by squeegeeing on a collage onto a piece of

276

	Prince
1	Prince
2	canvas. No one had ever done that before. That
3	was totally new and it was a very quick way to
4	add on an ingredient and make it into an entire
5	recipe.
6	Q. Okay. So let's talk about the
7	ingredients. These guitars that you say -- your
8	contribution to the Rastas was this introduction
9	of the guitar. Do you see where you said that?
10	MS. BART: Objection, form. I mean
11	there are --
12	MR. BROOKS: That's fine.
13	MS. BART: No, I just wanted --
14	MR. BROOKS: There are no speaking
15	objections.
16	MS. BART: I'm going to make my
17	comment for you --
18	MR. BROOKS: Don't make it for him.
19	MS. BART: He's not my client.
20	MR. BROOKS: I know that.
21	MS. BART: I'm making it for you.
22	There are a myriad of pictures in
23	this book, and to ask a blanket question
24	like that --
25	MR. BROOKS: No, I'm asking him

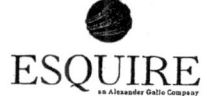

Toll Free: 800.944.9454
Facsimile: 212.557.5972

Suite 4715
One Penn Plaza
New York, NY 10119
www.esquiresolutions.com

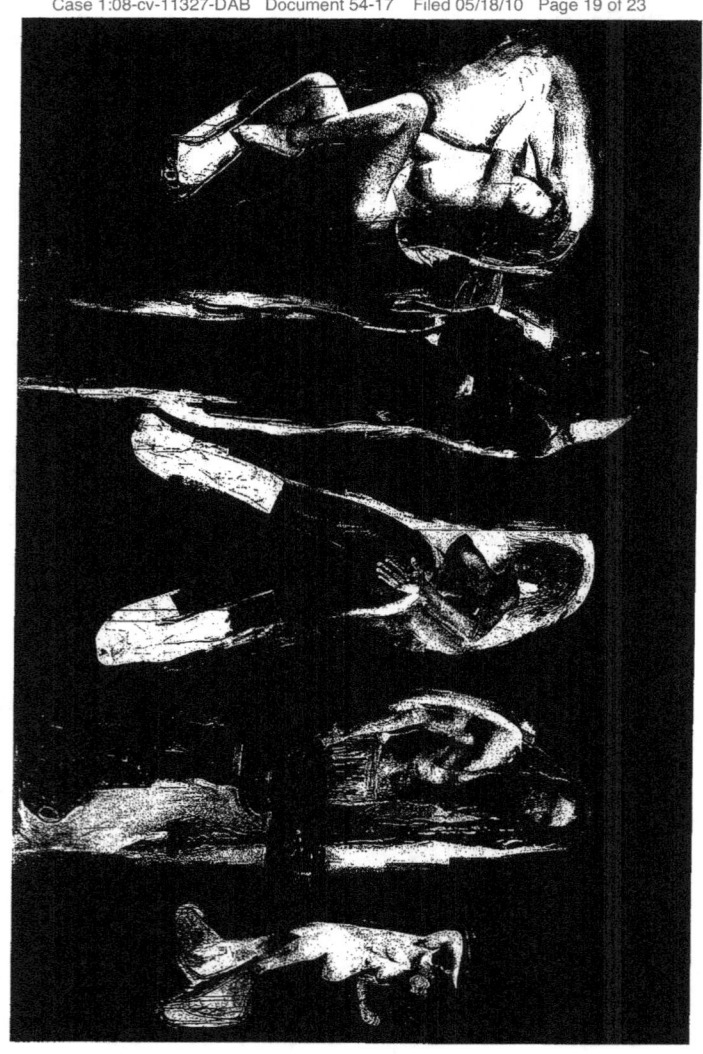

18   Specially Round Midnight

277

	Prince
1	Prince
2	about something he said in an interview.
3	He said and then my contribution to the
4	Rastas was this introduction of the
5	guitar.
6	BY MR. BROOKS:
7	Q. Do you see that?
8	A. Yes.
9	MS. BART: Still objection.
10	Q. Was the guitar one of the
11	ingredients in these paintings?
12	A. Yes.
13	MS. BART: I'm still objecting.
14	MR. BROOKS: Fine.
15	BY MR. BROOKS:
16	Q. Were the naked women an ingredient
17	in the paintings?
18	A. Yes.
19	Q. Were the Rastas --
20	MS. BART: Objection.
21	(Interruption by reporter.)
22	BY MR. BROOKS:
23	Q. Were the guitars that you introduced
24	an ingredient in these paintings?
25	MS. BART: Objection, form.

278

	Prince
1	Prince
2	MR. HAYES: Objection, form.
3	Q. You can answer.
4	A. Yes.
5	Q. Were the naked women that you found
6	in various places an ingredient in the
7	paintings?
8	MS. BART: Objection, form.
9	MR. HAYES: Objection, form.
10	Q. Were the Rastas an ingredient in the
11	paintings?
12	
13	MS. BART: Objection, form.
14	MR. HAYES: Objection, form.
15	A. Yes.
16	Q. Was the tropical foliage in the
17	background behind the Rastas in the Yes Rasta
18	photos, was that an ingredient in the paintings?
19	A. Yes.
20	MS. BART: Objection, form.
21	A. Sorry.
22	Q. What's the answer?
23	A. Yes.
24	Q. Were the paintings -- were any of
25	those things, the guitars, the naked women, the

279

	Prince
1	Prince
2	Rastas, or the tropical foliage, the subject
3	matter of the paintings?
4	MS. BART: Objection, form, compound
5	question.
6	MR. HAYES: Objection, form.
7	Q. You can answer.
8	A. Were any of those -- any of those
9	one -- I believe the primary subject, the
10	primary ingredient is probably the guitar.
11	Q. Okay. And what's the primary
12	subject of the paintings?
13	MR. HAYES: Objection to form.
14	MS. BART: Same.
15	A. I think the guitar. The guitar is a
16	brilliant, brilliant contribution.
17	Q. And, again, I know you testified to
18	this before, where did you find the guitars
19	again? I'm not trying to trip you up. Was it
20	one book or several books? I don't remember.
21	A. One source was Guitar Magazine.
22	Q. Okay. So there's kind of a
23	rock-and-roll theme to these paintings?
24	MR. HAYES: Objection to form.
25	MS. BART: Same.

280

	Prince
1	Prince
2	Q. You can answer.
3	A. I would say heavy metal, but, yes,
4	rock and roll.
5	Q. Sorry. Okay.
6	Can you look at page 77, which is
7	I think the last page of this interview.
8	I'm going to read this answer at the
9	top. Well, I should read the question on the
10	previous page. Why did you get sick of doing
11	the De Kooning paintings? It seemed like you
12	did more nurse paintings than De Koonings.
13	And then you answered, Yeah, I did
14	more nurses, but with De Koonings, I'd just done
15	it. I didn't like the idea that in the end I
16	had to pay attention to someone else's work.
17	And I wanted to get rid of the color. So the
18	thing is that, you know, two years of doing the
19	De Koonings was enough. It was enough of my
20	attention. The Rastas came really fast. And
21	they're going to be over really fast too.
22	Can you explain what you meant when
23	you said the Rastas came really fast and they're
24	going to be over really fast too?
25	A. The Rasta -- the Canal Zone

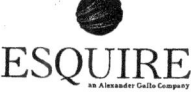

ESQUIRE
an Alexander Gallo Company

Toll Free: 800.944.9454
Facsimile: 212.557.5972

Suite 4715
One Penn Plaza
New York, NY 10119
www.esquiresolutions.com

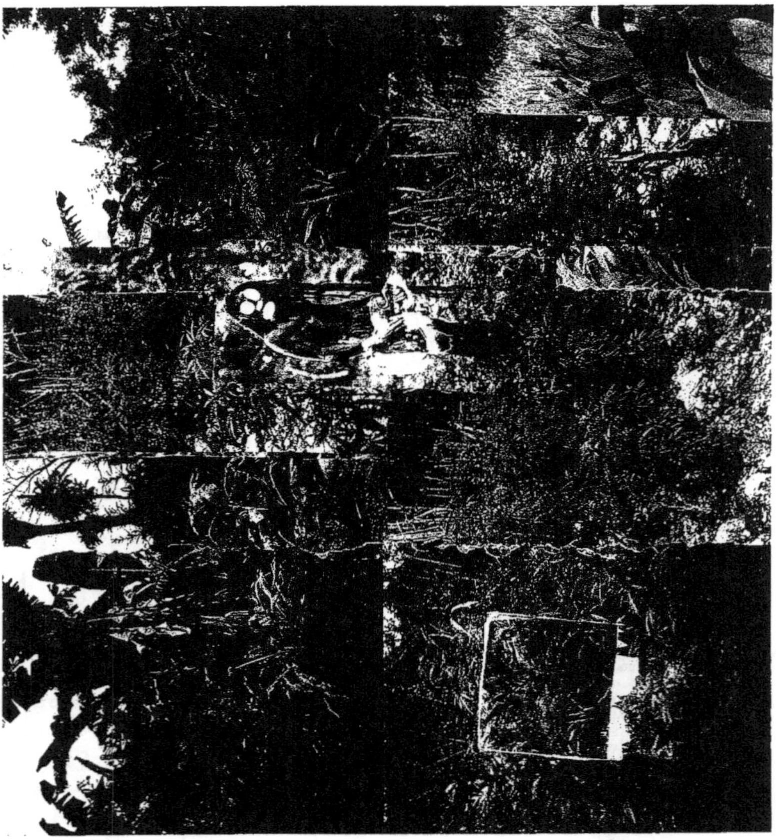

7   Canal Zone

281

1   Prince
2   paintings, which part of those paintings, an
3   element of those paintings are the Rastas.
4   The reason I believe they were
5   going -- they came really fast and they were
6   going to be over fast is I was in the middle of
7   other bodies of work that I needed to pay
8   attention to.
9   Q.   You needed to pay attention to the
10 other bodies of work?
11   A.   Yes.
12   (Discussion off the record.)
13   THE VIDEOGRAPHER: 4:25. Off the
14 record. End of tape 4.
15   (Recess taken: 4:25 p.m.)
16   (Proceedings resumed: 4:29 p.m.)
17   THE VIDEOGRAPHER: 4:29. On the
18 record. Beginning of tape 5.
19 BY MR. BROOKS:
20   Q.   In these paintings that you made for
21 the Canal Zone show were you commenting on the
22 Rasta photos in the Yes Rasta book?
23   A.   No.
24   Q.   Were you commenting on Mr. Cariou's
25 technique or methodology in taking those photos?

282

1   Prince
2   A.   No.
3   Q.   I know you don't have your own
4   plane, but you could fly commercial to Jamaica,
5   correct, if you wanted to?
6   MR. HAYES: Objection to form,
7   speculation.
8   A.   I suppose so.
9   Q.   So if you wanted pictures of Rastas
10 you could have flown to Jamaica and taken your
11 own pictures, correct?
12   MS. BART: Objection to form.
13   MR. HAYES: Objection.
14   Q.   You can answer.
15   A.   It's not how I make pictures though.
16   Q.   Right. Okay. You'd rather
17 appropriate than take your own pictures?
18   MR. HAYES: Objection --
19   MS. BART: Objection, form,
20 argumentative.
21   MR. HAYES: -- form and
22 argumentative.
23   Q.   You can answer.
24   A.   It's funny, a friend of mine who
25 is a photographer just went to Jamaica and sent

283

1   Prince
2   me pictures of, quote, I guess they were
3   Rastafarians, and said can you use these.
4   I said, you know, unfortunately, you
5   know, these types of situations inhibit me. And
6   I think it's an unfortunate circumstance that I
7   have to be -- think about these things.
8   But to answer your question, yes, I
9   suppose I could have gone. But it would never
10 occur to me to get on a plane and go to Jamaica
11 for the express purposes of taking photographs
12 of people who are alive.
13   I -- my way of taking a portrait is
14 to take something that's already been taken.
15   Q.   Right. And you still believe that
16 that makes it more believable if you've
17 appropriated it from someone else?
18   MR. HAYES: Objection as to form.
19   MS. BART: Objection to form, and
20 asked and answered.
21   A.   Well, everybody creates their own
22 artificial reality when they're making art. And
23 mine gets made in a studio. I'm the king of my
24 castle in my studio. I don't operate very well
25 out in the real world. I like a much more

284

1   Prince
2   private world.
3   And I'm a bibliophile. I collect
4   books. At any one time I have 20, 25 different
5   types of books laying about the studio.
6   Sometimes I pay attention to them, sometimes I
7   don't. I'm always ripping them up.
8   And, as I said, I sort of would
9   describe that practice as sort of deejaying
10 photographs --
11   Q.   You're not saying you have
12 agoraphobia --
13   A.   -- or pictures.
14   MR. HAYES: Let him finish the
15 question, if you don't mind. He's in the
16 middle of a question -- answer.
17   Let him finish.
18   Go ahead.
19   A.   I'm not sure what agoraphobia is,
20 but that idea of -- is it that thing where you
21 can't travel? My sister has that.
22   Q.   But you don't?
23   A.   I don't believe I have it.
24   MR. HAYES: Let the record reflect
25 the questioner interrupted the witness in

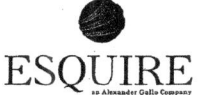

285

	Prince
1	Prince
2	the middle of answer.
3	So do you want to go back?
4	THE WITNESS: No, it's not
5	important.
6	Q. You said you were deejaying or
7	something? Do you have anything to add to that?
8	A. It's a figurative way --
9	MR. HAYES: Object to form.
10	A. -- to describe what I do.
11	Q. Have you ever heard of I guess it's
12	a website called iStockphoto.com?
13	A. No.
14	Q. Would it surprise you to know that
15	they have more than five-million royalty-free
16	non-copyrighted photos on their website?
17	MR. HAYES: Objection as to form.
18	A. I didn't know that.
19	Q. Would it surprise you to know that
20	the price of those photos is very, very modest?
21	MR. HAYES: Objection as to form.
22	A. I didn't know that.
23	Q. Would you -- and I invite you to do
24	this after the deposition, go to their website
25	iStockphoto.com, and you will see if you put in

286

	Prince
1	Prince
2	the search term Rastas you will find over 3,000
3	non-copyright pictures of Rastas, some black and
4	white, some color.
5	MR. HAYES: Is there a question
6	there?
7	Q. Would that surprise you to know
8	that?
9	MR. HAYES: Objection as to form.
10	A. It doesn't anymore.
11	Q. Because?
12	A. Because I believe the -- I think
13	things have changed since 1977. I've been slow
14	to change with them in terms of how I make my
15	images. I'm catching up. I believe that I'm
16	not very fluent with the computer.
17	But, as I said before, I think
18	rephotography could be called -- is a primitive
19	way of downloading an image. And there was a --
20	anyway, I believe in surrogate substitution,
21	simulants, robots, I believe in science fiction,
22	I believe in J.G. Ballard, the Concrete Jungle,
23	I believe that virtual reality is on our
24	doorstep. Cloning is right around the corner.
25	And I believe, even though I did

287

	Prince
1	Prince
2	this 30 years ago, I think it's here to stay.
3	And I am not surprised that there are -- there's
4	a website like this.
5	Q. Okay.
6	A. I don't believe there would have
7	been a website like this ten years ago. But I'm
8	happy to know this information.
9	Q. Well, I invite you to go to
10	iStockphoto.com.
11	A. Thanks.
12	MR. HAYES: Objection to the form,
13	if that was a question.
14	MR. BROOKS: Can we mark as
15	Exhibit Plaintiff's 29 a three-page
16	document GGP001421 and GGP00424 and 425.
17	(Plaintiff's Exhibit 29, three-page
18	document, was marked for identification,
19	as of this date.)
20	Q. Mr. Prince?
21	A. Yes.
22	Q. If you look at what's been marked as
23	Exhibit 29?
24	A. Mm-hmm, yes.
25	Q. We had talked about this before, at

288

	Prince
1	Prince
2	the bottom it says, Hi, Betsy, Richard said you
3	could hook us up with images for his interview.
4	I love the Rasta work and would like to run
5	several big pages. We are on a tight schedule.
6	What's the next step?
7	And it's signed Glenn. That's from
8	Glenn O'Brien, correct?
9	A. Yes.
10	Q. I think I had asked you about that
11	before. And then there's an e-mail from Betsy
12	your assistant or your studio manager to Melissa
13	and Gagosian saying per Glenn O'Brien's request
14	that they should send some high-resolution Rasta
15	works to Glenn O'Brien. Do you see that?
16	A. Yes.
17	Q. And then at the top I wanted to ask
18	you if you know what this is. It's from Melissa
19	Lazarov. It says see below, and it says I need
20	to send some JPEGs, J-P-E-G-S, to Glenn. Please
21	attach for me, from Melissa. Do you know what a
22	JPEG is?
23	A. Yes, I do.
24	Q. Can you tell me, please?
25	A. It's an image that you send through

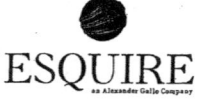

289

1	Prince
2	the computer.
3	Q. Is it different than a PDF?
4	A. I don't know what a PDF is.
5	Q. Is it high resolution and pretty
6	accurate depiction, a JPEG?
7	MS. BART: Objection, form.
8	MR. HAYES: Objection, form.
9	A. Again, I'm not that fluent in
10	computer. I do e-mail and that's about it.
11	Q. Okay.
12	A. I've never sent a JPEG myself to
13	anybody. And I've never sent, what is it
14	called, a PDF. So I'm not in a position to
15	answer that question.
16	Q. Fair enough.
17	If you look at the first page of
18	Exhibit 28, which is the interview that Glenn
19	O'Brien did with you. Do you remember we looked
20	at these already, these five images?
21	Simple question. Do you know
22	whether those are JPEGs?
23	A. What I'm looking at here?
24	Q. Those five images, correct, on the
25	first page of Exhibit 28.

290

1	Prince
2	A. No.
3	Q. You don't know?
4	A. I don't know.
5	Q. Okay, fine.
6	MR. BROOKS: Let's mark as
7	Plaintiff's Exhibit 30 a number of photos
8	printed out from iStockphoto.com.
9	(Plaintiff's Exhibit 30, photos from
10	iStockphoto.com, was marked for
11	identification, as of this date.)
12	Q. Have you seen Exhibit 30?
13	A. Have I seen this exhibit before?
14	Q. Well, look at it now. Have you had
15	an opportunity to look at it now?
16	A. No --
17	MR. HAYES: He wants you to take an
18	opportunity to look at it.
19	Q. Yes, please do.
20	MR. HAYES: Please take a look at
21	it.
22	A. Yes, I've looked at it now.
23	Q. So it's six photos?
24	A. Yes.
25	Q. I'm aware you weren't aware of

291

1	Prince
2	iStockphoto, but now that you see these photos
3	would these have been appropriate ingredients
4	for your Canal Zone paintings?
5	MR. HAYES: Objection as to form.
6	MS. BART: Objection, form.
7	Q. You can answer.
8	A. Not really because they're in color.
9	I guess I could have transformed
10	them to black and white. But, again, I wasn't
11	aware of this particular company.
12	Q. Well, I hear what you're saying.
13	One of them is black and white.
14	A. Oh, it is?
15	Q. I think the fourth one is black and
16	white.
17	A. A little lavender in it.
18	Q. Okay. So that one is not suitable
19	either?
20	MS. BART: Objection, form.
21	MR. HAYES: Same objection.
22	Q. Is that what you're saying?
23	A. I mean are you asking me if I had
24	seen this --
25	Q. Would you have used it?

292

1	Prince
2	A. -- like four years ago, three years,
3	two years ago, a year ago?
4	Q. Yeah.
5	MR. HAYES: Objection to the form of
6	the question. Calls for speculation.
7	A. I don't know.
8	Q. You might have used them?
9	A. It's possible.
10	MS. BART: Objection. Move to
11	strike as speculative.
12	MR. BROOKS: Let's mark as
13	Plaintiff's Exhibit 31 three pages from --
14	I believe from the Gagosian Gallery
15	website Bates stamped C8 through 10.
16	(Plaintiff's Exhibit 31, three pages
17	from Gagosian Gallery website, was marked
18	for identification, as of this date.)
19	Q. Mr. Prince, I've placed in front of
20	you Plaintiff's Exhibit 31. It says that the
21	Canal Zone show was going to be November 8th to
22	December 20th, 2008, is that your recollection?
23	A. Yes.
24	Q. And then under this picture, do you
25	know which painting that is, the one at the top?

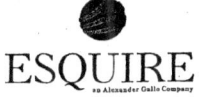

Toll Free: 800.944.9454
Facsimile: 212.557.5972

Suite 4715
One Penn Plaza
New York, NY 10119
www.esquiresolutions.com

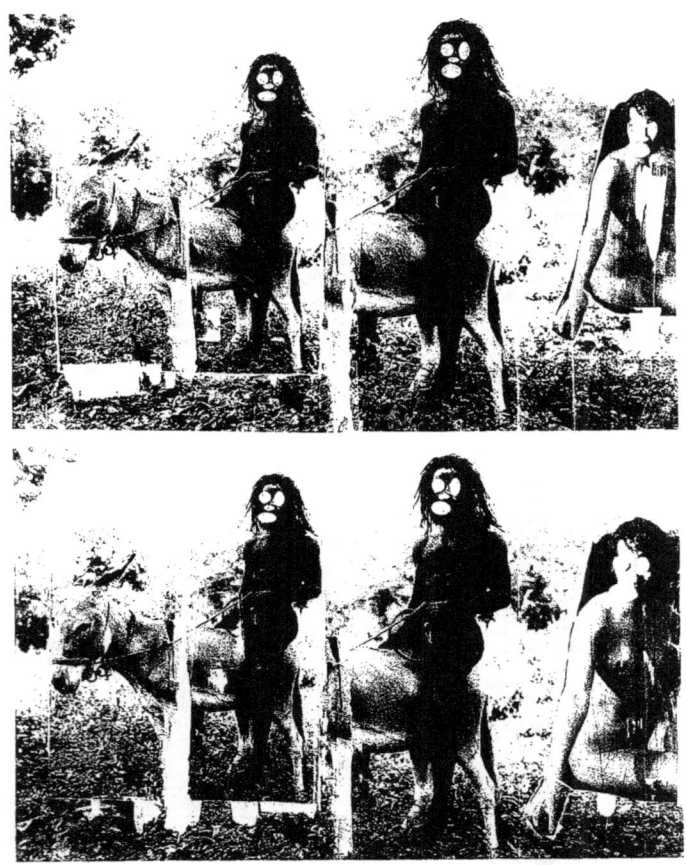

5   Charlie Company

293

Prince

1
2   A.   Is that the Garden of Eden? It's a
3   little fuzzy, so. I do know that it has --
4   anyway, is it --
5   Q.   I'm not sure. It's either the
6   Garden of Eden or Charlie Company.
7   A.   It's either one of those two. It's
8   a little -- my reproduction here is difficult to
9   see.
10   Q.   And then it says underneath that it
11   quotes you, the story was basically about a guy
12   that lands in St. Barth's, gets off the plane,
13   is immediately told that there's been a nuclear
14   holocaust in the rest of the world and he looks
15   at his family and says we can't go back.
16   So that's taken from your pitch I
17   assume?
18   MS. BART: Objection, form.
19   Q.   Is that taken from your pitch?
20   A.   It sounds like it's been taken from
21   my pitch, yes.
22   Q.   And then beneath that it says, two
23   paragraphs down, it says the Panama Canal Zone,
24   where he was born -- do you see that?
25   A.   Yes.

294

Prince

1
2   Q.   -- was until 1979 a political
3   exclave of the U.S., part colonial company
4   enclave and part socialist government
5   purportedly dominated by virulent separatist
6   racism.
7   Other than the fact that you were
8   born there and that it was not part of Panama
9   until 1979, do you agree with any of the balance
10   of this statement?
11   MS. BART: Objection, form.
12   A.   I've never --
13   Q.   You can answer.
14   A.   I've never seen this before. I
15   believe this is a press release.
16   Q.   This is taken from the Gagosian
17   Gallery website.
18   A.   Okay.
19   Q.   In connection with the opening of
20   your show.
21   A.   I've never seen this text.
22   MS. BART: In light of the witness's
23   answer I lodge an objection.
24   MR. BROOKS: Great.
25   MS. BART: Foundation.

295

Prince

1
2   BY MR. BROOKS:
3   Q.   Was the Panama Canal Zone a place
4   that was, to your knowledge, dominated by
5   virulent, separatist racism?
6   MS. BART: Objection to form.
7   MR. HAYES: Objection to form.
8   A.   I thought it was -- I always
9   associated it as a very cool place to live
10   except for that Noriega guy, but -- and a lot of
11   spooks.
12   Q.   Spooks meaning spies?
13   A.   KGB, CIA, yeah, I mean --
14   Q.   Those kind of spooks?
15   A.   Yeah. Spies.
16   Q.   But a convivial, pleasant place to
17   live?
18   A.   I mean my couple of days there was
19   very nice.
20   Q.   How about your six years?
21   A.   I only remember houses on stilts,
22   large insects, and palm trees.
23   Q.   Okay. On the next page of
24   Exhibit 31 it says -- in the middle paragraph it
25   says, towards the bottom of it, Canal Zone, this

296

Prince

1
2   orgiastic post-nuclear new order of civilization
3   as we once knew it takes its place among other
4   great modern visions of the apocalypse from
5   Joseph Conrad's Heart of Darkness and Pablo
6   Picasso's Guernica to the Beatles' Helter
7   Skelter and Michel Houellebecq's prophetic
8   Platform. Do you see that?
9   A.   Yes.
10   Q.   Do you agree with any of that?
11   MR. HAYES: Object to form.
12   MS. BART: Same.
13   A.   It's pretty good. I think Louise
14   Neri probably wrote this. I would say that
15   that's kind of an interesting take on what I
16   was -- let me just --
17   Q.   Go ahead.
18   A.   Canal Zone, this orgiastic
19   post-nuclear -- I like the Heart of Darkness.
20   Q.   Joseph Conrad?
21   A.   And I like the Guernica.
22   I've read Platform, but I'm much
23   more of a fan of Houellebecq's Atomised. He's a
24   French author. Terrific writer.
25   And Helter Skelter I would have

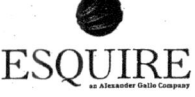

ESQUIRE
an Alexander Gallo Company

Toll Free: 800.944.9454
Facsimile: 212.557.5972

Suite 4715
One Penn Plaza
New York, NY 10119
www.esquiresolutions.com

297

1   Prince
2   substituted a Ramones song.
3   Q.   But you find this to be an apt
4   description of your paintings in the Canal Zone
5   exhibition?
6   MS. BART: Objection to form.
7   A.   It's not necessarily the way I would
8   have described it had they asked me to write the
9   press release. But I don't write press releases
10 and I don't read them.
11   Q.   And is this the first time --
12   A.   I find them -- sorry.
13   MS. BART: No, you were talking. He
14 interrupted you.
15   Q.   Go ahead.
16   A.   I find press releases incredibly
17 silly and boring, and I just don't -- I've never
18 wanted anything -- because they're really just
19 trying to hype the work. And I don't
20 particularly like to get involved in that.
21   Q.   And, again, is this the first time
22 you're seeing this press release?
23   A.   This is the first time I'm seeing
24 this.
25   Q.   On the last page it says that mining

298

1   Prince
2   images from mass media, advertising, and
3   entertainment since the late '70s, Prince has
4   redefined the concepts of authorship, ownership,
5   and aura. Do you see that?
6   A.   Yes.
7   Q.   Do you agree that you've redefined
8   the concept of authorship?
9   A.   I would hope that I've had some hand
10 in redefining the issues that have to do with
11 authorship.
12   Q.   How so?
13   A.   It has to do with that concept that
14 people really believe artists are special and
15 they have something special to say. There was a
16 time in the late '70s when I didn't go along
17 with that concept. And there was that essay by
18 Roland Barthes called Death of an Author, and it
19 was just an issue that was going around town.
20   And I think that I got caught up in
21 it and I got involved in it and I sort of
22 decided to do something about it in my own
23 particular little way.
24   And hopefully, yes, I hope that --
25 you know, I would have called it the death of

299

1   Prince
2   the ego, but I guess authorship is a fairly
3   accurate and it's an okay word.
4   I mean it's very -- all it is is
5   philosophical. And, you know, it's sort of like
6   someone writing a term paper, you know, it's
7   academic. You know, it's something that takes
8   place in October Magazine, which I don't
9   particularly like and Columbia University and,
10 you know, it's -- I'm much more of a -- well,
11 I'm much more interested in trying to make art
12 that stands up next to Picasso, De Kooning, and
13 Warhol. That's what I'm interested in.
14   MR. BROOKS: Let's mark as exhibit,
15 Plaintiff's Exhibit 32, a two-page
16 document GGP004298 and 99.
17   (Plaintiff's Exhibit 32, two-page
18 document, was marked for identification,
19 as of this date.)
20   Q.   Before we get to this, I just -- I
21 forgot to ask you a follow-up question before.
22   Do you remember you were looking at
23 that press release that mentioned Helter Skelter
24 and Guernica and Heart of Darkness?
25   A.   Yes.

300

1   Prince
2   Q.   Do you think that's a more apt
3   description of these paintings in the Canal Zone
4   exhibit than Manet's Luncheon On the Grass?
5   MS. BART: Objection to form.
6   MR. HAYES: Objection to form.
7   Q.   You can answer.
8   A.   Manet on the Grass isn't a bad
9   stretch.
10   Q.   Is or isn't? I didn't hear.
11   A.   I think it's a fairly good stretch
12 as a description. In comparison to Heart of
13 Darkness, Colonel Kurtz, Apocalypse Now.
14   Q.   The movie?
15   A.   Yeah, I mean it's -- they're all --
16 that's the great thing about making this kind of
17 art is that it has all these -- it can provide
18 different interpretations.
19   Q.   So it can be like Manet's Déjeuner
20 sur l'herbe, Lunch on the Grass, it can be like
21 Guernica?
22   MR. HAYES: Objection to form.
23   MS. BART: Join.
24   Q.   Sticking to paintings?
25   A.   I wouldn't -- I would rather have

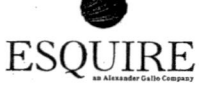

301

	Prince
1	
2	had Picasso's Mademoiselle d'Avignon. I think
3	it's a much more accurate painting because of
4	the masks and the revolutionary techniques and
5	the way he appropriated African imagery in that
6	painting than the Manet.
7	Also, it reminds me of the bands,
8	that Mademoiselle d'Avignon.
9	Q. Okay. I'm going to ask you to look
10	at the back of what's been marked as Exhibit 42,
11	which is the Canal Zone book, and tell me how
12	many --
13	MR. HAYES: I'm just taking off my
14	microphone so I can get it for you.
15	Q. Tell me how many paintings are
16	listed in the book. And we're starting with
17	page C210. You don't have to name them, I just
18	want you to tell me how many.
19	MS. BART: All of them or --
20	MR. BROOKS: All together.
21	MR. HAYES: You want him to count
22	them?
23	MR. BROOKS: No, they're numbered.
24	You don't have to count them.
25	MS. BART: Right. But not all of

302

	Prince
2	them are at issue in this lawsuit.
3	MR. BROOKS: I didn't ask him --
4	well, that's -- I'm not going to argue
5	with you about what's at issue in this
6	lawsuit. I'm asking him how many
7	paintings are in the book. That's all.
8	A. Well, it says here -- how many
9	paintings are in the Canal Zone exhibition?
10	Q. In that book.
11	A. It's funny, they didn't list -- I
12	just realized they didn't list a work.
13	Q. Yeah, they didn't list a few. But
14	I'm just asking you how many are listed in the
15	book?
16	A. 22.
17	Q. Now, there's a 23rd thing, but
18	that's not a painting at all, right, that's like
19	a car hood or something?
20	A. Yes.
21	Q. So if we're talking about paintings
22	it lists 22 paintings, correct?
23	A. I believe so, yes. I count 22. I
24	see 22.
25	Q. Right. Now, the actual exhibition

303

	Prince
1	
2	itself, could you take a look at Exhibit 32
3	which has just been handed to you?
4	A. Yes.
5	Q. Some kind of schematic of your show?
6	A. It looks like it's some kind of the
7	way we positioned --
8	Q. Exactly.
9	A. -- the paintings.
10	Q. Yes. And so if you add these up,
11	again, not counting the Dear Mary, the car, it's
12	part of a sculpture, part of a car. It looks
13	like there were only 15 paintings actually
14	exhibited during your show, is that correct?
15	A. I believe I -- yes, I count 15
16	paintings on this chart.
17	Q. And now I'm asking you a slightly
18	different question. Is that your recollection
19	of how many paintings were actually exhibited at
20	the show?
21	MR. HAYES: Objection as to form.
22	A. Is that my recollection? I never
23	really thought about it until you asked me the
24	question. I'm assuming, now that I look at this
25	chart, I can definitely say -- I believe I can

304

	Prince
2	kind of remember where every painting was hung.
3	And I believe, yes, it was 15 paintings.
4	Q. If you look on the second page at
5	the top, this is that painting we've been
6	talking about the four lesbians who took
7	over the Guanahani?
8	A. Yes.
9	Q. And the first one is Djuna,
10	D-J-U-N-A, Barnes.
11	A. Djuna Barnes.
12	Q. And then Natalie Barney?
13	A. Natalie Barney.
14	Q. Renée Vivien?
15	A. And Romaine Brooks.
16	(Clarification by reporter.)
17	Q. Romaine Brooks?
18	A. They have it spelled wrong here.
19	Q. I know.
20	Now, a number of these paintings
21	that are in Exhibit 32 are not listed in the
22	book that you were just looking at where it
23	lists 22 paintings, correct?
24	For instance, the very first one
25	Pumpsie Green is not listed, right?

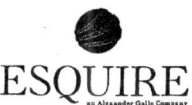

ESQUIRE
an Alexander Gallo Company

Toll Free: 800.944.9454
Facsimile: 212.557.5972

Suite 4715
One Penn Plaza
New York, NY 10119
www.esquiresolutions.com

305

Prince

2 MR. HAYES: He's asking you whether
3 they're listed at the back of the book, if
4 you want to compare them.
5 A. Oh, so Pumpsie Green is not in the
6 catalog?
7 Q. That's right.
8 A. I didn't really notice that, but if
9 you say -- yeah, I mean I can go back and check.
10 Q. Just check that one. The others,
11 the record will speak for itself.
12 A. I don't -- I've never really looked
13 at the back of this catalog.
14 Q. Right.
15 A. Pumpsie Green was in the show and
16 it's not listed in the catalog.
17 What page are we looking for?
18 MR. HAYES: 210 through 213.
19 210 through 212, I'm sorry.
20 A. I think what's listed here has to do
21 with the Canal Zone catalog.
22 Q. Right.
23 A. And what's listed here has to do
24 with the show.
25 Q. Right. So they're not -- there's

307

Prince

2 in gallery 3, number 5, but it's not in the book
3 either, is it?
4 A. There is a -- it's interesting,
5 there's a variation in the book.
6 Q. Ah.
7 A. And you would never know.
8 Q. I see. So it's a different painting
9 or is it --
10 A. It's the same painting.
11 Q. A different --
12 A. Do you want me to show you?
13 Q. We'll get to it.
14 And now, a Scapegoat is listed here
15 in gallery 3 as having been exhibited, but it's
16 not in the book either, is it?
17 A. Scapegoat -- no.
18 MR. BROOKS: In fact, let's mark
19 as Plaintiff's Exhibit 33 a number of
20 paintings that are not listed in the book?
21 MS. BART: This is 34?
22 MR. BROOKS: This is 33.
23 (Plaintiff's Exhibit 33, listing of
24 paintings, was marked for identification,
25 as of this date.)

306

Prince

2 some overlap --
3 A. I mean it's two separate --
4 Q. -- but there's also some paintings
5 that were exhibited that are not in the catalog,
6 right?
7 A. My feeling is there's -- yeah,
8 there's two -- yeah, two separate ways of
9 identifying really what's two separate ways of
10 contemplating the Canal Zone idea.
11 Q. So besides Pumpsie Green is it
12 correct that MC9 White Panthers is listed as
13 being in the show but -- in gallery three -- but
14 is not listed in the book?
15 A. Yes, MC9 was one of the last
16 paintings.
17 Q. Right.
18 A. It didn't make --
19 Q. Didn't make the cut?
20 A. Didn't make the cut for the catalog.
21 And I believe that's the painting
22 where Charles Company's daughter appears.
23 Q. MC9?
24 A. I believe so.
25 Q. How about Inquisition, that's listed

308

Prince

2 Q. All right. So Exhibit 33 contains
3 it looks like seven paintings that are not
4 listed in the Canal Zone book, correct?
5 I'll read them into the record.
6 MC9, paren, White Panthers.
7 Myrna Loy, Janet Flanner, et cetera,
8 et cetera, and Oscar Wilde's niece Dolly Wilde.
9 Pumpsie Green.
10 Uncle Tom, Dick, and Harry.
11 On the Beach, On the Beach.
12 Inquisition --
13 MR. HAYES: Tom, Dick, and Harry is
14 2008, right?
15 MR. BROOKS: They all are 2008.
16 BY MR. BROOKS:
17 Q. On the Beach, On the Beach.
18 Inquisition.
19 And Scapegoat.
20 These are in Exhibit 33, Mr. Prince,
21 and they're all not listed at the end of the
22 book, correct?
23 A. No, they're not.
24 Q. So then if my math is correct, if
25 you add 22 and 7 that means there were 29

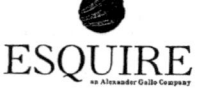

309

	Prince
2	paintings in all, right?
3	MS. BART: Objection to form.
4	A. In the Canal Zone series?
5	Q. Yes.
6	A. I don't really know how many are in
7	the Canal Zone.
8	Q. At least 29?
9	A. But if we've counted 29 there's at
10	least 29, yeah.
11	Q. 22 plus the 7 that are in
12	Exhibit 33, right?
13	A. Yes.
14	Q. Okay. Do you know of those 29 how
15	many were sold, do you know?
16	A. No, I don't.
17	Q. Let me ask you about the ones that
18	haven't been sold. Are they on public display
19	now or are they somewhere safe? Where are they?
20	A. In my racks in my studio.
21	Q. So they're not --
22	A. And I believe some are being
23	prepared to be -- I think some are in storage,
24	at the moment, I'm not positive about this,
25	either at Larry's storage or my storage in

310

	Prince
2	Brooklyn.
3	Q. All right. But they're not
4	somewhere where members of the public can view
5	them, is that right?
6	A. No, I haven't allowed anybody to
7	look at them in quite some time.
8	MR. BROOKS: Let's mark as
9	Plaintiff's 34 a letter dated
10	December 11th, 2008, Bates stamped C13
11	and 14.
12	(Plaintiff's Exhibit 34, letter
13	dated December 11, 2008, was marked for
14	identification, as of this date.)
15	(Discussion off the record.)
16	THE WITNESS: How long do we have?
17	MR. HAYES: He's guessing about an
18	hour. You may have to be somewhere --
19	THE WITNESS: I'm fried. I mean
20	this has been a long day. Is there any
21	way we can come back?
22	Or can you give me an idea of how
23	much more time and I can tell you?
24	MR. BROOKS: I said I think about an
25	hour.

311

	Prince
2	THE WITNESS: So about an hour more
3	until six?
4	MR. BROOKS: Well, you know, running
5	time -- how much running time do we have
6	left?
7	THE WITNESS: I can't go past -- I
8	don't know if I can go past six.
9	MR. BROOKS: Okay. How much running
10	time --
11	THE VIDEOGRAPHER: About five hours
12	and -- 5:45 exactly.
13	MS. BART: 5:45, right?
14	MR. BROOKS: So we have another hour
15	and fifteen minutes that we're entitled to
16	under the rules.
17	So I'm willing to accommodate you.
18	If you feel you want to stop now, with the
19	understanding that I've got another hour
20	and fifteen minutes to ask you questions?
21	MR. HAYES: And this gentleman
22	may --
23	THE WITNESS: I'll take your advice,
24	so.
25	MR. BROOKS: It's completely up to

312

	Prince
2	you.
3	THE WITNESS: Yeah, I mean I'm
4	comfortable. It's just that I have to be
5	at an opening tonight, and I promised my
6	daughter that I would be home.
7	MR. BROOKS: What time do you have
8	to leave here?
9	MR. HAYES: Now.
10	THE WITNESS: As I said, I have to
11	get home at six.
12	MR. BROOKS: All right. So let me
13	try --
14	MR. HAYES: But, you know, you call
15	it. I mean do you want to just get it
16	over with?
17	(Clarification by reporter.)
18	MR. BROOKS: So what did we say,
19	another hour and fifteen minutes?
20	I'm willing to do it tomorrow
21	morning and break right now --
22	MS. BART: I'm not available
23	tomorrow.
24	MR. BROOKS: Thursday morning we're
25	all scheduled to be here. Finish him and

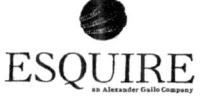

313		315	
1	Prince	1	Prince
2	then start.	2	you know, for these days, so I can't do
3	MS. BART: I'm not able to be here	3	Friday morning unfortunately.
4	because I'm going to be with Mr. Gagosian,	4	MR. HAYES: Monday morning?
5	so.	5	THE WITNESS: Monday is a holiday.
6	MR. BROOKS: Well, he's going to be	6	MS. BART: It is?
7	here having his deposition.	7	THE WITNESS: Yeah, it's Columbus
8	MS. BART: At 10. Yeah, I can't get	8	Day.
9	down here earlier than that.	9	MR. HAYES: What kind of good
10	MR. BROOKS: Well, I mean whatever,	10	Italian are you?
11	it's really --	11	THE WITNESS: I can do it -- well, I
12	MR. HAYES: He can stay until six.	12	can do it almost any day except Thursday
13	THE WITNESS: I can stay until six.	13	morning.
14	MR. BROOKS: Okay. Well, let's see	14	MR. BROOKS: Why don't we do this.
15	if we -- is that okay with you?	15	Why don't we start with him at 10 on
16	THE COURT REPORTER: That's fine	16	Thursday, we'll finish him --
17	with me.	17	THE WITNESS: I can't --
18	THE WITNESS: I only can stay until	18	MR. HAYES: That's the one day he
19	six if that's it. I don't want to come	19	can't do.
20	back for fifteen minutes --	20	THE WITNESS: I can do it in the
21	MR. BROOKS: I can't promise -- I	21	afternoon on Thursday.
22	can't control the objections --	22	MR. BROOKS: No, we're having
23	THE WITNESS: Then I can't promise	23	Mr. Gagosian's deposition on Thursday.
24	that I can stay until six. If you can't	24	MS. BART: And Mr. Gagosian flew
25	promise me, I can't promise you.	25	back from Europe specifically for this.

314		316	
1	Prince	1	Prince
2	MR. BROOKS: Well, it's not entirely	2	So I don't want to start him late.
3	in my control how long this takes. There	3	THE WITNESS: What's tomorrow?
4	are objections --	4	MR. HAYES: Tomorrow is Wednesday.
5	THE WITNESS: I thought that we --	5	MS. BART: I'm not available
6	MR. HAYES: He's up to -- he has an	6	tomorrow.
7	hour and 15 minutes left. He can do that	7	THE WITNESS: I can do it tomorrow.
8	if he wants.	8	MR. HAYES: Can you do it tomorrow
9	MR. BROOKS: The rule is seven hours	9	afternoon?
10	of actual testimony.	10	MS. BART: No.
11	THE WITNESS: Okay. Then let's do	11	MR. HAYES: That took care of that.
12	it --	12	Tuesday?
13	MR. BROOKS: I'll accommodate you.	13	THE WITNESS: Can you guarantee me
14	THE WITNESS: I'm in the city, I can	14	6:15 and that's it?
15	come back --	15	MR. BROOKS: Yes.
16	MR. HAYES: How is Thursday morning?	16	THE WITNESS: Promise?
17	THE WITNESS: Friday morning I	17	MR. BROOKS: Yes.
18	could, but I have to -- I can only do it	18	THE WITNESS: Okay, I can --
19	in the morning.	19	MR. BROOKS: Let's go then.
20	MR. BROOKS: It's an hour and	20	THE WITNESS: -- because I got the
21	fifteen minutes.	21	car service outside.
22	THE WITNESS: That doesn't concern	22	MR. BROOKS: All right.
23	me. It's tonight.	23	Let's mark as Plaintiff's 35 a
24	MS. BART: Friday morning I've got	24	document Bates stamped PR45 through 50.
25	client meetings that are already set up,	25	(Plaintiff's Exhibit 35, PR45

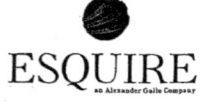

317

1   Prince
2   through 50, was marked for identification,
3   as of this date.)
4   (Discussion off the record.)
5   Q.   Let's go back to 34. It's a letter
6   dated December 11th.
7   A.   December 11th?
8   Q.   2008. From me. Do you see it?
9   A.   Yes, I do.
10   Q.   I only have one question.
11   Did you receive it?
12   A.   I'm not in a position to know if I
13   received it. I don't know.
14   Q.   Well, let me ask you this. Is that
15   your correct address on the letter?
16   A.   Yes, it is.
17   Q.   You just don't know if you received
18   it?
19   A.   I've never seen it before.
20   Q.   Okay. That's fine.
21   Take a look at 35. This is a
22   document that was produced by your counsel. Do
23   you know what it is?
24   A.   Yes.
25   Q.   What is it?

318

1   Prince
2   A.   It looks as if it's a guest list for
3   a party.
4   Q.   On November 8th, 2008?
5   A.   Yes, the party that was after the
6   show.
7   Q.   But it was in honor of the opening
8   of the show?
9   A.   Yes.
10   Q.   If you look at the very end, the
11   last page, do you see that Renée Zellweger was
12   one of the people invited?
13   A.   I see that her name is on the list,
14   yes.
15   Q.   Do you know her?
16   A.   No. I've met her.
17   Q.   Does she co-own a restaurant in
18   East Hampton called the Blue Parrot?
19   MR. HAYES: If you know.
20   Q.   If you know.
21   A.   I believe she's a co-owner in the
22   restaurant.
23   Q.   With Ronald Perelman and Larry
24   Gagosian and Bon Jovi?
25   A.   Yes, that's what I've heard.

319

1   Prince
2   Q.   And was there ever -- were you ever
3   approached about hanging your artwork in that
4   restaurant?
5   A.   Yes.
6   Q.   The Blue Parrot restaurant?
7   A.   Yes.
8   Q.   And is any of your artwork --
9   withdrawn.
10   Has any of your artwork been
11   displayed there since the restaurant reopened
12   last summer?
13   A.   Yes.
14   Q.   It wasn't any of the Canal Zone
15   paintings, was it?
16   A.   No.
17   Q.   Did the Bush daughters come to the
18   dinner, Barbara and Lauren Bush?
19   A.   Are they on the list?
20   Q.   Yes.
21   A.   I don't think so. I don't know
22   them. So, no. That's a lot of people there.
23   No.
24   Q.   Did Paul McCartney or Mick Jagger
25   come to the dinner?

320

1   Prince
2   A.   No.
3   Q.   Who is John Kern, is he an artist
4   who was represented by Gagosian, do you know?
5   A.   He's an artist. I don't know if
6   he's represented by Gagosian.
7   Q.   Steven Cohen, did he buy one of your
8   paintings?
9   A.   Yes.
10   Q.   Does he have a hedge fund called
11   SAC, Steven A. Cohen?
12   A.   I don't know what it's called. I
13   know he has a hedge fund.
14   Q.   Do you know who Leon Black is?
15   A.   Leon Black, no, I don't know who
16   that is.
17   Q.   How about Henry Kravis?
18   A.   I know Henry Kravis. I played golf
19   with him this summer.
20   Q.   He's a private equity person?
21   A.   I don't know what he does.
22   Q.   How about Jeanne Greenberg Rohatyn,
23   did she buy a painting from you?
24   A.   Yes.
25   Q.   Who is she?

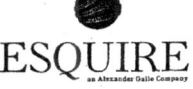

321	323
1 Prince	1 Prince
2 A. She's an art dealer.	2 I don't know if they say redacted on
3 Q. And I think we already talked about	3 them though. I don't know what that means.
4 Mr. Evans, he bought one of your paintings,	4 Q. I don't either.
5 right?	5 MR. HAYES: Redacted by my office
6 A. Yes.	6 because they redacted out the paintings
7 Q. His first name is Michael?	7 that were not related to Canal Zone.
8 A. Michael.	8 Q. So the first one is Canal Zone?
9 Q. There are two people listed there	9 A. Yes.
10 named Niarchos, N-I-A-R-C-H-O-S. Did either of	10 Q. So that was sold for $1.2 million
11 them buy one of your paintings from the Canal	11 dollars and you received $720,000, is that
12 Zone show?	12 right?
13 A. Philip Niarchos bought -- yes, I	13 A. If that's what it says, yes.
14 believe he did.	14 Q. RP share, that would be your share,
15 Q. You don't remember which painting?	15 right?
16 A. Yes, I do.	16 A. That would have been -- if it sold
17 I think he bought the Eden, the	17 for 1.2 I would have received -- I don't know if
18 Garden of Eden.	18 there was a discount. I very rarely pay
19 Q. The one from the 2007 show --	19 attention to what -- I don't pay any attention
20 withdrawn. Withdrawn.	20 to these kind of things, but if this is what
21 From the 2008 show?	21 they sent me, this is what happened.
22 A. No, I think it was the one from --	22 Q. Well, this came from your production
23 the one that was hanging -- I think it was -- I	23 so somebody must have sent it to you.
24 don't pay much attention to who buys what, but I	24 A. If Betsy sent it and if she says,
25 believe he bought number six -- Back to the	25 then I believe it.

322	324
1 Prince	1 Prince
2 Garden, I'm sorry, Back to the Garden.	2 Q. The next one is Other Side of the
3 Q. Back to the Garden.	3 Island, it indicates that that too was sold for
4 Do you know how much he paid for it?	4 $1,200,000 and that your share was $720,000,
5 A. No, I don't.	5 correct?
6 MR. BROOKS: Let's mark as	6 A. That's correct.
7 Plaintiff's Exhibit 36 a multipage	7 Q. And then this untitled Rasta was
8 document with some different accountings	8 sold for $400,000 and your share was $240,000?
9 that were sent to Mr. Prince by Gagosian	9 A. I'm not -- I don't -- I didn't
10 Gallery.	10 realize that painting had sold. But if that's
11 (Plaintiff's Exhibit 36, multipage	11 what it says, then it did.
12 accounting document, was marked for	12 Q. And then Naked Confessions?
13 identification, as of this date.)	13 A. Yes, I remember that painting.
14 Q. Mr. Prince, before I get to that, I	14 Q. You received 270,000 out of 450,000?
15 neglected to ask you, you know that painting on	15 A. Yes.
16 wood -- not a painting, a collage on wood from	16 Q. And the next one is Mr. Jones, that
17 the 2007 show that was called Canal Zone 2007?	17 one?
18 A. Yes.	18 A. Mr. Jones, yes.
19 Q. Did you sell that?	19 Q. That was sold for 2 million and you
20 A. No, that wasn't for sale.	20 received 1.2 million?
21 Q. You still have it?	21 A. Yes.
22 A. I have that.	22 Q. And the Scapegoat was sold for
23 Q. So now let's look at Exhibit 36.	23 2 million and you received 1.2 million, is that
24 Do you receive accountings like this?	24 right?
25 A. Yes, I believe -- yes, I do.	25 A. Yes.

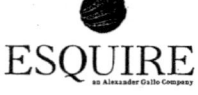

325

```
1              Prince
2    Q.   I didn't hear your answer.
3    A.   Yes.
4    Q.   And if you turn a few more pages to
5    page PR124 at the bottom?
6    A.   Yes.
7    Q.   You'll see Specially Round Midnight,
8    which was sold for it appears 2,430,000 and your
9    share was 1,458,000 dollars, is that correct?
10   A.   Wow -- yeah.  Yes.
11        MR. BROOKS:  Okay.  This is
12   Exhibit 40, we're skipping --
13        MR. HAYES:  A bunch.
14        MR. BROOKS:  We're skipping 37 and
15   38.
16        MS. BART:  And 39.
17        MR. BROOKS:  And 39.
18   In the hopes of expediting this --
19        MS. BART:  Thank you.
20        MR. BROOKS:  -- we're going to move
21   right to 40.
22        (Plaintiff's Exhibit 40, paintings
23   and photos juxtaposed, was marked for
24   identification, as of this date.)
25        MS. BART:  Mr. Brooks, can you just
```

326

```
1              Prince
2    tell me if this is something your office
3    prepared?
4         MR. BROOKS:  No, Mr. Cariou prepared
5    it with somebody else's help.  And it was
6    produced in our initial disclosure.
7         MS. BART:  No, I mean that I just
8    wanted to know the source of it.
9         MR. BROOKS:  We did not produce it.
10        MR. HAYES:  This is 40?
11        MR. BROOKS:  Yes.
12   BY MR. BROOKS:
13   Q.   Before we get to Exhibit 40, I'll
14   tell you what it is.  It's a juxtaposition I
15   guess of various of your paintings and various
16   of the photographs in Yes Rasta from which
17   images were taken in your paintings.  That's
18   what this is entitled -- that's what this is
19   intended to be.
20        At the end there are some other
21   images that maybe are not in the Canal Zone
22   book, but I'll get to those later, and they were
23   taken from the Yes Rasta book.
24        MS. BART:  And for the record, this
25   was done by Mr. Cariou and someone helping
```

327

```
1              Prince
2    him?
3         MR. BROOKS:  Yes, that's correct.
4    But as backup we have the Canal Zone
5    book and we have the Yes Rasta book.  So
6    if anything is incorrect then so be it.
7         THE WITNESS:  This could be a cool
8    book.
9         MS. BART:  Okay, stop.
10   BY MR. BROOKS:
11   Q.   Well, I'm not showing it to you in
12   your capacity as an artist.  You have to have
13   your witness hat on.
14   I'm going to ask you -- before we go
15   to this comparison, can you take the Canal Zone
16   book, which probably has been dismembered now.
17   A.   Oh, the Canal Zone book.  I don't
18   have a copy of that.
19        MS. BART:  Here.
20        THE WITNESS:  No, I need the book,
21   the actual book.
22        MR. HAYES:  They've told us this is
23   supposed to be a copy.
24        THE WITNESS:  You want the book
25   or -- oh, this?
```

328

```
1              Prince
2         MR. BROOKS:  Yes.  Go to page -- can
3    you help him, Mr. Hayes?
4         THE WITNESS:  Yeah, I got it.
5         MR. BROOKS:  Bates stamp page
6    C00118.
7         THE WITNESS:  118.
8         MR. BROOKS:  All right.  Now, just
9    keep your -- keep that place -- keep your
10   hand on there.  And, again, I'm going to
11   ask you to go back to the end of the book,
12   but don't lose that page.
13        MR. HAYES:  We got it.
14        MR. BROOKS:  Where -- the very last
15   page where there's a copyright notice.
16   Can you help him find that?  It's
17   C213.
18        MR. HAYES:  Sure.
19        THE WITNESS:  Got it.
20   BY MR. BROOKS:
21   Q.   Okay.  Now, it says that you -- all
22   artworks -- you're the copyright owner of all
23   artworks and of all insert images.  Do you see
24   that?
25   A.   Yes.
```

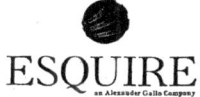
ESQUIRE
an Alexander Gallo Company

Toll Free: 800.944.9454
Facsimile: 212.557.5972

Suite 4715
One Penn Plaza
New York, NY 10119
www.esquiresolutions.com

329	331
Prince	Prince
1	1
2 Q. And, again, the inserts are those	2 You'll have to turn to the previous
3 smaller pages that are in this book?	3 page I guess C116.
4 A. Yes.	4 MR. HAYES: Yep.
5 Q. So if you go now to page C118?	5 A. Got it.
6 A. Yes.	6 Q. So C118 is taken from C116, right?
7 Q. This guy on the donkey, do you	7 A. Yes.
8 consider that to be an artwork that's in this	8 Q. And are you sure that that's a
9 book?	9 painting and not a reproduction of this
10 MR. HAYES: Objection to the form of	10 photograph from the Yes Rasta book?
11 the question, among other things, it's not	11 A. It's a painting.
12 one of the smaller inserts that's referred	12 Q. In what sense?
13 to, I don't think.	13 A. Based on a reproduction that I found
14 MR. BROOKS: I'm sorry?	14 in this Yes Rasta book.
15 MR. HAYES: You have the book in	15 Q. Which you're looking at now, right?
16 front of you. You asked the witness about	16 A. It's a lot of -- this is what I was
17 smaller inserts?	17 talking about earlier with this new technique,
18 MR. BROOKS: No, no, no. This is	18 this new medium that transferred his work, which
19 page C118. It's not an insert.	19 I don't think lost any of its original intent,
20 MR. HAYES: Oh.	20 because my work here is completely a different
21 A. And the question?	21 message and medium, it's a completely different
22 Q. Is this one of the artworks in this	22 look, and it's a completely different
23 book, this image on C118?	23 application, and it's a new way of collaging.
24 MR. HAYES: Object to the form.	24 There are several elements.
25 A. No.	25 There's also an image from Eric

330	332
Prince	Prince
1	1
2 Q. What is it?	2 Kroll. There's an image of a guitar from
3 A. It's part of an artwork that's in	3 George -- that's George Harrison's guitar with
4 the book. It's a detail.	4 his hands. And there are -- this painting on
5 Q. Are you the copyright owner, as you	5 top, it's not a photograph, it's an inkjet image
6 understand it, of this image on C118?	6 on canvas, which is a fairly new technique.
7 MR. HAYES: Objection as to form.	7 And then these lozenges are painted
8 MS. BART: Join.	8 directly on the canvas.
9 A. My answer to that is I guess so.	9 Q. Okay. You're talking about C116,
10 Q. Now, was this photo taken from the	10 right?
11 Yes Rasta book?	11 A. Yes, I am.
12 MR. HAYES: Object to the form.	12 Q. Now, can you turn to C118, which is
13 A. No, it's a painting. I mean I made	13 in your book?
14 a painting. Anyway, no.	14 A. Yes.
15 Q. This is a painting?	15 MR. HAYES: That's the detail.
16 A. Yes.	16 A. The detail.
17 Q. How did you make the painting, with	17 Q. C118.
18 a paint brush?	18 A. Yes. You can see it's ripped out of
19 A. Yes.	19 the book.
20 MS. BART: Objection, form, and	20 Q. But is it a painting or is it taken
21 argumentative.	21 from the book?
22 Q. I'm going to show you the photo of	22 A. This is a painting. The transfer,
23 this man on the donkey from the Yes Rasta book.	23 as you can see, it was -- the reproduction was
24 A. Can we see the whole painting?	24 taken from the book and then collaged next to an
25 Q. Of course.	25 additional image taken from the book, and it was

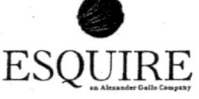

ESQUIRE
an Alexander Gallo Company

Toll Free: 800.944.9454
Facsimile: 212.557.5972

Suite 4715
One Penn Plaza
New York, NY 10119
www.esquiresolutions.com

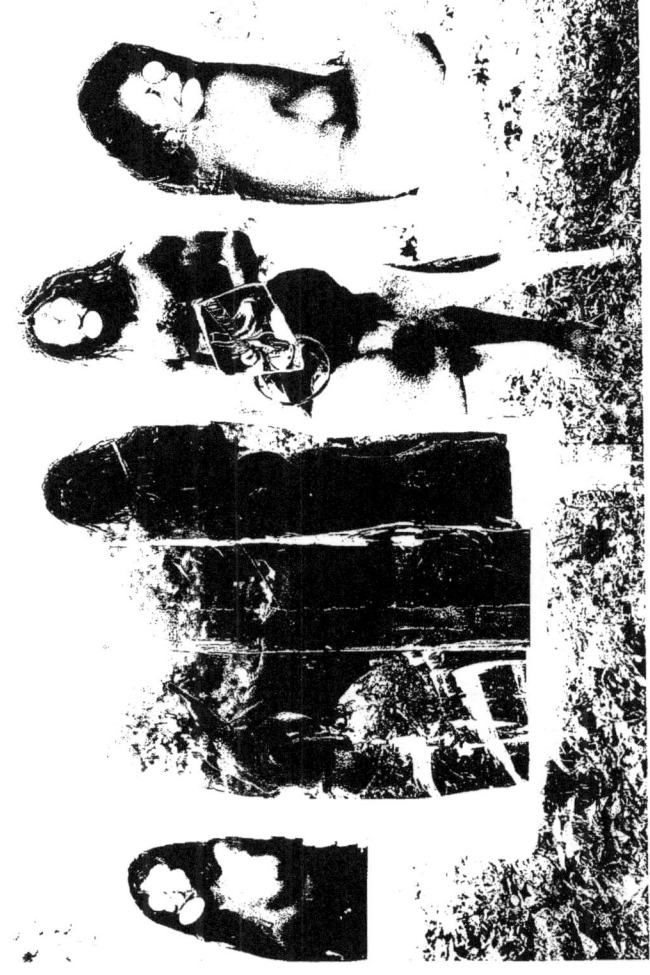

Richard Prince

October 6, 2009

333

Prince

1 a different tonality --
2 Q.   Okay --
3 MS. BART: Let him finish.
4 A.   Which I think is really important,
5 because this is a bit darker, this is lighter.
6 MR. HAYES: Let the record reflect,
7 referring to the man on the donkey and the
8 woman to the right.
9 A.   You know, the tonality here is quite
10 different. And this was a -- I mean this
11 collage was sent out to NancyScans.
12 Q.   Right.
13 A.   And then came back, as I believe, in
14 a fairly large canvas, which I then cut up the
15 canvas. These strips, as you see them here --
16 MR. HAYES: Referring to 118.
17 A.   This image then was transferred to
18 canvas and then I cut the canvas again in strips
19 and I squeegeed it. That was the new technique.
20 That's what made this painting very exciting for
21 me to paint because I couldn't control the
22 amount of paint that would come out from behind
23 the collage.
24 Q.   Right.

334

Prince

1 A.   This kind of -- no one -- I had
2 never seen that in a painting before. It was
3 almost a new way of silk screening.
4 Q.   Okay. Now, can I ask you to go back
5 to C118?
6 A.   Sure.
7 Q.   Which is what I was asking you
8 about. And I want you to look at that and then
9 compare it to the image in the Yes Rasta book.
10 And I'm just talking about those two.
11 A.   Yes.
12 Q.   I'm talking about a page in your
13 book.
14 A.   A page in my book.
15 MR. HAYES: Detail of the painting,
16 right?
17 Q.   Which you say you're the copyright
18 owner of?
19 A.   I don't say that I'm the copyright
20 owner.
21 Q.   No? Okay.
22 A.   In fact --
23 Q.   Let's just compare this image on
24 C118 with the photograph in the Yes Rasta book

335

Prince

1 because I'm very confused now.
2 Now, let's talk about C118. Are you
3 saying you painted this?
4 MS. BART: Objection, form.
5 A.   No, I just explained what I did.
6 MR. HAYES: He just told at some
7 length.
8 Q.   You cut it out of the book and then
9 squeegeed it on?
10 MR. HAYES: No, you want him to
11 explain it all again?
12 A.   You want me to --
13 Q.   I don't understand.
14 How is this a painting, that's what
15 I want to know, C118, in what way is it a
16 panting as opposed to a scanned photograph?
17 MR. HAYES: This is part of 116, you
18 got that, right?
19 Q.   I want to hear about 118.
20 A.   Again?
21 MS. BART: But it's a detail.
22 Q.   I'm aware of that, but I'm limiting
23 it to this page in your book.
24 MS. BART: Then I object to the

336

Prince

1 question.
2 A.   I understand, but I just explained
3 it. You want me to explain it again?
4 Q.   Did you paint the nose and the eyes
5 and the ears and the beard?
6 MR. HAYES: Explain it again.
7 A.   I painted on the nose and the eyes
8 and the ears.
9 Q.   Okay. So you took the photograph --
10 A.   And I also painted on the eyes and
11 the ears and the mouth of the image that was
12 next to him.
13 Q.   In 116?
14 A.   And I also painted the eyes and the
15 nose and the mouth on the women.
16 But to answer your question, yes,
17 it's -- on 118 this is a painting.
18 The process, you have to understand,
19 inkjet is four colors. Paint is mixed and it's
20 blown out on canvas. It's a completely
21 different type of texture when I receive it.
22 And then what I do is I start to
23 paint again. That's why you see all this paint
24 undemeath the image and on the image. I don't

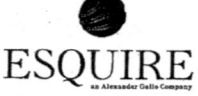

ESQUIRE
an Alexander Gallo Company

Toll Free: 800.944.9454
Facsimile: 212.557.5972

Suite 4715
One Penn Plaza
New York, NY 10119
www.esquiresolutions.com

	337		339
1	Prince	1	Prince
2	know how else to explain it.	2	kind of fantastic, absolutely hip, up to date,
3	Q. You said this has a different	3	contemporary take on the music scene. And it's
4	meaning than his photograph?	4	my way of dealing with this idea that I've
5	A. I believe so, yeah. It has a --	5	always had, which are the three relationships
6	Q. What's the meaning that's different?	6	that exist in the world, which are men and
7	MS. BART: Objection, form.	7	women, men and men, and women and women. It
8	MR. HAYES: Objection to form.	8	exists, therefore I try to reflect what I
9	A. I think my first reaction was a	9	think what interests me.
10	figure riding along the Nile in religious times,	10	I mean I don't necessarily think
11	something that I saw and that I took a picture	11	there's -- I'm not trying to -- in any artwork I
12	of years ago when I was traveling down the Nile.	12	don't think there's any one message. I'm not a
13	I was very surprised that -- it was	13	political artist. If you can tell me who the
14	the idea of transportation, that it's a type of	14	president of France was when Gauguin was in
15	transportation that I'm not familiar with.	15	Tahiti I'll give you a thousand dollars.
16	I mean that was my -- I suppose my	16	Politicians come and go, art comes and comes.
17	initial -- you know, and it gets back to this	17	Q. You mentioned the music scene.
18	idea of Back to the Garden, this kind of Adam	18	You'll notice in C116, the image of the
19	and Eve kind of thing I was thinking about.	19	Rastafarian on the donkey to the right, the one
20	I mean that was my -- those are my	20	with the paint --
21	kind of -- the way I riff on an image when I	21	A. The bleached out --
22	first come upon it.	22	Q. That one --
23	At least this is what -- again,	23	A. -- which is extremely, you know, I
24	there's many interpretations about any	24	thought about bleaching him out, getting him a
25	particular image. But this just happens to be	25	little lighter.

	338		340
1	Prince	1	Prince
2	mine.	2	Q. But that's not my question.
3	I know that that's not the original	3	A. Oh.
4	intent of the image, but I don't have any -- I	4	Q. This has a guitar, right?
5	don't have any really interest in what the	5	A. Yes.
6	original intent is because my -- because what I	6	Q. So is that what you were talking
7	do is I completely try to change it into	7	about, commenting on the music scene?
8	something that's completely different.	8	A. The guitar, again, is what I think
9	Q. And just again, what is your intent,	9	my contribution is to the image, one of the
10	what are you changing it into?	10	contributions to this particular image, just
11	A. To make great artworks that make	11	like the mask was my contribution to the nurse
12	people feel good.	12	paintings. Once I make some sort of connection.
13	Q. But is this -- let's take 116 since	13	Now, if that hadn't been made, this
14	you seem to prefer to talk about 116.	14	guitar, this collage, which turns this -- the
15	MR. HAYES: Object to the form, if	15	original intentions of this image into something
16	there's a question.	16	completely different, obviously, he's playing
17	Q. Which is this painting Back to the	17	the guitar now, it looks like he's playing the
18	Garden, right? Okay?	18	guitar, it looks as if he's always played the
19	A. Mm-hmm. Yes, I'm sorry.	19	guitar, that's what my message was.
20	Q. What is your message or what is the	20	Q. Okay.
21	meaning of this painting, what is it that you're	21	A. Is to sort of tell people, hey, this
22	trying to get across?	22	guy is playing the guitar.
23	A. I'm trying --	23	Q. Understood.
24	MR. HAYES: Object to the form.	24	A. And --
25	A. As I said, I'm trying to make a	25	Q. I'm kind of -- I don't mean to cut

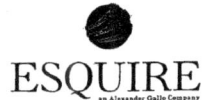

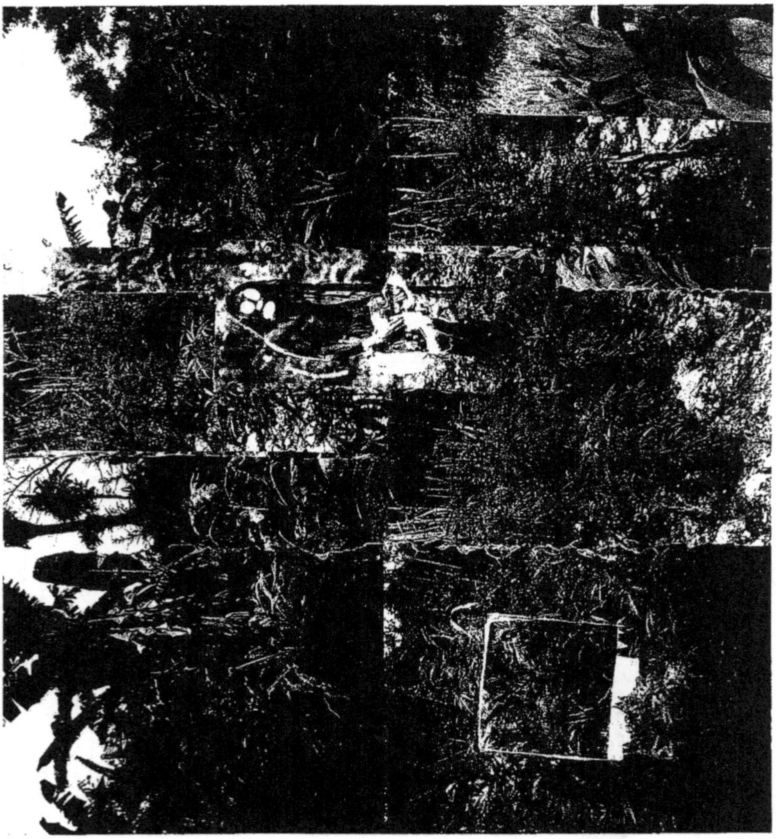

7   Canal Zone

341

1   Prince
2 you off, but I'm trying to finish by 6:15.
3   A.   Okay. I'm sorry.
4   Q.   I think you're answering the
5 questions but then you seem to feel you need to
6 give me more information.
7   A.   I'm sorry.
8   Q.   And if you have to, you have to, but
9 I'd like to get out of here at 6:15.
10   A.   Okay.
11   Q.   So on this painting C116, we talked
12 before about this post-apocalyptic vision?
13   A.   Yes.
14   Q.   Does this painting Back to the
15 Garden on C116 fit into that vision?
16   A.   I think so.
17   Q.   In what way?
18   A.   They don't have much clothes on.
19   Q.   Right. Well, the women don't have
20 any clothes on?
21   A.   He doesn't have much clothes on
22 either. And he's riding a donkey.
23   Q.   Right, so that's post-apocalyptic --
24   A.   So you can't fill up a donkey at the
25 gas tank.

342

1   Prince
2   Q.   Right.
3   A.   Maybe that has something to do with
4 it. I mean I don't think the original intent of
5 that image on a donkey ever thought about
6 filling up the donkey with a gas tank at the gas
7 station. I don't even know if there's gas
8 stations in Jamaica. You know, that's not my --
9   Q.   There are.
10   A.   That's not what I think about.
11   Q.   Okay.
12   A.   What I think about is how can this
13 collage form a new kind of band, and the band is
14 called Back to the Garden. I mean I think
15 there's even a song by Joni Mitchell called Back
16 to the Garden.
17   Q.   Right.
18   A.   It was at Woodstock. I see this as
19 a kind of a Woodstock picture. I went to
20 Woodstock --
21   Q.   And you took acid, so did Glenn
22 O'Brien, I read that.
23   A.   -- and I took one photograph.
24   Q.   With your last remaining --
25   A.   With my -- which is an important

343

1   Prince
2 point.
3   Q.   It is. No, never mind.
4   Does it relate to this painting?
5   A.   Again, it's a reading. This could
6 be about --
7   Q.   Taking acid at Woodstock?
8   A.   No, I didn't take acid at Woodstock.
9 I do think it could be a reading because of the
10 title and because Joni Mitchell wrote it.
11   I just -- actually, it didn't occur
12 to me until this moment that she wrote that.
13   Q.   Right. Okay. So this is supposed
14 to be a rock-and-roll band, these four people?
15   A.   Yes. Actually --
16   Q.   And the donkey, what instrument does
17 he play?
18   MR. HAYES: Objection.
19   A.   He's the roadie.
20   Q.   He's the roadie? Okay.
21   Now, take a look at this comparison
22 that we marked as Exhibit 40 before.
23   Now, these pages are Bates stamped
24 at the bottom. So could you turn to 39, C00039?
25   A.   Yes.

344

1   Prince
2   Q.   And this is taken from the insert in
3 your book?
4   A.   Yes. No, I had it right here.
5 There's another insert also.
6   Q.   There are three inserts?
7   A.   Yes.
8   Q.   But let's stick with this picture
9 here.
10   A.   Okay.
11   Q.   So the one on the bottom is a photo
12 in the Yes Rasta book?
13   A.   Yes, it is. It's a reproduction in
14 the book, yes.
15   Q.   Right. Of a photo.
16   And above looks like you've taken
17 that entire photo and put it in your studio?
18   A.   I've taken the entire photo and had
19 it, the inkjet process, blown up to a very large
20 scale on canvas and stretched it on stretcher
21 bars. That's what we're looking at on the top
22 of that photo.
23   Q.   Let me just find -- okay. Here is
24 the photo in the book. Here it is, okay?
25   A.   Yes.

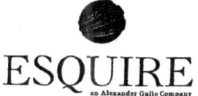

ESQUIRE
an Alexander Gallo Company

Toll Free: 800.944.9454
Facsimile: 212.557.5972

Suite 4715
One Penn Plaza
New York, NY 10119
www.esquiresolutions.com

Richard Prince   October 6, 2009

	345			347	
1	Prince		1	Prince	
2	Q. Do you agree that's the photo?		2	A. Yes.	
3	A. That's the photograph. That's the		3	Q. It's your studio. Okay.	
4	reproduction.		4	Now, this page from the insert in	
5	Q. Are you saying that the thing in		5	your Yes Rasta book, the top part --	
6	your -- is this in your studio?		6	A. Yes.	
7	A. Not any longer.		7	Q. -- of C39, how is it changing the	
8	Q. Well, where was this?		8	meaning of the photo on the bottom, if it is,	
9	A. Where was it?		9	can you explain that?	
10	Q. Yes.		10	A. I can. It will change.	
11	A. I'll show you.		11	Q. Right.	
12	This is --		12	A. Because this was a way of	
13	Q. No, no, no, no, no.		13	documenting how I transferred the original	
14	You misunderstand --		14	image. So on the next insert it's the same	
15	A. You asked me where the photograph		15	photo turned upside down, these lozenges were	
16	is.		16	then painted. Now, this is --	
17	Q. No.		17	Q. Just tell us the number of that	
18	A. And I'm answering you.		18	because no one will know what you're talking	
19	Q. No, no, no, no.		19	about.	
20	MR. HAYES: He's asking you whether		20	A. C00185.	
21	or not --		21	Q. Okay.	
22	Q. When this was taken -- I'm just		22	A. Now, this painting -- then I kept	
23	trying to explain what this is showing. That's		23	looking at it. And I wasn't satisfied with how	
24	all.		24	it looked.	
25	A. Okay.		25	Q. Right.	

	346			348	
1	Prince		1	Prince	
2	Q. I'm not asking you where it is.		2	A. This painting turned into this	
3	A. Okay. I thought you were asking me		3	painting which is called Inquisition.	
4	where it was.		4	This, it started out -- this is how	
5	Q. There is this picture in the		5	things start out. This is how -- these are the	
6	Yes Rasta book, right?		6	possibilities of appropriation. And this is --	
7	A. Yes.		7	it just happened that I documented -- I very	
8	Q. And now you, in the insert in your		8	rarely document the process.	
9	Canal Zone book, you are showing this entire		9	Q. Right.	
10	photo with some other things around it?		10	A. But this was what I got back from	
11	A. Yes.		11	the photo lab, then I painted -- I turned it	
12	Q. Can you explain to me -- maybe you		12	upside down thinking about George Baselitz the	
13	already did -- where this -- first, where was		13	painter, how he turns his images upside down.	
14	this taken, the photo in the top part of this?		14	I was sort of riffing on George Baselitz.	
15	MS. BART: Objection, form.		15	I painted my lozenger head to kind	
16	A. Where was it taken?		16	of obscure his face. I didn't particularly like	
17	Q. Okay. Let me show you --		17	it. And then I decided to -- there's only a	
18	A. It was taken from the -- the image		18	small remnant. I mean this is a bad	
19	was taken from the Yes Rasta book.		19	reproduction, but there's a small remnant of the	
20	Q. I understand. And then enlarged?		20	lozenger about here.	
21	A. Enlarged.		21	I then had -- I cut up -- this is a	
22	Q. And then placed in a room, I see		22	woman with a dog and a guitar, and these are	
23	behind there some bookshelf --		23	more -- these are more Rasta heads with crazy	
24	A. Yes, that's my studio.		24	De Kooning type of faces.	
25	Q. That's what I'm asking you.		25	Q. Okay. This image --	

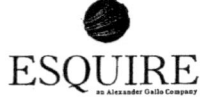

ESQUIRE
an Alexander Gallo Company

Toll Free: 800.944.9454
Facsimile: 212.557.5972

Suite 4715
One Penn Plaza
New York, NY 10119
www.esquiresolutions.com

349

	Prince
1	Prince
2	A. So this painting is what was -- this
3	was shown. This was shown at Gagosian.
4	Q. This, referring to C39?
5	A. Yes. But it was shown -- this is
6	the painting.
7	Q. And what are you referring to there?
8	A. I'm referring to Inquisition.
9	Q. Now, this gentleman here, getting
10	back to the Yes Rasta book, did you also use him
11	in the Canal Zone 2007 collage, the same guy?
12	A. 2007, I think I did.
13	Q. Take a look at Exhibit 14.
14	A. What was it, 2007 collage? Yeah.
15	Q. Take a look at Exhibit 14.
16	A. I did. I remember the hat.
17	Q. He's the same guy, right?
18	A. Well, it's the hat.
19	Q. Well, just take a look at it. I
20	don't want you to guess.
21	MR. HAYES: That's 15 but it's the
22	same painting.
23	MR. BROOKS: It's the same painting.
24	A. Yeah, I drew a face on him.
25	Q. Same guy though?

350

	Prince
1	Prince
2	A. I drew a very Picasso-like face.
3	Q. So you had actually changed him in
4	2007 before Canal Zone?
5	A. Well, I think it was the fact that
6	I found -- I sort of made a more -- a bigger
7	commitment because of the guitar.
8	Q. Okay.
9	A. That's when I started to make the
10	paintings.
11	Q. Do you agree with me that in C39 --
12	if you go back to C39?
13	A. Yes.
14	Q. This is in Exhibit 40.
15	A. Right.
16	Q. That this entire portrait of the
17	Rasta from Yes Rasta is depicted in its entirety
18	without having been changed?
19	And I know you did something later,
20	but in this picture.
21	MS. BART: Objection, form.
22	Q. You can answer.
23	A. It's different.
24	Q. How is it different?
25	A. It's bigger, it's on canvas, and

351

	Prince
1	Prince
2	it's been inkjetted.
3	Q. By who?
4	A. Inkjetted by NancyScans.
5	And then it's been stretched.
6	Q. Okay. Let's look -- now, I'm still
7	with Exhibit 40 here.
8	A. Oh, here we go.
9	There's the painting right here.
10	MR. HAYES: Get the number.
11	Q. Inquisition?
12	A. C40.
13	Q. That's Inquisition?
14	A. Yes.
15	Q. Okay. Now, let me ask you to look
16	at C24, Mr. Prince.
17	MS. BART: You said 24?
18	MR. BROOKS: 24, yes, in Exhibit --
19	MR. HAYES: 40.
20	MR. BROOKS: -- 40.
21	A. Yes.
22	Q. Now, this one has one of the Rastas
23	in the middle there, correct, your painting?
24	A. Yes.
25	Q. And this one is called Canal Zone,

352

	Prince
1	Prince
2	right?
3	A. Yes.
4	Q. And do you see that everything else,
5	all the squares of tropical landscaping around
6	it were all taken from Yes Rasta?
7	A. I can see that it's implied here,
8	yes.
9	Q. Well, isn't it -- in fact, that's
10	how you made this particular painting, right?
11	A. No.
12	Q. Are you saying there's landscaping
13	there that wasn't taken from Yes Rasta?
14	A. To my best recollection, there might
15	have been some Tahiti. I'm not saying this, but
16	there was a Tahiti book that I was also cutting
17	up at the same time, and some of the Tahiti
18	landscapes were getting into the paintings.
19	It's hard to see -- it's hard to
20	tell because of the reproduction is so small,
21	but it doesn't make any difference to me whether
22	it's the Tahiti landscape or the Yes Rasta
23	landscape. I mean to me the landscape was
24	Panamanian.
25	MR. BROOKS: Let's take a break.

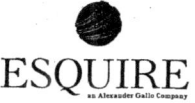

ESQUIRE
an Alexander Gallo Company

Toll Free: 800.944.9454
Facsimile: 212.557.5972

Suite 4715
One Penn Plaza
New York, NY 10119
www.esquiresolutions.com

Richard Prince. *Djuna Barnes. Natalie Barney. Renée Vivien and Romaine Brooks take over the Guanahani.* 2008. 52 1/4 x 90 1/2 inches (plate 14 in book)

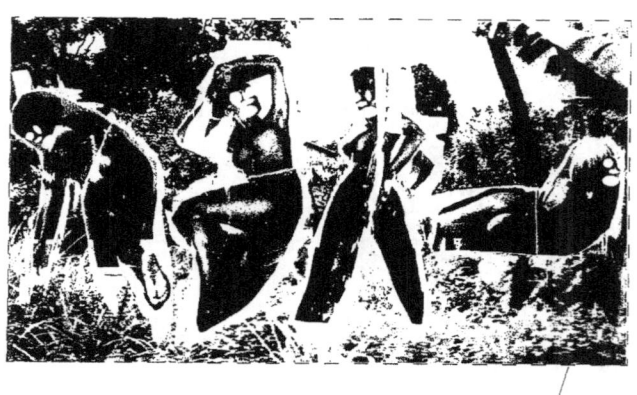

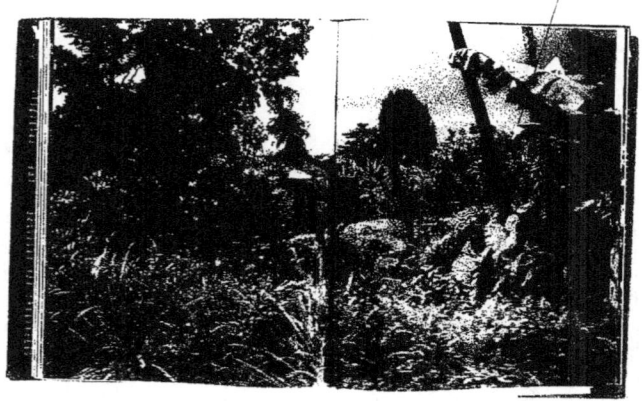

Yes Rasta! ©Patrick Cariou. 2000. Published by Powerhouse books. inc.

16

353		355	
1	Prince	1	Prince
2	THE VIDEOGRAPHER: 5:51. Off the	2	Q. Right. But any landscaping could do
3	record. End of tape 5.	3	that, right?
4	(Recess taken: 5:51 p.m.)	4	MS. BART: Object to form.
5	(Proceedings resumed: 5:55 p.m.)	5	MR. HAYES: Object to form.
6	THE VIDEOGRAPHER: 5:55. On the	6	A. Not really. I don't think my front
7	record. Beginning of tape 6.	7	lawn in Wainscott would do that trick.
8	BY MR. BROOKS:	8	Q. But any tropical landscape would be
9	Q. Now, this painting on C24 where you	9	able to do the same?
10	took landscapes from Yes Rasta and inserted one	10	MS. BART: Objection, form,
11	of the Rastas in the middle, what is the new	11	speculative.
12	meaning or message or artistic expression in	12	Q. You can answer.
13	that painting?	13	A. I don't know.
14	A. I was thinking about camouflage,	14	Q. Turn to C30 in the Exhibit 40. This
15	hiding in plain sight, thinking about Warhol's	15	is Djuna Barnes, Natalie Barney, et cetera.
16	camouflage paintings.	16	A. I've got the wrong one.
17	Q. Are you -- in this painting on C24	17	Which one?
18	are you commenting on any aspects of culture?	18	MR. HAYES: C30.
19	MS. BART: Object to form.	19	Q. C30.
20	A. I'm sorry, we're on the same	20	A. C30, yes.
21	painting?	21	Q. You have that?
22	Q. 24, C24.	22	A. Yes.
23	MR. HAYES: Object to form.	23	Q. The top part is your painting Djuna
24	A. I would say a musician is a solo	24	Barnes, Natalie Barney, et cetera, Take Over the
25	artist, maybe, if that's -- is that culture?	25	Guanahani, correct?

354		356	
1	Prince	1	Prince
2	Yeah.	2	A. Yes.
3	Q. So the musician is this Rasta with a	3	Q. And now beneath that do you see that
4	guitar?	4	the entire backdrop to those four women is taken
5	A. The musician is actually Neil Young.	5	from the Yes Rasta book?
6	Q. It's supposed to be Neil Young?	6	And here I've turned in the
7	A. Yes.	7	Yes Rasta book to that photo which takes up two
8	Q. Because it's called Canal Zone or	8	pages. Do you see that?
9	because of some other reason?	9	A. Yes --
10	A. It's Neil Young's guitar.	10	MR. HAYES: Objection, form.
11	Q. So you're not commenting on the	11	Q. What's the answer?
12	landscape in this painting, right?	12	A. Yes, I believe I used that
13	MR. HAYES: Objection to the form,	13	reproduction as a background material for this
14	asked and answered.	14	new painting.
15	Q. You can answer.	15	Q. For instance -- I'm sorry.
16	MS. BART: Same.	16	In the upper right there's a palm
17	A. I don't really make comments with	17	frond or something. Do you see that?
18	any of my work.	18	A. Yes.
19	Q. But the landscaping is not the	19	Q. It's very distinctive, right?
20	subject of this painting Canal Zone's page C24?	20	MR. HAYES: Objection to form.
21	MR. HAYES: Object to form.	21	MS. BART: Objection, form.
22	MS. BART: Same.	22	Q. You can answer.
23	Q. You can answer.	23	A. I don't --
24	A. Well, it helps to make it appear	24	Q. It's very noticeable, right?
25	like camouflage, the shapes.	25	MS. BART: Objection, form.

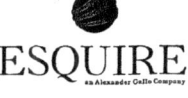

ESQUIRE
an Alexander Gallo Company

Toll Free: 800.944.9454
Facsimile: 212.557.5972

Suite 4715
One Penn Plaza
New York, NY 10119
www.esquiresolutions.com

357

```
1              Prince
2        MR. HAYES: Same.
3     A.   In the book?
4     Q.   Yes.
5     A.   Or in the painting?
6     Q.   Let's start with the book.
7     A.   Not really.
8     Q.   How about in your painting?
9     A.   Not really. No.
10    Q.   You notice it there, right?
11    A.   You're pointing it out to me, yes.
12    Q.   Well, you -- sir, you're the person
13    who took these pages from Yes Rasta and used it
14    as the backdrop for this painting called
15    Djuna Barnes, et cetera, Take Over the
16    Guanahani, right?
17    A.   Yes, I did.
18    Q.   Okay. Why?
19    A.   I wanted these women to take over
20    the Guanahani.
21    Q.   And where is the Guanahani?
22    A.   It's in St. Barth.
23    Q.   No, no, no. In this painting?
24    A.   It's behind the woman on the right.
25    She's covering it up.
```

358

```
1              Prince
2     Q.   So you can't see it?
3     A.   I was speaking figuratively. It's a
4     poetic title that refers to my impressions of
5     what I wanted to try to say in the painting.
6     Q.   Let's stick with what's actually
7     there.
8        MS. BART: Objection.
9        MR. HAYES: Objection to form.
10    A.   I'm not interested -- I've never
11    been interested in what's actually there.
12    Q.   Sir --
13    A.   I think these photographs are
14    interested in what's actually there. I've never
15    been interested in what's actually there. I
16    would like to make that point.
17       (Time noted: 6:00 p.m.)
18    Q.   I understand.
19       Just explain to me why you took
20    these four images -- these are supposed to be
21    the four lesbians, correct?
22    A.   They're supposed to be, yes.
23    Q.   And behind them you have taken a
24    tropical landscape from Yes Rasta, correct?
25       MS. BART: Objection, form.
```

359

```
1              Prince
2        MR. HAYES: Objection, form.
3     A.   I've used this particular image as
4     part of a collage in creating the painting Djuna
5     Barnes, Natalie Barney, Renée Vivien, Romaine
6     Brooks Take Over the Guanahani.
7     Q.   When you say you've taken this image
8     or this the photograph, you're pointing to the
9     Yes Rasta book, correct?
10       MS. BART: Objection, form.
11    A.   I said I used --
12    Q.   You said this --
13    A.   This image.
14    Q.   And that means this image in the
15    Yes Rasta book that you're pointing to?
16    A.   Yes.
17    Q.   And tell us why you did that.
18       MR. HAYES: Objection to form, asked
19    and answered.
20    A.   To make the painting called Djuna
21    Barnes, Natalie Barney, Renée Vivien, Romaine
22    Brooks Take over the Guanahani. I don't know
23    how else to explain it.
24    Q.   Isn't that kind of reductive?
25       MS. BART: Objection, form, and
```

360

```
1              Prince
2     argumentative.
3     A.   You're right. This is a very
4     reductive painting. This is very minimal --
5     Q.   I meant your answer. Never mind.
6     You said you did it because you did
7     it and I'm trying to understand why you did it.
8        MR. HAYES: Objection to form.
9        MS. BART: And asked and answered.
10    Q.   Let me withdraw that.
11    A.   Okay. I can answer it.
12    Q.   No, let me withdraw it. I'm going
13    to ask you more specific questions.
14       In superimposing these four images
15    over the landscape from Yes Rasta, right, were
16    you commenting on any aspects of culture?
17    A.   No.
18    Q.   Were you trying to create anything
19    with a new meaning or a new message?
20    A.   No.
21       MS. BART: Objection, form.
22    Q.   Were you trying to create something
23    new and unique?
24       MS. BART: Objection, form.
25       MR. HAYES: Objection, form.
```

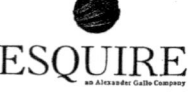

ESQUIRE
an Alexander Gallo Company

Toll Free: 800.944.9454
Facsimile: 212.557.5972

Suite 4715
One Penn Plaza
New York, NY 10119
www.esquiresolutions.com

	361			363
1	Prince		1	Prince
2	A. Yes.		2	Q. You put a guitar on and some paint
3	Q. What?		3	on the face, right?
4	A. A balls-out, great, unbelievably		4	A. I collaged the guitar and I painted
5	looking great painting that had to do with a		5	the face, yes.
6	kind of a rock-and-roll painting on the radical		6	Q. And what new meaning or artistic
7	side, and on a conservative side something to do		7	expression have you added to the Yes Rasta
8	with Cézanne's bathers.		8	photo?
9	Q. Okay.		9	MS. BART: Objection, form.
10	A. So the melding of the two left wing,		10	MR. HAYES: Object to form.
11	right wing, would maybe make a middle wing. I		11	A. That's pretty simple. I was
12	guess that's the way I could explain it.		12	thinking about the guitar as the new fig leaf,
13	Q. All right.		13	which I think is an interesting idea.
14	Can you take a look at C18?		14	I don't see a fig leaf on this
15	MR. HAYES: C what?		15	particular image. I'm referring to the image
16	Q. C0018.		16	that's a reproduction in Yes Rasta.
17	Do you see that, C18?		17	Q. Could you look at C32?
18	A. Yes.		18	Is that Tales of Brave Ulysses?
19	Q. This particular Rasta, would you		19	A. Yes.
20	agree you used him a number of times in the		20	Q. Now, there you've used that same
21	Canal Zone paintings?		21	Rasta four times but haven't painted on his face
22	A. Yes.		22	or put on a guitar, correct?
23	Q. In fact, you also used him, among		23	A. That's correct.
24	other places, in C23?		24	Q. So how have you added a new meaning
25	A. Yes.		25	or message or commented on aspects of culture in

	362			364
1	Prince		1	Prince
2	Q. Now, which of these, C18 or C23, was		2	your painting as compared to the photo from
3	the basis for the invitation to the Canal Zone		3	Yes Rasta?
4	show, if you know?		4	MS. BART: Objection to form.
5	A. C18.		5	MR. HAYES: Objection, form.
6	Q. The first one?		6	A. I'm not sure if I have to comment on
7	A. Oh, no.		7	culture with every single painting.
8	Q. One is called Graduation and the		8	Q. Well, I'm just asking you about this
9	other is called Meditation.		9	painting?
10	A. I believe it was C18, but I could be		10	A. I think the -- Tales of Brave
11	mistaken. But my feeling is it's C18.		11	Ulysses was written by the Cream, the group.
12	Q. It's one of those two?		12	Q. The Cream?
13	A. I believe so, yes.		13	A. The Cream.
14	Q. So let's take C18. What is the		14	Q. So this is another music --
15	different message or meaning of your painting as		15	A. It was a musical band that I really
16	opposed to this photograph?		16	like and I really like that song. And the
17	MS. BART: Objection, form.		17	rhythm, the repetition of the images, the
18	A. I don't see any photograph.		18	different scales, I wanted to kind of get this
19	Q. The image on the bottom is taken		19	idea of the rhythm of how that song -- what
20	from Yes Rasta, correct?		20	impression that song makes to me when I was
21	A. Yes, it is.		21	listening to it I believe.
22	Q. And the image at the top is your --		22	Q. Which song?
23	is a reproduction of your painting, right?		23	A. Tales of Brave Ulysses.
24	A. Yes.		24	Q. So this -- your painting, what is
25	MS. BART: Objection, form.		25	the Rasta and these women, is supposed to

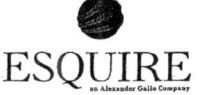

Toll Free: 800.944.9454
Facsimile: 212.557.5972

Suite 4715
One Penn Plaza
New York, NY 10119
www.esquiresolutions.com

Richard Prince

October 6, 2009

365

1   Prince
2   conjure up that song?
3   MR. HAYES: Object to the form.
4   MS. BART: Join.
5   A.   I tried, yes, to conjure up the
6   feeling I had for that song.
7   Q.   Now, does this painting Tales of
8   Brave Ulysses fit into the post-apocalyptic
9   theme that we discussed before?
10   A.   Yes.
11   Q.   Are you implying in this painting
12   that these black Rastafarians are potentially
13   dangerous to these naked white women, that they
14   might rape them?
15   MR. HAYES: Objection, form.
16   MS. BART: Objection, form.
17   Q.   You can answer.
18   A.   No.
19   Q.   Not at all?
20   MR. HAYES: Objection, form.
21   A.   No.
22   Q.   What, if anything, are you -- what
23   is your message, if any, with respect to the
24   juxtaposition of this Rasta and these naked
25   women? Without any guitars, right?

366

1   Prince
2   A.   My daughter would say I was slapping
3   the bass.
4   Q.   What does that mean?
5   A.   I don't believe I have to interpret
6   or explain slapping the bass. It's a reggae
7   term.
8   Q.   Well, just enlighten us --
9   A.   As far as I know --
10   Q.   Enlighten us since we're not --
11   A.   It's about jamming. I'm jamming.
12   Q.   Okay.
13   A.   I believe that this is a kind of
14   painting that suggests, or I would hope that it
15   would suggest that type of activity.
16   Q.   All right.
17   A.   I mean you've --
18   Q.   Seeing these people as a band, a
19   rock-and-roll band?
20   A.   Yes.
21   MR. BROOKS: Last exhibit, 41?
22   (Clarification by reporter.)
23   MR. BROOKS: This will be 43.
24   (Plaintiff's Exhibit 43, pictures
25   from Yes Rasta, was marked for

367

1   Prince
2   identification, as of this date.)
3   Q.   Mr. Prince, these let me explain
4   what these are, although you may know.
5   But these were made available to us
6   by your attorney. And Mr. Boden here went over
7   there and looked at what you had written in the
8   Rasta book, Yes Rasta book.
9   Remember you said you had it and
10   were writing in it and cutting things out?
11   And so this is what was made
12   available to us.
13   MR. BROOKS: And we asked for these
14   to be copied, am I right, Mr. Hayes?
15   MR. HAYES: You're right that he
16   took photographs of them. I don't think
17   we copied them. You took photos?
18   MR. BODEN: Yes.
19   MR. BROOKS: But these were made
20   available by you, right?
21   MR. HAYES: I assume so, yes. I
22   have no reason to doubt it --
23   THE WITNESS: Why are they all
24   upside down?
25   MR. HAYES: I don't think they were

368

1   Prince
2   made available in this form or this
3   order --
4   (Clarification by reporter.)
5   MR. HAYES: I can't say that they
6   were made available in this form or this
7   order, but I certainly accept the
8   representation by Eric that he made
9   photocopies of them -- he made photos of
10   them at my office.
11   BY MR. BROOKS:
12   Q.   Anyway, we'll let you decide,
13   Mr. Prince, what this is. Maybe you'll say I
14   never saw this before.
15   So I'm led to believe this was a
16   production made from your documents from your --
17   what you wrote in the book. But --
18   A.   These things? They're all
19   different. I mean --
20   MR. HAYES: That's not true.
21   A.   -- there are a whole bunch of
22   different --
23   MR. HAYES: Ask Eric if he copied
24   them.
25   MR. BROOKS: Well, let's look at the

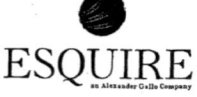

ESQUIRE
an Alexander Gallo Company

Toll Free: 800.944.9454
Facsimile: 212.557.5972

Suite 4715
One Penn Plaza
New York, NY 10119
www.esquiresolutions.com

Richard Prince. *Tales of Brave Ulysses*. 2008. 84 x 132 inches (plate 16 in book)

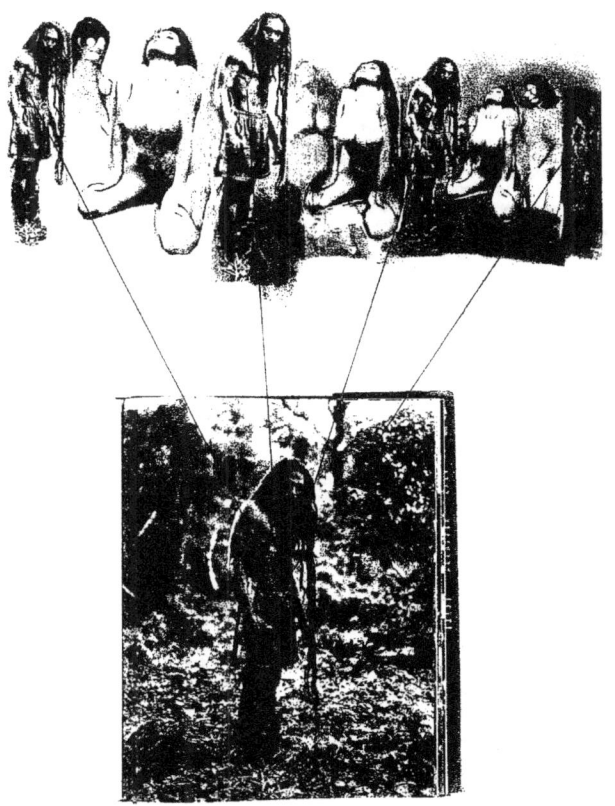

Yes Rasta! ©Patrick Cariou, 2000. Published by Powerhouse books, inc.

18

369

Prince

1   first one since time is passing.
2   (Clarification by reporter.)
3   THE WITNESS: They were not handed
4   to me --
5   MR. BROOKS: Can I just see that to
6   make sure we're talking about -- okay.
7   MS. BART: Oh, so there's no
8   Bates Numbers on them?
9   MR. BROOKS: No, because they
10 weren't produced. They were just --
11 You copied them with a digital
12 camera from Mr. Hayes's files?
13 MS. BART: Are there any others
14 besides these that have not been produced?
15 MR. BODEN: We didn't produce them.
16 MR. HAYES: I think she's asking the
17 question just to clarify. Are there other
18 photos, Eric, that were taken that are not
19 part of this package?
20 MR. BODEN: Yes.
21 RQ MS. BART: I'm going to call for
22 their production so everybody has the same
23 thing.
24 MR. BROOKS: You can go over there

370

Prince

1   like we did and inspect and copy. That's
2   all we did.
3   MR. HAYES: She's asking for
4   production of whatever Eric --
5   MS. BART: I want the copies --
6   MR. BROOKS: Let's not waste time.
7   MR. HAYES: Go ahead. Ask your
8   question.
9   BY MR. BROOKS:
10 Q. So the first page, what is that?
11 A. The first page?
12 Q. Yeah.
13 A. It looks to me like drawing --
14 drawings on images that appeared in the
15 Yes Rasta book.
16 Q. Drawings by whom?
17 A. Myself.
18 Q. Okay. So what are you showing on
19 this first page, how have you changed this Rasta
20 with your drawing?
21 MS. BART: Objection, form.
22 MR. HAYES: Objection, form too.
23 Q. You can answer.
24 A. How have I changed it?

371

Prince

1   Q. Yes.
2   A. I changed it with oil crayon.
3   Q. I don't mean the materials. What
4   are you -- what is the meaning of these two
5   drawings?
6   A. There is no meaning.
7   MS. BART: Objection, form.
8   Q. Are you showing a monkey-like look?
9   A. No.
10 Q. Is there a picture in here of
11 Bob Marley or one of his children?
12 A. Right here. Bob Marley.
13 Q. That is Bob Marley?
14 A. Yes.
15 Q. And I think there's another one too.
16 So did you use that Bob Marley image
17 in the Canal Zone book?
18 A. In the Canal Zone book, the catalog,
19 no.
20 Q. Or in the show?
21 A. No.
22 Q. Let me ask you to look at this one.
23 Is that somebody from the Yes Rasta book?
24 MS. BART: How are we going to

372

Prince

1   create a record as to what this one is?
2   I can't even find the one about
3   Mr. Marley, I can't find that one because
4   they're not numbered.
5   MR. BROOKS: Right.
6   MR. HAYES: That's a problem.
7   MS. BART: I'm not sure I have a
8   complete exhibit.
9   MR. BROOKS: Mark this as 43A.
10 (Discussion off the record.)
11 MR. HAYES: It's 6:15.
12 MR. BROOKS: I'm just going to ask
13 him about these four paintings and then
14 we'll leave.
15 MR. HAYES: You've got to ask them
16 quickly because we had a deal. It's
17 6:15 --
18 MR. BROOKS: But there was a break
19 and there were a lot of objections.
20 THE WITNESS: No, we had a deal --
21 MR. HAYES: There was no objections.
22 We took a break because the videotape guy
23 had to change it.
24 MR. BROOKS: I'm just going to ask

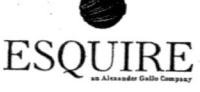

Richard Prince   October 6, 2009

373	375
1 Prince	1 Prince
2 him to identify these documents and	2 Here's 43C. Is that the picture of
3 then --	3 Bob Marley?
4 THE WITNESS: I'm sorry, you	4 A. Yes.
5 promised 6:15. I'm sorry.	5 Q. And where -- that wasn't in the
6 MR. BROOKS: So you're leaving?	6 Yes Rasta book, was it?
7 (Interruption by court reporter.)	7 A. No.
8 MR. HAYES: Stop marking the	8 Q. That came from your files?
9 documents for a moment.	9 A. Yes.
10 Give him the documents, ask him if	10 Q. And you were thinking of using this
11 he can identify them, we'll mark them	11 in the Canal Zone show?
12 after he leaves.	12 A. I don't know.
13 MS. BART: Fine with me.	13 Q. Here's 43A. What is this?
14 MR. BROOKS: Well, I didn't think	14 A. It's a collage. It's hard to say.
15 that was fine with you.	15 It's a collage of female genitalia, four
16 MS. BART: Well --	16 collages of female genitalia, on what, I don't
17 MR. BROOKS: You seemed extremely	17 know. I believe it's on a landscape image that
18 upset about it --	18 came from the Yes Rasta book.
19 (Multiple speakers talking at once.)	19 Q. And this is the last thing. So we
20 MS. BART: It's highly improper to	20 have 43A, B, and C. The first page that you
21 put this out here without giving it to	21 looked at that was part of 43, I want to make
22 everyone in advance.	22 that 43D, just that one page, because the whole
23 BY MR. BROOKS:	23 thing is dismembered.
24 Q. Let me see one at a time, and I'm	24 MR. HAYES: That one?
25 just going to ask you a simple question about	25 MS. BART: This one?

374	376
1 Prince	1 Prince
2 each.	2 MR. BROOKS: Correct. Yes, we'll
3 All right. Let's take this one,	3 make this one --
4 which is going to be 43B, a picture of a	4 (Multiple speakers talking at once.)
5 Rastafarian holding something.	5 MR. BROOKS: We'll make that one
6 43B, write that down.	6 43D. And you already testified about
7 Is that something you did in the	7 that.
8 Yes Rasta book?	8 MR. HAYES: You're done.
9 A. No.	9 MR. BROOKS: The two faces.
10 Q. Do you know what that is?	10 (Multiple speakers talking at once.)
11 A. Yes.	11 THE VIDEOGRAPHER: This concludes
12 Q. What is it?	12 the deposition of Richard Prince. The
13 A. It's a collage.	13 time is 6:20 p.m. End of tape number 6.
14 Q. That you did?	14 Off the record.
15 A. Yes.	15 (Discussion off the record.)
16 Q. And the image of the Rastafarian,	16 (Plaintiff's Exhibit 43A, landscape
17 did that come from the Yes Rasta book?	17 from Yes Rasta with female genitalia, was
18 A. Yes.	18 marked for identification, as of this
19 Q. And you added in a cartoon or --	19 date.)
20 A. It's called a hippie drawing.	20 (Plaintiff's Exhibit 43B, picture of
21 Q. A hippie drawing.	21 Rasta holding hippie drawing, was marked
22 That you did or --	22 for identification, as of this date.)
23 A. Yes.	23 (Plaintiff's Exhibit 43C, picture of
24 Q. -- that you found?	24 Bob Marley, was marked for identification,
25 Okay. So that's 43B.	25 as of this date.)

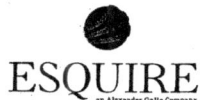

377

1   Prince
2   (Plaintiff's Exhibit 43D, two
3   pictures drawn on from Yes Rasta, was
4   marked for identification, as of this
5   date.)
6   MR. BROOKS: This is not part of the
7   video record.
8   We've agreed that I'm withdrawing
9   what had been marked as Exhibit 43, which
10   was a multipage document, and instead
11   we've marked four documents, which the
12   witness looked at and identified.
13   43D is what was originally the first
14   page of 43. It's two pictures drawn on
15   from Yes Rasta.
16   We're going backwards in order.
17   43C is a picture of Bob Marley that
18   he identified.
19   43B is a picture of a Rasta holding
20   a hippie drawing.
21   MS. BART: That's what he described
22   it as.
23   MR. BROOKS: And 43A is a landscape
24   from Yes Rasta and superimposed on it are
25   female genitalia, four of them.

378

1   Prince
2   That's it.
3   (Time noted 6:27 p.m.)
4
5   _____
6   RICHARD PRINCE
7
8   Subscribed and sworn to
9   before me this _____ day
10   of _____, 2009.
11
12   _____
13
14
15
16
17
18
19
20
21
22
23
24
25

379

1   Prince
2   CERTIFICATE
3
4   STATE OF NEW YORK)
5   )ss:
6   COUNTY OF NEW YORK)
7
8   I, BRYAN NILSEN, a Notary Public
9   within and for the State of New York, do
10   hereby certify:
11   That RICHARD PRINCE, the witness
12   whose deposition is hereinbefore set
13   forth, was duly sworn by me and that such
14   deposition is a true record of the
15   testimony given by such witness.
16   I further certify that I am not
17   related to any of the parties to this
18   action by blood or marriage and that I am
19   in no way interested in the outcome of
20   this matter.
21   IN WITNESS WHEREOF, I have hereunto
22   set my hand this ___ day of _____, 2009.
23
24
25   BRYAN NILSEN, RPR

380

1   Prince
2   ------------------ I N D E X ------------------
3   WITNESS   EXAMINATION BY   PAGE
4   RICHARD PRINCE   MR. BROOKS................7
5
6
7
8   -------------- INFORMATION REQUESTS ------------
9   REQUESTS: PAGE
10   Photos taken but not produced..............369
11
12
13   MOTIONS:
14   Motion to strike..........................241
15   Motion to strike..........................292
16
17
18
19
20
21
22
23
24
25

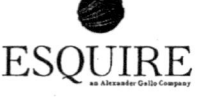

Richard Prince   October 6, 2009

381

1   Prince
2   ------------- EXHIBITS -------------
3   PLAINTIFF'S   FOR ID.
4   1 Amended complaint......................21
5   2 Answer to amended complaint..............22
6   3 Two-page printout from website..........32
7   4 Interview................................47
8   5 Interview in French.....................53
9   6 English translation of portion of
10   French interview........................56
11   7 Two-page article.........................68
12   8 Interview................................88
13   9 Article................................108
14   10 Copyright Litigation Blog...............123
15   11 Article................................135
16   12 Le Figaro interview in French...........146
17   13 English translation of portion of
18   Le Figaro interview 147
19   14 GGP003781..............................179
20   15 GGP004296..............................183
21   16 Series of e-mails.......................184
22   17 E-mail.................................188
23   18 E-mail dated July 26, 2007.............191
24   19 GGP004330 and 4332.....................196
25   20 Article from Art Newspaper.............198

382

1   Prince
2   -------------- EXHIBITS (Cont'd.) -----------
3   PLAINTIFF'S   FOR ID.
4   21 NOT MARKED
5   22 Pitch..................................207
6   23 E-mails................................213
7   24 PR88 through 91........................219
8   25 PR92 through 95........................223
9   26 E-mail.................................254
10   27 PR38...................................237
11   28 Interview in Interview Magazine.........242
12   29 Three-page document....................287
13   30 Photos from iStockphoto.com.............290
14   31 Gagosian Gallery website pages..........292
15   32 Two-page document.......................299
16   33 Listing of paintings....................307
17   34 Letter dated December 11, 2008..........310
18   35 PR45 through 50.........................316
19   36 Multipage accounting document...........322
20   37 NOT MARKED
21   38 NOT MARKED
22   39 NOT MARKED
23   40 Paintings and photos juxtaposed.........325
24   41 Yes Rasta book.........................239
25   42 Canal Zone book.........................86

383

1   Prince
2   -------------- EXHIBITS (Cont'd.) -----------
3   PLAINTIFF'S   FOR ID.
4   43 WITHDRAWN - pictures from Yes Rasta.....366
5   43A Landscape from Yes Rasta with female
6   genitalia.............................376
7   43B Picture of Rasta holding hippie drawing.376
8   43C Picture of Bob Marley...................376
9   43D Two pictures drawn on from Yes Rasta....377
10
11   ** EXHIBITS RETAINED BY COUNSEL **
12
13
14
15
16
17
18
19
20
21
22
23
24
25

384

1   DEPOSITION ERRATA SHEET
2   RE: Esquire Deposition Solutions
3   File No. 13829
4   Case Caption: PATRICK CARIOU
5   vs. RICHARD PRINCE, et al.
6   Deponent: RICHARD PRINCE
7   Deposition Date: October 6, 2009
8   To the Reporter:
9   I have read the entire transcript of my Deposition taken
10   in the captioned matter or the same has been read to me.
11   I request that the following changes be entered upon the
12   record for the reasons indicated. I have signed my name to
13   the Errata Sheet and the appropriate Certificate and
14   authorize you to attach both to the original transcript.
15
16   Page No._____Line No._____Change to:_____
17
18   Reason for change:_____
19   Page No._____Line No._____Change to:_____
20
21   Reason for change:_____
22   Page No._____Line No._____Change to:_____
23
24   Reason for change:_____
25

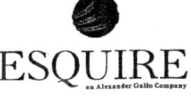
ESQUIRE
an Alexander Gallo Company

Toll Free: 800.944.9454
Facsimile: 212.557.5972

Suite 4715
One Penn Plaza
New York, NY 10119
www.esquiresolutions.com

Richard Prince   October 6, 2009

1   Prince

2   That's it.

3   (Time noted 6:27 p.m.)

4

5

6   RICHARD PRINCE

7

8   Subscribed and sworn to

9   before me this _2 4__ day

10   of _November_, 2009.

11

12   _Jacqueline Bogardus_

13

14   Jacqueline Bogardus
            Notary Public State of New York
15   No. 01BO6068591
            Qualified in Greene County
            Commission Expires 12-31-09

16

17

18

19

20

21

22

23

24

25

UNITED STATES DISTRICT COURT
SOUTHERN DISTRICT OF NEW YORK

--X

PATRICK CARIOU,

                            Plaintiff,

            -against-

RICHARD PRINCE, GAGOSIAN GALLERY, INC.,
LAWRENCE GAGOSIAN, and RIZZOLI
INTERNATIONAL PUBLICATIONS, INC,

                        Defendants.

--X

08 CIV 11327 (DAB)

**AFFIDAVIT OF DEFENDANT
RICHARD PRINCE
IN SUPPORT OF
DEFENDANTS' MOTION FOR
SUMMARY JUDGMENT**

RICHARD PRINCE, being duly sworn, deposes and says:

1.   I am an artist living in New York City and Rensselaerville, New York, but maintain my principal studio in Rensselaerville.

2.   I submit this affidavit in support of Defendants' Motion for Summary Judgment.

3.   I have been an artist for nearly 40 years, and have consistently aspired to create beautiful pieces of art to convey a distinct message or creative concept. My work has been displayed in, and is part of the permanent collection of major museums around the world, including the Solomon R. Guggenheim Museum in New York; Whitney Museum of Art; the San Francisco Museum of Modern Art; Museum Boijmans van Beuningen, Rotterdamn; Museum für Gegenwartskunst, Basel; and Kunstmuseum Wolfsburg. As an example, in late 2007, the Solomon R. Guggenheim Museum in New York presented a major retrospective of my work, which filled the entire rotunda and two tower galleries.

4.   My works are sought after by significant collectors and galleries of contemporary art worldwide, and are regularly offered at auction.

5.   My career as an appropriation artist dates back to 1977, when I was working in the tear-sheet department of Time-Life magazine, clipping and filing articles for its editors. While working at Time-Life, I would re-photograph discarded advertising imaged that I salvaged. I also made collages using clippings from various advertising images, and combined them as if they were freeze frames from the same movie.

6.   Ultimately, I began using photographic images of artists, and re-photographing them by changing the context in which they appear.

7.   In 1984, I began creating exact re-drawings of cartoons that elicited a mix of cultural preferences, human desires and biases. This process inspired me to paint and so I began to add painterly elements to my works to evoke the styles of Robert Rauschenberg and other well-known appropriation artists.

8.   My style of appropriation evolved further with my "Hippy Drawings" consisting of stick figures with abstract, mask-like faces onto which I painted circles over the eyes, nose, and mouth, which are known as my signature "lozenge" faces.

9.   After this body of work, I increasingly began using bright colors, drip painting, bold brush strokes, and other painterly elements to create layered effects, which spoke to my expressive and gestural styles.

10.   My next body of work was my sequential series, which included *Nurses* (2002-04), the *Check Paintings* (2004-05), the *de Kooning Paintings* (2007-07), and the *Canal Zone* (2008) series.

11.   I tend to create artwork in series and/or groups, as I believe things are best understood in relation to other things. My work that falls under the grouping and repetition categories include *Untitled* (four women with hats) (1979-80); *Untitled* (three hands with watches) (1980); *Cowboys* (1980-2003); *Gangs* (1984-86); *the Monochrome Jokes* (1985-89); and the *White Painting* (1990-95). Similarly, the *Canal Zone* Paintings were done as a group.

12.   My style is highly inspired by popular culture. Guitars frequently appear as a subject in my work, and they represent my love for rock music, which began in 1973 when I moved to New York City and immersed myself in its downtown music and arts scenes. At the time, I was enamored with Andy Warhol, and especially interested in the punk rock movement.

13.   In the work I have done as an appropriation artist, including the *Canal Zone* series, I look at pre-existing images of all types and see what I can contribute to make something new, distinctive and hopefully visually beautiful with one or more messages to be found in the work by the viewer. It is all about what contribution I can bring as an artist in all of my work. Often I adopt a unique persona to go along with my works of art often portraying myself as a rebel, an outsider, or an outlaw. Adopting this unique persona allows me to discover and create new things.

14.   I like to use other people's work to incorporate facts into my work to reduce speculation and make them more genuine, but I am not interested in what is actually there. Instead, I am interested in making art that transforms something that already existed without involving myself in the original intent of the image. I ultimately believe

3

that artists should be as free as possible in their studio because art is about freedom of expression and not being restricted.

15.   Although my primary artistic practice has been as a painter, sculpture and re-photographer, I have long had an interest in writing. I have collected first editions and other literary works for many years and have also authored a number of works both real and fictitious.

16.   My development of the *Canal Zone* series began in part with a literary creation rather than the paintings themselves. The *Canal Zone* developed from the storyline of a cinematic pitch I wrote from 2007 through 2008 called *Eden Rock*. *Eden Rock* describes a fantasy account of survivors of a nuclear attack whose cruise ship ends up in St. Barts. The survivors in the story form gangs and tribes, taking over the resort hotels on the island, and create their own post-apocalyptic society. The tribes and gangs include "Charlie Company," the family unit; the "Backpackers," who are college students on spring break; the "Rastas or Reggae," who play in cruise ship band; lesbian "Amazons" who escaped from the cruise ship; and a group of affluent individuals dubbed, the "Ultimate Ones." I was also affected by a trip I made to Panama (where I was born) in about 2005 and wanted to do a painting series set in a tropical location, as in the pitch described above.

17.   Around the same time, I was visiting St. Bart, where I rent a home for two weeks each year, and found a copy of *Yes Rasta* in a bookstore on the Island. I had never seen the book in any other bookstore and assumed it was an out of print book. I saw the documentary images in the book and made a connection to the tropical settings I had seen on my visit to Panama. The day before I had also seen cruise ships in the harbor of St.

4

Barts and thought they should be in my screenplay. I also had envisioned that one of the tribes in my screenplay would be a reggae band that was on the cruise ship and certain of the Rastafarians looked like males that would fit into my screenplay. At the time, I had also been listening to Radiodread, an album that sampled and replicated Radiohead in a reggae manner, and was very much into that album. When I walked into the bookstore the next day and saw the book with Rastas, I thought something was in the air. At the time that I painted my de Kooning series, I was already thinking about the *Canal Zone* Series, and therefore, I had also been looking for black and images of figures of men that I could put next to my de Kooning women.

18.   I began drawing in *Yes Rasta* itself like I had done before in a book of de Kooning's works, and making notations and sketches, which I eventually incorporated into portions of into my *Canal Zone* paintings. When I began to do this, I was simply making random drawings as I tend do wherever I am, at home or on vacation, as part of the creative process. I continued to draw on the faces for two or three years. I was inspired by the images because it was a subject matter that I knew nothing about, a position that I often put myself in to discover new things.

19.   In creating the *Canal Zone* paintings, I was influenced by a combination of events. The paintings are in part inspired by my trip to the former *Canal Zone* in Panama, and depict portions of my storyline from the Eden Rock screenplay. The screenplay was the starting point for the *Canal Zone* series. Therefore, while the plot and characters in the screenplay were in my head when I created the paintings, my paintings do not depict every aspect of the storyline. In creating a painting series there are many

5

ingredients and influences that go into the germination and creation of works of art in the studio, and portions of the screenplay story line are among those ingredients.

20.   I named the series the *Canal Zone* because I was very intrigued by the fact that the name of the place I was born in, *Canal Zone*, had disappeared, and was renamed Panama.

21.   In addition, I sought to pay homage and refer back to Willem de Kooning, Cezanne, Warhol and Picasso through my paintings in the *Canal Zone* series (collectively, the "Paintings"). For example, I sketched out enlarged hands and feet on some of the images in the *Yes Rasta* book in de Kooning-esque fashion, as a transition from my previous *de Kooning* series (which I had been working on when I began drawing in the *Yes Rasta* book), and to emulate the style of de Kooning hybrid creatures. This is also a reference to Cezanne's abstracted bathers paintings from the 1930's and his exaggerated drawings of hands and feet. I also abstracted the faces found in many of the *Canal Zone* Paintings with painterly elements, such as dripping paint, use of oil stick crayon and other media, and lozenge-face circles to emulate the style of de Kooning's contorted facial features and Picasso's primitive masks and unique ways of drawing parts of figures. I further transformed the images found in *Yes Rasta* by painting images onto the canvas and then painting over them again to create a ghost-like effect. I organized images of nude figures next to one another and drew Picasso-like primitive masks on some of the images that appear in the Paintings. Finally, the repetition that appears throughout the *Canal Zone* series refers to the iconic style of Andy Warhol. Such references to the history of art are a significant part of my work. Other artists such as Picasso have been noted for the art historical references in their work.

6

22.   I added images of guitars to my paintings to establish groupings of men and
women as contemporary musical bands in order to create a rock and roll theme
throughout the paintings in the *Canal Zone* series. Each Painting represents different
musical bands or aspects of my ideas conveyed in my screenplay pitch as one of the
ingredients in the Painting. My creative message for the *Canal Zone* series was to have
music groups and music itself be the surviving, if not redeeming, fact of life in the post-
apocalyptic world I imagined in my screenplay. The redemptive value of music is one of
the important concepts and messages of this series.

23.   I used images of Rastas from *Yes Rasta* because they looked primitive, and like
the type of man that might appear in my post-apocalyptic screenplay. The landscapes in
Canal Zone merely served as background for my creative expression. The images served
as one ingredient in my entire recipe.

24.   To create the *Canal Zone* series, which I created alone, I appropriated, in the
tradition of Duchamp, 41 images from *Yes Rasta*, two adult books from an art publishing
company called Taschen, images of rock guitars and musician hands from contemporary
music magazines, images from anatomy books that I bought at the art supply store, and
an image from a book or magazine on Bob Marley.

25.   When creating the paintings, I had at least 25 or more books and magazines in
front of me and would randomly take images that fit into my artistic vision and message
for each work.

26.   With the exception of *Canal Zone,* 2007, which I created using portions of pages
torn from *Yes Rasta* onto which I drew masks in the style of Picasso (*see* ¶ 21 above), I
digitally scanned and resized the *Yes Rasta* images, some of which I scanned directly

7

onto the canvas while others I fixed onto a canvas with glue, scotch tape or paint, and then used them either as background for collaging or as collage elements, creating a layering effect. In some of the Paintings, I affixed the collaged elements to other images with scotch tape for further scanning, and in others I applied the collage elements directly to the canvas using a squeegee technique in which elements are affixed to the canvas with paint to create a layered effect. Thus, in making the *Canal Zone* Paintings, I sought to make a totally new artistic contribution using what I call ingredients.

27.   I also created the works to convey specific messages, such as historical art references as an homage to master painters whose works I admire, such as Cezanne, Picasso, Warhol and de Kooning, and the fictional world on a tropical island where bands of individuals form musical groups that live and interact (as reflected in part of my screenplay pitch.) These ideas are combined with art techniques of collage, layering use of different media (acrylic paint, oil stick, graphite, inkjet printing and images from numerous photographic books) to create entirely new and different works of art that I hope are interesting and contribute to the dialogue of art.

28.   Larry Gagosian and I withdrew the balance of the *Canal Zone* paintings that remained for sale from the market pending the resolution of this lawsuit.

29.   Although the *Canal Zone* Paintings were done as part of one artistic conception, I have set forth in detail below, what I did – and why – in creating each of the Paintings in the *Canal Zone* series.

30.   To appreciate the various elements, or ingredients, that appear in each of the Paintings, and in turn, their transformative nature, the defendants have compiled, as an aid to the Court, the Composite Exhibit attached hereto as Exhibit A, which contains the

8

images taken from the *Yes Rasta* book, and corresponding Painting(s) in which the image appears, a summary of the various elements (or ingredients) and the techniques I used to create each Paintings and a summary of Mr. Cariou's testimony explaining why he took the particular *Yes Rasta* images.

31.   As the various layering effects and elements are not readily ascertainable from the images reproduced in the Composite Exhibit, Mr. Gagosian and I respectfully invite the Court for a private viewing of the Paintings to be held at the Court's convenience either at a gallery space in New York City or in my studio in Rensselaerville, New York, where most of the remaining Paintings are located.

Individual Paintings in the *Canal Zone* Series

32.   *Graduation*, **2008**. To create *Graduation*, I tore pages from the *Yes Rasta* book and had it scanned, enlarged in a bluish tint. I also had the background landscape dimmed and deemphasized. I painted a Picasso-inspired, blue lozenge facemask directly onto the canvas on the Rastafarian's face, not only to pay homage to Picasso, but also because musicians often wear face masks while performing, and thus, the mask was another way of illustrating his identity and carrying out my theme for the series. I collaged a picture of a blue electric guitar, which I cut out of a guitar aficionado magazine, onto the Rastafarian's body, and also replaced his hands with enlarged ones. I painted a small dot of blue pigment on the Rasta's forehead. These elements were then rescanned and printed directly onto the canvas. In furtherance of my music-inspired message, I added the guitar to this image to transform the identity of the Rastafarian to a contemporary musician who represented the lead guitarist of one of the bands.

9

33.   *Meditation, 2008*. In creating *Meditation*, I used the same image of the guitar-playing Rastafarian found in *Graduation*. I rotated, and altered the size of, the image, and taped it onto a plain white canvas. I painted a white lozenge facemask on the Rastafarian's face, collaged proportional size hands and a different guitar onto the image, and added hints of blue on the four edges of the painting. The male who appears in *Meditation* represents the same musician that appears in *Graduation*. However, I switched the direction he was facing, and the guitar, as musicians often switch instruments as part of a performance, to further my reference to an ongoing musical performance in this series of Paintings.

34.   *Canal Zone, 2008*. In creating *Canal Zone*, 2008 I used the same image that appears in *Graduation* and *Meditation*, but once again, I replaced the guitar with a different one and affixed different hands instead. In this painting, the Rastafarian is cut out and placed among a grid-like landscape, which is created from torn, scanned, altered, and reassembled images of foliage I took from various pages in *Yes Rasta* and, if I recall correctly, may include portions from a book on Tahiti I had come across. I used the photographs of different landscapes because I wanted the painting to appear like a camouflage backdrop, with the guitarist in the midst of lush foliage that has taken control of my fictional island. I also was inspired by Andy Warhol's camouflage paintings, and his use of grids, so in this respect, I paid homage to him. The Rastafarian in the painting, symbolizes a musician who is a solo artist, and is actually a reference to musician Neil Young (deliberately using a black man as a stand in for Young). He is holding an appropriated image of Neil Young's guitar with proportional hands, and I added a white lozenge facemask as a reference to Picasso. Absent from this painting is any architecture

or buildings to create a sense that nothing has survived after the apocalypse, except this man and his guitar and music.

35.   *The Ocean Club*, **2008.** I named this painting after a club on Chambers Street in Manhattan, New York. To create *The Ocean Club*, I cut up different images of green landscapes from *Yes Rasta* and possibly a book on Tahiti , and recombined them on a canvas with tape and paint. I then cut out an image of a Rastafarian from *Yes Rasta* and added white lozenge faces. I also cut out an image of a nude female figure on the beach from another book, and added pink lozenge faces. I duplicated and enlarged the images of the Rastas and the nude women and then pasted them, using white paint, in alternating order onto the canvas over the background images of the landscape. The repetition in this painting is similar to the repetition that I utilize in many of my works of art, and is an homage to Warhol's style of repetition. I also chose *Ocean Club* as the title for this painting because Warhol used to go to the Ocean Club, a club I would also go to when I was a young artist, and I envisioned that the females in the painting were on the beach.

36.   *Charlie Company*, **2008.** In *Charlie Company*, I tore pages bearing an image from *Yes Rasta* and cut out the image of a Rastafarian riding a donkey, had it scanned and enlarged, and then reassembled it side by side with tape, and glued it twice on top of the image that was scanned on to the canvas as background. During the scanning process, I had the image cropped on the left side and tinted in sepia tones. I then pasted an image of a nude female figure next to the image of the Rastafarian riding a donkey. I attached the images to the canvas with white paint, which I applied with the use of a squeegee. I also painted lozenge facemasks on the Rastafarian and the nude female figure. The repetition and juxtaposition of images in this painting is a reference to Warhol, while the fracturing

11

of the image is a reference to Picasso's cubism. The woman in this painting represents a tourist and the black man represents a native, and they are juxtaposed because they are helping each other to survive. Again, absent from this painting is anything mechanical or man-made to illustrate the post-apocalyptic world in which they now exist.

37.   ***Back to the Garden, 2008***. In creating *Back to the Garden*, I first scanned and enlarged the image of the Rastafarian on a donkey along with the background landscape onto a canvas. To this altered image, I added a collaged guitar and a white lozenge mask to make it seem as though the Rastafarian is playing the guitar. Next I cut out the same image of the Rastafarian on a donkey, and cropped, scanned, and tinted it to sepia, and then superimposed it over the image on the canvas. Before applying it, I tore it into three pieces and then reassembled and affixed it using white paint onto the canvas. I also affixed the images of two nude women, which were also scanned in a sepia tone, on each end of the two Rastafarian images, and added lozenges facemasks to the women's faces. I was thinking about Adam and Eve when I painted *Back to the Garden* since they were in the Garden of Eden and my post-apocalyptic screenplay takes place in a tropical jungle garden. This painting also is a take on the music scene, by combining the guitar and hands with the collaged man on the donkey, while highlighting three different human relationships in the universe: women with women, women with men, and men with men. The landscape represents the idyllic setting at Woodstock, and again, included nothing man-made. The man in the painting is playing "Back to the Garden" at Woodstock on George Harrison's guitar and has become a "Beatle" in furtherance of my message that music is the only redeeming thing to have survived.

38.   *Cheese and Crackers*, 2008. In creating *Cheese and Crackers*, I first scanned images of three nude women onto the canvas. Next I painted, drew, and collaged onto their bodies enlarged hands and feet, and also obscured their faces. I cut out a portion of a scanned and enlarged image of the Rastafarian found in *Graduation*, and applied it to the canvas using white paint. I obscured his face as well with paint. For one of the Rastafarian's hands, I applied a scanned, enlarged image of a hand onto the figure, and for the other hand, I drew on it with an oil stick crayon. I also altered the Rastafarian's feet by painting enlarged feet over them. I painted the background with bright, heavy colors. This painting, especially the wine colored background, is heavily influenced by de Kooning's techniques, and is stylistically very similar to my de Kooning series. I consider *Cheese and Crackers* a bridge between my de Kooning paintings and the *Canal Zone* Paintings. This painting is also influenced by Picasso's well-known 347 series of etchings and Cezanne's bathers. I essentially took different elements from art history and attempted to update them, and make them a part of this painting in order to pay homage to these particular artists. In particular, the feet and primitive facemasks are a historical reference to Picasso while the cartoon, lozenge faces reference de Kooning. I titled this painting *Cheese and Crackers* because I envisioned that that this was the name of the band.

39.   *Mr. Jones*, 2008. Mr. Jones was influenced by Picasso's famous painting *Demoiselles d'Avignon* now in the Museum of Modern Art in New York, and is very similar to *Cheese and Crackers*. The images of the nude female figures were scanned onto the original canvas. The male figure that appears in the painting was a cut out of a scanned and enlarged image of the Rastafarian in *Graduation* that I affixed to the canvas

13

using paint. I painted a de Kooningesque mask over the face of the male figure, and added images of oversized hands, feet, and an arm on the image of the Rastafarian. I added similar oversized hands and feet to the nude females that appear on each side of the male figure. I also added pigment to the lower portion of the male figure that continues downward to the bottom of the canvas. This painting is stylistically similar to *Cheese and Crackers* in that it is heavily influenced by de Kooning's techniques, Picasso's 347 series and Cezanne's bathers. I used these elements from art history, again, to pay homage to these particular artists.

40.   ***The Other Side of the Island*, 2008.** In creating this painting, I scanned images of different female figures onto the canvas and painted yellow lozenge facemasks over their faces. Then I cut out, scanned, and enlarged two images of Rastafarians from *Yes Rasta*, the one from *Graduation* and a different one. In obscuring the images of the Rastafarians in this painting, I painted de Kooningesque style masks on their faces, covered half their bodies with paint, and painted and drew enlarged hands on them. I made the background of this painting dark with a hint of orange and purple swirls. This painting is stylistically similar to *Cheese and Crackers* in that it is heavily influenced by de Kooning's techniques, Picasso's 347 series and Cezanne's bathers. I used these elements from art history, again, to pay homage to these particular artists.

41.   ***Naked Confessions*, 2008.** In creating this painting, I used images of three female figures, and a male Rastafarian figure from a page torn from *Yes Rasta*. I painted the background with darker shades of black and dark red swirls. I collaged an electric guitar onto the Rastafarian figure and then scanned and enlarged the combined image, and affixed it to the canvas. I then obscured the face of the male figure by painting a mask-

like eyes and lips. I also collaged a guitar on the Rastafarian's hands. I replaced the landscape that appeared in the background of the photograph of the male Rastafarian with a background of white and pink paint. I altered the images of the nude females by adding either lozenge masks or for the figure on the right, a fully drawn de Kooning-like face and enlarged hands and feet. This painting is stylistically similar to *Cheese and Crackers* in that it is heavily influenced by de Kooning's techniques, Picasso's 347 series and Cezanne's bathers. I used these elements from art history, again, to pay homage to these particular artists. I also juxtaposed these historical references with the guitar, which is a contemporary reference.

42.   *Specially Round Midnight,* **2008.** In creating *Specially Around Midnight,* I painted the background with dark colors before affixing scanned and enlarged cutouts of the images of three nude female figures and the two images of Rastafarians, which also appear in *The Other Side of the Island.* Around the two male figures, I painted haloes of white paint. I collaged an image of a guitar over the hands of one of the male figures. To this same male figure I also added exaggerated painted boots to his feet and painted a white mask on his face. On the other male figure, I drew distorted eyes and a mouth over his face and added black stripes to his sleeve. I also obscured the bottom half of his figure by darkening it. On the female figures, I drew and collaged enlarged feet and drew over their faces to obscure them. I also painted haloes of white paint around two of the female figures. This painting is stylistically similar to *Cheese and Crackers* in that it is heavily influenced by de Kooning's techniques, Picasso's 347 series and Cezanne's bathers. I used these elements from art history, again, to pay homage to these particular artists. The title for this painting refers to Miles Davis who had a song and album entitled

15

"Round About Midnight." The man in the painting represents the lead guitarist who is playing that song, and the four others that appear symbolize the other members of the band.

43.   *Zipping the System, 2008.* In creating *Zipping the System*, I first primed the canvas and then collaged onto the canvas enlarged and cutout scans of three nude females and the same two male Rastafarian figures that appear in *The Other Side of the Island.* I outlined the collaged images with white, pink and grey paint. I altered each Rasta figure by drawing and painting enlarged hands, facial features, and for one of the figures, a sketch of enlarged feet over the existing image. I obscured the bottom half of one of the male figures by cutting off the image at the bottom and painting over it with black paint. I also drew enlarged feet and hands on the female figures and altered their faces by drawing and collaging different eyes and mouths. The up and down style in this painting is a reference to Barnett Newman's famous zip paintings (areas of vertical color separated by thin lines).

44.   *Color Me Mine, 2008.* In creating *Color Me Mine*, I used four scanned and enlarged cutouts of nude female figures, and a scanned and enlarged partial image of a male Rastafarian figure taken from a page torn from *Yes Rasta,* and collaged them onto a primed canvas. Before affixing the image of the Rastafarian, I collaged together four separate bodies before scanning it into a single image. I added a guitar on the image with the Rastafarian head in furtherance of my music-inspired theme and obscured the face by painting it with white paint and an oil stick. To the female images, I added pink lozenge facemasks and sketched enlarged hands for one of them. I also collaged a pair of feet that appears below one of the female figures. I painted the background of the painting with

16

purple and white brushstrokes. This painting is heavily influenced by de Kooning's style.
The melding of the white and black person together is also a reference to Basquiat.

45.   *James Brown Disco Ball*, 2008. To create this painting, I scanned and enlarged
cut outs of images of five nude figures and headshots of two male Rastafarian images,
taken from pages torn from *Yes Rasta*. I affixed portions of these images to the canvas,
and layered the background with strokes of purple, pink and white paint. Almost all the
images in this painting have been cut and reassembled onto the canvas. On top of one of
the nude figures, I pasted an altered and bleached image of a Rastafarian head and added
white lozenge eyes, a cut out of an enlarged foot, and white paint around the top of the
head. I placed the other image of the Rastafarian's head on top of another nude figure
and added a primitive-looking facemask to his face. I also painted black lozenge
facemasks on the faces of the female figures, and collaged onto them different scanned
and altered images of hands and feet. The bodies in this picture represent disco balls,
while the painting itself is a poetic reference to James Brown whose disco ball I had
recently purchased at auction. I used the headshots of the Rastafarian men because they
typified another black man, but in this painting, he is in a funk band, as evidenced by the
title, which again references my musical theme. However, the only visible trait of the
Rastafarian images are their dreadlocks, which I used because they give the illusion of
dripping paint, a technique that refers to the Japanese photographer Araki who would put
black paint on black and white photographic images.

46.   *Inquisition*, 2008. To create this painting, I scanned and enlarged an image of a
nude female figure onto which I had drawn a lozenge facemask and then collaged an
image of a blue electric guitar and an image of a dog on to this image. I scanned,

17

enlarged, and cut out portions of images of Rastafarian figures taken from pages torn from *Yes Rasta* and onto which I had drawn primitive and de Kooning style masks and pasted them around her. I affixed these images with white paint, which I applied with a squeegee. Each element in this painting has been collaged, scanned, and then collaged and reworked. I also included an upside-down image as a reference to Georg Baselitz, although it is completely obscured by other images layered on top of it. Again I entitled this painting, *Inquisition*, to draw upon its theme of world domination which related to the post-apocalyptic, island/jungle theme and the message of my pitch.

47.   ***Uncle Tom, Dick, and Harry, 2008***. In creating this painting, I constructed layers with some of the images being scanned directly onto the canvas and others cutout and affixed directly on top. The four images of Rastafarians taken from pages torn from *Yes Rasta* were scanned with a blue tint, and then I cut out portions and altered the images by adding lozenge facemasks and de Kooningesque style masks over their faces. I affixed one of the images of male figures upside down. I also added black lozenge faces to the nude female figure. I painted the background white, with strokes of blue, and added an enlarged image of a marijuana cigarette. The upside-down image is a reference to the contemporary artist, Georg Baselitz. The title was influenced by the spies that are in my screenplay.

48.   ***Canal Zone, 2007***: To create this collage, I created a grid of collaged and obscured portions of images of landscapes and Rastafarians taken from pages torn from *Yes Rasta.* I altered each of the images that appear in this collage by drawing lozenge and primitive facemasks on some of the Rastafarian's faces, and other features with magic marker, crayons, pencil, and white acrylic paint. For others, I obscured their facial

18

image entirely with paint or other techniques. The images were rearranged in a big grid and thumb tacked to a piece of plywood. *Canal Zone* was exhibited during the first unveiling of the pitch at the Eden Rock Hotel in St. Bart, and was a way of introducing some of the characters, components, and players in the screenplay that I envisioned would be a part of the *Canal Zone* series.

49.   *Tales of Brave Ulysses, 2008.* In creating this painting, I layered cutout portions of images of nude female figures and a male Rastafarian onto a canvas. I scanned, enlarged, and applied as collage three of the four Rastafarian figures (the same image as is found in *Graduation*), and varied each of the sizes of the images. I scanned and enlarged the fourth one directly onto the canvas, and also altered its size to be smaller than the other three. To affix the collage elements, I used white paint, which I applied with a squeegee. In fact, on the largest male image, the squeegee marks still appear. On the smallest Rastafarian image, I drew enlarged hands. I also varied the size of the female images. I painted the bodies of the female figures, and added white, lozenge eyes to three of the six female images. I painted the background with a combination of light yellow, orange and red. I named the painting after a song by one of my favorite groups, Cream. The repetitive images seek to capture the rhythm of Cream's song, *Tales of Brave Ulysses*, and are also homage to Warhol and a reference Cezanne's Bathers. The figures, which are a band, are jamming, but the male figure does not yet have a guitar because he has not been the lead yet.

50.   *Escape Goat, 2008.* I painted the background of this painting a whitish-blue color. I then scanned, enlarged, and collaged onto the canvas five images of a portion of the same Rastafarian figure that appears in the *Graduation* in varying sizes and forms.

19

On the smallest figure to the far left, I collaged an image of enormous hands on the body and a blue lozenge facemask. To the next figure to the right, I added blue lozenge facemasks and an enlarged painted hands. I sketched over his feet with an abstract drawing. I collaged blue lozenge facemasks and a blue, electric guitar to the central male figure. I created this central figure by first collaging the mask and guitar and then scanning it. I also blackened out and enlarged his feet with paint and oil stick crayon. I created the fourth male figure by affixing collaged sections with white paint and then adding white lozenge eyes and sketching over his hands and feet. The last image is identical to the one with the collaged blue guitar and blue lozenge facemask, but I drew different feet on him. I also affixed cutouts of four nude female figures, and painted different colored lozenge facemasks on them as well. I outlined some of figures using a hint of green and gray paint. This painting references Cezanne's bathers.

51.   _On the Beach_, **2008.** In creating this painting, I cut out, scanned, and enlarged fragments of images of seven nude female figures and a fragment of an image of the same Rastafarian male that appears in _The Other Side of the Island, Specially Round Midnight, Canal Zone,_ 2007 and _Zipping the System._ For the background, I scanned and enlarged a landscape image taken from pages in _Yes Rasta,_ and affixed the other scanned images on top of it using white paint that I applied with a squeegee, which created a layered effect. On the images, I also drew white and mustard yellow lozenge facemasks. The lozenge faces are a reference to de Kooning, and the title reference Nevel Shutes's novel _On The Beach._ The composition of images comes from multiple sources, such as Richard Kern, German nudist books, and a book called "Paradise." These elements added to my vision of a post-apocalyptic world in my screenplay.

20

52.   *Cookie Crumbles*, **2008.** In creating *Cookie Crumbles*, I cut out canvases of
scanned and enlarged images of four nude female figures, and one image of a male
Rastafarian taken from a page torn from *Yes Rasta*, and then collaged them directly onto
another canvas. I affixed the images by first applying black paint with a squeegee and
then sticking the images to the black paint. I replicated the image of the male Rastafarian
three times in the painting, and juxtaposed these images with images of the nude women.
I painted a mask over the male Rastafarian and added enlarged hands and other drawings
in oil stick crayon. I also scribbled on the stomach of each of these images and altered
the man's seashell pendant into a peace sign. I also added white and black lozenge
facemasks to the faces of the female figures, and painted parts of their bodies. I painted
the background pastel yellow, with a splash of pink and grey. The images in this painting
refer to dance and evoke a kind of musical rhythm. The images of women come from
four different books, but I repeated the image of the male Rasta in different scales and
tones and with different masks to suggest that they are twin brothers who would also be
members of the same group on the Island. The repetition also is a reference to Warhol.

53.   *It's All Over*, **2008.** To create this painting, I first cut out, scanned, and enlarged
portions of images of three nude female figures, and a portion of the male Rastafarian
figure that appears in *On the Beach, On the Beach, The Other Side of the Island,
Specially Round Midnight, Canal Zone*, 2007 and *Zipping the System*. For the
background, I used an enlarged image of a landscape from *Yes Rasta*, but then painted
over it with white and pink paint obscuring the landscape. I drew black, pink, and white
lozenge facemasks on all the images. I affixed the images with black, white, pink, and
orange paint. I collaged guitars on two of the four Rastafarian images, which represented

21

George Harrison's guitars, which refers to the musical theme in my screenplay, and drew enlarged feet on them as well, as a historical art reference to deKooning and Picasso. I drew on the images of the female bodies using drip paint. I also included three of my *Hippie Drawings* in this painting. The repetition of different sized images that appears in this painting is a reference to Warhol. I highlighted the dreadlocks as a painterly form of drips, which also references the Japanese photographer, Araki who would put black paint on black and white photographic images.

54.   *Ile de France,* **2008.** To create this painting, I affixed directly to an unprimed canvas scanned, enlarged, and cutout portions of images of three nude female figures and a Rastafarian that appears in *Canal* Zone, 2007. To affix the images, I applied paint with a squeegee and then stuck the images on top of the paint. On the female figures I painted black and white lozenge faces, and added strokes of white, black, and grey paint over their bodies. I had portions of the image of the Rastafarian scanned in a bluish tint, and I cropped the lower portion of his body. I attached the cropped Rastafarian figure to the canvas with white, black, and grey paint, which is evident from the layers of paint that appear on the figure. This painting represents another aspect of the screenplay in which the hotel on St. Bart (named Ile de France) has been occupied by a band of people.

55.   *Djuana Barnes, Natalie Barney, Renee Vivian and Roman Brooks Take Over the Guanahani,* **2008.** For the background of this painting, I used a photograph of a tropical landscape taken from pages torn from *Yes Rasta,* had it scanned, cropped, and enlarged in a pinkish tone. I collaged images of cutouts of portions of four nude female figures onto the canvas using pink and white paint to affix them. I also added pink and white lozenge faces to the female figures. I named this painting after four famous literary

lesbians. This painting portrays the women taking over the Guanahani. This painting represents another element of my screenplay in which early 20th century novelists, poets, and expatriates, who had a lesbian salon in Paris, take over the Guanahani on St. Bart. I also wanted to portray a rock and roll theme on the one hand and also make reference to Cezanne's bathers. The background is a stereotypical, generic tropical jungle, which is the setting for my screenplay.

56.   *Mina Loy, Janet Flanner, Radcylffe Hall, Una Towbridge and Oscar Wilde's niece Dolly Wilder, 2008.* In creating this painting, which I named after lesbian writers in reference to the lesbian characters in my screenplay, I had scanned and enlarged cutouts of the images of six nude female figures, the male Rastafarian figure that appears in *Graduation*, and portions of images of landscapes, dreadlock hair and necklaces, which were torn from the pages of *Yes Rasta*. Before affixing the collage of images to the canvas, I cut up and reassembled all of the images such that they differed from their original composition and added white lozenge faces to many of the figures. Once assembled, I had them scanned. I then affixed and layered these scanned images onto the canvas using white paint. I painted the background of the painting with pastel blue paint. I used different scales, masks, and tattoos in this painting to create an all over abstract painting. The women in this painting represent lesbian writers from the 20th century.

57.   *Quarry, 2008.* In creating this painting, I had scanned and enlarged images of four nude female figures, and an image of the male Rastafarian figures, necklace and landscape that appear in *Mina Loy, Janet Flanner, Radcylffe Hall, Una Towbridge and Oscar Wilde's niece Dolly Wilder*, and the marijuana cigarette that appears in *Uncle Tom, Dick and Harry*. I cut up the scanned images of the male Rastafarian and landscape and

23

affixed portions of the, along with cut out images of a marijuana cigarette, hemp leaves and a necklace, on top of the images of the female figures. I added white lozenge facemasks to the images. The tattoo in this painting is a reference to the idea of Polynesia and idea that they are shipwrecked. In creating this painting, I was thinking about Marlan Brando and Clarke Gabel sailing. I was also thinking about Tahiti and the oceanic art. The collage of the male and female figures was a way for me to fuse the two together in a new inventive way. The repetition is a reference to Warhol.

58.   *Untitled, 2008.* In creating this painting, I had scanned and enlarged an image of a nude female, and a landscape and the necklace found on the male Rastafarian in *Quarry*. I had the enlarged image of the landscape scanned onto the canvas, and then I affixed with paint the enlarged chest of the female figure on top of the landscape. I then affixed the cropped image of a Rastafarian's chest wearing a medallion necklace on top of the female figure. This painting depicts a contemporary band. All the *Untitled*, 2008 paintings (including those described in paragraphs 57 and 58 below) relate to comparisons between and relationships among the males and females occupying my fictional tropical island.

59.   *Untitled (Rasta), 2008*. To create this painting, I cut out, enlarged and scanned onto a canvas images of two nude female figures, to which I added pink and black lozenge faces, and a collaged the image of the Rastafarian male found in *Graduation* to which I had added a white lozenge mask, guitar and a cut out of hands. I then affixed with paint these sheets of canvas to another unprimed canvas. This painting is a sister painting to my other untitled works, and also depicts a contemporary band.

24

60.   *Untitled (Rasta),* 2008. I used similar techniques to create this painting as I used
to create the other *Untitled (Rasta)*. To create this painting, I cut out, enlarged and
scanned onto a canvas images of three nude female figures, to which I added white
lozenge face. I also collaged a cut out the image of the Rastafarian found in *Graduation*
to which I had added a white lozenge mask, guitar and a cut out of hands. I then affixed
with paint these sheets of canvas to another unprimed canvas. This painting also depicts
a contemporary band, with the Rastafarian representing the lead male in the band.

61.   *Ding Dong the Witch is Dead,* 2008. In this painting I have used a number of
raw materials and other elements using many of the same techniques as those found in
the rest of the *Canal Zone* series. None of the images found in *Yes Rasta* appear in this
work. There is, however, an image I took from a book about Bob Marley to further my
artistic concept of post-apocalyptic bands, and my message of equality between the sexes.

Other Matters Related to the *Canal Zone* Series

62.   I did the paintings in the *Canal Zone* relatively quickly both because I often do
paintings in a day or less (something which many other artists such as Picasso are also
known for) and because I had been working for quite some time on the de Kooning series
and felt that I need a break and so I began to prepare these paintings in the summer of
2008 with the idea of using them for a show in the fall of 2008 in lieu of another show
that had been planned.

63.   The images in the *Yes Rasta* book, in which I had been drawing figures and ideas
for some time, fit into my ongoing vision composed of an homage to Cezanne, de
Kooning, Warhol, Picasso and others, as well as the screenplay pitch I prepared and my

25

desire to combine these elements with strong references to music and the people who
play music in a tropical setting similar to Panama where I was born. As I said before, in
my use of any images whether photographic or otherwise, I do this to use an ingredient in
a work and to transform the work into something to which I have made a contribution and
which I believe contributes to the dialogue among artists through their work while
providing an interesting new experience for people to see the work and may be interested
in purchasing it.

64.   It is true that I have made several million dollars from the sale of the *Canal Zone*
paintings. However, the sales of the *Canal Zone* paintings are not at any higher level for
similar-sized paintings that I have done in other series and indeed, have sold for less
based on such comparisons. I believe that the value contained in the paintings is that
which I brought to it by my contribution as an artist as well as the obvious benefit to my
name and place in contemporary art as an enticement to collectors to purchase my
paintings. In creating these paintings, I changed the use of the images in Mr. Cariou's
book of documentary photographs into part of a fictional environment which related to
my screenplay pitch, and my desire to do a series of paintings in a tropical setting with an
emphasis on musical groups, while still making strong art historical references. Whether
a particular viewer likes my work or not, I believe that, when compared to Mr. Cariou's

photographs, it is evident that what I have done is a highly individualistic, proprietary and, I believe, transformative use of images, techniques and a variety of other sources to create works which are unique, creative and utilize a visual vocabulary that is uniquely mine.

65.   The catalog for the show contained an essay by James Frey, an American author. It is common to have essays contained in art show catalogs, sometimes by the scholars but often by the writers or others whose essays are included in order to add an extra element to the catalog. I asked Mr. Frey initially to do this for me and he did it as a favor. When I received the actual essay, I was not pleased by it, because although some elements of my pitch were referred to in the essay, I felt that he had done an entirely different work and that ultimately the themes contained in his essay had nothing to do with my paintings. However, since he had done the essay for me as a favor, and since I felt that the paintings stood on their own in any event, I agreed to the essay being included.

66.   I do see my work as continuing within prior artistic traditions of offering homages to prior artists, utilizing a variety of images and media in new and different ways and bringing my own artistic concepts, message and fantasies to visual expression as part of an ongoing dialogue of art.

RICHARD PRINCE

Subscribed and sworn to before me
this 13th day of May, 2010

Notary Public

STEVEN M. HAYES
Notary Public, State of New York
No. 4968850
Qualified in Nassau County
Commission Expires Oct. 31, 19___ 2013

27

"Attached hereto as Exhibit N are copies of the 22 paintings depicted in the Canal Zone Catalogue."
- Daniel J. Brooks, Declaration in support of the plaintiff's motion for summary judgment, p. 4 of 9

Exhibit N

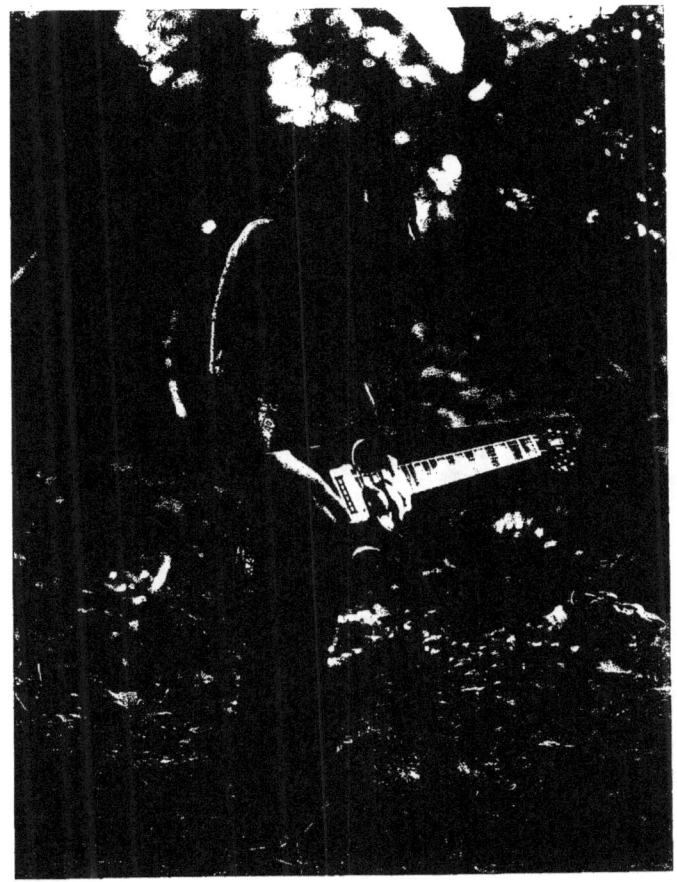

1   Graduation

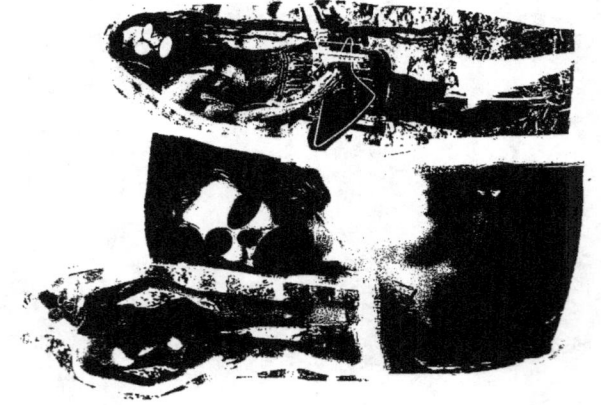

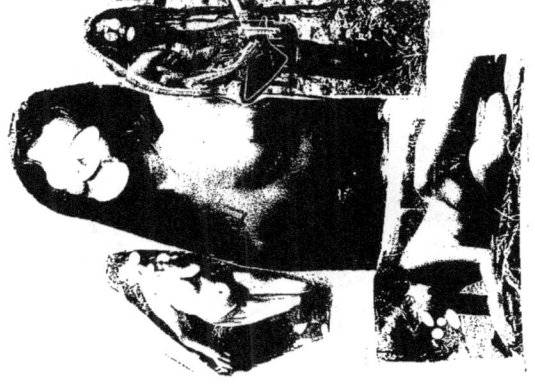

3   Untitled (Rasta)

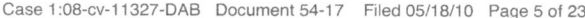

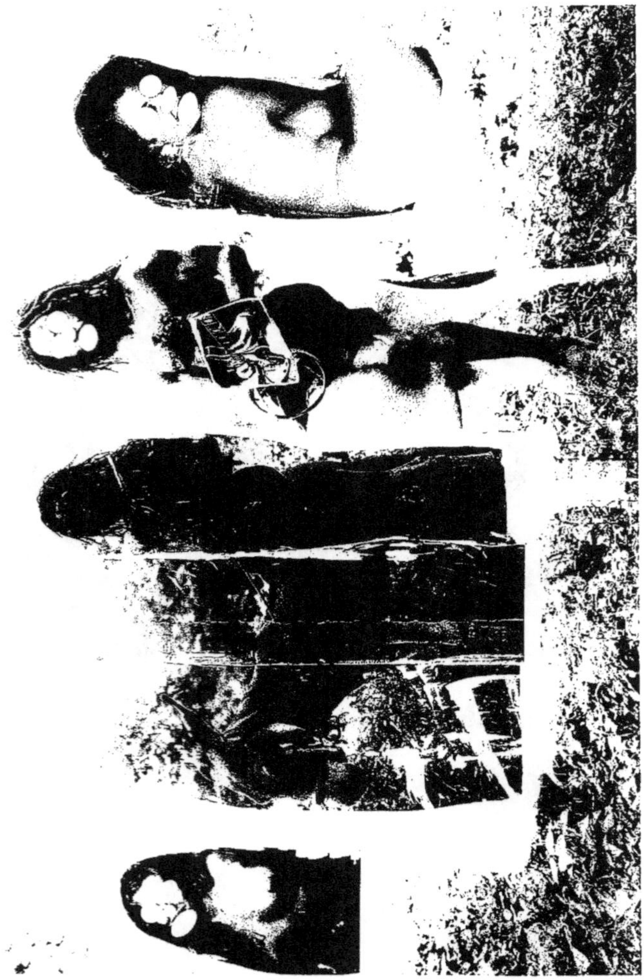

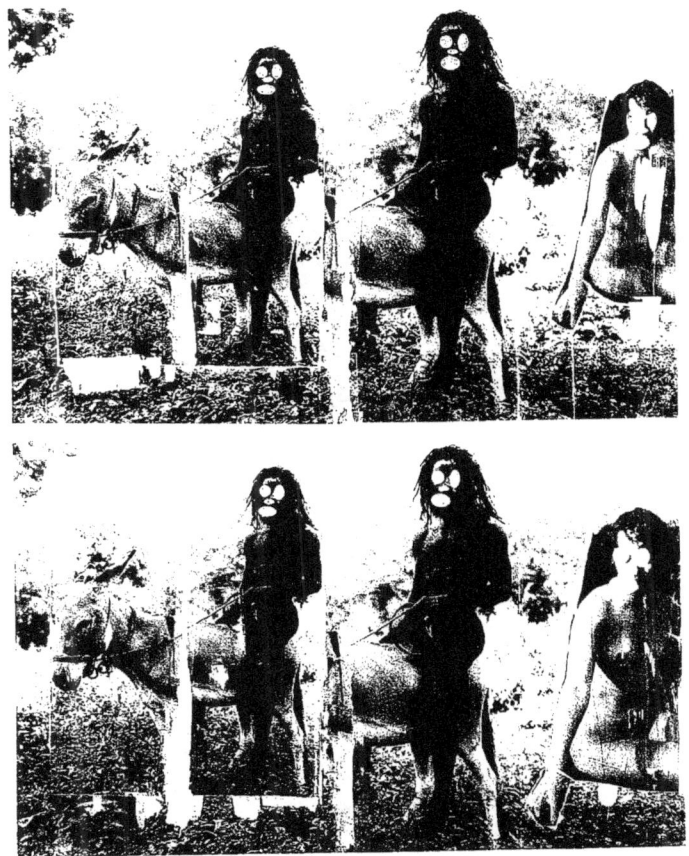

5   **Charlie Company**

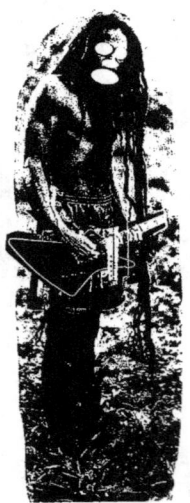

6   Meditation

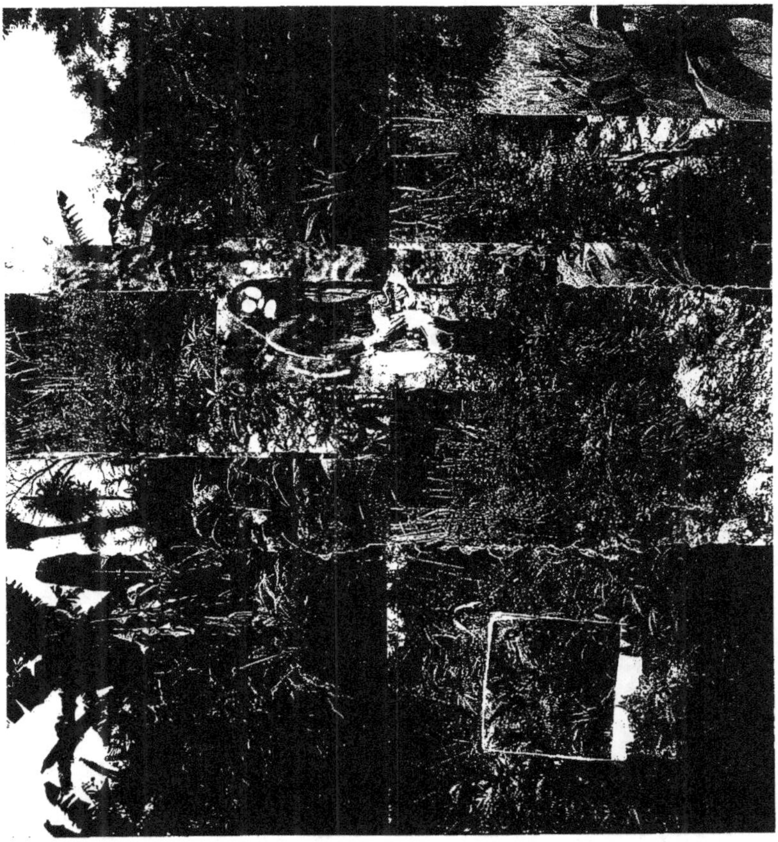

Canal Zone

7

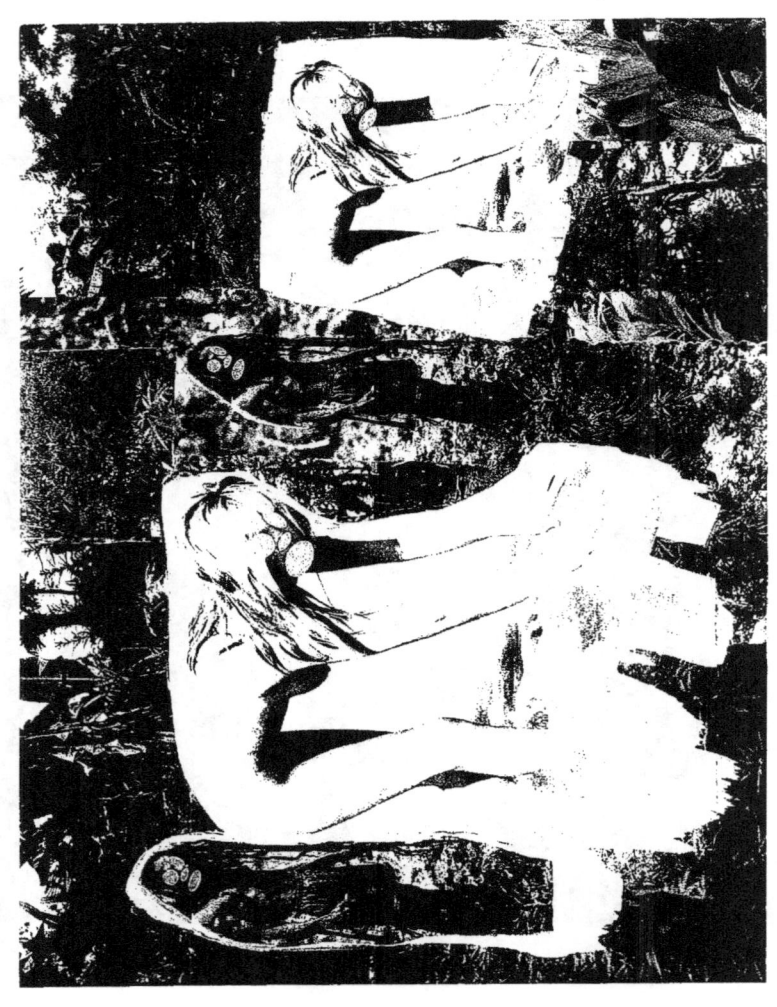

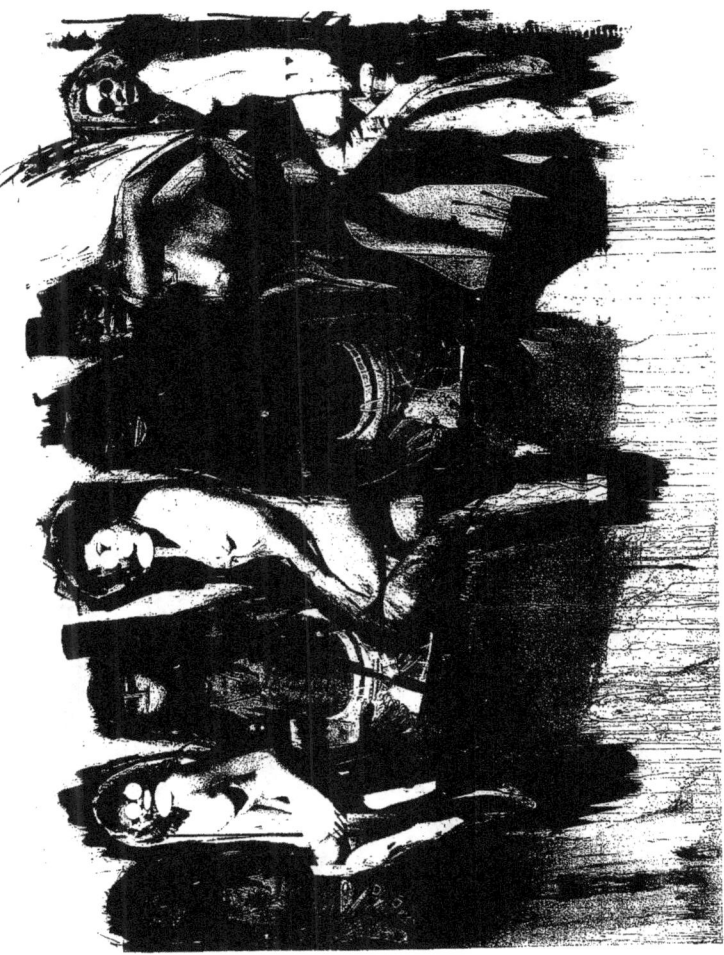

9   Cookie Crumbles

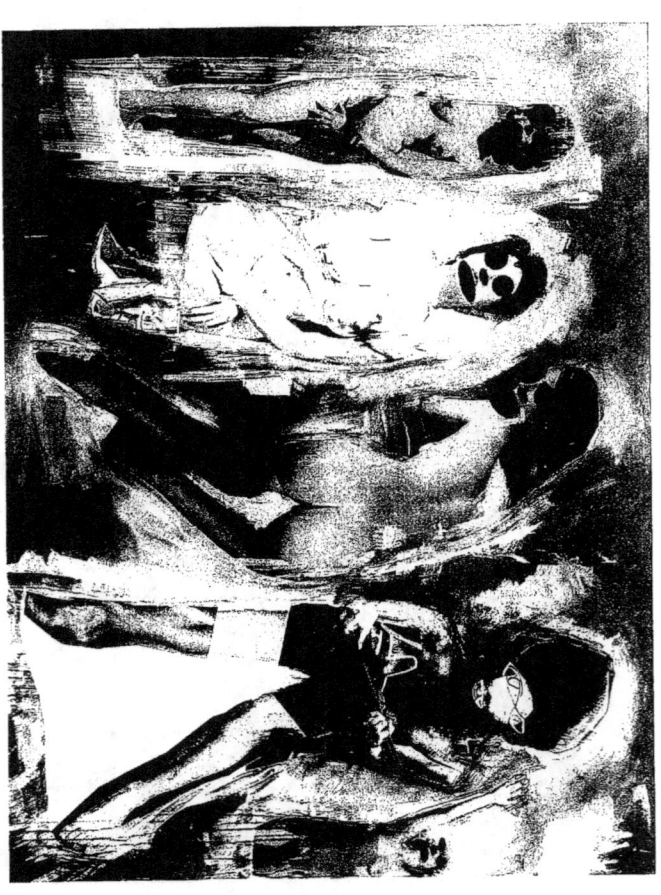

10   Color Me Mine

11   James Brown Disco Ball

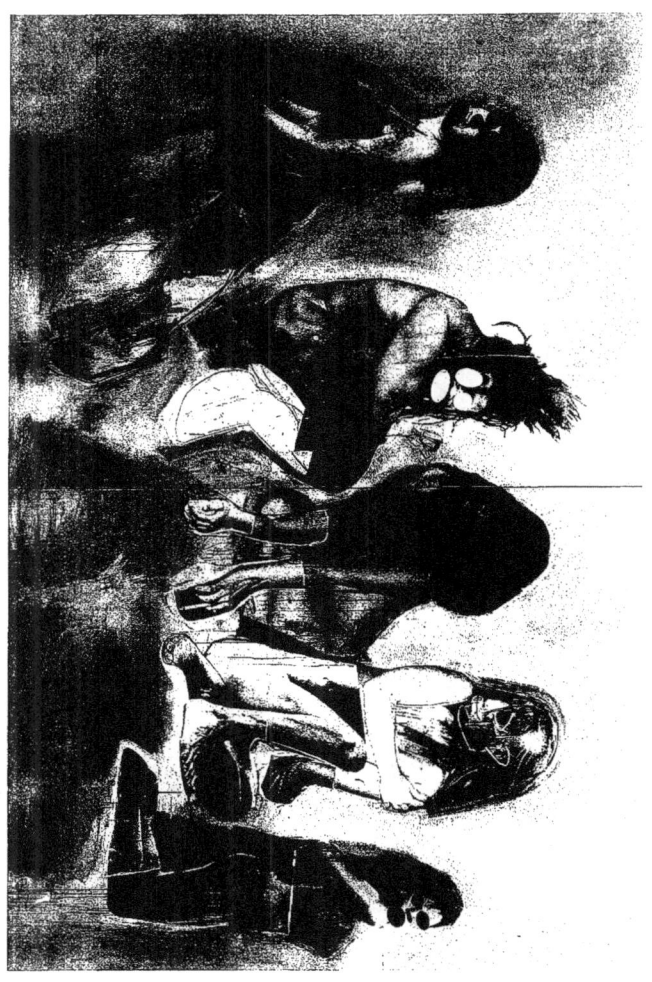

12   Ile de France

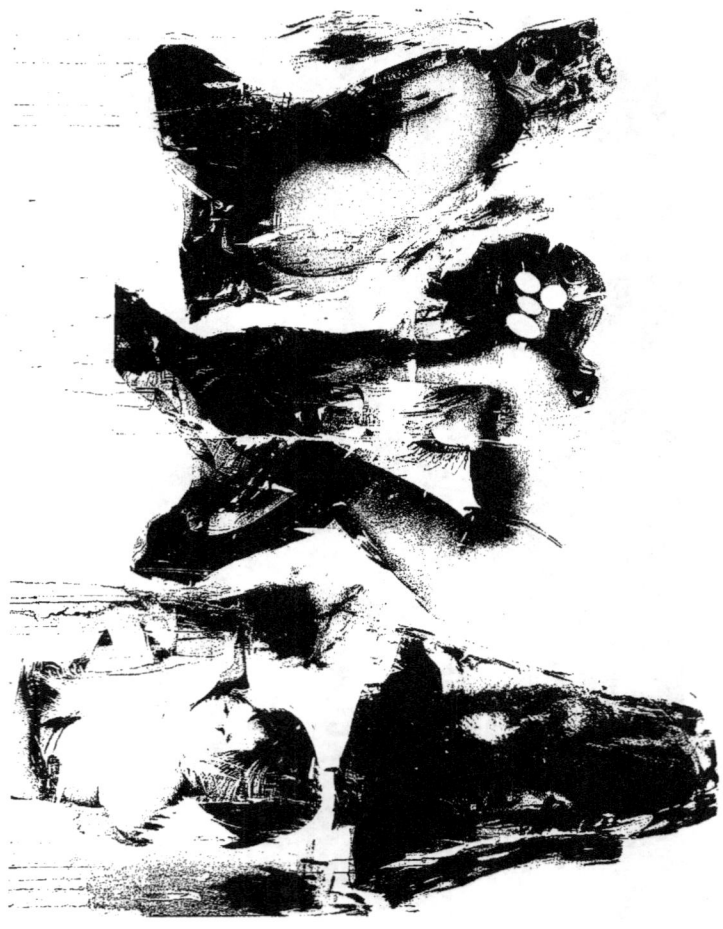

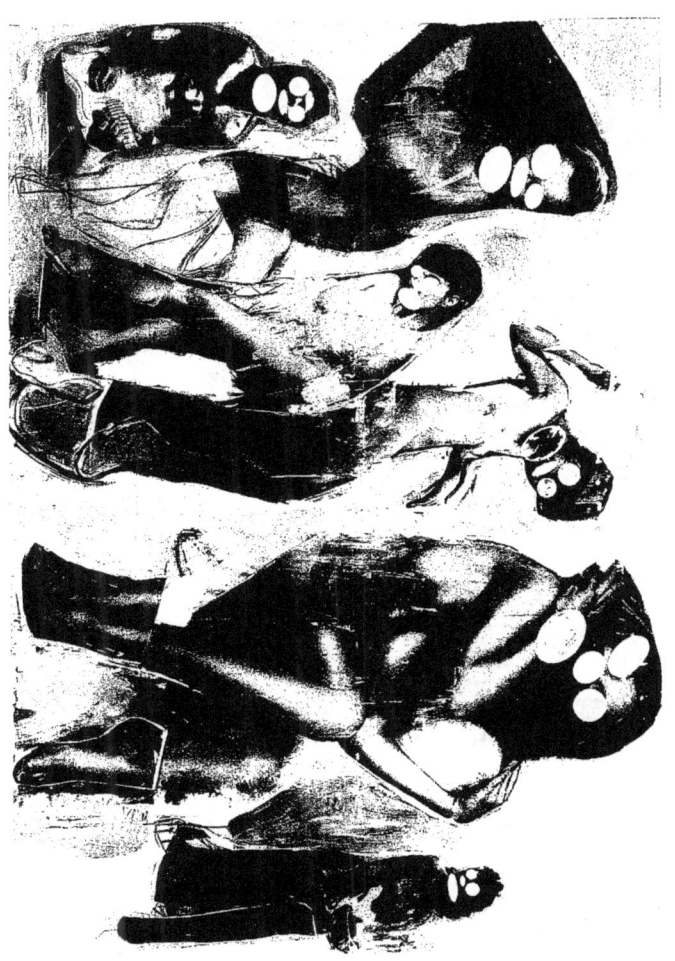

13   Ding Dong the Witch Is Dead

14   Djuna Barnes, Natalie Barney, Renée Vivien, and Romaine Brooks Take Over the Guanahani

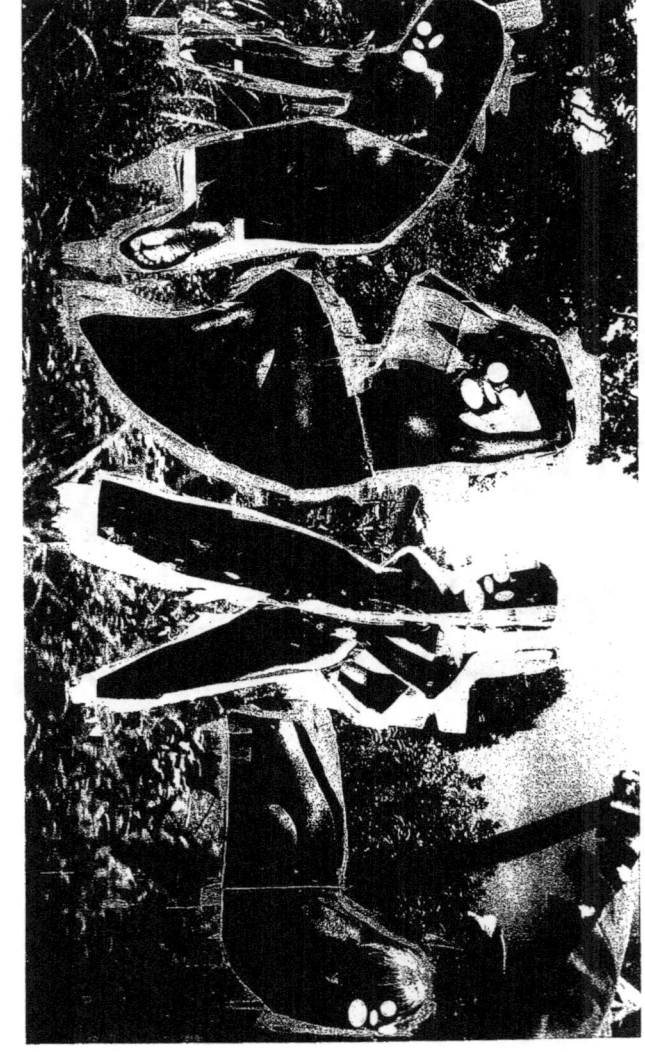

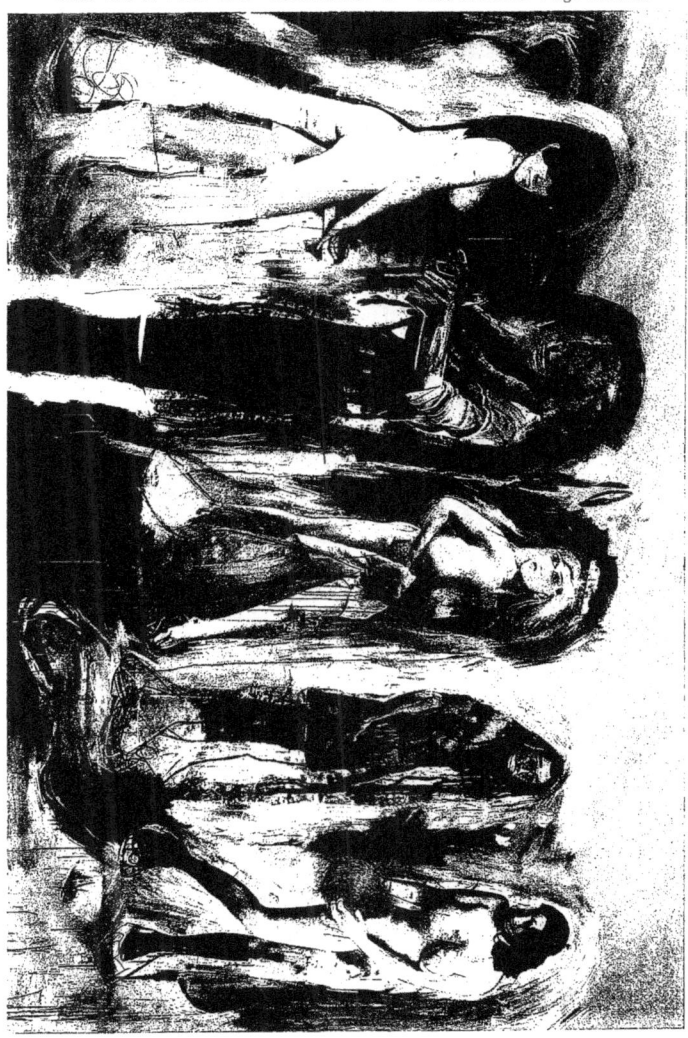

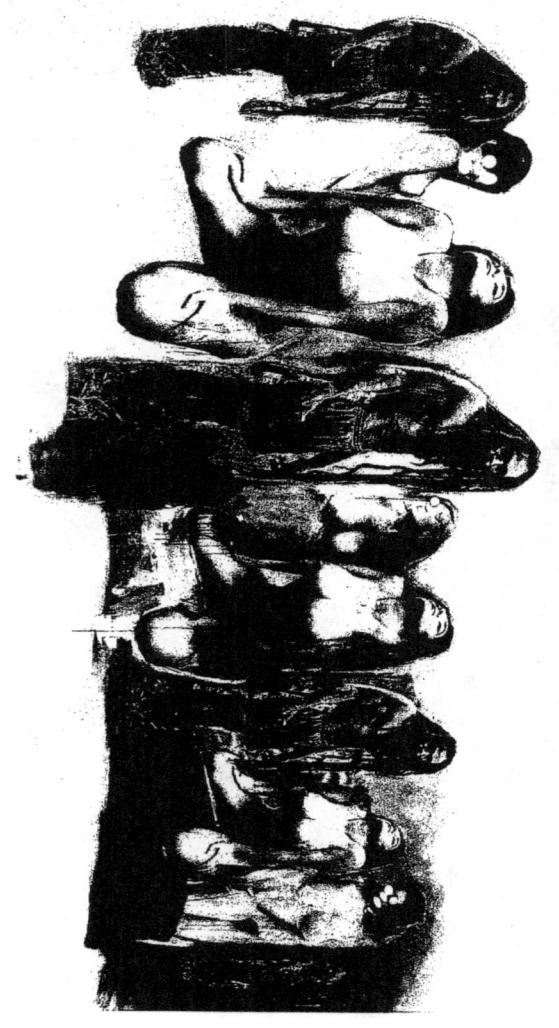

16   Tales of Brave Ulysses

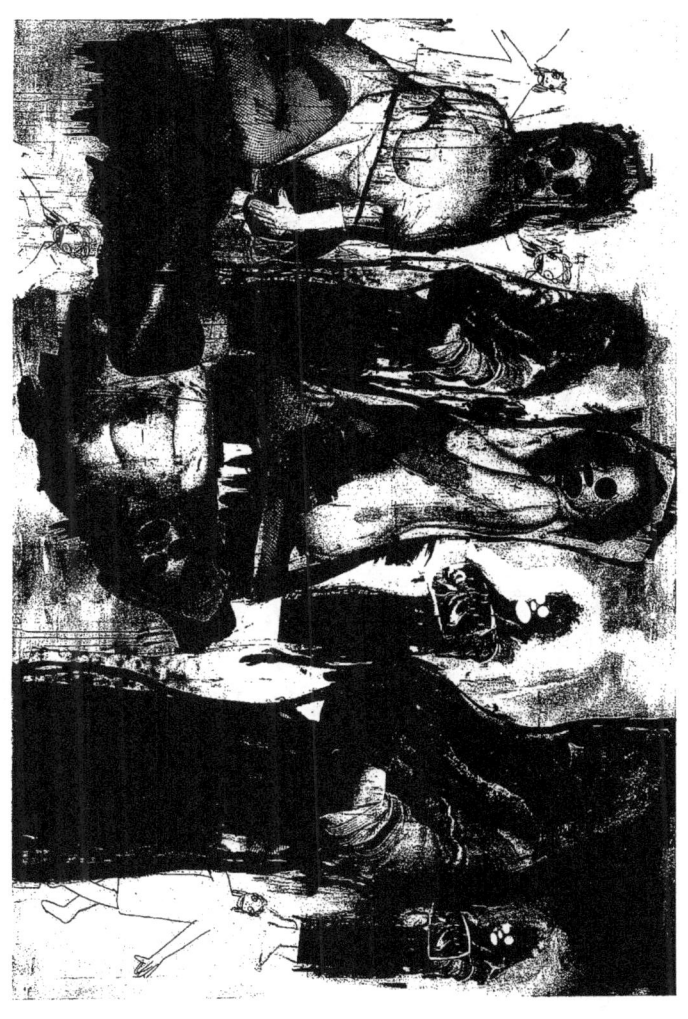

17 It's All Over

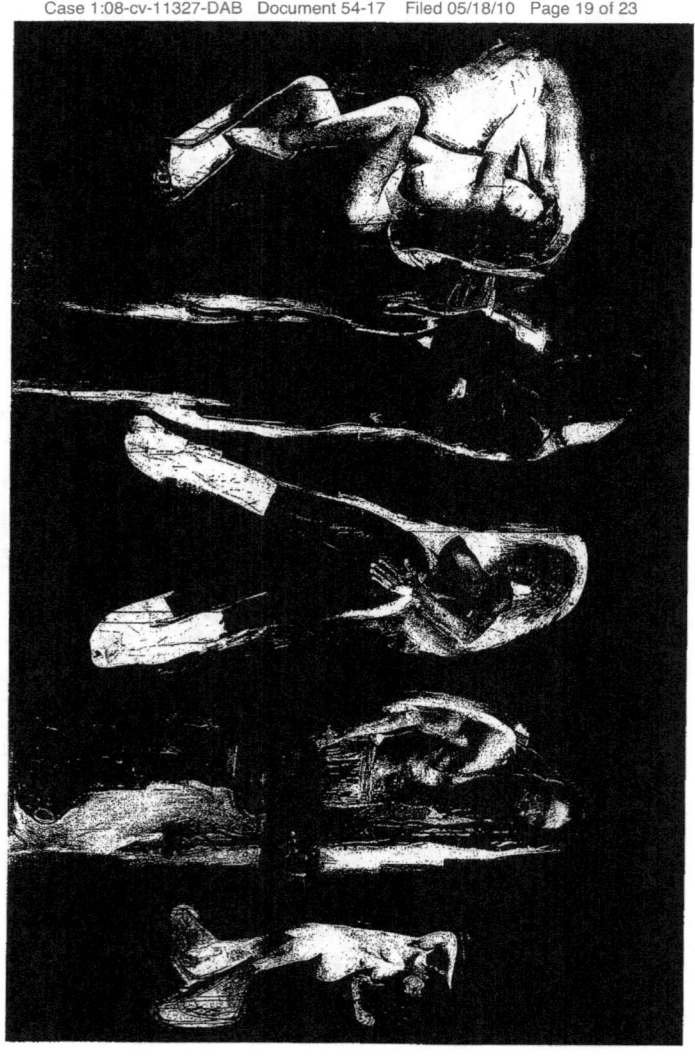

18 Specially Round Midnight

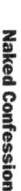

19   Naked Confessions

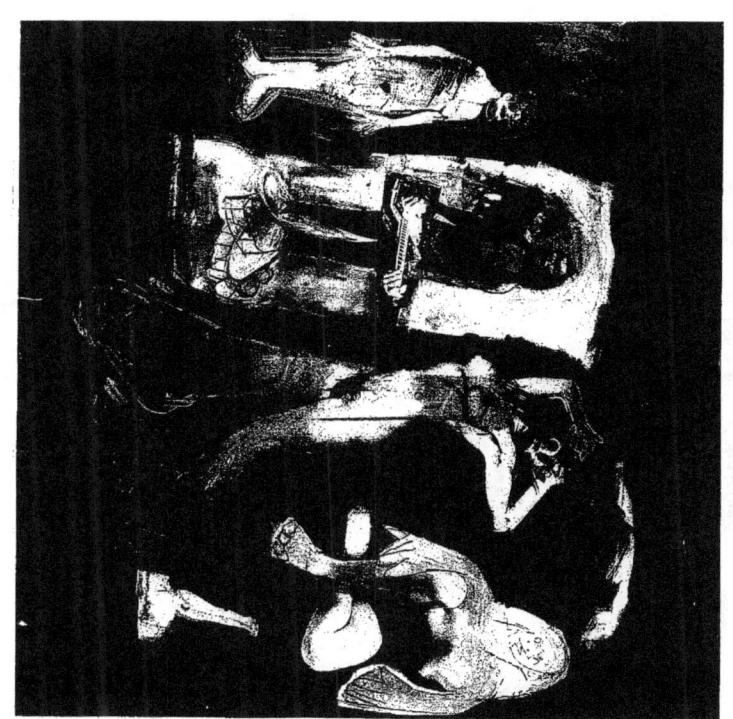

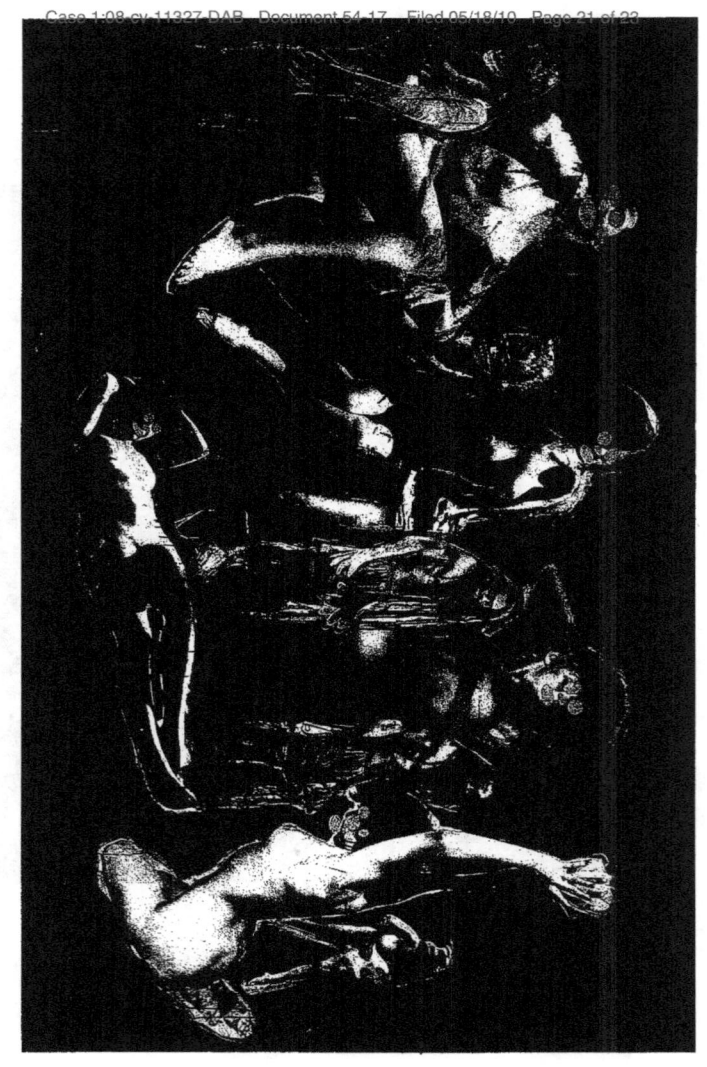

20   The Other Side of the Island

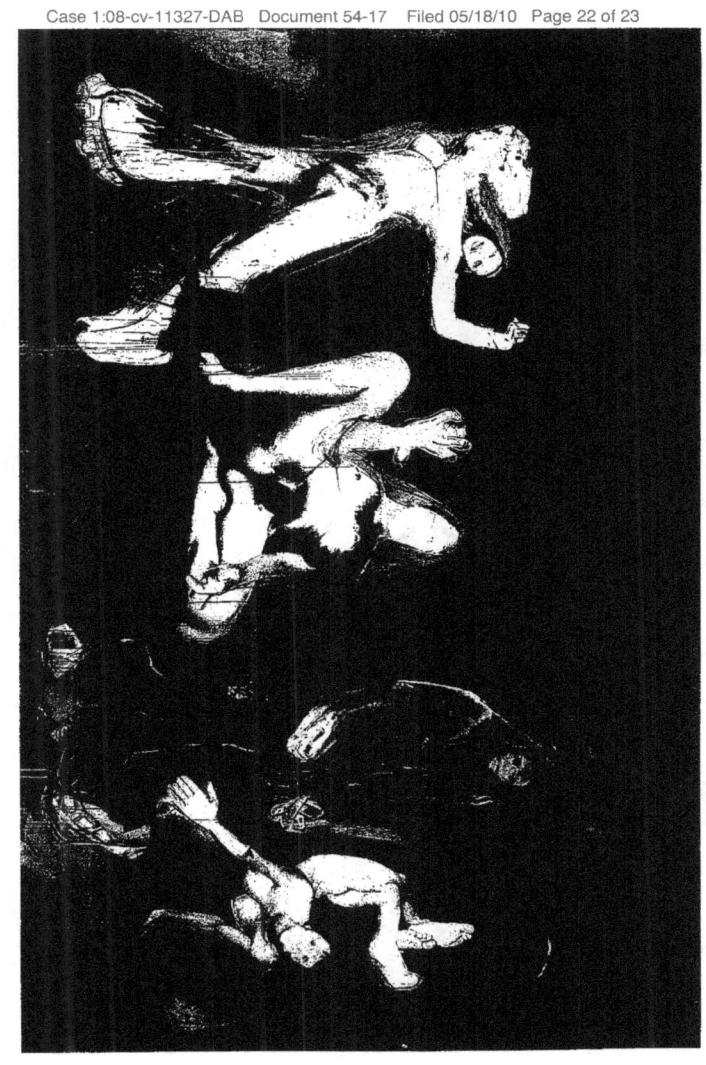

21   Cheese and Crackers

22   Mr. Jones

"Attached hereto as Exhibit O are copies of seven additional Prince paintings, which are not depicted in the Canal Zone Catalogue, which were marked as Exhibit 33 in the Prince deposition."
- ibid., p. 4.

Exhibit O

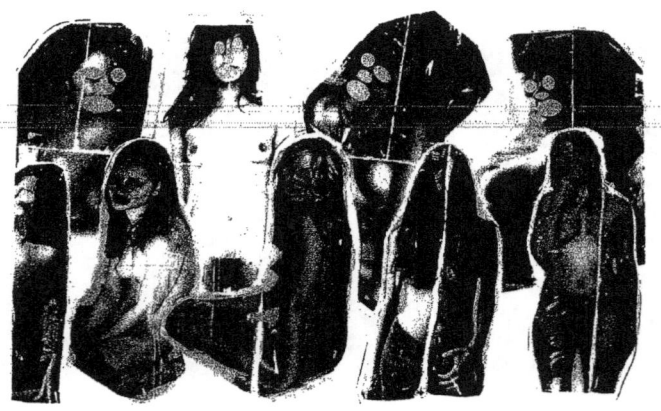

Richard Prince
MC9 (White Panthers), 2008
Ink jet, acrylic and collage on canvas
98 x 132 inches
248.9 x 335.3 cm
(Inv# RPS590)

Δ(π)EXHIBIT 33
Deponent PRINCE
Date 10/06/09 Rptr. Bm
www.DEPOBOOK.COM

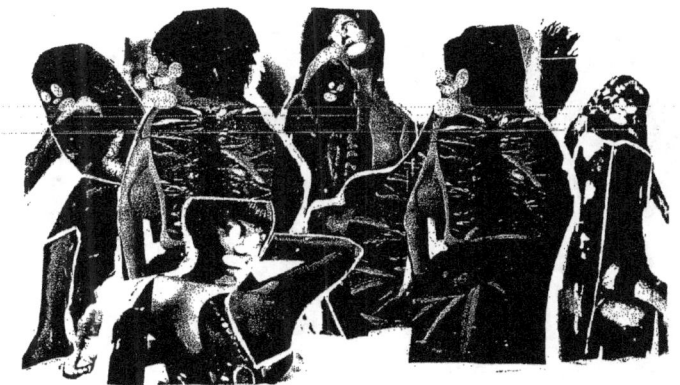

Richard Prince
Mina Loy, Janet Flanner, Radclyffe Hall, Una Trowbridge and Oscar Wilde's niece Dolly Wilde, 2008
Ink jet, acrylic and collage on canvas
77 1/2 x 120 1/2 inches
196.9 x 306.1 cm
(Inv# RPS606)

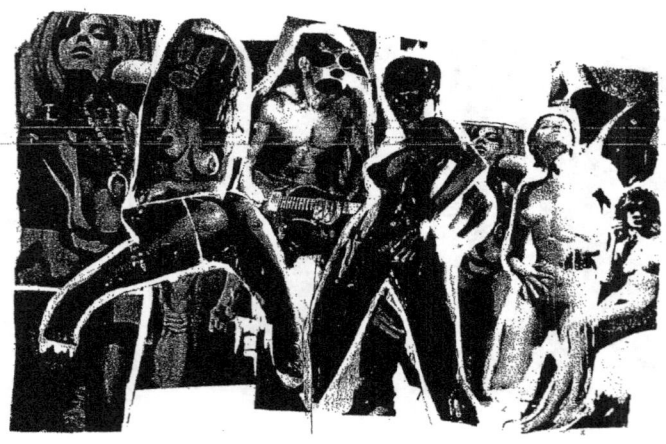

Richard Prince
Pumpsie Green, 2008
Ink jet, acrylic and collage on canvas
77 x 100 1/2 inches
195.6 x 255.3 cm
(Inv# RPS587)

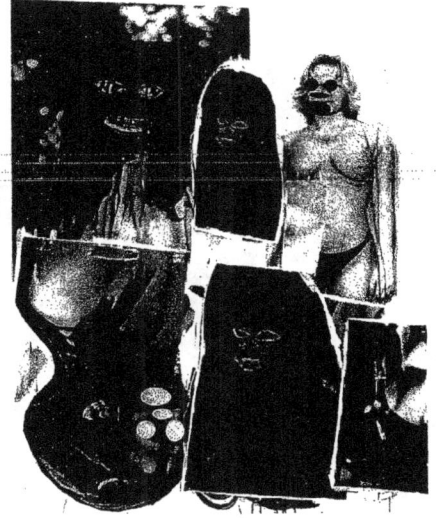

Richard Prince
Uncle Tom, Dick and Harry, 2008
Ink jet, acrylic and collage on canvas
81 1/2 x 57 1/2 inches
207 x 146.1 cm
(Inv# RPS589)

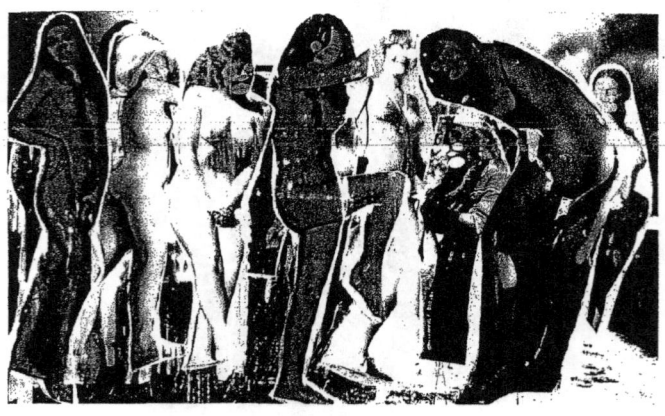

Richard Prince
On The Beach, On The Beach, 2008
Ink jet, acrylic and collage on canvas
59 x 90 1/4 inches
149.9 x 229.2 cm
(Inv# RPS591)

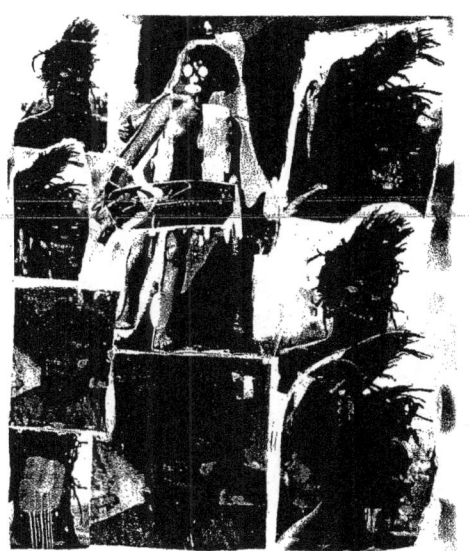

Richard Prince
Inquisition, 2008
Ink jet, acrylic and collage on canvas
100 1/2 x 77 inches
255.3 x 195.6 cm
(Inv# RPS592)

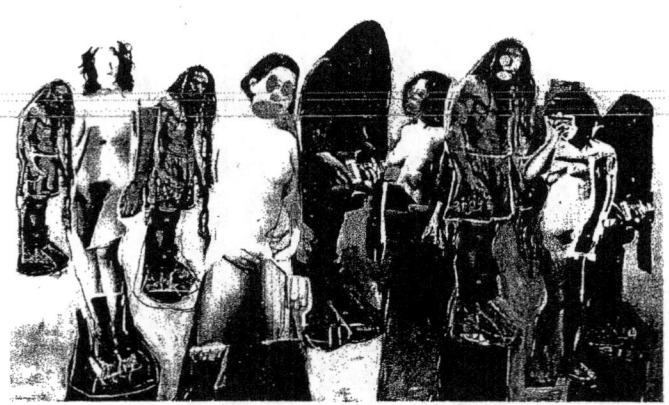

Richard Prince
Escape Goat, 2008
Ink jet, acrylic and collage on canvas
92 x 122 inches
233.7 x 309.9 cm
(Inv# RPS607)

"Attached hereto as Exhibit V is a copy of Prince painting entitled, Canal Zone 2007, which consists of 35 pages from Yes Rasta collaged on a plywood board. This document was marked as Exhibit 14 to the Prince deposition."
- ibid., p. 5 of 9.

Exhibit V

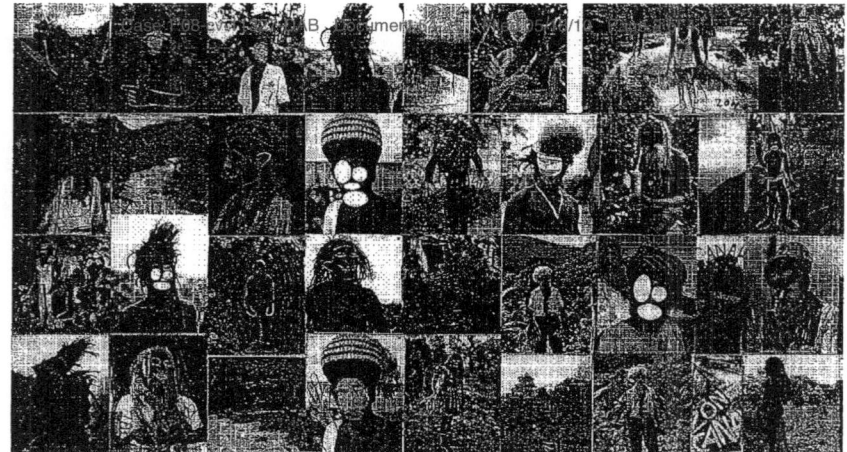

RICHARD PRINCE *The Canal Zone*, 2007   Mixed media on homosote,   48 x 82 3/4 inches, (121.9 x 210.2cm)   PRINC 2007.0033

GAGOSIAN GALLERY

"Attached hereto as Exhibit V-1 is a copy of Canal Zone 2007 as it was exhibited in late 2007 in St. Barth's. This document was marked as Exhibit 15 to the Prince deposition. - ibid., p. 5 of 9.

Exhibit V-1

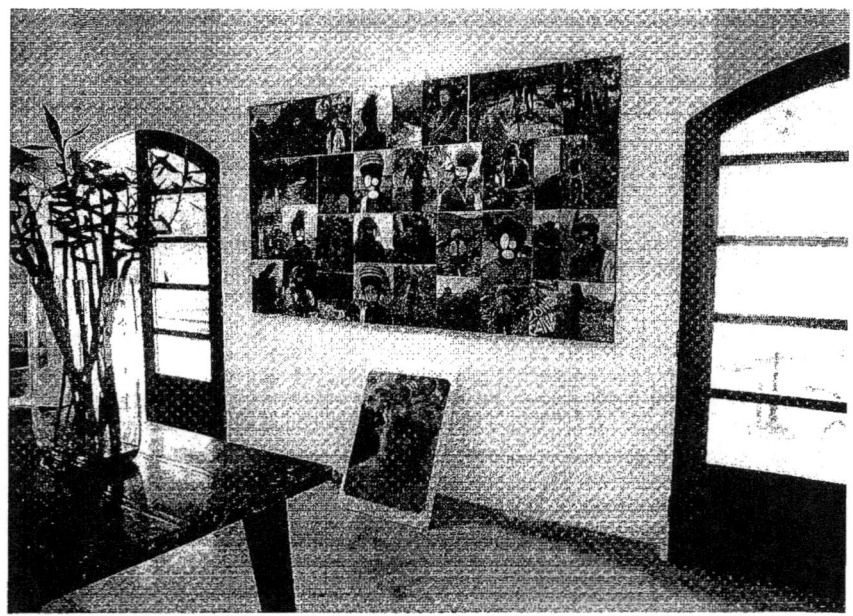

Δ (Z) EXHIBIT 15
Deponent PRINCE
Date 10/06/09 Rptr Bm
WWW.DEPOBOOK.COM

GGP004296

The Pitch

Charles Company, his wife, son and daughter arrive at the St. Barts airport, late afternoon two days before Xmas, he's meeting up with his brother and sister-in-law… staying on the island for a couple of weeks…vacation…
As he's landing, he sees out the window a lot of people running around…general commotion.
As the plane taxis up to the gate he asks the pilot what's going on…
As the Company family disembarks the plane, there's more pandemonium…
People grabbing, shouting, some hysterical…it's a tiny airport, but there's an overload of people waiting to get thru customs and many people literally "crying"…they're "crying" because there are no planes going out…no planes returning to St. Martins…returning to Miami…returning to NYC…returning to London…returning anywhere…
There are no returning flights because these cities and many other major "areas" in the continental U.S. and Western and Eastern Europe have just been obliterated by nuclear attack.
Charles Company and his family are informed of this fact and seemed to melt into the tarmac under 88 degree temps…holding their bags, their backpacks…what will come to be as all their worldly possessions.
They hook up with Charles's brother, who will fill them in with a bit more detail of the events "round" the world. "What are we suppose to do?" is Charles's wife's first question…
"There's nowhere to go", is the first answer.
A good part of the world, "most" of the world, has been nuked and they are here on a tiny French island in the middle of nowhere…which in a year's time will become part *On the Beach*, part *Lord of the Flies*.

Background: Charles is 55, has no military background, is pretty much out of shape…makes his living as an architect.

To make this pitch even shorter I'm going to cut to a year later…

People on the island have broken up into "tribes"…most of the houses have been ransacked and all of the hotels occupied.
Charles Company is now Charlie Company. He has been exercising. Hes also learned to load a weapon, field dress a wound, cook without a fire. His daughter is the #1 scavenger…
He, his wife, son and daughter, brother and sister-in-law, (along with several followers) have taken over the Eden Rock Hotel. It's headquarters.

Stockpiled. A Mini-Mart. As best a fortress as can be under the circumstances. Everything is rationed, everything is "used"...

Next:

Charles's son is standing lookout. Thru his telescope out in the ocean he sees what appears to be a periscope...he sounds the alarm...

The movie is called Eden Rock...

Tuesday, October 21, 2008 2:07 PM

Subject: RE: "The Pitch"
Date: Tuesday, October 7, 2008 4:41 PM
From: Louise Neri
To: Betsy Biscone

Dear Betsy—

Thanks so much for all this.

I definitely want to talk to Richard, but let me get started. Would be great if we can schedule something in on Thursday, then I can get done by the end of the week.

regards and see you soon!

Louise

Louise Neri
Gagosian Gallery
555 West 24th Street,
New York NY 10011

Think before you print.

From: betsy biscone [mailto:
Sent: Tuesday, October 07, 2008 4:29 PM
To: Betsy Biscone; Louise Neri
Cc: Melissa Lazarov
Subject: Re: "The Pitch"

Dear Louise,
I hope this finds you well. Per Richard's request, please find attached *The Pitch*, which was displayed on the wall at the Eden Rock Hotel in Saint Barth for last December 2007, *Eden Rock* Show. Also, you'll find below additional writing Richard did this past Spring '08.

I understand you would like to talk with him at some point. Tell me know what you are thinking so I can schedule something in.
Do let me know if there is any question or if I can be of further assistance.
All best,

Betsy Biscone
--
Prince Studio Manager
R'ville, NY 12147
T:
F:

-- Additional Eden Rock/Pitch Material written MARCH 2008 --

More on Eden Rock

1. Rastas and Reggae... they escape from one of the Cruise ships, (they were the band aboard the ship) three days after the bombs went off. They go to the Hotel Manapany. Six band members, two roadies and a manager.

2. The Backpackers... these are college kids, use to spring breaks, know nothing of responsibility or the real world.

Page 1 of 2

' They gather first in bars then take over a small hotel just above Shell Beach. They keep partying, drinking, smoking... they are the first to "go native"... the first to smear "war paint" on their bodies... they're also the first to get wiped out....

3. The Amazons... Four Lesbians who escape a second Cruise ship, who bring along part of the crew and take over the Guanahani Hotel. These are large well built women along the lines of Shena Queen of the Jungle, Wonder Woman, Cat Woman, think Raquel Welch meets Linda Hamilton in the Terminator. Their outfits, hair and make-up remind us of Road Warriors....

4. The Ultimate Ones... this tribe is made up of rich, affluent, masters of the universe... these are guys who own the huge private boats parked in Gustavia... they have the loyalty of their crews, they have their own weapons and in the beginning access to food and water. They quickly make deals with the local St. Bart police force. They stay on their boats at first but then take over the Ill de France hotel... these guys are use to privilege and shaping the future... they don't take "no" for an answer... they believe they "own" the island and everyone is their subject... several come to be assassinated, held hostage, and hanged upside-down... in an opening scene one of them is pictured buried up to his head in the sand at Saline Beach with the tide coming in...

These are the four main tribes along with Charlie Company...

Charlie Company represents "family"
Rastas and Reggae represents "the disenfranchised"
Backpackers represent "alternative"
Amazons represent "sex"
Ultimate Ones represent "power"

Richard Prince

------ End of Forwarded Message

WITHERS BERGMAN LLP
Hollis Gonerka Bart (HB-8955)
Dara G. Hammerman (DH-1591)
Azmina Jasani (AJ – 4161)
430 Park Avenue, 10ᵗʰ Floor
New York, New York 10022
212.848.9800 (p)
212.848.9888 (f)
Attorneys for Defendants Gagosian Gallery, Inc.
and Lawrence Gagosian

SHERIDAN FISHER & HAYES LLP
Steven M. Hayes, Esq.
Hanly Conroy Bierstein
112 Madison Avenue
New York, NY 10016-7416
(212) 784-6414
Attorneys for Defendant Richard Price

UNITED STATES DISTRICT COURT
SOUTHERN DISTRICT OF NEW YORK
---X

PATRICK CARIOU,   08 CIV 11327 (DAB)

                                      Plaintiff,

                     -against-

RICHARD PRINCE, GAGOSIAN GALLERY, INC.,
LAWRENCE GAGOSIAN, and RIZZOLI
INTERNATIONAL PUBLICATIONS, INC.,

                                      Defendants.

---X

**MEMORANDUM OF LAW IN SUPPORT OF
DEFENDANTS' JOINT MOTION FOR SUMMARY JUDGMENT**

document number: NY23802/0005-US-863030/4

TABLE OF CONTENTS

i

ii

TABLE OF AUTHORITIES

Cases

Other Authorities

Preliminary Statement

In creating the *Canal Zone* paintings, Richard Prince drew inspiration from the world around him to develop his artistic vision for a fantastical, post-apocalyptical world where all that remained was music and the bands to play it. In expressing that vision, Prince, in the tradition of other acclaimed appropriation artists, used raw materials appropriated from many sources, including pages torn from *Yes Rasta,* a book of photographs taken by Patrick Cariou of Rastafarians in their native Jamaican landscape, to convey new insights with a wholly new expressive meaning and message, the redemptive value of music and equality between the sexes. Through the use of established appropriative techniques, Prince expressed this genuine creative rationale, by collaging and scanning rescaled, altered, cropped images to which he added images of guitars, painterly elements, and historical art references as an homage to master painters he admires. In doing so, Prince achieved his goal of using only what was needed to transform the raw elements into a beautiful, completely new and contemporary take on the music scene having nothing to do with Rastafarians in their Jamaican landscape. As such, the exhibition and sale of the *Canal Zone* paintings by Prince, through the efforts of Gagosian Gallery and its owner, Lawrence Gagosian, does not compete with, and therefore could not ursurp the market for, Cariou's *Yes Rasta* images. Indeed, as of November 2008, when the *Canal Zone* exhibition opened, the market for Cariou's images was virtually non-existent due solely to choices Cariou made, and not any bad faith or unlawful conduct by defendants. When viewed in light of defendants' contribution to the broader public benefit of art, then, Prince's use of the *Yes Rasta* images was fair. The goal of copyright law to promote the progress of the arts would be better served by allowing Prince's use of the Images because to hold otherwise would effectively stifle, if not foreclose, an established art form that has been firmly entrenched in society and art history.

1

FACTUAL BACKGROUND

A. **Appropriation Art, an Established Art Form**

Appropriation art can be traced back to the late 19th century when authors, composers and artists began borrowing from existing artworks, using fragments of them to create their own. Kenly Ames, *Beyond Rogers v. Koons: A Fair Use Standard For Appropriation*, 93 Colum. L. Rev. 1473, 1478 (Oct. 1993) ("Ames"). By the 20th century, incorporation of elements of popular culture and of existing works had become routine. *See* Ex A (Tate Collection Glossary definition of Appropriation Art).[1] In appropriating artwork, artists "encompass a wide variety of methods, ranging from the incorporation of a single element into a much larger work through collage techniques to the reproduction of an image without physical alteration, but reattributed to the appropriating artist." Ames at 1479. The collage technique takes pieces of photographs, fabric and other raw materials that are organized together and affixed to a surface, often a canvas, creating a layered effect, to produce a completely new work. *See* Ex B (Tate Collection Glossary definition of collage). By reusing a work and removing it from its usual context, appropriation artists aim to give new meaning to the work, questioning "the most fundamental perceptions, both literal and symbolic, on which society is based." Id. at 1482.

Some examples of the most celebrated appropriation art include Dadaist Marcel Duchamp's Fountain (1917), in which he used a readymade urinal, rotated it ninety degrees and signed it with a pseudonym "R. Mutt," to reference a popular cartoon character. *See* Ex C (Tate

---

[1] "Ex __ " refers to the exhibits attached to the accompanying Affidavit of Hollis Gonerka Bart ("Bart Aff."). "RP Aff." or "Prince Affidavit" refers to the accompanying Affidavit of Richard Prince in Support of Defendants' Joint Motion for Summary Judgment. "RP Tr." refers to the transcript of the Prince deposition taken on October 6, 2009, "LG Tr." refers to the transcript of the deposition of Lawrence Gagosian taken on October 8, 2009, "AP Tr." refers to the transcript of the deposition of Anthony Petrillose, taken on October 23, 2009, "PC Tr." refers to the transcript of the deposition of Patrick Cariou taken on January 12, 2010, "CC Tr." refers to the transcript of the deposition of Christiane Celle taken on January 26, 2010, excerpts of which are attached to Bart Aff. as Exhibits G, L, R, U, Y, respectively.

Collection description of Marcel Duchamp). Another is pop-artist Andy Warhol, who created iconic paintings using popular, commercial images and portrait paintings and recreated them using bright colors, repetition, and his signature grid. *See id.* at Ex D (MOMA description of Warhol's Gold Marilyn Monroe 1962). Other well-known appropriation artists include Pablo Picasso, Georges Braque, Jasper Johns, Robert Rauschenberg, Sherrie Levine, Salvador Dali, Jeff Koons and Prince. *See* Ex A; *see also* Ex E, ¶ 18; Ex F (Guggenheim Release on Prince).

B.   Richard Prince, a World-Renowned Appropriation Artist

Prince's career as an appropriation artist began in 1977, when he re-photographed discarded advertising images he salvaged while working in the tear-sheet department of Time Life. RP Aff. ¶ 5; RP Tr. 12-13, 48-49; *see also* RP Tr. 46. Initially, Prince made collages with the clippings, combining the images as if they were freeze frames from the same movie. RP Aff. ¶ 5. Over time, he began working with other artists' photographic images and re-photographing them to place them in a wholly different context. *Id.* at ¶ 6; *see also* RP Tr. 13-16. In 1984, Prince began a new body of works consisting of exact re-drawings of cartoons that evoke a mix of cultural preferences, human desires and prejudices. *Id.* at ¶ 7. These works eventually led to his pursuit of painting and the addition of painterly elements to his work. *Id* at ¶ 7. In the ensuing years, his techniques expanded with his scribbled "Hippy Drawings" consisting of stick figures with abstract, mask-like faces onto which he would paint circles over the eyes, nose and mouth, known as his "lozenge" faces. RP Aff. ¶ 8. This body of work was followed by sequential series such as the *Nurses* (2002-04), the *Check Paintings* (2004-05), the *De Kooning Paintings* (2007-07), and the *Canal Zone* (2008). RP Aff. ¶ 10. With each successive series, Prince broadened his gestural style with bright colors, dripping paint, bold brush strokes and other painterly elements to create a layered effect. *Id.* at ¶ 9. Historically, Prince has gravitated

3

toward repetition, groupings and categories as he expresses himself taxonomically, based on the belief that objects are best understood in relation to other objects. *Id.* at ¶ 11.

Prince's appropriative style also is informed by trends in popular culture. *Id.* at ¶ 12. Prince's works feature guitars as a repetitive element, representing his love for music. *Id.* at ¶ 12. Prince is "always trying to hook [his] art up with musical terms." RP Tr. 43; *see also id.* at 125-26. Prince frequently pays homage in his works to master painters whose work he respects. RP Aff. ¶¶ 21, 27; RP Tr. 165-67; Ex F (Guggenheim Release on Prince). Prince aspires to create beautiful pieces of art, and believes that "artists ... should be as free as possible... in their studios." Price Aff. ¶ 3; RP Tr. 123. "Art is about freedom. It's not about being restricted. If I was restricted, then I couldn't transform these images . . . I believe artists   . . . should be as free as possible, yes, in their studios." *Id.* at 120-21.

Prince's works are considered among the most innovative art produced in the past 30 years. Ex F; *see also* Ex E at ¶ 28 (Prince is "an accomplished, educated and informed artist"). The work of Prince has been widely exhibited and is found in the permanent collections of major museums around the world. RP Aff. ¶ 3. In late 2007, the Solomon R. Guggenheim Museum in New York presented a major retrospective of his work, which filled the entire rotunda and two tower galleries. *Id.* at ¶ 3. *See also* Ex F. Prince's works also are sought by significant collectors. RP Aff. ¶ 4. He has an active and strong primary gallery market, with a strong secondary market at auctions and in private sales. *See* Ex H, Ex I. In 2008, *Overseas Nurse* sold at auction in London for approximately $8.4 million, the highest price for a work by Prince to date. *See* Ex J, Ex K.

C.   Prince's Creation of the *Canal Zone* Series

As detailed further in his affidavit, Prince's creation of the *Canal Zone* series evolved from the storyline of a cinematic "pitch" he began writing in 2007 entitled, *Eden Rock.* *See* RP

Aff. Ex A; *see also* RP Tr. 218, 232. The screenplay is his fantastical account of survivors of a worldwide nuclear attack whose cruise ships end up in St. Barts. *Id.; see also* RP Tr. 30, 192, 207-208. Forming separate "tribes" or "gangs," these survivors take over the resort hotels on the island and create their own post-apocalyptic society. *Id.* at ¶ 16; *see also* RP Tr. 207-08, 214-18.

For Prince, the creation of the *Canal Zone* series was the culmination of a confluence of events that came together when he heard his stepson playing the alternative music of the Easy Star All-Stars band in the album *Radiodread.* RP Aff. ¶ 17; RP Tr. 263-64, 266. The next day, Prince found a copy of *Yes Rasta* in a bookstore on St. Barts (Ex EE), and was drawn to the images in the book, given his inclusion of a reggae band as the Rastafarian "tribe" in his screenplay. RP Aff. ¶ 17; RP Tr. 150-51, 153-58, 158, 266. Drawing inspiration from his birthplace, the Panama Canal Zone, where he had recently visited, and the storyline of his *Eden Rock* screenplay, Prince imagined a make-believe, post-apocalyptic enclave, the Canal Zone, in which bands and music are the only things to survive. RP Aff. ¶ 16; RP Tr. 7, 30, 207-08, 218, 232, 251-52. As Prince explains it, "the redemptive value of music is one of the important concepts of this series." *Id.* at ¶ 22; *see also* RP Tr. 251-52 (Prince's *Canal Zone* Paintings represent a musical band).

To convey his message, Prince, in the tradition of Duchamp, used appropriated imagery, which included 41 images torn from the pages of *Yes Rasta* (collectively, the "Images"), and images of naked women, rock guitars and musicians' hands taken from several other sources. RP Aff. ¶ 24; PR Tr. 30 (Images were but one of the "recipe ingredients" that became the *Canal Zone* series); *see also* RP Tr. 170-71, 277-80 (guitars, naked women and Rastas were all ingredients in the Paintings, with the guitar being the primary one). In all but one of the works, *Canal Zone,* 2007, Prince digitally scanned and enlarged the images, applying some directly to the canvas as a backdrop for collaging, and others as cut-out collage elements. RP Aff. ¶ 26; RP

5

Tr. 40; 168-69. In some of the works, Prince affixed the collage elements to other images with scotch tape for further scanning, and in others he would apply the collage elements directly to the canvas using his squeegee technique in which elements are affixed to the canvas with paint.[2] RP Aff. ¶ 26; *see also* RP Tr. 168-69; 331-37. *Canal Zone*, 2007 consists of portions of 35 Rastafarian faces torn from pages in *Yes Rasta* and onto which Prince drew and painted facemasks. RP Aff. ¶ 48. These were reordered and tacked to a board as means for Prince to introduce the likely characters of his next series, the *Canal Zone*. *Id.*

Stylistic references to the history of art are a hallmark of Prince's *Canal Zone* Paintings in which he pays homage to artists such as de Kooning, Cezanne, Warhol and Picasso. RP Aff. ¶ 21; RP Tr. at 165-66; 300-01. For example, the enlarged hands in several Paintings represent a transition from the *De Kooning* series, which emulated the compositional style of De Kooning's hybrid creatures, and also is a reference to Cezanne's *Bathers*. RP Aff. ¶ 21; *see also* RP Tr. 156, 166-67, 251-52; 264-65. In the style of de Kooning's contorted facial features and Picasso's primitive masks, Prince abstracted the faces found in many of the *Canal Zone* Paintings with painterly elements, oil stick crayon, and the application of his signature "lozenge-face" circles. RP Aff. ¶ 21; *see also* RP Tr. 172-73. As Prince explained in his deposition, he was attempting to create an "unbelievably looking great painting that had to do with a kind of rock-and-roll painting on the radical side, and on a conservative side, something to do with Cezanne's *Bathers*." *Id.* at 361. "As I said, I'm trying to make a kind of fantastic, absolutely hip, up to date, contemporary take on the music scene. And it's my way of dealing with this idea that I've always had, which are the three relationships that exist in the world, which are men and

---

[2] For a more detailed description of the transformative nature of the various elements and techniques Prince used in the Paintings in the *Canal Zone* series, the Court is respectfully referred to the Prince Affidavit at paragraphs 32 through 61 and Exhibit A thereto, which is a Composite Exhibit describing the transformative elements of each of the Paintings, and contrasting Cariou's stated purpose for each of the Images Prince lawfully appropriated from *Yes Rasta*.

women, men and men, and women and women." *Id.* at 338-39. In the *Canal Zone series,* Prince emphasized equality between the sexes. RP Aff. ¶ 61.

D.   Gagosian Gallery's *Canal Zone* Exhibition

Lawrence Gagosian is the founder and owner of the Gagosian Gallery, a leading contemporary art gallery with eight locations worldwide. Ex L at LG Tr. 16, 18-19. Throughout its history, Gagosian Gallery has dedicated itself to organizing important exhibitions of contemporary art. *See,* www.gagosian.com. Since approximately 2005, Gagosian Gallery has represented Prince in the marketing and exhibition of his artwork. LG Tr. 24.

From about November 8, 2008 through December 20, 2008, Gagosian Gallery held the *Canal Zone* Exhibition (the "Exhibition") at its gallery in Chelsea, featuring 22 of the 29 Paintings in the *Canal Zone* series. Ex M; LG Tr. 25. Gagosian Gallery sold 14 of the Paintings through its promotion of the exhibition. Ex N at Ex A. Gagosian Gallery purchased four of the Paintings, and some were traded in non-cash transactions for other works. *Id.*

Gagosian Gallery spent approximately $434,730.47 organizing and marketing the Exhibition. Ex O at GGP0043144. Advertisements for the Exhibition were featured in various publications. Ex P at GG0071-79. Marketing efforts primarily targeted prominent collectors, gallerists and museums, as they are the predominant market for Prince's artwork. *See* Ex H. Invitations to the Exhibition were sent to target consumers. *See* LG Tr. 59-60; Ex Q. Gagosian Gallery also created a catalogue entitled *Canal Zone,* featuring Paintings in the Exhibition. Bart Aff. Ex M. Rizzoli International planned to publish *Canal Zone* for distribution that was scheduled to begin in September 2009, but Rizzoli backed out because of plaintiff's lawsuit.[3] *See* AP Tr. 24. Though not legally obligated to do so, Defendants withdrew the unsold Paintings, pending this case. RP Aff. ¶ 28.

---

[3] Plaintiff has since dismissed all claims against Rizzoli with prejudice. *See* Ex S.

E.   Cariou's Career as a Photographer

Cariou is a Paris-based photographer who has published a number of photography books, including *Yes Rasta*, published in 2000 by powerHouse Books, Inc. ("powerHouse"). PC Tr. 45-46, 280, 285; Ex T ¶ 3; Ex E ¶ 3. For the past 20 years, Cariou has focused on portraiture photography and landscapes. PC Tr. 45-6, 280, 285. Sometime before 2004, Cariou stopped accepting commercial free-lance photography assignments to focus solely on his photography projects. PC Tr. 282. Two other books, entitled *Surfers* and *Trench Town Love*, containing Cariou's portraiture-style photographic images have been published. According to Cariou, his fourth book, featuring his Gypsy project, was finished in the fall of 2008, however, as of January 2010, he had no plans to publish this book. PC Tr. 286-7; *but see* CC Tr. 43-44. A few images from Cariou's *Yes Rasta* book and *Surfers* book were exhibited at a gallery in Paris in 2000. PC Tr. 234-235, 288-89. Images from his *Trench Town Love* series were exhibited in a small museum in Paris named La Villette for two months in 2009 as part of a group show. Ex V at 3(f); PC Tr. 288-90.

F.   Cariou's Creation of the Images in *Yes Rasta*

According to Cariou, the approximately 100 images that appear in *Yes Rasta* were taken over a six-year period, during which time he continued his career as a professional photographer. AC at ¶ 16; PC Tr. 39-40. Cariou testified that he wanted to photograph Rastafarians in Jamaica because of his love for Reggae music, Jamaica, its culture, the "look" of the Rastafarians and because "no book ha[d] ever been done about Rastafarians." PC Tr. 35-6; Ex E ¶ 16; Ex Z. His intent was to document the Rastafarian culture and the surrounding landscapes, and to capture as closely as possible the subject being photographed. PC Tr. 36, 40-43, 45, 110, 166, 171; 172-73; 176-78; 265-66; *see also id.* at 120; 185-86 ("What I'm into is to make beautiful books."); [4]

---

[4] None of the images in *Yes Rasta* have titles. PC Tr. 77; *but see* RP Tr. 248-49 (for Prince, titles to the Paintings are an important component to the works and to "recontextualizing the image" and "create[] another type of subtext that you can read into the painting.").

8

GGP0043115-6; *but see* RP Tr. 357-58 (in contrast to Cariou's images which capture what is actually there, Prince has "never been interested in what's actually there."). Cariou described the *Yes Rasta* project to powerHouse Books, in this way: "I told them that I wanted to have a book of photographs,...of portraiture, and I didn't want that book to look pop culture at all . . . ." *Id.* at 187. Cariou testified that powerHouse marketed *Yes Rasta* to consumers of artist books. *See id.* at 188; *but see* Ex W.

Cariou describes his portraiture style as "a static way of taking a picture of when someone is looking at you;" that is, it is staged and the subject knows he/she is being photographed. *Id.* at 45-46. To Cariou, it is the combination of the way the subject looks at the viewer, the way his body looks, the lighting and the quality of the black and white that make his images strikingly original. *See, e.g.,* PC Tr. 80-81; *but see* Ex CC (similar images from Internet).

Cariou explained that sometimes he would just snap a landscape shot while on his way to another destination, and sometimes he would choose background settings because he thought they would make a beautiful portrait, they suited the subject, were visually compelling, or created a tropical feel, or because they just "felt good" or it "felt right" and not because of any specific attribute about the particular setting. *Id.* at 51, 74, 84, 109-10, 112, 115; 151. Cariou also included photographs of marijuana plantations to depict a prominent feature of the Rastafarian and Jamaican cultures. *Id.* at 114-15; 118. Many of the Images were taken in the towns of Negril and Lucille and in other public places. *Compare* PC Tr. 6, 36-37, 73-74, 83-84, 128 *with* Ex E at ¶ 16. In many instances, Cariou blurred the landscape background to make the subject stand out. *See, e.g.,* PC Tr. 53-55, 123-24; 140-41. Cariou believes his landscape images in *Yes Rasta* are distinctive because they are his and because of the way the tropical landscape is organized in the book, adjacent to the portraiture shots. *Id.* at 67-68, 109; *see also id.* at 171. As

9

Cariou explained it, the reader must view the whole book to get the feel of the subject matter of each of the individual images in *Yes Rasta*.[5] *Id.* at 81.

G.   By Cariou's Own Design, the Market for his Images is Virtually Non-Existent

Cariou has utilized an unconventional business model to manage and advance his career as a photographer, such that as of November 2008, the market for his photographic images was virtually nonexistent. Information about Cariou's career as well as images from his books can be found at the website he set up years ago, www.patrickcariou.com. Cariou says he does not maintain or monitor this website or check the email address listed on the webpage to see if he has had any inquiries concerning his work. PC Tr. 239. Visitors to Cariou's website can only purchase photographs if they contact him directly via the website. *Id.* at 238-39. Cariou testified that since its creation, no one has contacted him through the website to purchase any of his photographs. *Id.* at 239-40, 254, 260.

Cariou has only sold a few photographs, and by choice, all of these sales were to his friends or to people he liked depending on his mood. Ex V at 1(c); *see also* PC Tr. 89, 92, 126, 157-58, 161, 237, 283-84. In each instance, Cariou arbitrarily decided the price. *See* PC Tr. 92. *Id.* at 221. Moreover, in selecting artist editions for the works he sold, Cariou said he did not really give much thought to which photographs to select. *Id.* at PC Tr. 93-94. Likewise, Cariou has made little attempt to market the *Yes Rasta* images, and he has not given any of the 70 copies of *Yes Rasta* that he received free from the publisher to people who could help market the book. *Id.* at 103, 109, 116, 118, 121, 128, 129, 134, 139, 140, 142, 144, 153, 159, 221.

Cariou is not listed in the 2009 Art in America guide to galleries, museums and artists. *See generally* www.artinamerica.com. Cariou also is not included in either of the Artnet

---

[5] For a detailed recitation of Cariou's stated reasons for photographing the Images, the Court is respectfully referred to the Composite Exhibit attached to the Prince Affidavit as Exhibit A.

databases, which is a valuable resource utilized by art appraisers, art dealers, museum curators, auction experts, and collectors to find artists. *See* www.artnet.com. Cariou's website does not list museum exhibitions featuring his work. Ex X at GG004340 – 43143. Other than the exhibition at Gallerie 213, Paris, Cariou has not exhibited or actively sought to exhibit the *Yes Rasta* Images in an effort to promote their sale. PC Tr. 232, 234-235, 288-89.

According to Cariou, exhibiting his works at the Clik Gallery was the first opportunity he considered to exhibit and sell the *Yes Rasta* Images. *Id.* at PC Tr. 95. Cariou testified that Christiane Celle ("Celle") planned to represent him on an exclusive basis for the exhibition. *Id.* Cariou claims that Celle backed away from doing the *Yes Rasta* show because she did not want to look opportunistic and ride on Prince's fame while his work was being exhibited at Gagosian. *Id.* at 100. Celle, however, has not foreclosed working with Cariou on future projects, and has even requested proofs from Cariou for other shows, but Cariou has not followed through with finalizing her representation of him. Bart Aff. Ex Y, CC Tr. 106, 133, 149; *see also* PC Tr. 103. After deciding not to move forward with the *Yes Rasta* exhibition, Celle also reached out to Cariou to inform him of her decision. CC Tr. 63. However, Cariou never responded. CC Tr. 63-65, 71. It was not until they spoke months later, when he called to ask her for help with this lawsuit, that Celle first informed Cariou that she had, for her own professional reasons, decided not to proceed with a show featuring the Images in *Yes Rasta*. *Id.* 71-73. Cariou has not approached anyone else about the possibility of helping him implement his plan to sell prints from his various bodies of work, including invoking his right under his agreement with powerHouse Cultural Entertainment, Inc. ("powerHouse") to permit others to publish his Images. *Id.* at 103, 230-231.

Cariou was not involved in the marketing, advertising, or publicity of *Yes Rasta*. *See id.* at 185, 212, 224. Cariou did not know how many *Yes Rasta* books were sold, whether it was out

11

of print, how many copies powerHouse still has available for sale, or whether powerHouse has received inquires about the possible sale of *Yes Rasta*. *Id.* at 211, 218, 230, 268; *see also* RP Tr. 236 (*Yes Rasta* was out of print when Prince started to create the *Canal Zone* series). Discovery obtained from powerHouse shows that the market for *Yes Rasta* is very small. *See* Ex T at ¶ 4. powerHouse published one edition of *Yes Rasta*, and has only sold 5,791 copies. *Id.* at ¶ 2, 3. Cariou has earned $8,087.75 in royalties from the sale of *Yes Rasta*. *Id.* at 214-215; Ex T at ¶¶ 2, 3, and 6. Although powerHouse has not foreclosed working with Cariou on future projects, a hard cover edition of Yes Rasta is out of stock and a limited number of copies are available for sale through the powerHouse website. *Id.* at Ex T, ¶¶ 8-9, 11. Cariou claims his ability to sell copies of *Yes Rasta* or to earn revenues from derivative works based on the Images has been damaged due to defendants' alleged conduct. Ex E at ¶ 14. Cariou, however, never intended to continue with portrait photography, and it was not until recently that he allegedly "decided" he was finally ready to market and sell his images. PC Tr. 94-95, 235, 284-85, 286.

ARGUMENT

PRINCE'S APPROPRIATIVE USE OF THE *YES RASTA* IMAGES WAS FAIR

Section 107 of the Copyright Act is a codification of the common law tradition of fair use adjudication, and requires courts to avoid a rigid application of the copyright statute that "would stifle the very creativity which that law is designed to foster." *Campbell v. Acuff-Rose Music, Inc.*, 510 U.S. 569, 577 (1994). *See also* Pierre N. Leval, *Toward a Fair Use Standard*, 103 Harv. L. Rev. 1105, 1107 (1990) ("Leval") ("Fair use should be perceived . . . as a rational, integral part of copyright, whose observance is necessary to achieve the objectives of that law."). "The ultimate test of fair use . . . is whether the copyright law's goal of 'promoting the Progress of Science and useful Arts,' . . . 'would be better served by allowing the use than by preventing it.'" *Blanch v. Koons*, 467 F.3d 244, 251 (2d Cir. 2006) (citations omitted).

12

In determining fair use, courts rely on four *non-exclusive*, statutory factors: 1) "the purpose and character of the use," 2) "the nature of the copyrighted work," 3) "the amount and substantiality of the portion used in relation to the copyrighted work as a whole," and 4) "the effect of the use upon the potential market for or value of the copyrighted work." 17 U.S.C. § 107. Since "no generally applicable definition [of the fair use doctrine] is possible . . . each case raising the question must be decided on its own facts." *Harper & Row, Publishers, Inc. v. Nation Enters.*, 471 U.S. 539, 560 (1985). *See also Blanch*, 467 F.3d at 251 (*citing Campbell*, 510 U.S. at 577-78) ("determination of fair use defense is an open-ended and context-sensitive inquiry."). "Although '[f]air use is a mixed question of law and fact,' this court has on a number of occasions resolved fair use determinations at the summary judgment stage where . . . there are no genuine issues of material fact." *Blanch*, 467 F.3d at 250. When viewed in light of the pivotal role of the fair use defense in promoting the progress of arts and the public exhibition of art, Prince's appropriation of plaintiff's *Images* should be considered fair use as a matter of law.[6]

A.   **Because the Paintings in Prince's *Canal Zone* Series Were Created With New Insights, a Different Purpose, Message and New Meaning, the Character and Purpose Prong of the Fair Use Defense Weighs Decidedly in Defendants' Favor**

The first factor, the purpose and character of the use, lies at the heart of the fair use inquiry, and is often considered the key factor in determining fair use. *See Campbell*, 510 U.S. at 579. In evaluating the purpose and character prong, courts in this Circuit consider whether the use was transformative, for a commercial purpose, and in bad faith, as well as the rationale for the use. *See, e.g., Blanch*, at 476 F.3d at 251-56.

---

[6] Plaintiff's Fifth Claim for Relief, "Conspiracy by [Defendants] to Violate Plaintiff's Rights Under the Copyright Act" must be dismissed because there is no cause of action under New York for conspiracy to violate the Copyright Act, and such claims are preempted by the Copyright Act. *Calloway v. Marvel Entm't. Group*, 1983 U.S. Dist. Lexis 10506, at **14-15 (S.D.N.Y. 1983); *Irwin v. ZDF Enters. GMBH*, 2006 U.S. Dist. Lexis 6156, at *9 n.1, 11-14 (S.D.N.Y. 2006).

13

1.   Prince's Use of the Images was Transformative

In determining whether the secondary work is transformative, the central inquiry is

whether it "merely 'supersedes the objects' of the original creation, or instead adds something

new, with a further purpose or different character, altering the first with new expression,

meaning, or message…in other words, whether and to what extent the new work is

'transformative.' Although such transformative use is not absolutely necessary for a finding of

fair use, the goal of copyright, to promote science and arts, is generally furthered by the creation

of transformative works. Such transformative works thus lie at the heart of the fair use

doctrine's guarantee of breathing space." *Id.* at 251 *quoting Campbell*, 510 U.S. at 579 (citations

omitted). The secondary use adds value where the copyrighted expression in the original work

"is used as raw material, transformed in the creation of new information, new aesthetics, new

insights and understandings – this is the very type of activity that the fair use doctrine intends to

protect for the enrichment of society." *Id.* (citations omitted).

Here, Cariou's stated goal was to create a beautiful portraiture book, which accurately

depicts members of the Rastafarian culture in their native Jamaican landscapes. PC Tr. 35-36,

51, 132, 134, 141, 186, 265-66; *see also* Ex 2. In other words, Cariou's objective in taking the

Images was to document the Rastafarian culture as reality. *See, e.g.*, Ex AA. Prince, in contrast,

is "not interested in what is actually there," and is instead "really interested in making art

that…transforms something that's already existed without getting involved in the original intent

of the image." RP Tr. 167, 358.

In furtherance of that artistic purpose, Prince appropriated the Images, along with other

raw materials, and used them for an entirely different artistic and expressive purpose, which was

to create his vision of a fantastical post-apocalyptical world set in a place which no longer exists,

while paying homage to master painters. RP Aff. ¶ 21; *see, e.g.* RP Tr. 30, 165-67; 341, 365.

One of his creative message for the *Canal Zone* series was to have "music groups and music

14

itself be the surviving, if not redeeming, fact of life in the post-apocalyptic world I imagined in my screenplay. The redemptive value of music is one of the important concepts and messages of this series." RP Aff. ¶ 22; *see also* RP Tr.338-40. Prince added guitars to the Paintings to establish groupings of men and men, men and women, and women and women as musical bands, to connote equality between the sexes (RP Aff. ¶ 22) and to further the band and music theme that was one of the centerpieces of his *Canal Zone* series (RP Tr. 279; 338-39. RP Aff. ¶¶ 22 , 32, 44, 45, 46, 53, 55, 65 and Ex A to RP Aff.).

As detailed further in the Prince Affidavit, Prince's juxtaposition of collaged and other elements in each of the Paintings combined to create a fictionalized world that transforms the individual raw elements used in the Painting into a completely new expression and a different message that had nothing to do with capturing as accurately as possible the Rastafarian culture in native landscapes in Jamaica.[7] On this record, the first, and arguably most compelling, fair use factor, weighs decisively in favor of a finding that Prince's appropriative use of rescaled, altered, cropped reproductions of the Images as raw materials in the Paintings, is transformative and should therefore be considered fair use. *See, e.g., Blanch*, 467 F.3d at 252-53 (use of copyrighted work as "raw material" to further creative objectives "sharply different" from those of copyright owner "confirms the transformative nature of the use."); *Bourne Co. v. Twentieth Century Fox Film Corp.*, 602 F.Supp. 2d 499, 509-10 (S.D.N.Y. 2009) (Batts, J.) ("The Second Circuit found it 'plain' that superimposing the face of Leslie Neilsen on a photographed body intended to look like Demi Moore's was 'transformative' of Leibovitz's original photograph.") citing *Leibowitz v. Paramount Pictures Corp.*, 137 F.3d 109, 114 (2d Cir. 1998).

---

[7] As the layering of the raw materials and other elements used in the Painting is difficult to appreciate from a view of the *Canal Zone* book or the photographs attached to the Prince Affidavit, the defendants invite the Court to inspect the Paintings in person at either Prince's studio in Rensselaerville, New York or in a gallery space in Manhattan should the Court wish to confirm Prince's sworn statements concerning the manner in which he used the Images.

2.   The Broader Public Benefit of the Public Exhibition, and Progress,
of Art Outweighs the Commercial Exploitation of the Paintings

While courts will consider the commercial nature of the secondary use when it is an

untransformed duplication of the original, any significance attributable to the commercialism

factor should be discounted where, as here, the second use is demonstrably transformative. *See*

Blanch v. Koons, 467 F.3d 244, 254 (citing *Campbell,* 510 U.S. at 579) ("The more

transformative the new work, the less will be the significance of other factors, like

commercialism, that may weigh against a finding of fair use."); *see also* Point A(1). In any

event, given the importance placed on encouraging the creative expression of art, the net

economic gains derived from the Paintings to which defendants stipulated (*see* Ex N), should

give way to the broader public benefits to be derived from the public exhibition of works of art

by Prince. *See id.* at 253-54 ("courts are more willing to find a secondary use fair when it

produces a value that benefits the broader public interest . . . Notwithstanding the fact that artists

are sometimes paid and museums sometimes earn money, the public exhibition of art is widely

and we think properly considered to 'have value that benefits the broader public interest.'"). As

such, little weight, if any, should be afforded to the commercialism factor.

3.   Although Not Dispositive, Prince Acted Properly and in Good Faith

Although consideration of the propriety of an alleged infringer's conduct is an integral

part of the analysis, it is not, even when undertaken in bad faith, dispositive of either the first

factor or the fair use defense. *NXIVM Corp. v. Ross Inst.* 364 F.3d 471, 479 (2d. Cir. 2004)

citing *Campbell,* 510 U.S. at 585 n.18. In any event, as Prince did not act in bad faith when he

used the Images to create the Paintings, the good faith factor weighs in Prince's favor.

Cariou readily admits that Prince is a well-known appropriation artist. (Ex E ¶ 18).

"Appropriation art" is defined as taking "possession of another's imagery (or sounds), often

without permission, reusing it in a context which differs from its original context, most often in

16

order to examine issues concerning originality or to reveal meaning not previously seen in the original." Ex BB. Thus, appropriation art necessarily entails a taking and repurposing of another image and turning it into something else – a construct that is the very essence of the fair use doctrine. As such, Prince's use of the Images was consonant with an established art form for which he is well-known; that is, taking raw elements and turning them into something new. *See, e.g.,* RP Tr. 120-21, 123. Indeed, that Prince would not object to his own images being copied and sold for a profit, illustrates his belief in appropriation art as an art form, his commitment to the promotion of the arts, and in turn, his lack of bad faith. RP Tr. 88 ("I'm all for it."), 123 (artistic freedom is for all artists: "It could be an art student. I would encourage it.").

In any event, Cariou's claim that Prince appropriated the Images without Cariou's permission (Ex E ¶ 19; RP Tr. 28), in itself, does not constitute bad faith. *Blanch,* 467 F.3d at 256 ("We are aware of no controlling authority to the effect that the failure to seek permission for copying, in itself, constitutes bad faith and the cases addressing bad faith tend to arise in circumstances strikingly different from the situation here."). Even plaintiff's allegation of "continued distribution" of Prince's work after plaintiff notified him of his copyright infringement claim (Ex E ¶ 27), "is of no relevance to the fair use equation . . . because [i]f the use is otherwise fair, then no permission need be sought or granted . . . ." *Id.* Besides, upon learning of this lawsuit, defendants pulled the remaining Paintings pending resolution of this lawsuit out of respect for the judicial process. RP Aff. ¶ 28.

    4.   Prince Had a Genuine Creative Rationale for Appropriating the Images

For Prince, his decision to appropriate the Images was part of a fluid creative process that was inspired by a series of chance events, which happened while he was working on his *Eden Rock* screenplay. *See* RP Tr. 266; RP Aff. ¶ 16. Specifically, when Prince first saw a copy of *Yes Rasta,* he immediately made a connection between the images in the book and the jungles he

17

had seen on a recent visit to Panama. RP Tr. 158, 161; RP Aff. ¶ 17. The day before, he had seen "monumental cruise ships" in the harbor in St. Barts and he thought they should be in the screenplay. RP Tr. 266; RP Aff. ¶ 17. In thinking about who should be on the ship, the idea of a reggae band popped into his head. *Id.* At the time, he had been listening to Radiodread, an album that sampled and replicated Radiohead, in a reggae manner. RP Tr. 263-64; RP Aff. ¶ 17. As Prince explained, "I was very much into that album, I played it over and over. And then the next day I walk into a bookstore and what do I pick up, a book that had pictures of Rastas in them and I said to myself, hmm, something is in the air. It was pure chance." *Id.* "It's that notion of when worlds collide." RP Tr. 263; RP Aff. ¶ 17. Prince had been looking for black and white images of figures so that he could put them next to his *de Kooning* women, as a transition from that series. RP Tr. 264, 251; RP Aff. ¶ 17.

At the time he was painting his *de Kooning* series, Prince was already thinking about the *Canal Zone* series, and his desire to pay homage to de Kooning through that series. RP Tr.156-57, 165-66; RP Aff. ¶¶ 21, 38, 39, 40, 41, 42, 43, 46, 47, 51, 53, 62, 63. Working in the style of de Kooning, Picasso, and Warhol, and using the composition of Cezanne's *Bathers* along with other raw elements (*i.e.*, "ingredients"), Prince transformed the images he had torn from the pages in *Yes Rasta.* RP Tr. 167, 264, 277-79; RP Aff. ¶¶ 27, 42, 53, 63; *see also* Point A(1). The sincerity of Prince's artistic vision is further confirmed by the fact that he also used an image of a Rastafarian he came across in a book on Bob Marley. *Id.* at 162, 263; *see also* RP Aff. ¶ 24 and Ex M at p. 13-14. Prince, who two years earlier, had "started drawing directly in the book like [he] had done before in a book of De Kooning's work" (RP Tr. 151), was inspired by the Images because the Rastafarian culture was a subject he knew nothing about, and Prince often puts himself in a position to discover new things. *Id.* at 156. Thus, Prince's explanation for using the Images, particularly when viewed in light of the entirely different expressive

18

purpose of the *Canal Zone* series (*see* A(1)), reveals a genuine creative rationale for his appropriative use of the Images that supports a fair use defense.[8] *See Blanch*, 467 F.3d at 255 (Koon's sworn explanation for use of original work sufficient to carry justification prong of first fair use factor) cited in *Bourne*, 602 F.Supp.2d 499, 507-08 ("Second Circuit has given weight to an artist's own explanation of their creative rationale when conducting fair use analysis").

**B.   The Nature of Cariou's Work – Depicting, as Accurately
         as Possible, Real-Life Images – Weighs in Favor of Fair Use**

Because Prince's use of the Images was transformative, the second fair use factor, the nature of the work, arguably is of limited usefulness since the use was intended to further a wholly different artistic purpose, and not to exploit the "creative virtues" of the Images. *See Blanch v. Koons*, 467 F.3d 244, 257 citing *Bill Graham Archives v. Dorling Kindersley Ltd.*, 448 F.3d at 612-13. In any event, because the images in Cariou's *Yes Rasta* book were published with the stated goal of depicting real-life images of Rastafarians in their native Jamaican landscape (*see* Ex Z), which, according to Cariou, are destined to have historical significance (PC Tr. 284-86), the second prong should weigh in favor of fair use. *See Blanch*, 467 F.3d 256 ("greater leeway being allowed to a claim of fair use where the work is factual or information, and [] the work is published"); *see also Blanch v. Koons*, 396 F. Supp. 2d 476, 481-82 (S.D.N.Y. 2005)(fair use factor favored defendant where image "not sufficiently original to deserve much copyright protection."); CC Tr. 160.

C.   The Amount and Substantiality of the Images Prince Used was Reasonable

The third fair use factor considers whether "'the quantity and value of the materials used,' are reasonable in relation to the purpose of the copying." *Campbell*, 510 U.S. at 586. *See*

---

[8] Cariou has suggested in his February 8, 2010 letter to the Court (Ex Z) that a work must comment on the original work to be transformative. This is not the law. While a transformative work may comment on the original work, it is not a prerequisite to finding that the secondary work is transformative. *See Blanch*, 467 F.3d at 255.

also Blanch v. 467 F.3d 244, 257 (whether copying was "excessive, beyond his 'justified' purpose for doing so."). This analysis focuses not only on the quantity of the materials used, but also their quality and importance. *Campbell*, 510 U.S. at 587; *Graham*, 448 F.3d 608, 613. The analysis "must take into account that 'the extent of permissible copying varies with the purpose and character of the use'" and the review is undertaken in reference to the original work.[9] *Graham*, 448 F.3d 608, 613 (citing *Campbell*, 510 U.S. at 586-87).

In this case, then, analysis of the amount and substantiality prong must begin with Cariou's testimony that the images in his *Yes Rasta* book need to be viewed as a whole in order to appreciate the distinctiveness of the individual images. PC Tr. 61-62, 81, 117. By his own admission, then, the individual Images are not particularly distinctive. Indeed, images strikingly similar to Cariou's images of Rastafarians, tropical landscapes and marijuana plantations can be readily found on the Internet (Ex CC), thereby demonstrating that the importance of the individual Images is marginal. *See Blanch*, 396 F. Supp. 2d at 467 at 482. Cariou's testimony also shows that the importance of the Images is as part of a collection of approximately 105 images in the *Yes Rasta* book, for which the copyright was registered as a compilation (Ex DD). Prince's use is thus diminutive and becomes inconsequential when viewed in light of Prince's overall creative and artistic purpose for the *Canal Zone* series. *See, e.g., NXIVM Corp.*, 364 F.3d at 481 (rejected "heart of the work" theory where plaintiff conceded book was an assemblage, and it reflected "no objective core").

Even when viewed individually, however, the quantity and value of the Images Prince used in his Paintings are reasonable to carry out that artistic purpose, particularly given the importance placed on the furtherance of the arts. Though Cariou has represented to this Court that Prince engaged in wholesale copying of entire original works, it is important to note that

---

[9] As such, Prince's enthusiastic appreciation for the images in *Yes Rasta* is not determinative, as plaintiff urges in his February 8, 2010 letter to the Court. *See NXIVM Corp.*, 364 F.3d at 480-81.

20

none of the Paintings incorporate the actual original works, the photographs themselves. Rather, the appropriative use was made of Images which plaintiff had already reproduced, altered and published in book format in *Yes Rasta*. *See* PC Tr. 204-205. Moreover, as can be readily seen from a comparison of the Images in *Yes Rasta* and those use in the *Canal Zone* series (*see* PR Aff. Ex A), in all but three of the Paintings, *Djuna Barnes, Natalie Barney, Renee Vivien and Romaine Brooks*, 2008, *On the Beach, On the Beach,* 2008, and *Graduation*, 2008, Prince appropriated only portions of the Images, and in all instances, did so solely to the extent necessary to further his unique artistic purpose and message. *See id. at* ¶¶ 55, 51, 32 and Ex A to Prince's Aff.

In the three instances where Prince used an entire Image, the amount and substantiality of the Images used is not fatal to defendants' fair use defense because Prince's artistic expression in those three Paintings, a fantastical post-apocalyptical survivor society on St. Barts, is entirely different from Cariou's artistic purpose of creating a beautiful book containing images that depict as realistically as possible Rastafarians in their native Jamaican landscapes. *See Field v. Google Inc.*, 412 F. Supp. 2d 1106, 1121 (D. Nev. 2006); *see also Leibovitz* (fair use found even where entire photograph replicated to look precisely like original). Moreover, these three Images were altered, cropped and used solely as a backdrop for other raw elements painterly techniques. *Campbell*, 510 U.S. at 586-87 ("[T]he extent of permissible copying varies with the purpose and character of the use"; therefore, this inquiry requires the court to return to the first factor).

Given the purpose of the copyright law to progress the arts and encourage artistic freedom, the amount and substantiality factor should weigh in favor of fair use, particularly since, as demonstrated below, there has been no usurpation of the market for Cariou's *Yes Rasta* book or the photographs contained therein. *See* Leval at 1123-24 (amount and substantiality factor must be evaluated "in relation to the copyright objectives; they must consider the

21

justification for the secondary use and the *realistic risk* of injury to the entitlements of authorship.") (emphasis added).

D.   Prince's Use of the Images Did Not Usurp the Potential Market For, or Value of, the *Yes Rasta* Images

In his February 8 letter to the Court, Cariou points to Celle's decision not to go forward with a six-week show featuring Cariou's *Yes Rasta* images to support his view that the exhibition of the Paintings has resulted in "Potential Harm to the Market for Plaintiff's Photographs and Prints." Ex 2; PC Tr. 98-100. However, even if Celle's testimony about her reputational concerns of not wanting to be seen as riding on Prince's coattails (CC Tr. 88-90) can be reconciled with her testimony that she went with another artist due to timing constraints because Cariou did not respond for months to her attempts to reach him (*id.* at 64-65), Celle's decision is not the sort of harm the Copyright Act protects. *See NXIVM Corp.,* 364 F.3d at 482 (affirming holding that Goldie Hawn's cancellation of visit with plaintiff after defendants disseminated allegedly infringing materials is not a cognizable harm under Copyright Act). "In considering the fourth factor, our concern is not whether the secondary use suppresses or even destroys the market for the original work or its potential derivative, but whether the secondary use usurps the market of the original work." *Id.* at 481-82 (citing *Campbell,* 510 U.S. at 593). "The focus here is whether defendants are offering a market substitute for the original." *Id.* at 481. Here, there is no evidence that Prince's creation or defendants' exhibition and sale of the Paintings usurped, or was offered as a substitute for, Cariou's *Yes Rasta* images.

At the time the *Canal Zone* series was exhibited at Gagosian Gallery, the market for Cariou's *Yes Rasta* images was virtually non-existent. Other than the creation and publication of the image in the *Yes Rasta* book in 2000 and his non-committal communications with Celle about a possible show in the spring of 2009 (CC Tr. 66), Cariou has not actively tried to license, market, promote, exhibit or actively sell any of the *Yes Rasta* images. *See supra* Factual

22

Background G. Instead, Cariou intentionally limited the sale of his works to his friends or people he likes. Ex V at 1(c); PC Tr. 89, 92, 126, 157, 158, 161. To date, Cariou has only sold six *Yes Rasta* images for €1,500 to €2,000. Cariou purportedly had no intention of making any of his portraiture work available to the public until his fourth and final book of *Gypsies* portraits was completed, which (purportedly) happened in the fall of 2008. PC Tr. 286; *but see* CC Tr. 43-44 (Cariou told her it was not done as of the fall 2008). Cariou, having completed the last book, intends to move on from portraiture photography altogether. PC Tr. 286. Thus, it was factually impossible to usurp a market that, by Cariou's own design did not exist.

Second, even if Celle's speculation that she would have done well with Cariou's *Yes Rasta* images (CC Tr. 82) could be spun as a forecast of the potential market for those images, Cariou cannot show that the *Canal Zone* Paintings compete in the same market. *See Consumers Union of the United States, Inc. v. Gen. Signal Corp.,* 724 F.2d 1044, 1051 (2d Cir. 1983) ("[w]here the copy does not compete in any way with the original, this concern [regarding usurping the market] is absent."); *accord Video-Cinema Films, Inc. v. Cable News Network, Inc.,* 2001 U.S. Dist. LEXIS 25687 *29 (S.D.N.Y. 2001) ("If the allegedly infringing use is not in competition with the copyrighted use, the fair use defense is ordinarily sustained.") (citations and internal quotations omitted). Prince is a well-known appropriation artist whose wholly fictionalized works containing pop cultural messages are displayed in major museums around the world. AC ¶ 18; RP Aff. ¶¶ 3, 12. Consumers of his works are museums, galleries and private collectors of contemporary art, and his works are regularly offered at auction. RP Aff. ¶ 3. Four of the Paintings were sold for prices ranging between $400,000 and $2,430,000. Ex N. Cariou, in contrast, is an established portraiture photographer, who has had a couple of shows in the last ten years, and who is known for creating beautiful photography books that capture with great accuracy the essence of his subjects. PC Tr. 45-46, 288-90; *Yes Rasta* (inside jacket cover); CC

23

Tr. 42-46. As there is no similarity between the styles, concepts, mediums, price ranges or the markets of Cariou and Prince, the *Canal Zone* Paintings in no way compete with the *Yes Rasta*, and certainly are not a substitute for them.[10]

Moreover, as Prince intended to, and did, create Paintings that were transformative (RP Aff. ¶¶ 21, 64), there is no derivative market for Cariou to tap into that is in any way related to Prince's use of portions of the Images. *Blanch*, 467 F.3d at 258 (existence of derivative market for original work must be related to use by defendant); *see also Campbell*, 510 U.S. at 59 (where second use is "transformative," "market substitution is at least less certain, and market harm may not be so readily inferred.").

Finally, the record reveals that notwithstanding Celle's stated reluctance to proceed with a *Yes Rasta* show due to professional considerations, she was quite adamant when she finally spoke to Cariou on or about February 2009, that he do his own *Yes Rasta* show; she urged him to do a reprint of *Yes Rasta* (it was out of print) "because it is a very important book;" she was insistent on purchasing additional *Yes Rasta* books; she felt she could sell prints of images from *Yes Rasta* for between $3,000 and $20,000, depending on the size; and she remained willing to represent him, even though it took him several months to return her call. *See* CC Tr. 52-53, 82, 102, 104-05, 107-08, 155. As Celle put it, "I was very committed, I wanted to represent him. We agree on it but we never really pursue it." *Id.* at 133. PC Tr. 286-7 (powerHouse also is still interested in working with Cariou). On this record, then, the fourth factor weighs in favor of

---

[10] While Celle (also represented by plaintiff's counsel) testified that her recently-opened (June 2009) gallery, which sells prints of photographic works ranging from $3,000 to $20,000, also markets to entertainers, people in the fashion industry, decorators and others (CC Tr. at 67-68, 128, 137, 154-155; *see also* Ex Z), any evidence of an actual overlap between the consumers of the Paintings and consumers of prints of the images in the *Yes Rasta* book (and none was adduced) does not show that in marketing and exhibiting the Paintings, defendants were offering a market substitute for Cariou's *Yes Rasta* prints.

24

Prince, as his use of the Images did not usurp the potential market for or value of the *Yes Rasta* images. *See Blanch*, 467 F.3d at 258; *NXIVM Corp.*, 364 F.3d at 481-82.

CONCLUSION

When weighed in light of the purposes of copyright to progress the arts, Prince's use of portions of Cariou's Images should be considered fair because, as demonstrated herein and in the accompanying exhibits, Prince's Paintings, having been created in good faith and a with genuine creative rationale to convey new insights, a different purpose and new meaning, are transformative and contribute to the broader public benefit of art; and the quantity and value of the Images Prince used in his Paintings was reasonable to carry out his genuine artistic purpose, which was to transform Cariou's fact-based Images into a completely different expressive purpose that does not compete with and therefore does not usurp Cariou's market for the Images. Accordingly, for all of the reasons set forth herein and in the accompanying exhibits, defendants Prince, Gagosian Gallery and Lawrence Gagosian respectfully request that the Court enter an order granting them summary judgment on their fair use defense and dismissing plaintiff's conspiracy claim as it is frivolous and preempted by federal copyright law, and for such other and further relief to which the defendants are entitled.

25

Dated: May 14, 2010
     New York, New York

WITHERS BERGMAN LLP

By: _____

Hollis Gonerka Bart (HB-8955)
Dara G. Hammerman (DH-1591)
Azmina Jasani (AJ- 4161)
430 Park Avenue, 10th Floor
New York, NY 10022-3505
Phone: (212) 848-9800
Fax: (212) 848-9888
*Attorneys for Defendants Gagosian Gallery
Inc. and Lawrence Gagosian*

By: _____

Steven M. Hayes, Esq. (SH-2926)
Hanly Conroy Bierstein
Sheridan Fisher & Hayes LLP
112 Madison Avenue
New York, NY 10016-7416
(212) 784-6414
Attorneys for Defendant Richard Prince

26

UNITED STATES DISTRICT COURT
SOUTHERN DISTRICT OF NEW YORK
---x
PATRICK CARIOU,   :
                                                     :
                             Plaintiff,   :
                                                     :   08 Civ. 11327 (DAB)
              -against-   :
                                                     :
RICHARD PRINCE, GAGOSIAN GALLERY,   :
INC., LAWRENCE GAGOSIAN and RIZZOLI   :
INTERNATIONAL PUBLICATIONS, INC.,   :
                                                     :
                             Defendants.   :
---x

MEMORANDUM OF LAW IN OPPOSITION TO
DEFENDANTS' MOTION FOR SUMMARY JUDGMENT

SCHNADER HARRISON SEGAL & LEWIS LLP
140 Broadway, Suite 3100
New York, New York 10005-1101
Telephone: 212-973-8000
Facsimile: 212-972-8798
Attorneys for Plaintiff Patrick Cariou

On the Brief:
Daniel J. Brooks, Esq.
Eric A. Boden, Esq.

TABLE OF CONTENTS

i

TABLE OF AUTHORITIES

CASES

ii

iii

STATUTES

OTHER AUTHORITIES

PRELIMINARY STATEMENT

The memorandum of law of defendants Richard Prince, Gagosian Gallery, Inc. and Lawrence Gagosian in support of their motion for summary judgment ("Def. Mem."), claims that Prince's extensive copying of plaintiff Patrick Cariou's photographs (the "Photographs") is protected by the fair use doctrine, even though Prince's paintings (the "Paintings") do not in any way comment on or relate to the Photographs. Defendants' arguments, which distort the law and the factual record, are: (1) as an "appropriation artist," Prince was entitled to take whatever images he wanted, without limit and for any or no reason, and to remain willfully ignorant of the identities and rights of the victims of his piracy, failing which his creativity and ability to "convey new insights" would be "stifled"; (2) Cariou's "factual" photographs of real people can be stolen with impunity; (3) as long as Prince did not appropriate the entire *Yes Rasta* book, he was entitled to take as many Photographs as he needed to produce his "fantastical post-apocalyptical" vision; and (4) Christiane Celle's irrevocable decision to cancel Cariou's show the instant she learned of Prince's plagiarism (and the resulting cognizable harm to the market for Cariou's Photographs) can be disregarded because Cariou did not promptly return the phone call Celle made to announce that irrevocable decision. *See* Def. Mem. at 1, 19, 20-21, 22.

In opposition to defendants' motion, Cariou respectfully submits this memorandum of law, counter-statement of undisputed facts pursuant to Local Rule 56.1 and declaration of Daniel J. Brooks, dated June 11, 2010 ("Brooks Opp. Dec.") and exhibits thereto, in order to address the misleading legal and factual contentions -- including assertions in Richard Prince's moving affidavit contradicting his own sworn deposition testimony -- which permeate defendants' motion. As demonstrated below, defendants' motion should be denied because it is both unfounded in law and unsupported by the factual record.

ARGUMENT

POINT I

ALL FOUR STATUTORY FACTORS WEIGH HEAVILY AGAINST DEFENDANTS' FAIR USE DEFENSE

A.   First Fair Use Factor: Prince's Status as an Appropriation Artist Does not Render "Transformative" Defendants' Commercial Exploitation of Cariou's Work

1. As a Matter of Law, Prince's Appropriation Was Not Transformative

Defendants rely on a student note, *Beyond Rogers v. Koons: A Fair Use Standard for Appropriation*, 93 COLUM. L. REV. 1473, 1478, 1479, 1482 (1993) (the "Note"), to trace the tradition of "appropriation art," through which, "[b]y reusing a work and removing it from its usual context, appropriation artists aim to give new meaning to the work, questioning 'the most fundamental perceptions, both literal and symbolic, on which society is based.'" Def. Mem. at 2 (quoting the Note). Defendants neglect to advise the Court that, according to the author of the Note, the fair use doctrine affords no protection to this "post-modernist" artistic tradition.

As the Note acknowledges: "[C]urrent fair use doctrine does not adequately protect the work of artists who use this creative method [of appropriation]. Instead, artists who appropriate are quite vulnerable to legal sanctions based on their choice of copyrighted subject matter." Note, at 1484. Indeed, the purpose of the Note was to propose a new fair use standard to protect visual artists engaged in the practice of appropriation (*id.* at 1515-16) – a standard which has been adopted neither by Congress nor by the Courts – because "[t]he current copyright law, and especially the fair use doctrine, are ill-equipped to handle the challenge posed by appropriation in the visual arts. In its current form, the fair use doctrine, copyright's accommodation of certain unauthorized secondary uses that accord with the aims of copyright, does not afford much protection to artists who appropriate." *Id.* at 1498.

The lack of protection provided by fair use has been recognized by appropriation

2

artists themselves, who, with the exception of Jeff Koons, have an "artistic tradition" of not only appropriating other artists' work, but also, when threatened with a lawsuit or sued by those artists, of paying for or ceasing the appropriation, rather than defending it as a matter of principle. When they were caught taking other artists' works and were threatened with lawsuits or sued for copyright infringement, Robert Rauschenberg, Sherrie Levine and David Salle, all well-known appropriation artists, settled without attempting to litigate any fair use defense. *Id.* at 1480, 1484-85.

   Even Andy Warhol and/or his assigns have capitulated to lawsuits or threats of lawsuits for copyright infringement rather than zealously pressing a fair use defense. Warhol settled a threatened lawsuit by Patricia Caulfield, the copyright holder of the photograph Warhol appropriated in making his well-known *Flowers* paintings, making a payment and giving Caulfield royalties on the print edition of *Flowers*. *See* Note, at 1484. Another instance is described in an article by William M. Landes, the Clifton R. Musser Professor of Law & Economics at the University of Chicago Law School and a co-author with Seventh Circuit Judge Richard A. Posner of numerous books and articles on intellectual property.[1] As explained by Professor Landes in the article (William M. Landes, *Copyright, Borrowed Images, and Appropriation Art: An Economic Approach*, 9 GEO. MASON L. REV. 1 (2000) ("Landes")), after Warhol's death, Henri Dauman, a French photographer, came to realize that Warhol's famous *Jackie* series of silkscreen prints appropriated Dauman's copyrighted photograph of Jackie Kennedy, taken at President Kennedy's funeral, that had appeared in *Life Magazine* in 1963. Landes at 18. Dauman sued the Estate of Andy Warhol, the Andy Warhol Foundation for the

---

[1] *See, e.g.,* William M. Landes & Richard A. Posner, *The Economic Structure of Intellectual Property Law* (Harvard Univ. Press 2003); William M. Landes & Richard A. Posner, *An Economic Analysis of Copyright Law*, 17 J. LEGAL STUD. 325 (1989).

3

Visual Arts and the Andy Warhol Museum (collectively, "Warhol"). Landes at 19.

Notably, rather than vigorously mounting a fair use defense, Warhol entered into protracted settlement discussions and a tolling agreement with Dauman. *Andy Warhol Foundation for the Visual Arts, Inc. v. Federal Insurance Co.*, 189 F.3d 208, 213 (2d Cir. 1999). When Dauman ultimately sued (*id.*), Warhol first moved unsuccessfully to dismiss the complaint (*Dauman v. Andy Warhol Foundation for the Visual Arts, Inc.*, No. 96 Civ. 9219 (TPG), 1997 U.S. Dist. LEXIS 8606, at *6 (S.D.N.Y. June 18, 1997)) and then, in order to obtain coverage, brought a declaratory judgment action against his liability insurance carrier, which was dismissed, but reinstated on appeal. *Andy Warhol Foundation*, 189 F.3d at 214, 218. Having obtained insurance coverage, Warhol then settled with Dauman. Landes at 19.

As Professor Landes explains: "Some appropriation art does not implicate copyright law at all. For example, Marcel Duchamp exhibited ready-made objects such as a urinal, bicycle wheel, and snow shovel as works of art. But when the borrowed image is copyrighted, appropriation art risks infringing the rights of the copyright owner." Landes at 1. It is at the intersection of appropriation and copyright that "[a]rtists and judges have very different views regarding how the law should treat appropriation art." *Id.* In outlining how the "artist perceives legal restraints on borrowing as a threat to artistic freedom[,]" Professor Landes provides a "typical" quote from an artist (Richmond Burton), which could have come from Prince himself: "I feel very free to take and change whatever I want, and that includes borrowing from my contemporaries. If some people are upset because my work has similarities to what they're doing, that's their problem. And if they take from me, that's great! I don't respect these artificial boundaries . . . erect[ed] to keep you in a certain category." *Id.*; *compare* Prince's virtually identical deposition testimony (declaration of Daniel J. Brooks, dated May 7, 2010, in

4

support of plaintiff's motion for summary judgment ("Brooks Dec."), Ex. E at 118-21). But, according to Professor Landes: "The law takes a more traditional view of appropriation art. Artists receive no special privileges to borrow copyrighted material." Landes at 1-2.

As mentioned above, one appropriation artist who has litigated fair use issues is Jeff Koons. In three cases, where it was found that his secondary works did not comment on the images he appropriated, his fair use defense was rejected because, if artistic expression alone justified the random taking of unrelated copyrighted work, there would be no limit to what could be appropriated and the fair use doctrine would "eviscerate the protection afforded by the Copyright Act." *United Feature Syndicate, Inc. v. Koons*, 817 F. Supp. 370, 379 (S.D.N.Y. 1993) (also stating: "The fact that the infringing copy can be classified as 'art' or as being part of an 'artistic tradition' cannot be used as a shield to salvage an otherwise defective fair use defense."); *see also Rogers v. Koons*, 960 F.2d 301, 310 (2d Cir.) ("If an infringement of copyrightable expression could be justified as fair use solely on the basis of the infringer's claim to a higher or different artistic use – without insuring public awareness of the original work – there would be no practicable boundary to the fair use defense."), *cert. denied*, 506 U.S. 934 (1992); *Campbell v. Koons*, No. 91 Civ. 6055 (RO), 1993 WL 97381, at *1 (S.D.N.Y. Apr. 1, 1993) (Koons' role in "conceiv[ing]" and "oversee[ing]" production of sculpture which appropriated photograph of a pig and boy, added an angel and transformed the boy into an angel was not fair use).

Only in *Blanch v. Koons,* 467 F.3d 244 (2d Cir. 2006) – where Koons explained, without contradiction, that he appropriated an advertisement for Gucci sandals from a glossy fashion magazine in order to use the "typicality [of the ad] to further his purpose of commenting on the 'commercial images . . . in our consumer culture'"; "to 'comment on the ways in which

5

some of our most basic appetites . . . are mediated by popular images'"; "to satirize life as it appears when seen though the prism of slick fashion photography"; and to "comment upon the culture and attitudes promoted and embodied in [the magazine containing the ad]" (*id.* at 247, 248, 255) – was Koons' fair use defense upheld. Remarkably, given that the Court emphasized Koons' comment on the appropriated image as having "established a 'justif[ication for] the very act of [his] borrowing[,]'" (*id.* at 255) (citation omitted), defendants, citing *Blanch*, 467 F.3d at 255, claim the case holds that "[w]hile a transformative work may comment on the original work, it [a comment] is not a prerequisite to finding that the secondary work is transformative." Def. Mem. at 19, n.8. *Blanch* says nothing of the sort. Instead, after noting the clear and articulate way in which Koons explained his reasons for appropriating the Gucci ad, the Court stated in a footnote (to which defendants are presumably referring): "Koons's clear conception of his reasons for using 'Silk Sandals,' and his ability to articulate those reasons, ease our analysis in this case. We do not mean to suggest, however, that either is a *sine qua non* for a finding of fair use - - as to satire or more generally." *Blanch,* 467 F.3d at 255, n.5.

Thus, while *Blanch* stands for the proposition that a clear, articulate explanation of the appropriator's reasons for commenting on the appropriated image is not a prerequisite to a finding of a transformative purpose, *Blanch* does not dispense with the requirement that there be a comment, or some other recognized justification for the appropriation of the specific image that was taken. Simply stealing for the sake of stealing – as Prince admitted he prefers doing (Brooks Dec. Ex. Q; Ex. R, at 2; Ex. E, at 34-35, 44, 48-49) – clearly does not suffice.

In addition to *Blanch*, defendants cite *Bourne Co. v. Twentieth Century Fox Film Corp.,* 602 F. Supp. 2d 499 (S.D.N.Y. 2009) and *Leibovitz v. Paramount Pictures Corp.,* 137 F.3d 109 (2d Cir. 1998) in support of their contention that "Prince's appropriative use of

6

rescaled, altered, cropped reproductions of the [Photographs] as raw materials in the Paintings, is transformative and should therefore be considered fair use." Def. Mem. at 15. Neither *Bourne* nor *Leibovitz*, however, holds that the random taking of copyrighted materials in order to alter them, without in any way commenting on them, is transformative. To the contrary, in *Bourne*, 602 F. Supp. 2d at 507, the Court found that the secondary use was a parody in which the defendants "were clearly attempting to comment" on the "hopeful" scene associated with the song *When You Wish Upon a Star* in the plaintiff's film *Pinnocchio*. Similarly, in *Leibovitz*, the superimposition of Leslie Neilsen's smirking face on a movie poster depicting a photographed body intended to look like the nude, pregnant Demi Moore in the plaintiff's well-known photograph was held to be transformative, but not merely because the original image was altered. *Leibovitz*, 137 F.3d at 111-12, 114. As the Second Circuit explained, the secondary use was transformative because it was a parody of the "seriousness, even the pretentiousness, of the original[,]" commenting on it by holding it up to "ridicule." *Id.* at 114. As the Court stated: "Being different from an original does not inevitably 'comment' on the original. Nevertheless, the ad is not merely different; it differs in a way that may reasonably be perceived as commenting, through ridicule, on what a viewer might reasonably think is the undue self-importance conveyed by the subject of the Leibovitz photograph. A photographer posing a well known actress in a manner that calls to mind a well known painting must expect, or at least tolerate, a parodist's deflating ridicule." *Id.* at 114-15.

As explained in *Castle Rock Entertainment, Inc. v. Carol Publishing Group, Inc.*, 150 F.3d 132, 143 (2d Cir. 1998), because one of the "exclusive rights" of a copyright owner is the right "to prepare derivative works based upon the copyrighted work" (17 U.S.C. § 106(2)) and a "derivative work," in turn, includes any "form in which a work may be recast, transformed,

7

or adapted" (*id.* § 101), merely transforming a copyrighted work without commenting on it may be derivative, but it is not transformative. Prince, by doodling on Cariou's Photographs, and all the defendants, by exhibiting, offering for sale and selling the Paintings, infringed Cariou's exclusive rights to reproduce, prepare derivative works based upon, distribute and display his copyrighted work (17 U.S.C. §§ 106(1), (2), (3), (5)), even if Prince's artistic techniques altered Cariou's images in order to create a "fantastical, post-apocalyptical world." *See* Def. Mem. at 1, 15. An analogous situation was presented in *Gaylord v. United States,* 85 Fed. Cl. 59 (2008), where a postage stamp depicting the Korean War Veterans Memorial which allegedly infringed the copyright of the Memorial's sculptor was described by the Court of Federal Claims as having drastically altered the appearance of the Memorial by "providing a different expressive character," "transform[ing] [the Memorial's] expression and message, creating a surrealistic environment with snow and subdued lighting where the viewer is left unsure whether he is viewing a photograph of statues or actual human beings[,]" giving the viewer "a feeling of stepping into the photograph, being in Korea with the soldiers, under the freezing conditions that many veterans experienced[,]" and "creating a nearly monochromatic image" that was "grayer" and "colder" than the Memorial. *Id.* at 68-69. Although the Court of Federal Claims found the stamp to be transformative (*id.*), on appeal, the Federal Circuit reversed, holding that the stamp's appropriation of the Memorial was not transformative or fair use because it lacked any commentary or criticism relating to the original work. *Gaylord v. United States,* 595 F.3d 1364, 1372-73, 1376 (Fed. Cir. 2010).

In reaching this conclusion, the Federal Circuit distinguished several cases, including: *Blanch,* 467 F.3d at 248 (where Koons' incorporation of "a woman's feet adorned with glittery Gucci sandals" into a collage "commenting on the 'commercial images . . . in our

8

consumer culture[]'" was transformative); *Bill Graham Archives v. Dorling Kindersley Ltd.*, 448

F.3d 605, 609 (2d Cir. 2006) (where Grateful Dead concert posters were incorporated into a

biographical work, a form "'of historical scholarship, criticism, and comment that require[s]

incorporation of original source material for optimum treatment of [its] subjects.'"); and *Lennon*

v. Premise Media Corp., 556 F. Supp. 2d 310, 323 (S.D.N.Y. 2008) (where a movie espousing

religion used a clip from John Lennon's song *Imagine*, which "envisioned a world without

religion," in order to "'criticize what the filmmakers see as the naiveté of John Lennon's

views.'"). *Gaylord*, 595 F.3d at 1373 & n.3. As the Court noted: "By contrast, here the stamp

did not use the [Memorial] as part of a commentary or criticism." *Id.* at 1373.

       Defendants warn that protection of Cariou's copyright in this case "would

effectively stifle, if not foreclose," Prince's creative activities. Def. Mem. at 1. That is not true,

although Prince will have to modify his business model. The next time Prince, by "pure chance"

(Brooks Dec. Ex. E at 264), finds a book containing images whose "look" he "loves" (Brooks

Dec. Ex. T at C000675; Ex. E at 261-62), he simply will have to look at the colophon page (there

is one not only in *Yes Rasta*, Brooks Dec. Ex. L-2, but also in the Canal Zone Catalogue, Brooks

Dec. Ex. M-4) in order to determine whether the images are copyrighted. If they are

copyrighted, and if Prince does not intend to criticize, comment upon, report upon, teach about,

engage in scholarship about, or research those images, or undertake a "remotely similar" use (*see*

Ringgold v. Black Entm't Television, Inc., 126 F.3d 70, 78-79 (2d Cir. 1997)) he will simply

have to contact the copyright owner and attempt to obtain a license to use the images. If he

cannot obtain a license, he will have to either take his own photograph or avail himself of the

vast quantities of public domain stock photos which are available on the Internet; *see*

http://www.istockphoto.com (a website with thousands of royalty-free photos of Rastas, one of

9

which Prince admitted he possibly could have used in the Paintings (Brooks Dec. Ex. E at 286,

290-92)); *see also* Ex. CC to the affidavit of Hollis Gonerka Bart, sworn to May 14, 2010 ("Bart

Aff."), depicting images of Rastas "culled from the internet from a myriad of websites."

While this new business model will entail some additional steps, that burden will

be far from insuperable for Prince, who employs four full-time assistants. Brooks Dec. Ex. E at

173-74. By following these simple steps, Prince will be able to appropriate images, combine

those images with other "raw materials appropriated from many sources," with a "new

expressive meaning and message" and "genuine creative rationale, by collaging and scanning

rescaled, altered, cropped images," with "painterly elements," and "historical art references as an

homage to master painters he admires" (Def. Mem. at 1), to his heart's content, all without

running afoul of the Copyright Law. Showing this modicum of respect for fellow artists will not,

therefore, stifle Prince's creativity. What it will do is prevent him from stealing for the sake of

stealing, a practice he has admitted he prefers (Brooks Dec. Ex. E at 44), and which he flaunts in

the Canal Zone Catalogue (*see* Brooks Dec. Ex. Z, showing the process of stealing in three

photographs of canvases in Prince's studio containing unaltered images of Cariou's Rastas). The

right to steal, however, is not one of the interests safeguarded by the fair use doctrine.

2. Prince's Improper Attempts to Change His Deposition Testimony

As a matter of law, the first fair use factor weighs heavily against the defendants,

even if the assertions contained in the moving affidavit of Richard Prince, sworn to May 13,

2010 ("Prince Aff."), could be reconciled with his deposition testimony. That, however, is not

the case.

In his affidavit, Prince claims that his *Canal Zone* Paintings "developed from the

storyline of a cinematic pitch [he] wrote from 2007 through 2008" involving "a fantasy account

of survivors of a nuclear attack" who end up in St. Barth's, where they "form gangs and tribes,"

10

take over resort hotels, and create a "post-apocalyptic society." Prince Aff. ¶ 16; *see* Brooks

Dec. Exs. DD, EE, FF (the pitch; additions to the pitch written in March 2008; description of the

pitch on Gagosian Gallery website). Prince claims that he found a copy of *Yes Rasta* in a

bookstore in St. Barth's "[a]round the same time." Prince Aff. ¶ 17. Prince contends that he had

already "envisioned that one of the tribes in [his] screenplay would be a reggae band," had

recently been listening to reggae music, and that when he "walked into the bookstore the next

day and saw the book with Rastas, [he] thought something was in the air." *Id.* Based on this

account in Prince's affidavit, defendants assert that the *Canal Zone* Paintings "evolved from the

storyline of [Prince's] 'pitch,'" and downplay the importance of Cariou's Photographs by

repeating Prince's claim that he only found the copy of *Yes Rasta* after he had already written his

screenplay in 2007. Def. Mem. at 4-5.

This narrative flatly contradicts Prince's deposition testimony. First, he testified

that his "pitch" was merely a "subtext." Brooks Dec. Ex. E at 30. Second, Prince testified

unequivocally that he actually found and purchased the copy of *Yes Rasta* in 2005, two years

before he wrote the pitch, when he was on vacation in St. Bart's, and made drawings in the book

"for two weeks out of every year for two years." Brooks Opp. Dec. Ex. A at 153-54. Therefore,

the claim in Prince's affidavit that he found the copy of *Yes Rasta* in 2007, after he had already

completed his screenplay, is at odds with his deposition testimony and must be disregarded. *See*

Sauerhaft v. Bd. of Educ. of the Hastings-On-Hudson Union Free Sch. Dist., No. 05 Civ. 09087

(PGG), 2009 U.S. Dist. LEXIS 46196, at *30 (S.D.N.Y. June 2, 2009) (disregarding portions of

affidavits filed in support of motion for summary judgment that were inconsistent with

witnesses' deposition testimony).

In his affidavit, Prince provides elaborate explanations of how he chose some of

11

the titles for his *Canal Zone* Paintings. Prince Aff. ¶¶ 35, 37, 38, 42, 45, 46, 47, 49, 51, 54, 55, 56. Defendants claim that titles are an important component of Prince's work and differentiate Prince's Paintings from Cariou's Photographs, which have no titles. Def. Mem. at 8, n.4. While Prince did testify that the titles were an important subtext that helped in the transformation and recontextualization of Cariou's images (Brooks Dec. Ex. E at 248-49), that testimony was belied by his inability, during the deposition, to remember titles of the Paintings, including some of the titles he explains in his affidavit.

For example, before the opening of the *Canal Zone* show, Prince was interviewed in *Interview Magazine*, which published details from five of the Paintings on the first page of the interview. Brooks Dec. Ex. T, C00065. Prince correctly identified the Painting at the left of the top row, but could not recall the title of the Painting at the right of the top row, which was *Tales of Brave Ulysses* (Brooks Dec. Ex. E at 244-45; Ex. T, C00065), a Painting whose title Prince carefully explains in his affidavit (Prince Aff. ¶ 49). Nor could Prince correctly name the Painting at the right of the bottom row, calling it *On the Beach*, when in fact the correct title was *The Ocean Club*, as Prince admitted, explaining his mistake by saying: "I think I just named them pretty close. The Ocean Club I was off a little bit. It did have something to do with a beach." Brooks Dec. Ex. E at 245-48. Significantly, *On the Beach* and *The Ocean Club* are two of the titles that Prince explains in his affidavit. Prince Aff. ¶¶ 35, 51.

Similarly, when asked whether a particular collector had bought one of his *Canal Zone* Paintings, Prince recalled that the collector had "paid around two million dollars," testified that he could "visualize" the Painting, and stated: "I mean I know the painting, I just don't recall the title." Brooks Opp. Dec. Ex. A at 190. Nor, according to one of his assistants, could Prince, in response to a request from Gagosian Gallery, remember the titles of at least two other

12

Paintings (Brooks Dec. Ex. MM at GGP004072); as the assistant stated: "[P]lease check the title on back of painting – Richard couldn't remember which was which." *Id.* Finally, with respect to his Painting *Back to the Garden*, Prince claims, in his affidavit, that he intended the title to refer to a song by that name that was performed at Woodstock (Prince Aff. ¶ 37), yet, during his deposition, Prince testified: "I mean I think there's even a song by Joni Mitchell called Back to the Garden" (Brooks Opp. Dec. Ex. A at 342), which "didn't occur to me until this moment." *Id.* at 343. In sum, Prince's facile recollection and explanation of the titles of his Paintings in his affidavit is inconsistent with his deposition testimony, is an improper attempt to rehabilitate his memory lapses and should be disregarded. *See Raskin v. The Wyatt Co.*, 125 F.3d 55, 63 (2d Cir. 1997) (disregarding declaration recounting what was discussed at a meeting when the witness, in his deposition, had been unable to remember the points that were covered during that meeting); *Federal Deposit Insurance Corp. v. Wrapwell Corp.*, Nos. 93 Civ. 859 (CSH), 94 Civ. 5574 (CSH), 2002 U.S. Dist. LEXIS 76, at *47-49 (S.D.N.Y. Jan. 3, 2002) (same).

A recurrent theme in defendants' motion is the assertion that Prince's message in the *Canal Zone* Paintings was "the redemptive value of music and equality between the sexes." Def. Mem. at 1, 7, 15; *see* Prince Aff. ¶¶ 22, 61. In his deposition, however, when asked what his message was in producing the Paintings, Prince testified: "I don't really have a message" (Brooks Dec. Ex. E at 45-46), later adding that "[t]he message is to make great art that makes people feel good" (*id.* at 267), and to do so with "a completely different look, and . . . a completely different application, and . . . a new way of collaging (*id.* at 331). He also said that his message in the Painting *Back to the Garden*, in addition to making a "fantastic, absolutely hip, up to date, contemporary take on the music scene" (*id.* at 338-39) was, with respect to the Rastafarian on the donkey with a guitar: "hey, this guy is playing the guitar" (*id.* at 340). Not

13

once in his deposition did Prince testify that his message was either "the redemptive value of music" or "equality between the sexes." The only deposition testimony cited by defendants regarding either of these "messages" (Def. Mem. at 15, citing pp. 338-40 of Prince's deposition transcript) contains no such statement.

Nor can either of these messages be found in Prince's "pitch" (Brooks Dec. Exs. DD, EE), the supposed source of Prince's inspiration for the Paintings, or in James Frey's adaptation of the pitch. Prince acknowledged that Frey's essay, *Ding Dong the Witch Is Dead*, which is included as an insert in the Canal Zone Catalogue (Brooks Dec. Exs. M, M-4), was "essentially based on [Prince's] pitch[,]" was written after Frey saw the pitch and some of the Paintings in Prince's Long Island studio in the summer of 2008, and that "parts of [Frey's] essay . . . are fairly close to [Prince's] original pitch." Brooks Dec. Ex. E at 201-02, 231. Frey's essay (the first insert in the Canal Zone Catalogue) makes no mention of the "redemptive value of music" (or music) and, far from envisioning "equality between the sexes," describes the post-apocalyptic environment this way: "Women become slaves. Some cook, some clean, some carry children, some take care of children, some care for the sick and the wounded, some care for prisoners. Some of the women become objects of pleasure and they are defiled, defiled every day, defiled in every way you can image." *See* Brooks Dec. Ex. M. Not surprisingly, given its repellent nature, Prince distances himself and his Paintings from Frey's oeuvre (Brooks Dec. Ex. E at 235; Prince Aff. ¶ 65), but the fact remains that the defendants chose to include the essay in the Canal Zone Catalogue, making sure that Frey's name appeared on the title page (Brooks Dec. Ex. M-2), so it would "come up if you Google James Frey." Brooks Dec. Ex. II. In any event, whether or not Frey's essay mirrors Prince's "message," the salient point is that neither the essay, nor Prince's pitch, nor Prince's deposition testimony makes any mention of the contrived

14

messages – the redemptive value of music and equality between the sexes – first enunciated in

Prince's affidavit. Because these messages are merely *"post hoc* rationalizations," *Castle Rock,*

150 F.3d at 142, they should be disregarded.

3. Commerciality and Bad Faith on the Part of the Defendants

Seeking to minimize commerciality and negate bad faith on their part, defendants

claim that, "upon learning of this lawsuit, [they] pulled the remaining Paintings pending

resolution of this lawsuit out of respect for the judicial process." Def. Mem. at 16-17; *see also*

Prince Aff. ¶ 28. This self-serving assertion is false and misleading. The lawsuit was

commenced on December 30, 2008, but Canal Zone Catalogues were sold through February

2009. Brooks Dec. Ex. P, ¶ 4. Four Paintings were traded for a Larry Rivers painting valued at

$3 or $4 million on March 13, 2009. Brooks Dec. Ex. P, ¶ 3(a) & Ex. A, at 2; Ex. F at 136-37.

The Painting *Inquisition* was sold on June 8, 2009 for $800,000. Brooks Dec. Ex. P, Ex. A, at 4.

Another Painting, *It's All Over*, was sold in August 2009 for $1.1 million. Brooks Opp. Dec. Ex.

B at 141-44.

B.   Second Fair Use Factor: The Nature of Cariou's Work is Expressive and Creative, Fitting Squarely Within the Core of Copyright Protection

While claiming that Prince's practice of ripping pages out of *Yes Rasta* and

sending them to a commercial laboratory to be scanned and printed with an ink jet printer is

highly creative, defendants contend that Cariou's Photographs, because they depict "real-life

images of Rastafarians in their native Jamaican landscape," are "factual or informational," rather

than creative. Def. Mem. at 19. Defendants also insist (incorrectly) that "[m]any of the

[Photographs] were taken in the towns of Negril and Lucille and in other public places[,]" Def.

Mem. at 9, presumably making those Photographs less worthy of copyright protection. And,

defendants contend that Cariou's Photographs "are not particularly distinctive" and that "images

15

strikingly similar to Cariou's images of Rastafarians, tropical landscapes and marijuana

plantations can be readily found on the Internet[,]" Def. Mem. at 20; Bart Aff. Ex. CC,

purportedly making them "'not sufficiently original to deserve much copyright protection'"

(quoting *Blanch v. Koons*, 396 F. Supp. 2d 476, 481-82 (S.D.N.Y. 2005)). Def. Mem. at 19.

  "[P]hotographs taken for aesthetic purposes [] are creative in nature and thus fit

squarely within the core of copyright protection." *Elvis Presley Enters. v. Passport Video*, 349

F.3d 622, 629 (9th Cir. 2003), *as amended*, 357 F.3d 896 (9th Cir.), *cert. denied*, 542 U.S. 921

(2004); *see also Rogers v. Koons*, 960 F.2d 301, 310 (2d Cir.) ("As an original expression

[plaintiff's photograph] has more in common with fiction than with works based on facts . . .

[and it] was creative and imaginative . . . ."), *cert. denied*, 506 U.S. 934 (1992); *Baraban v. Time

Warner, Inc.*, No. 99 Civ. 1569 (JSM), 2000 WL 358375, at *4 (S.D.N.Y. Apr. 6, 2000)

("Although photographs are often 'factual or informational in nature,' the art of photography has

generally been deemed sufficiently creative to make the second fair use factor weigh in favor of

photographer-plaintiffs.") As Judge Lynch recently stated in *Sarl Louis Feraud International v.

Viewfinder Inc.*, 627 F. Supp. 2d 123, 128 (S.D.N.Y. 2008) (quoting a prior decision in the same

case): "'[T]he notion that photographs merely reproduce reality, and do not apply a creative, or

even distorting, eye to the events is long discredited. The photographer selects the image to be

reproduced, capturing a particular angle of view, and that image conveys . . . at best a partial,

two-dimensional impression of the [original] . . . .'"

  As support for their claim that "many" of the Photographs were taken in Negril,

Lucille and "other public places," defendants cite pages 6, 36-37, 73-74, 83-84, and 128 of

Cariou's deposition transcript. Page 6 consists of defense counsel introducing herself to Cariou

and eliciting the fact that he is a French citizen; pages 36-37 establish that Cariou spent "most of

16

the time . . . in the mountains," but "[s]ometimes we had to go back to town to get some, you know, food or whatever we needed. Sometimes I needed batteries or whatever"; pages 73-74 do indeed discuss a photograph taken in Negril; pages 83-84 discuss a photograph of a man "in the middle of his plantation"; and page 128 describes someone who purchased two prints of Cariou's Photographs. Needless to say, the cited pages of the deposition transcript do not support defendants' claim that the Photographs were taken in populated areas. Nor would it matter. "[P]hotographic images of actual people," even taken in public places, such as Alfred Eisenstaedt's *V-J Day in Times Square*, "the classic image of a thrilled sailor exuberantly kissing a woman in Times Square on V-J Day," *see* Brooks Opp. Dec. Ex. D, "may be as creative and deserving of protection as purely fanciful creations." *Monster Communications, Inc. v. Turner Broad. System, Inc.*, 935 F. Supp. 490, 494 (S.D.N.Y. 1996).

Photographs that are "creative" or "expressive" lie within the core of copyright protection. *Blanch*, 467 F.3d at 256. Although the amended complaint alleges that Cariou's Photographs are "strikingly original" and "distinctive" (Brooks Dec. Ex. A, ¶ 16) – allegations that Cariou stands by and that are evident to anyone who peruses *Yes Rasta* – there is no requirement that photographs be unique or distinctive in order to be sufficiently creative to make the second fair use factor weigh in favor of the copyright owner. Therefore, the fact that other photos of Rastas and their environment may be available on the Internet is irrelevant to this analysis. Moreover, defendants' reliance on the statement by the District Court in *Blanch* that the plaintiff's photo was "not sufficiently original to deserve much copyright protection" is badly misplaced, to put it mildly; as the Second Circuit said on appeal of that decision, "[W]e disagree with the district court's characterization of Blanch's photograph as 'banal rather than creative.'" *Blanch*, 467 F.3d at 257. The Court then went on to explain, however, that, even though

17

Blanch's Gucci ad was a "creative work," this was of "'limited usefulness where the creative

work of art is being used for a transformative purpose.'" *Id.* (citation omitted). Since Prince's

Paintings are not transformative, the creative nature of Cariou's Photographs weighs heavily

against the fair use defense in this case.

C.   Third Fair Use Factor: Prince's Appropriation Was Excessive and Unreasonable, Even if He Did not Take the Entire *Yes Rasta* Book

Defendants argue that, because the copyright for Cariou's work was registered as

a compilation and Cariou supposedly testified that the images needed to be viewed as a whole in

order to be appreciated, "the importance of the individual [Photographs] is marginal," and Prince

acted reasonably in taking entire Photographs "to the extent necessary to further his unique

artistic purpose and message." Def. Mem. at 20, 21.

Defendants' contention that Cariou testified that the Photographs in *Yes Rasta*

needed to be viewed as a whole in order to be appreciated (citing pp. 61-62, 81 and 117 of

Cariou's deposition transcript) is disingenuous at best. Significantly, none of the testimony cited

by defendants pertains in any way to Cariou's photographic portraits of Rastafarians.

At pp. 61-62, Cariou was asked what instructions he gave to his laboratory for

processing a specific Photograph and Cariou explained that he had given the same overall

instructions for "the book as a whole." Cariou then responded affirmatively when asked: "[I]s it

fair to say then once you developed the technique that you wanted to create the certain dark look

with accents, that is how all of the images that appear in the *Yes Rasta* book were developed?"

The fact that Cariou wanted a uniform look throughout his book is a far cry from saying that

each Photograph was of marginal importance and could only be appreciated if one viewed the

book as a whole.

At p. 81, Cariou was asked, with respect to a landscape background that had been

18

"blurred out": "[I]s this just another example of you have to look at the whole book to get what's distinctive about the landscape?" and he responded, "Yeah, you have to look at the whole book in order to get a better feel of the place than looking at one picture, definitely." Similarly, at p. 117, Cariou responded affirmatively when asked: "And this is just another photograph of a landscape that you shot, again, to create this whole feeling of the whole book?" Cariou also explained that it took him time to frame this particular shot properly and find the proper light and that, by showing banana trees in proximity to "ganja [marijuana]," it showed "how intertwined ganja is with Jamaica. It's everywhere." Brooks Dec. Ex. D at 117-18.

Thus, while some of the landscapes, which are often in the background and out of focus, are better appreciated when viewed as a whole, that does not mean that Cariou agreed that each landscape was of marginal importance and could only be appreciated by viewing the entire book.[2] Nor, of course, does the cited testimony have any bearing at all upon the Photographs of Rastas which Prince appropriated in their entirety, often cropping out the background landscapes. Cariou never testified that his photographic portraits of individual Rastafarians could only be appreciated by viewing the entire *Yes Rasta* book.

The fact that *Yes Rasta* was registered as a compilation is also irrelevant. Where, as here, the registrant of the compilation is also the sole author and owner of its constituent parts, as evidenced by Cariou's certificate of copyright registration (Brooks Dec. Ex. K), he can bring an action for infringement of each copyrightable component of the compilation and is not limited

---

[2]   Cariou described some other landscapes that he shot: "[T]he countryside was beautiful and the light was amazing. I waited until the light was perfect . . . You can see there is a tropical storm coming in, and I was waiting for that storm to get at the right place[]"; "I think the sky is quite amazing and, you know, the light. Once again, the tropical storm makes extremely specific light. And the sugar cane, the sun on the sugar cane, and the really dark sky picture Jamaica very well I think[]"; "I took a lot of time to find the perfect lighting, the perfect depth of field in order to have the leaves that I really like in the background to be the way they are." Brooks Dec. Ex. D at 133-34, 143-44, 155.

to suing only for infringement of the entire compilation. *See Woods v. Universal City Studios, Inc.*, 920 F. Supp. 62, 64 (S.D.N.Y. 1996) (rejecting claim that copyright registration for a collective work only covers the selection and arrangement of its constituent illustrations and holding that the owner of a copyright for a collective work also owns copyrights for its constituent parts); *Heyman v. Salle*, 743 F. Supp. 190, 193 (S.D.N.Y. 1989) (copyright protection in a compilation of photographs extends to each copyrightable photograph contributed by the author of the compilation); *see also Eastern Am. Trio Prods., Inc. v. Tang Elec. Corp.*, 97 F. Supp. 2d 395, 416-17 (S.D.N.Y. 2000) (same). This being so, defendants' fair use defense must be evaluated with respect to each copyrightable Photograph which Prince appropriated. To hold otherwise would mean that it would be permissible for someone to pirate one song from an album as long as the entire album was not copied or to reproduce one copyrightable passage from a book as long as the entire book was not taken. *Cf. Harper & Row, Publishers, Inc. v. Nation Enters.*, 471 U.S. 539, 565 (1985) (taking 300 or 400 words from President Ford's memoirs relating to his pardon of former President Nixon was not fair use).

Nor does *NXIVM Corp. v. Ross Institute*, 364 F.3d 471 (2d Cir.), *cert. denied*, 543 U.S. 1000 (2004), which defendants cite (Def. Mem. at 20), support their argument. In that case, the defendants, "cult de-progammers," quoted sections of plaintiffs' course manual in order to expose the manual as a form of "mind control." *Id.* 364 F.3d at 475. The Court found that the third fair use factor did not favor the plaintiffs because the portions of the course manual that were taken were not "separately copyrightable" and the manual itself had no "objective core of expression." *Id.* at 481. Here, by contrast, each of Cariou's Photographs is creative and, therefore, copyrightable and Prince took the heart of each of those copyrightable images.

Defendants argue, finally, that Prince's appropriation was quantitatively

20

reasonable given his "unique artistic purpose and message." Def. Mem. at 21. The implication –

that the extent of Prince's appropriation was carefully calibrated to accomplish his artistic

purpose – is specious. As Prince admits: "When creating the paintings, I had at least 25 or more

books and magazines in front of me and would *randomly* take images that fit into my artistic

vision and message for each work." Prince Aff. ¶ 25 (emphasis supplied). Prince's own

description of his creative process distinguishes his random taking from the measured

appropriation in *Bourne Co. v. Twentieth Century Fox Film*, 602 F. Supp. 2d at 509, where the

facts made "it clear that the Defendants thought about how much of the original song was

necessary to make the object of their parody recognizable." As the Court stressed, "The internal,

creative dispute over how much of the original to use demonstrates that Defendants were

concerned about taking just enough of the original to make their point clear." *Id.* at 510.

Whatever Prince's point may have been – and, unlike the defendants in *Bourne*, it certainly was

not to comment on Cariou's work – it is clear that Prince gave no thought to "taking just enough

of the original" to make that point. Instead, Prince admits that he randomly took as much as he

felt like taking in the moment, as was his right as a renowned "appropriation artist."

D.   **Fourth Fair Use Factor: The Harm to the Potential Market for Cariou's Work Was Caused by the Defendants' Copyright Infringement, not by any Delay by Cariou in Responding to Christiane Celle, and Is Cognizable under the Copyright Act**

Seeking to evade responsibility for the potential, but very concrete, harm they

caused to the market for Cariou's work – lost sales of prints at prices ranging from $3,000 to

$20,000 per print; lost introductions to clients of Christiane Celle who are drawn to images of

Rastas; and a foregone book signing of Cariou's reprinted book in conjunction with an exhibition

opening a new gallery (Brooks Dec. Ex. J at 40-42, 45-46, 66-69, 87-88, 127-28, 130-31, 153-56,

158-59) – defendants attempt to blame the victim. As defendants would have it, Celle's decision

to cancel Cariou's show and open her new gallery with another artist was "due to timing

21

constraints" because Cariou did not respond promptly to her attempt to reach him when she learned that the Gagosian Gallery was exhibiting Paintings by Prince which plagiarized Cariou's Photographs. Def. Mem. at 22. Defendants also claim that this harm is not "cognizable" under the Copyright Act and that Prince did not usurp the market for Cariou's work because the Paintings do not compete in the same market as the Photographs. Def. Mem. at 22, 23.

Celle testified that when she found out about the *Canal Zone* show, in November or December 2008, she called Cariou and left a message for him to call her back. Brooks Dec. Ex. J at 63-64, 71. She did not speak to Cariou until late January 2009, perhaps because she went to St. Barth's on December 17, 2008, where she had an art gallery (but where her cell phone did not work), remaining there for the holidays. *Id.* at 36-37; Brooks Opp. Dec. Ex. C at 103, 104, 111. Celle called Cariou right after receiving an e-mail from him on January 29, 2009, advising that he had filed a lawsuit against Prince. Brooks Opp. Dec. Ex. C at 74-77; Brooks Dec. Ex. J at 107-08. Contrary to defendants' assertion (Def. Mem. at 11), Cariou's e-mail did not ask Celle for "help with this lawsuit." Brooks Opp. Dec. Ex. C at 75-77.

Celle never testified that she cancelled Cariou's show because of "timing constraints" or because he did not reply to her promptly. *Cf.* Def. Mem. at 22. In fact, due to construction delays, her new gallery did not actually open until June 2009. Brooks Dec. Ex. J at 65-66. Celle testified that, as soon as she learned of the *Canal Zone* show, she thought: "[I]f it's done already I'm not going to do now a Rasta show . . . It looks like I'm trying to take advantage of the success of Richard Prince . . . So at the time I knew that if I will do something with Patrick it will be probably the Surfer. But I could not do anymore the Rasta because it was already in Chelsea, a beautiful gallery in Chelsea." *Id.* at 89. When asked whether, by the end of January 2009, she had made any arrangements for advertising Cariou's show, Celle responded: "No,

22

because the minute I figure out that there was a Chelsea show of his work, you know, I knew that it was over." *Id.* at 91. Again, when asked whether it was in January 2009 that she decided not to proceed with the Cariou exhibit, Celle unequivocally replied: "No, actually I decided the end of November, December, and I met - - at the time when I saw the Richard Prince situation, I committed with another photographer called Lyle Owerko . . . [and] I just opened my gallery with [Owerko's] show." *Id.* at 123-24. Any delay by Cariou in responding to Celle's phone call was, thus, unrelated to the cancellation of his show.

Defendants contend that this harm is "not cognizable" under the Copyright Act, Def. Mem. at 22, citing *NXIVM*, 364 F.3d at 482. In that case, however, the defendants took portions of plaintiffs' course manual in order to criticize it as a cult, causing some individuals, including the actress Goldie Hawn, not to attend plaintiffs' seminars, a "sort of harm . . . not cognizable under the Copyright Act. If criticisms on defendants' websites kill the demand for plaintiffs' service, that is the price that, under the First Amendment, must be paid in the open marketplace for ideas." *Id.* Like parody, criticism, a form of expression specified in the preamble to the fair use statute, 17 U.S.C. § 107, is not likely to "affect the market for the original in a way cognizable under [the fourth fair use factor], that is, by acting as a substitute for it ('supersed[ing] [its] objects')." *Campbell v. Acuff-Rose Music, Inc.*, 510 U.S. 569, 591 (1994) (citation omitted). "[W]hen a lethal parody, like a scathing theater review, kills demand for the original, it does not produce a harm cognizable under the Copyright Act. Because 'parody may quite legitimately aim at garroting the original, destroying it commercially as well as artistically,' . . . the role of the courts is to distinguish between '[b]iting criticism [that merely] suppresses demand [and] copyright infringement[, which] usurps it.'" *Id.* at 591-92 (citations omitted). Criticism and parody are considered fair use because few creators will develop or license others

23

to produce "critical reviews or lampoons of their own productions." *Id.* at 592.

Here, conversely, the harm was caused not by any criticism of Cariou's work, but by the very act of appropriating it, as Celle testified. Nor is the harm mitigated, as defendants argue, because the Paintings and Photographs do not compete in the same market. Def. Mem. at 23. The cases cited by defendants for this argument are distinguishable. In *Consumers Union of the United States, Inc. v. General Signal Corp.*, 724 F.2d 1044, 1051 (2d Cir. 1983), not only was there no competition between the copyright owner and the copier, "but the owner does not even allege injury to any work currently copyrighted." In *Video-Cinema Films, Inc. v. Cable News Network, Inc.*, No. 98 Civ. 7128 (BSJ), 2001 U.S. Dist. LEXIS 25687, at *29-30 (S.D.N.Y. Nov. 28, 2001), not only was there no competition between the defendants' obituaries and the plaintiff's film, but the plaintiff "acknowledged that the obituaries did not have an impact on the market for the entire original film." Even without competing in the same market, a secondary use can potentially harm an original work, tipping the fourth factor against fair use. *See, e.g., Twin Peaks Productions, Inc. v. Publications Int'l, Ltd.*, 996 F.2d 1366, 1377 (2d Cir. 1993) (book containing detailed plot summaries of television episodes could lead someone who had missed an episode to refer to the book instead of renting the videotape of that episode).[3]

POINT II

CARIOU'S FIFTH CLAIM FOR RELIEF SHOULD NOT BE DISMISSED

In a footnote, defendants contend that Cariou's fifth claim for relief must be dismissed "because there is no cause of action under New York [law] for conspiracy to violate

---

[3] In arguing that they did not harm the market for Cariou's work, defendants improperly refer to a "stipulation" the Gagosian defendants entered into with Cariou's publisher, powerHouse Cultural Entertainment, Inc. *See* Def. Mem. at 12, citing Bart Aff. Ex. T. This "stipulation," to which Cariou was not a party, is rank hearsay, containing unsworn statements by a non-party whose deposition defendants did not bother to take, and references to it should be disregarded.

24

the Copyright Act, and such claims are preempted by the Copyright Act." Def. Mem. at 13, n.6.
The claim, however, is brought under the Copyright Act, not New York law. *See* Brooks Dec.
Ex. A at 13. Although the Copyright Act does not explicitly proscribe conspiracy to infringe, it
also does not explicitly proscribe contributory or vicarious infringement, yet both of those
"doctrines of secondary liability emerged from common law principles" and are well recognized
in copyright. *Metro-Goldwyn-Mayer Studios Inc. v. Grokster, Ltd.*, 545 U.S. 913, 930 (2005).
See 3 Melville B. Nimmer and David Nimmer, NIMMER ON COPYRIGHT § 12.04 (Matthew
Bender, Rev. Ed.) ("conspiracy to infringe may indeed be a cognizable claim"); *Astor-Honor,
Inc. v. Grosset & Dunlap, Inc.*, 441 F.2d 627, 629 (2d Cir. 1971) (Friendly, J.) (same) (*dictum*);
Universal City Studios, Inc. v. Am. Invsco Mgmt, Inc., No. 80 C 1241, 1981 U.S. Dist. LEXIS
14225, at *15 (N.D. Ill. May 26, 1981) (denying motion for summary judgment dismissing
copyright conspiracy claim due to a disputed issue of material fact).

CONCLUSION

For the foregoing reasons, defendants' motion should be denied in all respects.

Dated: New York, New York
       June 14, 2010

SCHNADER HARRISON SEGAL & LEWIS LLP

By: _____

Daniel J. Brooks
Eric A. Boden
140 Broadway, Suite 3100
New York, New York 10005
(212) 973-8000
Attorneys for Plaintiff Patrick Cariou

25

"Attached hereto as Exhibit U is a comparison document Cariou created juxtaposing images from the paintings by Prince with photographs by Cariou in order to show which of Cariou's images were appropriated by Prince in each of those paintings and in an insert in the Canal Zone Catalogue depicting one of Cariou's photographs on a canvas in Prince's studio."
- ibid., p. 5.

Exhibit U

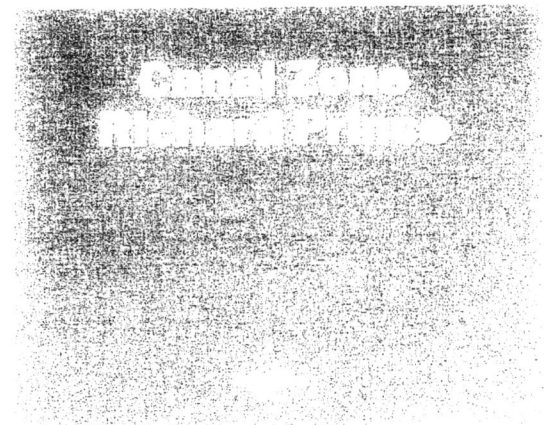

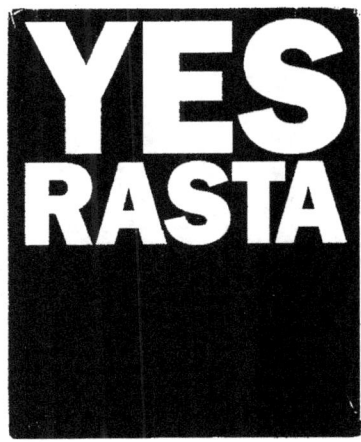

Richard Prince, *Graduation*. 2008. 72 3/4 x 52 1/2 inches (plate 1 in book)

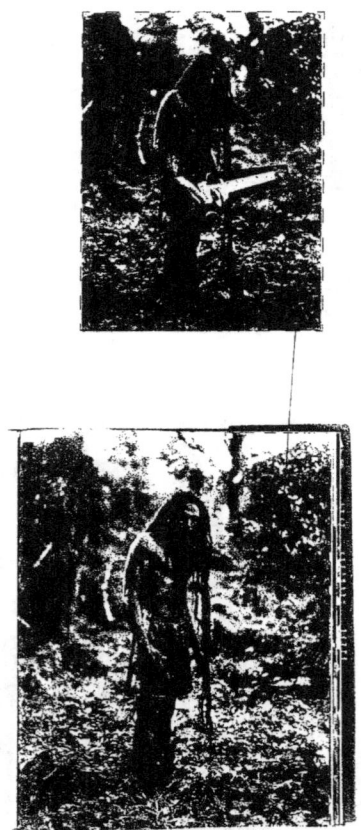

Yes Rasta! ©Patrick Cariou. 2000. Published by Powerhouse books, inc.

2

Richard Prince, *Untitled (Rasta)*, 2008. 40 x 30 inches (plate 2 in book)

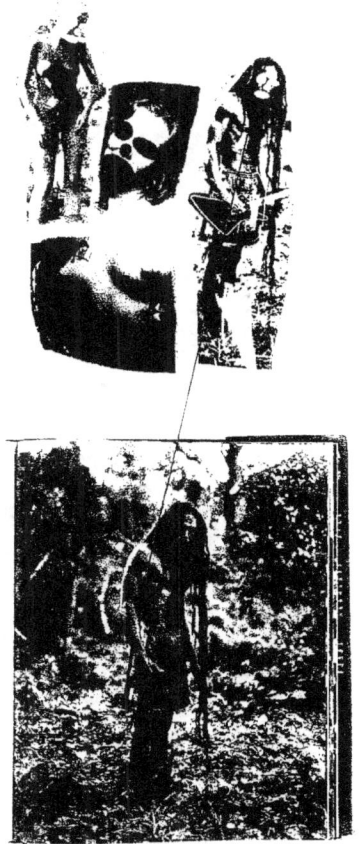

Yes Rasta! ©Patrick Cariou. 2000. Published by Powerhouse books, inc.

3

Richard Prince. *Untitled (Rasta)*. detail. 2008. 40 x 30 inches (plate 3 in book)

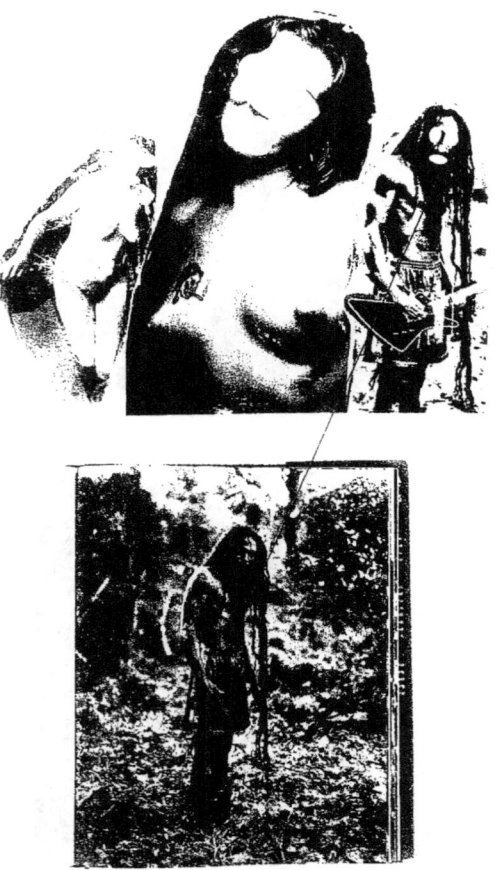

Yes Rasta! ©Patrick Cariou. 2000. Published by Powerhouse books. inc.

4

Richard Prince. *Back to the garden*. 2008. 80 x 120 inches (plate 4 in book)

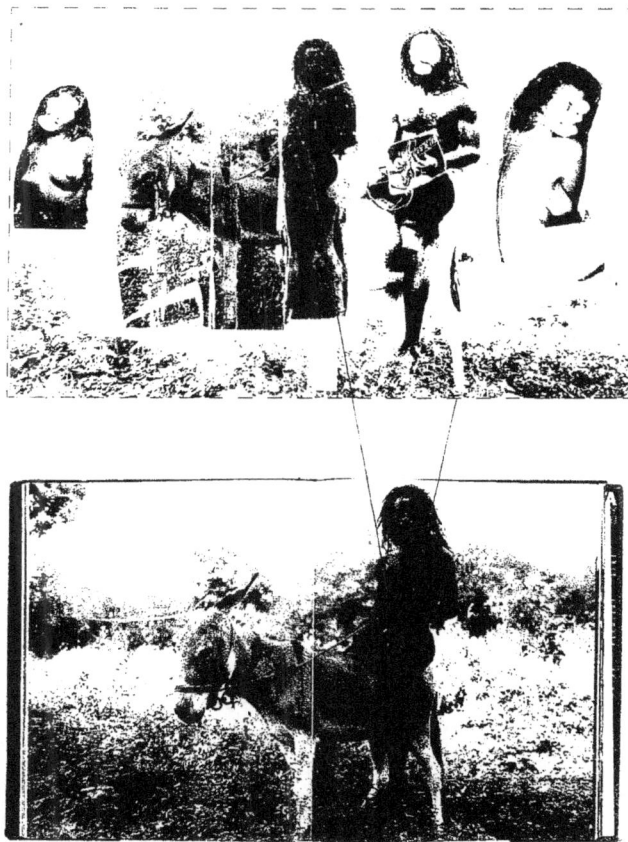

Yes Rasta! ©Patrick Cariou. 2000. Published by Powerhouse books. inc.

5

Richard Prince. *Charlie Company*. 2008. 131 x 100 inches (plate 5 in book)

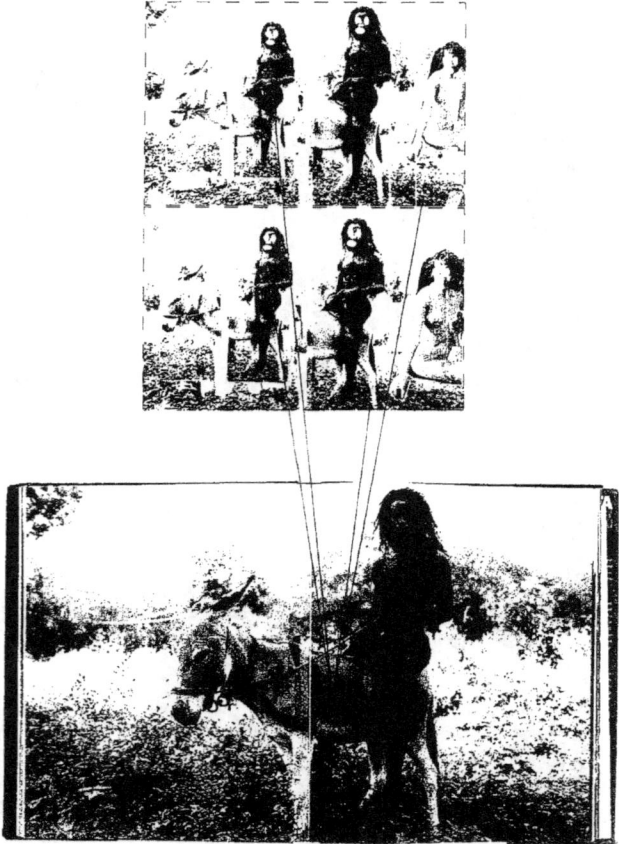

Yes Rasta! ©Patrick Cariou. 2000. Published by Powerhouse books, inc.

6

Richard Prince. *Meditation*. 2008. 58 x 46 inches (plate 6 in book)

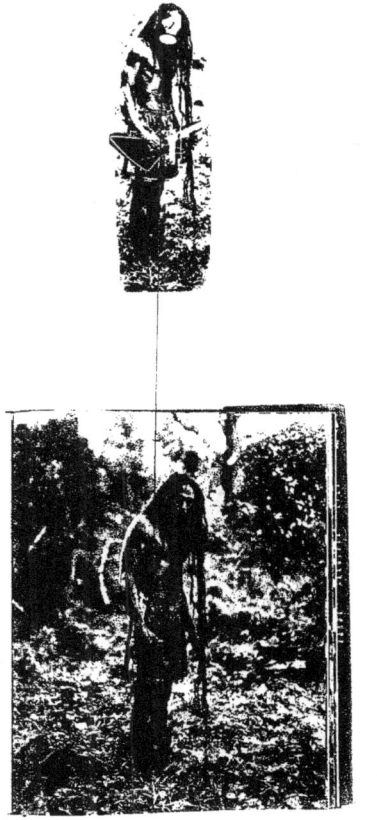

Yes Rasta! ©Patrick Cariou, 2000. Published by Powerhouse books, inc.

7

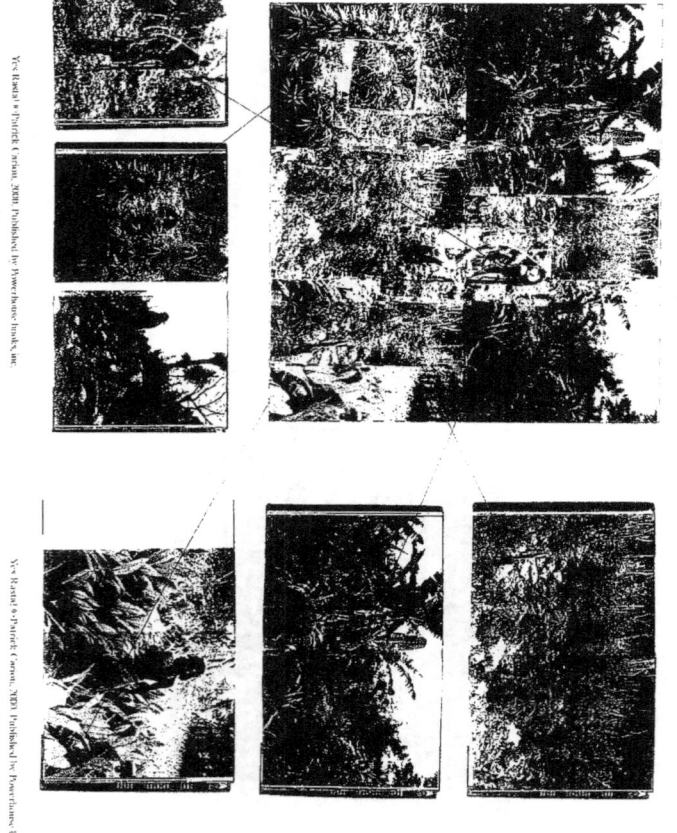

Richard Prince, *Canal Zone*, 2008, 102 x 119.5 inches (plus 7 inches)

Yves Rossier & Patrick Cramer, 2000. Published by Powerhouse Books, inc

Yves Rossier & Patrick Cramer, 2000. Published by Powerhouse Books, inc

Richard Prince, *The Avenue Club*, 2008, 45 1/2 x 90 1/4 inches (plate 8 in book)

Yes Rasta! "Patrick Cariou, 2000. Published by Powerhouse books, inc.

Yes Rasta! "Patrick Cariou, 2000. Published by Powerhouse books, inc.

Richard Prince, *Cookie Crumbles*. 2008. 76 x 100 1/2 inches (plate 9 in book)

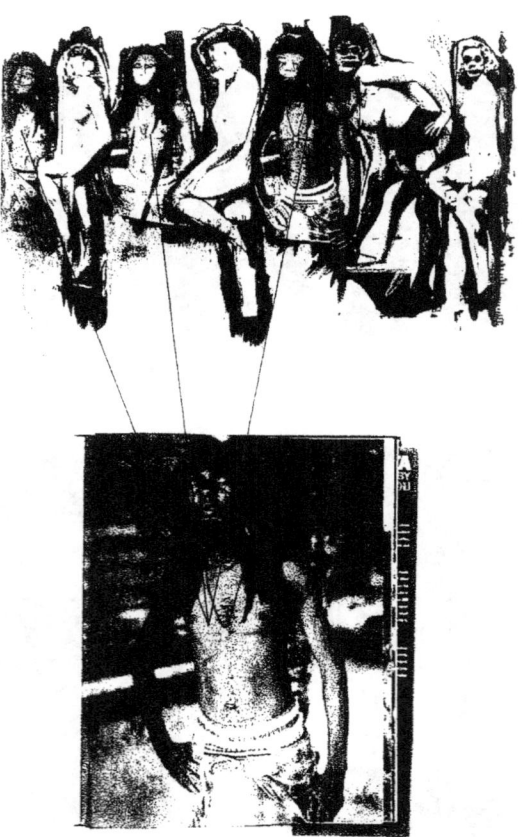

Yes Rasta! ©Patrick Cariou. 2000. Published by Powerhouse books. inc.

12

Richard Prince, *Color Me Mine*, 2008. 59 1/4 x 80 1/2 inches (plate 10 in book)

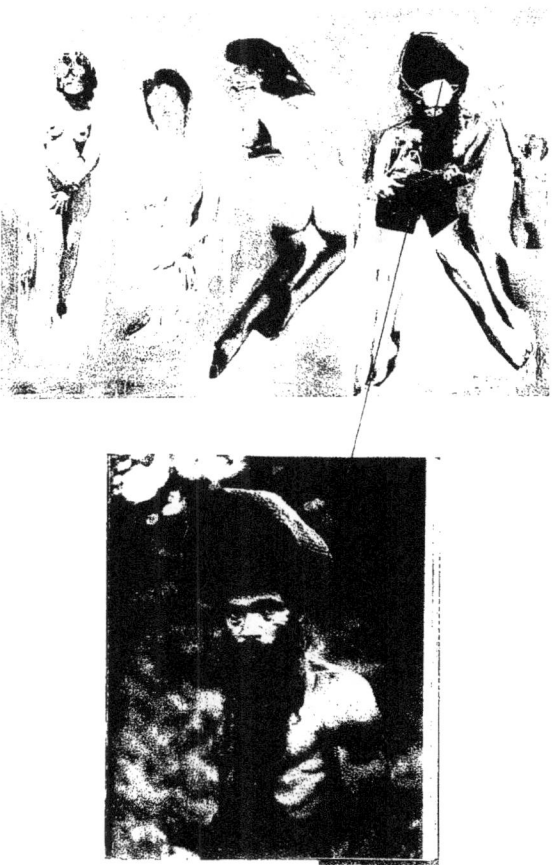

Yes Rasta! ©Patrick Cariou, 2000. Published by Powerhouse books. inc.

13

Richard Prince, *James Brown Disco Ball*, 2008, 100 1/2 x 154 1/2 inches (plate 11 in book)

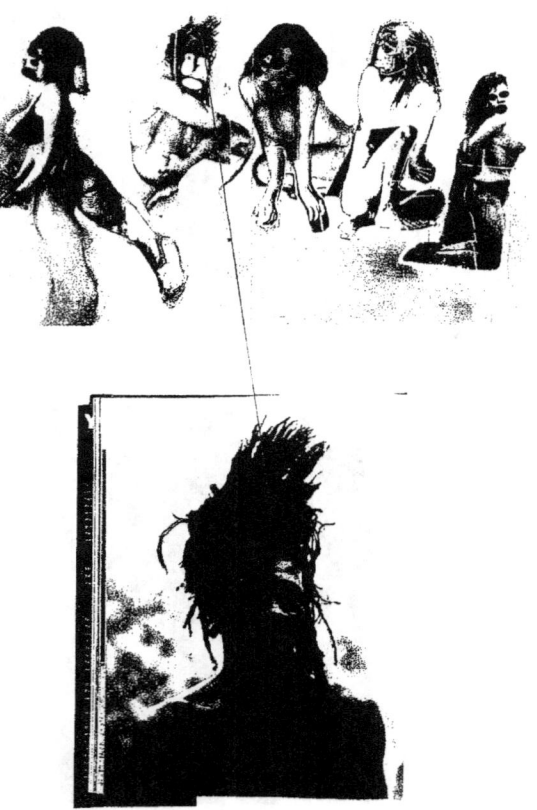

Yes Rasta! ©Patrick Cariou, 2000. Published by Powerhouse books, inc.

14

Richard Prince. *Ile de France*. 2008. 77 1/4 x 100 1/2 inches (plate 12 in book)

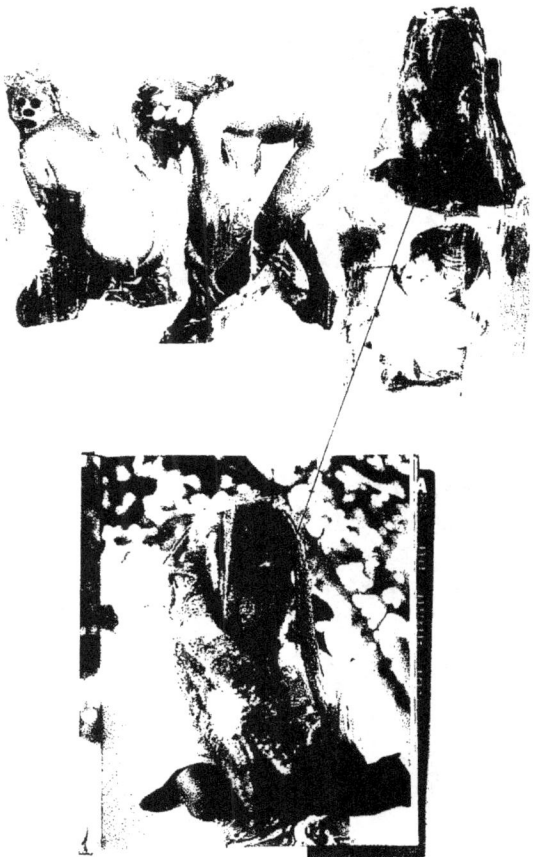

Yes Rasta! ©Patrick Cariou. 2000. Published by Powerhouse books, inc.

15

Richard Prince. *Djuna Barnes, Natalie Barney, Renée Vivien and Romaine Brooks take over the Guanahani*. 2008. 52 1/4 x 90 1/2 inches (plate 14 in book)

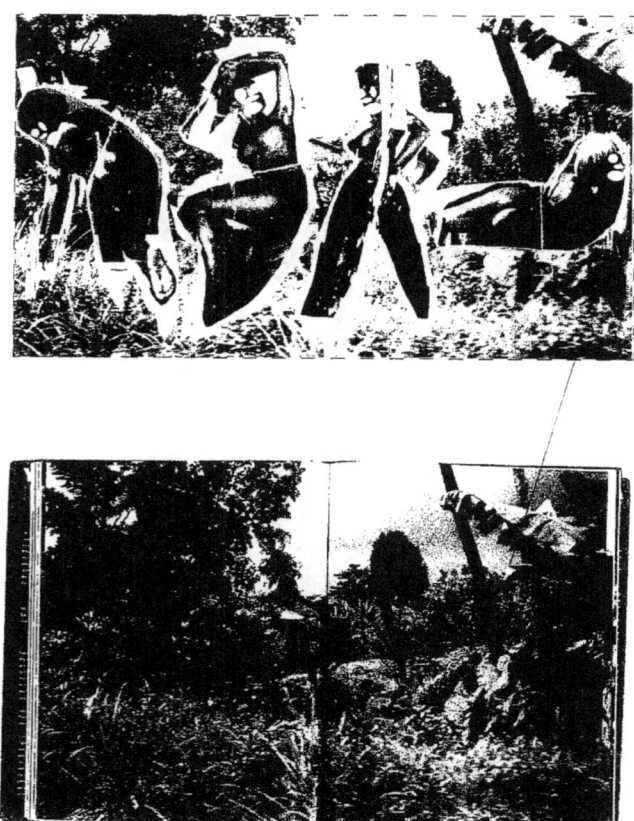

Yes Rasta! ©Patrick Cariou. 2000. Published by Powerhouse books, inc.

16

Richard Prince. *Zipping the System*, 2008. 71 1/2 x 110 1/2 inches (plate 15 in book)

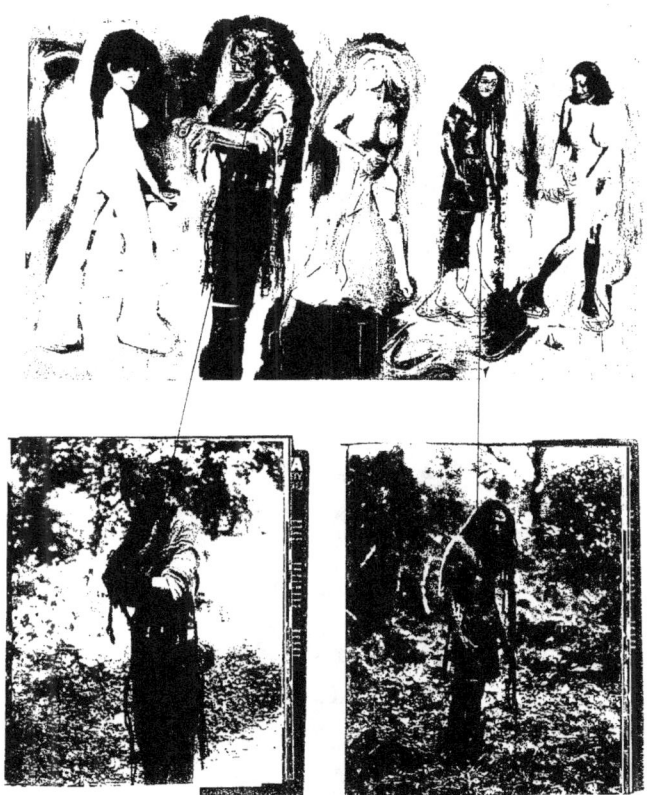

Yes Rasta! ©Patrick Cariou. 2000. Published by Powerhouse books. inc.

17

Richard Prince. *Tales of Brave Ulysses*. 2008. 84 x 132 inches (plate 16 in book)

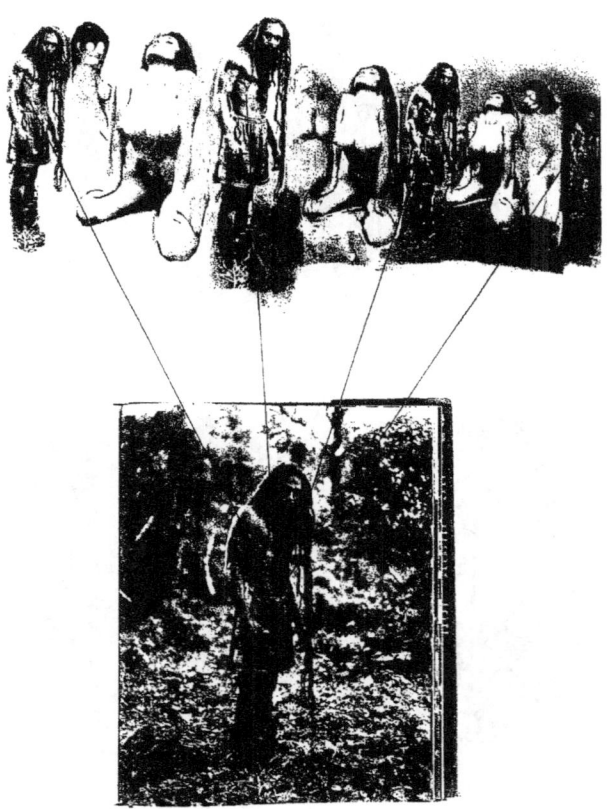

Yes Rasta! ©Patrick Cariou, 2000. Published by Powerhouse books, inc.

18

Richard Prince, *It's All Over*, 2008, 80 x 120 1/4 inches (plate 17 in book)

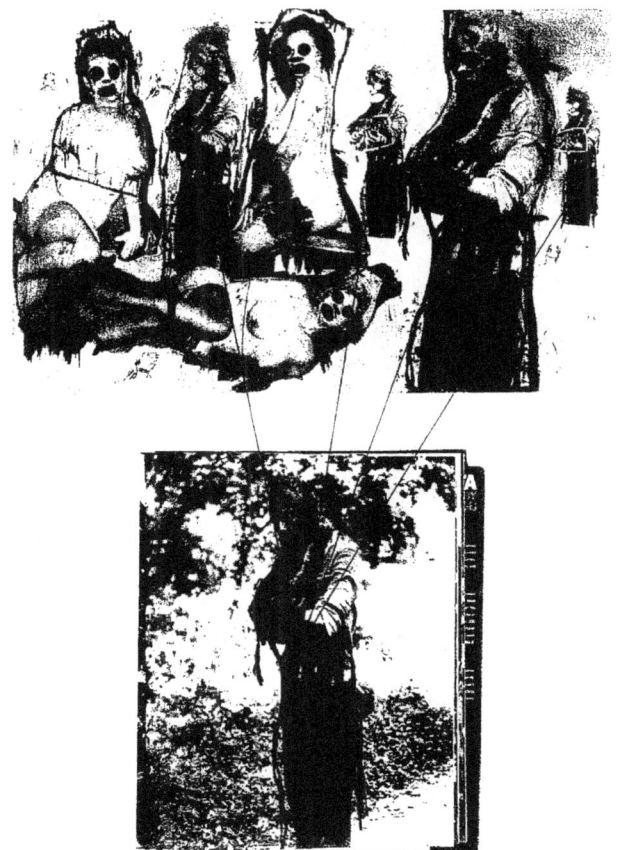

Yes Rasta! ©Patrick Cariou, 2000. Published by Powerhouse books, inc.

19

Richard Prince, *Specially round Midnight*. 2008. 100 1/2 x 154 inches (plate 18 in book)

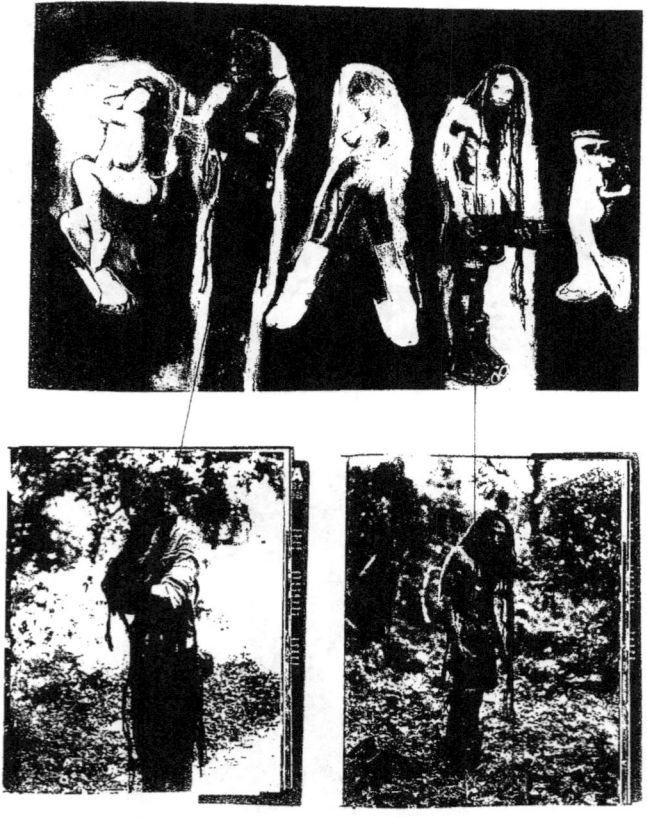

Yes Rasta! ©Patrick Cariou. 2000. Published by Powerhouse books, inc.

Richard Prince. *Naked Confessions*. 2008. 45 1/4 x 46 inches (plate 19 in book)

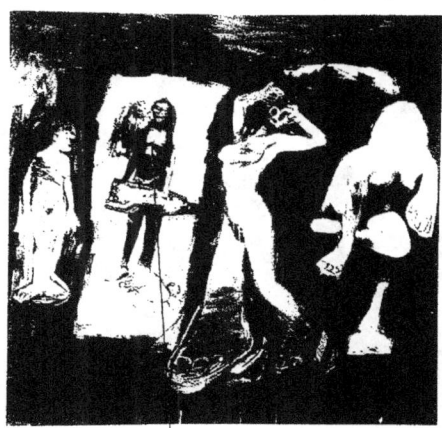

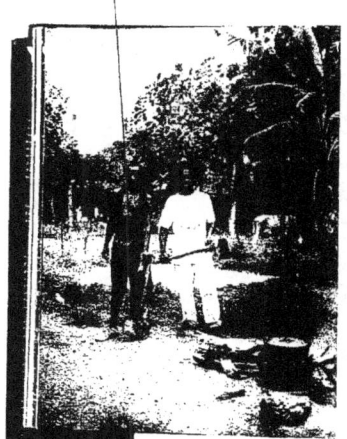

Yes Rasta! ©Patrick Cariou. 2000. Published by Powerhouse books. inc.

21

Richard Prince. *The Other Side of the Island*. 2008. 84 x 132 inches (plate 20 in book)

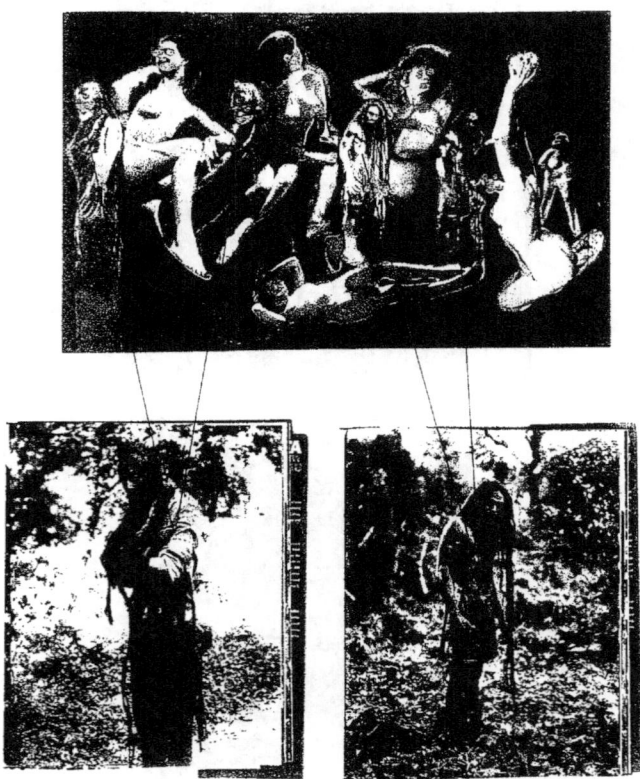

Yes Rasta! ©Patrick Cariou. 2000. Published by Powerhouse books. inc.

22

Richard Prince. *Cheese and Crackers*, 2008. 91 1/2 x 140 1/4 inches (plate 21 in book)

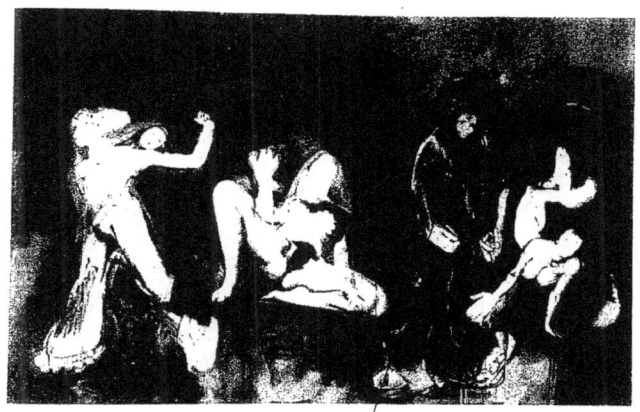

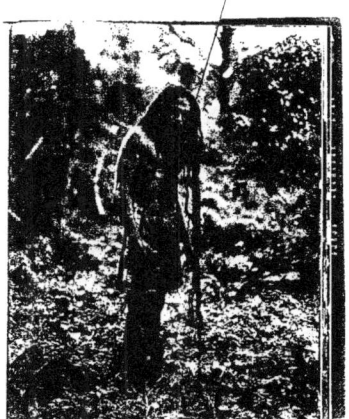

Yes Rasta! ©Patrick Cariou, 2000. Published by Powerhouse books, inc.

23

Richard Prince, *Mr Jones*, 2008, 91 1/2 x 128 inches (plate 22 in book)

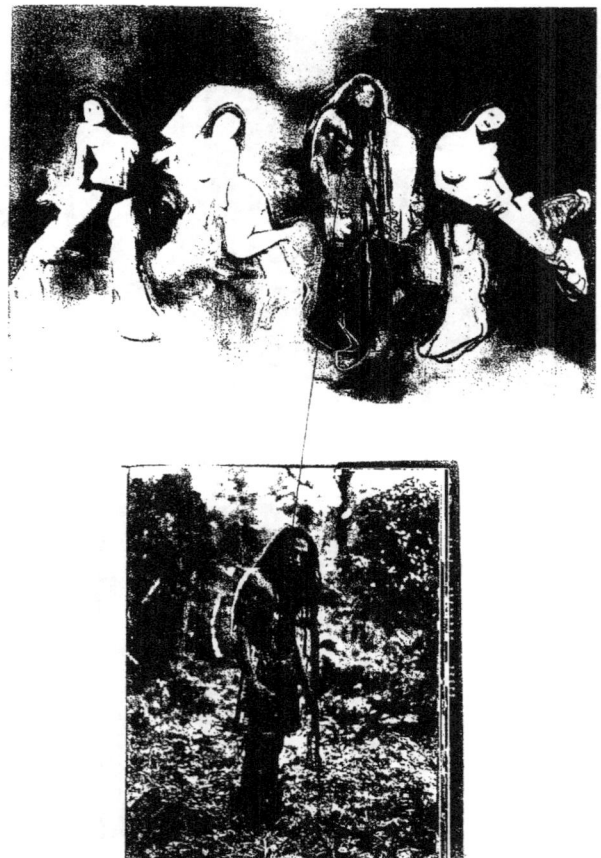

Yes Rasta! ©Patrick Cariou, 2000. Published by Powerhouse books, inc.

24

Richard Prince. book insert page

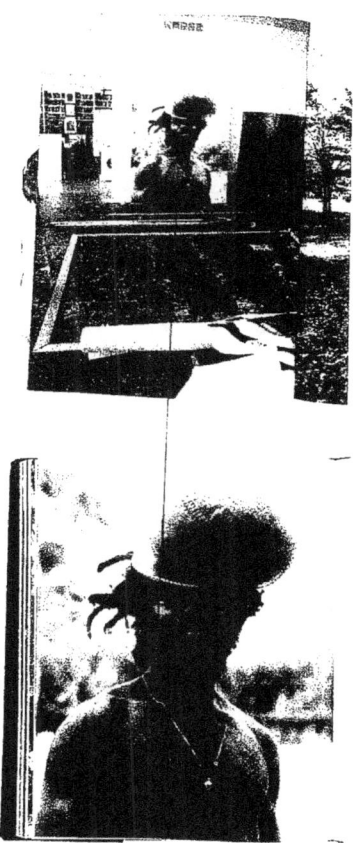

Yes Rasta! ©Patrick Cariou, 2000. Published by Powerhouse books, inc.

25

Richard Prince. *Inquisition*. 2008. 100 1/2 x 77 inches (from www.gagosian.com)

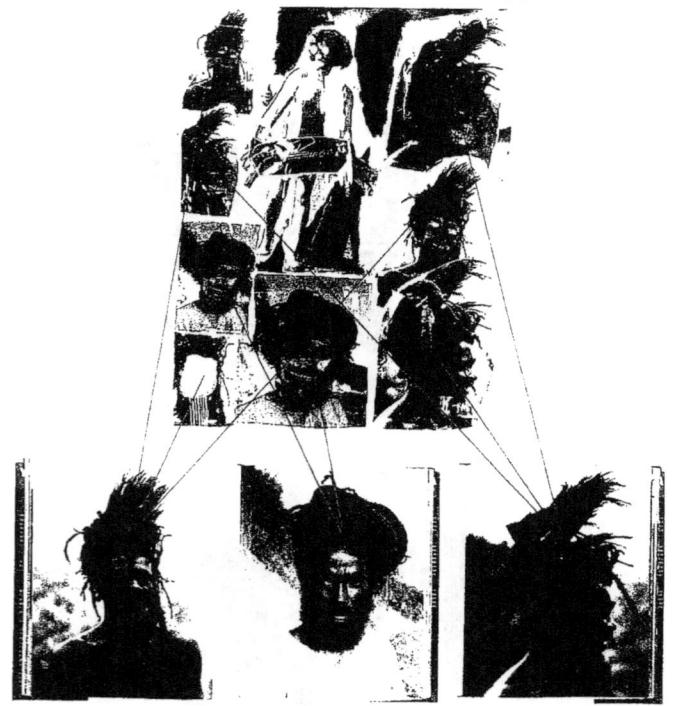

Yes Rasta! ©Patrick Cariou. 2000. Published by Powerhouse books, inc.

26

Richard Prince, *On the Beach, On the Beach,* 2008, 50 x 90.4 inches (from www.gagosian.com)

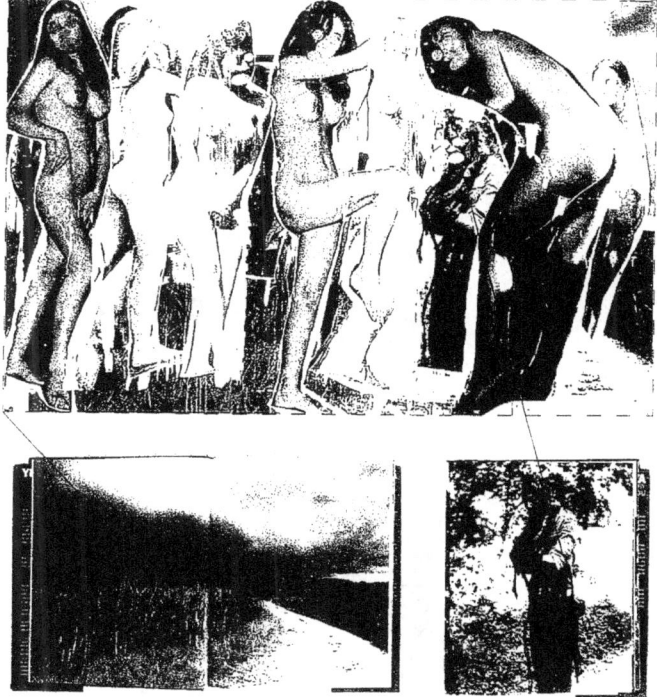

Yes Rasta! ©Patrick Cariou, 2000. Published by Powerhouse books, inc.

Richard Prince, from the series *Canal zone* (photograph of the exhibition)

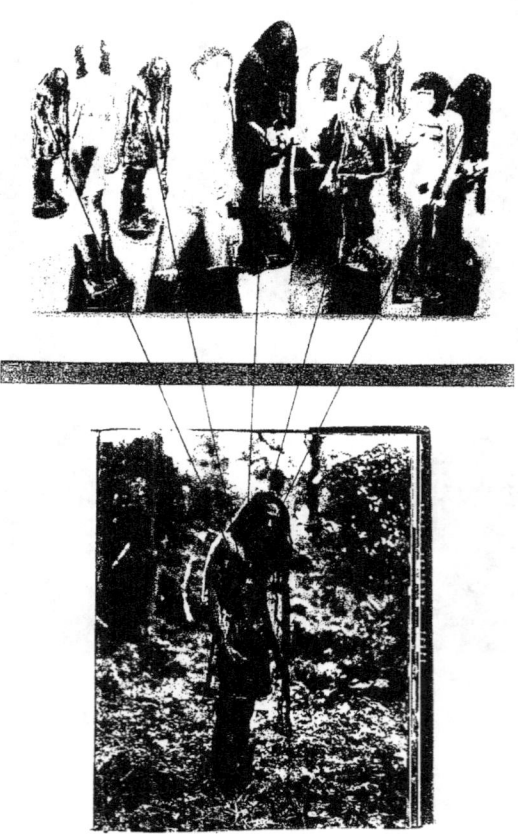

Yes Rasta! ©Patrick Cariou, 2000. Published by Powerhouse books, inc.

28

Richard Prince, from the series *Canal Zone*
(from Art Newspaper website – http://www.theartnewspaper.com/article.asp?id=16821)

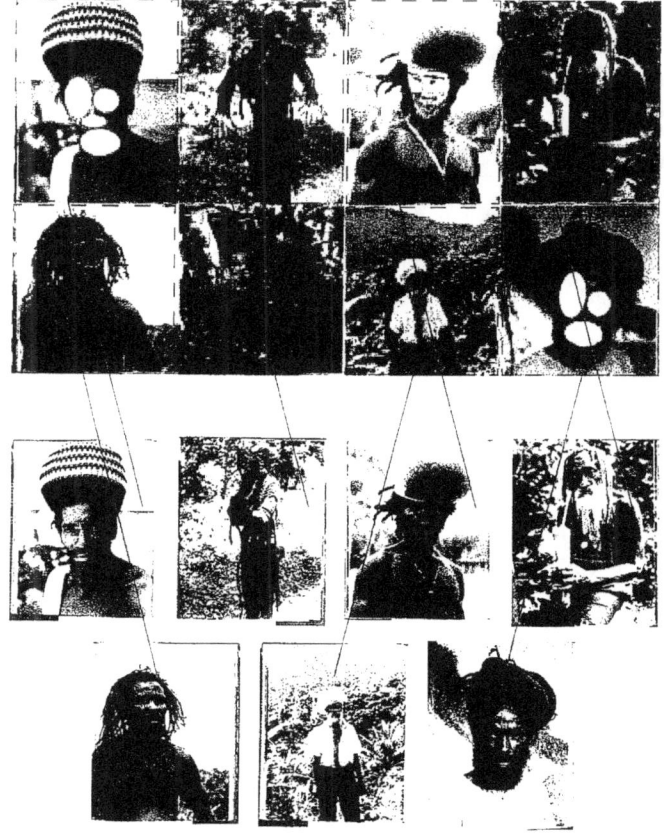

Yes Rasta! ©Patrick Cariou, 2000. Published by Powerhouse books, inc.

29

WITHERS BERGMAN LLP
Hollis Gonerka Bart (HB-8955)
Dara G. Hammerman (DH-1591)
Azmina Jasani (AJ-4161)
430 Park Avenue, 10th Floor
New York, New York 10022
212.848.9800 (p)
212.848.9888 (f)
*Attorneys for Defendants Gagosian Gallery, Inc.
and Lawrence Gagosian*

**HANLEY CONROY BIERSTEIN
SHERIDAN FISHER & HAYES LLP**
Steven M. Hayes (SH-2926)
112 Madison Avenue
New York, NY 10016-7416
(212) 784-6414
Attorneys for Defendant Richard Prince

UNITED STATES DISTRICT COURT
SOUTHERN DISTRICT OF NEW YORK
---X

PATRICK CARIOU,   08 CIV 11327 (DAB)

                            Plaintiff,

             -against-

RICHARD PRINCE, GAGOSIAN GALLERY, INC.,
LAWRENCE GAGOSIAN, and RIZZOLI
INTERNATIONAL PUBLICATIONS, INC,

                            Defendants.

---X

**MEMORANDUM OF LAW IN OPPOSITION TO
PLAINTIFF'S MOTION FOR SUMMARY JUDGMENT**

TABLE OF CONTENTS

TABLE OF AUTHORITIES

Cases

Preliminary Statement

Relying principally on his status as the compilation copyright holder and a presumption of infringement; snippets of testimony quoted out of context; and language lifted from cases without discussion of its application to the true facts of this case, Cariou's moving papers confirm that he cannot, as a matter of law, sustain his burden, as movant, to show that the Images are sufficiently original to warrant much, if any copyright protection, or that the use of the Images satisfies the "improper appropriation" prong of his copyright infringement claim (which is not even pled in his Amended Complaint), or that the use of the Images was not fair. Moreover, having failed to come forward with any evidence that either of the Gagosian defendants had any control over Prince's creation of the Images, Cariou's vicarious liability claim must be dismissed as frivolous. Nor is it enough to say that because Prince is a well-known appropriation artist, the Gagosian defendants knew or should have known that Prince had (allegedly) infringed Cariou's copyright, such that they should be held contributorily liable. As Cariou's moving papers also confirm that he cannot rebut the showing defendants have made in their opening brief and in this opposition that each of the determinative fair use factors weighs in favor of defendants, their summary judgment motion should be granted, particularly in light of Prince's transformative use of the Images to create a wholly new and different expression, meaning and message.[1]

---

[1] "P. Mem." refers to the referenced page of the Memorandum of Law in Support of Plaintiff's Motion for Summary Judgment. "D. Mem." refers to the referenced page of the Memorandum of Law in Support of Defendants' Motion for Summary Judgment. "RP Supp. Aff." refers to the accompanying Supplemental Affidavit of Defendant Richard Prince in Opposition to Plaintiff's Motion for Summary Judgment and in Further Support of Defendants' Motion for Summary Judgment. "Supp. Aff. Ex ___" refers to the exhibits attached to the accompanying Supplemental Affidavit of Defendant Richard Prince. "Opp. Aff. Ex. __" refers to the exhibits attached to the accompanying Affidavit of Hollis Gonerka Bart in Opposition to Plaintiff's Motion for Summary Judgment. All other references mentioned in this Memorandum remain the same as Footnote 1 of the Memorandum of Law in Support of Defendants' Joint Motion for Summary Judgment.

POINT I
CARIOU HAS NOT SHOWN THAT THE USE OF THE IMAGES SATISFIES THE
IMPROPER APPROPRIATION PRONG OF HIS COPYRIGHT INFRINGEMENT CLAIM

In his opening brief, Cariou assumes that because he owns the compilation copyright in

the images in *Yes Rasta*, he is entitled to the "core protection" of the copyright laws as to the

entirety of the Images. P. Mem. 1-2, 20. However, to prevail on an infringement claim, the

owner also must show actual copying *and* "improper appropriation" of constituent elements of

the work that are original. *See Feist Publ'ns., Inc. v. Rural Tel. Serv. Co., Inc.*, 499 U.S. 340,

348 (1991) (*"Feist"*) ("The mere fact that a work is copyrighted does not mean that every

element of the work may be protected. Originality remains the *sine qua non* of copyright;

accordingly, copyright protection may extend only to those components of a work that are

original to the author.").

While the techniques Cariou chose to shoot images depicting Rastafarians in their native

Jamaican landscape may be enough to satisfy the minimum standard for originality (P. Mem. 2,

20), "[n]o one may claim originality as to facts. This is because facts do not owe their origin to

an act of authorship. The distinction is one between creation and discovery. . . . The discoverer

merely finds and records." *Feist*, 499 U.S. at 347 (internal citations omitted). As such, the fact-

based images of Rastafarians in their Jamaican landscape that Cariou depicted as realistically as

possible, are not protectable as a matter of law. *Id; see also, Maxtone-Graham v. Burtchaell*,

803 F.2d 1253, 1262-63 (2d Cir. 1986); P. Mem. 1-2.

Though Cariou claims to have "staged" many of the pictures he took (P. Mem. 2), these

images along with the tropical and ganja-filled landscapes which surround them are non-

protectable *scenes a faire* typical of images of this type and thus, are not original. *Bill Diodato*

Photography, LLC v. Kate Spade, LLC, 388 F. Supp.2d 382, 392 (S.D.N.Y. 2005) (*"Diodato")*

("Sequences of events that necessarily result from the choice of a setting or situation do not

2

enjoy copyright protection.") (citations omitted). In capturing the Jamaican Rastafarian culture,

it is commonplace to incorporate pictures of Rastafarians with dreadlocks. Indeed, plaintiff

concedes in his Opening Memorandum that images of Rastafarians such as those found in *Yes*

Rasta can be readily found in stock photos. *See* P. Mem. 8; *Diodato* at 393 (photographs not

original where stock photos similar to ones at issue were readily available, and were found in

films and other media); *see also* Ex. CC; Opp. Aff. ¶ 2, Ex. A (a search on YouTube also yields

homemade videos by tourists filming ganja plantations in Jamaica, the details of which are

accessible via Google search, and footage of Rastas in their natural habitat). These materials also

confirm that it is common to include shots of tropical vegetation, ganja plantations, vegetation,

and scenes of mountains, villages and towns such as Negril and Kingston, in attempting to

capture the Jamaican Rastafarian culture. *See id.; see also Diodato* at 392 ("elements of an

image that flow naturally and necessarily from the choice of a given concept cannot be claimed

as original."); *Arden v. Columbia Pictures Indus., Inc.*, 908 F. Supp. 1248, 1259 (S.D.N.Y. 1995)

("depictions of drunks, prostitutes, rodents, and abandoned cars were unprotectable scenes a

faire") (citing *Walker v. Time Life Films, Inc.*, 784 F.2d 44, 50 (2d Cir. 1986)).

 The manner in which Cariou posed his subjects also is not a protectable element.

Diodato at 393 ("a plaintiff's copyrights cannot monopolize the various poses used") (internal

citations omitted). Nor does Cariou have a protectable monopoly on the technique commonly

used by photographers to blur the background, so as to bring the subject into sharp focus.

Diodato, 388 F. Supp. 2d at 392.

 Even Cariou's position that his work must be viewed as a compilation to appreciate the

distinctiveness of the *Yes Rasta* images (PC Tr. 61-62, 81) does not warrant copyright protection

as to the entirety of each Image. While the arrangement of elements in a compilation may give

rise to originality (*Feist*, 499 U.S. at 348), Prince used the Images as raw elements in the

Paintings without regard to how they are organized in *Yes Rasta*. In any event, as the Supreme

Court has observed:

> No matter how original the format, however, the facts themselves do not become original through association. . . . This inevitably means that the *copyright in a factual compilation is thin.* Notwithstanding a valid copyright, a subsequent compiler *remains free to use the facts contained in another's publication to aid in preparing a competing work,* so long as the competing work does not feature the same selection and arrangement. As one commentator explains it: "No matter how much original authorship the work displays, the facts and ideas it exposes are *free for the taking.* . . . The very same facts and ideas may be *divorced from the context* imposed by the author, and restated or reshuffled by second comers, even if the author was the first to discover the facts or to propose the ideas."

Id. at 349 (emphasis added) (internal citations omitted).

Where, as here, the works contain both protectable and unprotectable elements, the

court's "inspection must be more discerning; [it] must attempt to extract the unprotectable

elements from [its] consideration and ask whether the *protectable elements, standing alone,* are

substantially similar." *See Diodato at* 390 (citing *Knitwaves, Inc. v. Lollytogs, Ltd.,* 71 F.3d 996,

1002 (2d Cir. 1995)) (emphasis in original). As most of the elements in the Images are non-

protectable, Cariou cannot show an improper appropriation (an element not pled in his Amended

Complaint) since the only arguably protectable elements in the Images, *standing alone*, are not

substantially similar to the scanned, enlarged, altered and re-contextualized images in the

Paintings. *See id.* at 390 (to satisfy improper appropriation requirement, copyright owner must

demonstrate that "'substantial similarities' as to the protected elements of the work would cause

an average lay observer to 'recognize the alleged copy as having been appropriated from the

copyrighted work.'"). Cariou has conceded that the only elements of his photographs that fall

"within the core protection of copyright" are his choice of "camera, lenses, film, angle, lighting

and exposure" and his oversight of film development to "exacting specifications." P. Mem. 20.

Thus, when stripped of the non-protectable elements (fact-based images documenting

4

Rastafarians in their Jamaican landscape), it is not possible for an average observer to recognize

the remaining protectable elements as having been appropriated from *Yes Rasta*. *See Diodato*,

388 F. Supp. 2d at 390 ("When similar works resemble each other only in unprotected aspects –

for example, when similarities inhere in … expression that is not proprietary to plaintiff –

defendant prevails.") (citing 4 Melville B. Nimmer & David Nimmer, *Nimmer on Copyright* §

13.03[B][2]).

POINT II
CARIOU HAS FAILED TO SUSTAIN HIS BURDEN, AS MOVANT, THAT
HE IS ENTITLED TO SUMMARY JUDGMENT ON THE ISSUE OF FAIR USE

Even if Cariou could make out a copyright infringement claim, he would not be entitled

to summary judgment on his claim that defendants are not entitled to invoke the fair use defense.

As is evident from his opening brief, Cariou cannot rebut the showing defendants have made on

their motion for summary judgment seeking a determination that the use was fair. *See Bourne

Co. v. Twentieth Century Fox Film Corp.*, 602 F. Supp. 2d 499, 503 (S.D.N.Y. 2009) (Batts, J.)

(non-movant may not rely on conclusory allegations, speculation or conjecture. "Instead, when

the moving party has documented particular facts in the record, 'the opposing party must set

forth specific facts showing that there is a genuine issue for trial.'") (citation omitted).

A.   Cariou Has Not Proffered Any Basis to Defeat Defendants' Showing
that Prince's Use of the Images was Transformative as a Matter of Law

Cariou begins his discussion of the transformative prong by reciting the standard in

Campbell v. Acuff-Rose Music, Inc., 510 U.S. 569, 579 (1994) for determining whether the

"challenged use is transformative"; that is, "whether the new work merely 'supersede[s] the

objects of the original creation . . . or instead *adds something new*, with a *further purpose* of

different character, altering the original with *new expression, meaning or message*; it asks, in

other words, whether and to what extent it is 'transformative.'" P. Mem. 14 (emphasis added).

Though this standard clearly requires a comparison of the original and challenged work, Cariou does not explain why he feels Prince's use of the Images as raw elements in each of the Paintings is not transformative. *See id.* Instead, Cariou spends six pages attempting, unsuccessfully, to discredit Prince in the style and manner in which he works as an appropriation artist, attributing arguments to defendants they have never made, applying inapplicable legal theories quoted out of context, and chastising the Gagosian defendants for doing their job to promote a facially transformative body of works by Prince. *Id.* at 14-19. As such, none of Cariou's theories undermine the showing defendants made in their opening brief that Prince's use of the Images as raw elements to create an entirely new expression, meaning and message that was transformative as a matter of law. *See* D. Mem. 14-16; *see also* PR Aff. Ex. A.

> 1.   Evidence that Prince Worked Quickly in Implementing His
>   Creative Expression is Irrelevant to the Fair Use Analysis

Cariou cites no case to support his vague suggestion that the speed with which Prince completed the Paintings somehow casts doubt as to their transformative nature. P. Mem. 17. As Prince explained (in that portion of his deposition which Cariou omits): "I like when I do things fast. I think they should be done quickly. I think when they drag on, you know, you can over think it. I don't like a painting that's overcooked." RP Tr. 274. Indeed, some of the great masters, such as Cy Twombly and Picasso, to which Prince pays homage in the Paintings (RP Tr. 165-67), created many masterpieces in a matter of hours.[2] *See* Opp. Aff. Ex. B. The issue, however, is not how long it took Prince to complete each Painting, only the transformative nature of result of that process. *See, e.g., Mannion v. Coors Brewing Co.,* 377 F. Supp. 2d 444, 451 (S.D.N.Y. 2005) ("'Sweat of the brow' is not the touchstone of copyright. Protection derives

---

[2] Cariou's views about the speed with which Prince works stand in contrast to his statement that the shots he staged in 15 minutes took him a "considerable" period of time. *See* P. Mem. 2.

from the features of the work itself, not the effort that goes into it."). In any event, the irrefutable record is clear that the genesis of the Paintings was the result of a two-year creative process, which was informed by a trip Prince took to Panama, sketches he made in a copy of *Yes Rasta* he purchased while on vacation, and a screenplay he had been writing long before he began working on the Paintings. RP Tr. 8-9, 152-54, 265-66; *see also* P. Mem. 3, 8.

2.   Prince's Creation of the Paintings in the Tradition of Appropriation
        Artists Does Not Foreclose a Fair Use Defense, As Cariou Urges

In their opening brief, defendants show that appropriation art, an established and respected art form, by its very nature, involves a taking of an original work for the purpose of transforming into a new expressive meaning and purpose. *See* D. Mem. 14-16); *see also Rogers v. Koons,* 960 F.2d 301, 303 (2d Cir. 1992) ("*Rogers*") (defining appropriation art, as follows: "when the artist finishes his work, the meaning of the original object has been extracted and an entirely new meaning set in its place."). This is the very essence of fair use. Defendants then showed, in painstaking detail, precisely why Prince's use of the Images satisfies each element of their fair use defense. D. Mem. 14-24; *see also* RP Aff. Ex. A. On this record, then, the Court should ignore Cariou's unsubstantiated, and demonstrably false, accusation that Prince claims he is "excused" from (allegedly) infringing another artist's copyright simply "by following in that artistic tradition." P. Mem. 17. In making this argument, Cariou quotes language out of context from the *Rogers* case to urge that *Rogers* applies here. In *Rogers*, the artist, Jeff Koons "argue[d] that his sculpture is a satire or parody of society at large." *Rogers*, 960 F.2d at 309. Here, there is no claim that the Paintings are a satire or a parody. Thus, the holding in that case (also cited out of context in Cariou's Memorandum (P. Mem. 17-18)), requiring that the copied work must be the object of the parody to ensure "public awareness of the original," is limited to works involving parody. *Rogers* at 310 ("By requiring that the copied work be an object of the parody, we merely insist that the audience be aware that underlying the parody, there is an original and

separate expression, attributable to a different artist."); *see also United Feature Syndicate, Inc. v.*

Koons, 817 F. Supp. 370 (S.D.N.Y. 1993) (after completing its analysis of the four fair use

factors (Point IIIA), court turned to Koons' claim that works were a parody or satire (Point IIIB),

noting: "It is well recognized that there is a branch of the fair use doctrine which deals

specifically with the use of a copyrighted work for purpose of parody or satire.").

    In the same way, *United Feature Syndicate, Inc.,* also relied on by Cariou, is inapplicable

because it is another parody case that rejects the same art as a defense theory that has not been

advanced by the defendants in this case. P. Mem. 15. In any event, as both *Rogers* and *United*

Feature Syndicate were decided before the Supreme Court issued its landmark fair use decision

in *Campbell,* they are of limited precedential value on this point, since neither of these cases

address the transformative nature of the works at issue in those cases, focusing instead on

commercialism, a factor which *Campbell* teaches is of lesser significance than the transformative

nature of the new work. *Campbell,* 510 U.S. at 579.

    3.   Neither Section 107 Nor the Cases Construing It Require the Secondary User
          to Comment on the Original Work in Order to Satisfy the Transformative Prong

    In his opening brief, Cariou lifts snippets of Prince's testimony out of context to argue

that Prince's creation of the Paintings lack a message and do not comment. P. Mem. 6-7, 15, 17.

However, as shown in Defendants' Memorandum, Prince's creation of the Paintings was

informed by certain core meanings or messages he intended to convey through them:

> • Prince's concept of a fantastical post-apocalyptical world, where music was the
> only redeeming thing to survive, as shown through repetitive use of the guitar,
> figures as band members, and rhythm as expressed through various painterly and
> collaging techniques. *See, e.g.,* RP Aff. ¶¶ 22, 27, 32-61; *see also* RP Tr. 338-39
> ("I'm trying to make a kind of fantastic, absolutely hip, up to date contemporary
> take, on the music scene."), 359-61 ("unbelievably looking great painting that had
> to do with a kind of rock-and-roll painting on the radical side, and on a
> conservative side something to do with Cezanne's bathers."); P. Mem. 7, 8.

8

- An ongoing exploration of the relationships that exist in the world, which are men and men, men and women, and women and women. RP Aff. ¶ 37; RP Tr. 338-39.

- Equality between the sexes, as shown through their nudity and roles as band members. RP Aff. ¶ 61.

- To pay homage to master painters whose works Prince admires. *Id.* at ¶¶ 21, 27, 32, 34, 35, 38-42, 63, 66; *see also* RP Tr. 165-67.

See also RP Tr. 339 ("in any artwork I don't think there's any one message."). In using altered, scanned and enlarged copies of the Images as raw materials alone or in combination with other raw materials and painterly elements to communicate these meanings or messages, Prince has created an entirely new and different creative expression, such that his use of the Images in the Paintings is substantially transformative as a matter of law.[3] *See* D. Mem. 5-7, 14-24; *see also Reyes v. Wyeth Pharm., Inc.*, 603 F. Supp. 2d 289, 296-97 (D. P.R. 2009) (though actual sculpture was pictured without alteration, secondary work found "somewhat transformative" because message of the sculpture had nothing to do with message conveyed in ad).

In his opening brief, Cariou cites to Prince's deposition testimony that he does not make comments with any of his works (P. Mem. 7),[4] and then urges this Court to impose a further requirement that in expressing these meaning or messages, Prince must also comment on the Images or on culture generally, or his use must fit within one of the other illustrative purposes listed in Section 107. *See* P. Mem. 15-16. Cariou, however, makes no attempt to harmonize his

---

[3] Prince testified that his message is further expressed in the titles he gave to the Paintings. *See* RP Tr. 249; RP Aff. ¶¶ 35, 38, 42, 45-47, 51. Though Cariou tries to discredit this testimony by pointing out Prince's inability to recall specific titles for each of the Paintings (P. Mem. n.2), any perceived deficiencies in his ability to remember with precision all 29 titles does not diminish the importance Prince placed on those titles to convey his transformative message at time the works were created.

[4] It is worth noting that when viewed in the context of the questions and answers which preceded this answer that Prince struggled with the examiner's use of the word "comment," but he was steadfast in his responses that his message is about music and its reference to pop culture. *See* RP Tr. 353-55. This sequence also came on the heels of testimony in which Prince stated he is not a "political artist" (*id.* at 338-39), thereby suggesting that he understood the use of the term "comment" to mean political comment, a fact which he confirms in his Supplemental Affidavit. Supp. RP Aff. 7.

insistence on a strict application of Section 107 with the admission in his Memorandum that

purposes listed in Section 107 are "illustrative" (P. Mem. 14), or with the cases he cites, each of

which expressly adopt the holding in *Campbell* that Section 107 "employs the terms 'including'

and 'such as' in the preamble paragraph to indicate the 'illustrative and not limitative' function

of the examples given, which thus provide only general guidance about the sorts of copying that

courts and Congress most commonly had found to be fair uses."[5]   *Campbell*, 510 U.S. at 577-78

(internal citations omitted). Had Congress intended to impose a requirement that all secondary

works must comment, it could have done so by adding a comment requirement as a conjunctive

element, or by providing that only those activities listed in Section 107 can qualify as fair use, a

construction that was soundly rejected in describing the legislative intent:

> The statement of the fair use doctrine in Section 107 offers some guidance to
> users in determining when the principles of the doctrine apply. However, the
> endless variety of situations and combinations of circumstances that can [a]rise in
> particular cases precludes the formulation of exact rules in the statute. The bill
> endorses the purpose and general scope of the judicial doctrine of fair use, but
> there is no disposition to freeze the doctrine in the statute, especially during a
> period of rapid technological change. Beyond a very broad statutory explanation
> of what fair use is and some of the criteria applicable to it, the courts must be free
> to adapt the doctrine to particular situations on a case-by-case basis. Section 107
> is intended to restate the present judicial doctrine of fair use, not to change,
> narrow, or enlarge it in any way.

H. R. Rep. No. 94-1476 at 66 (1976); S. Rep. No. 94-473, p. 62 (1975). *See also* H.R. Rep. No.

94-1476, at 65; S. Rep. No. 94-473 at 61 (examples in Section 107 "are by no means

exhaustive").

---

[5] In keeping with his practice of using appropriated images as raw elements, Prince used the Images to provide unassailable authenticity to the creative expression and message of Rastafarian band members in a post-apocalyptic world set on a tropical island. *See* RP Tr. 43-44 ("I like to get as much fact into my work and reduce the amount of speculation. I believe there's too much – I like an artwork where that when you see something, like a cowboy or a girlfriend, I mean these are, in fact, true."); RP Aff. ¶ 14. It was in this sense that Prince finds it more satisfying to appropriate than to create his own work, not because he wanted to "avoid the drudgery in working up something fresh," as Cariou suggests. P. Mem. 3, 15 (quoting *Campbell*). As such plaintiff's attempt to cram this case into the facts of *Campbell* is unavailing.

Unlike the parody cases on which Cariou relies, in which the point of the parody can only be appreciated by commenting on the underlying work, there was no need for Prince to comment on the Images since his intent was to re-contextualize them into an entirely new expression, thereby rendering their original meaning irrelevant. RP Aff. ¶¶ 26, 27, 32-61; RP Tr. 361-61. In any event, even in a parody case, the Second Circuit has found the use transformative where the artist was commenting generally, and not on the underlying works. *See Blanch v. Koons,* 467 F.3d 244, 252-53 (2d Cir. 2006) (use transformative where artist used image "as fodder for his commentary on the social and aesthetic consequences of mass media.").

Even if this Court were to interpret Section 107 to impose a commenting requirement, it could nonetheless find that Prince, through his appropriative techniques, effectively comments generally on aspects of society and the music scene through the meaning and messages which inspired the creation, and informed the expression, of the Paintings. *See, e.g., Rogers,* 960 F.2d at 304 (appropriation art, which dates back to beginning of 20th century, defines its efforts as follows: "when the artist finishes his work, the meaning of the original object has been extracted and an entirely new meaning set in it place."); *see also Blanch,* 467 F.3d at 254-55 (in deciding that Koons's work appeared more properly classified as a satire than a parody, the Second Circuit noted that "[a]lthough it seems clear enough to us that Koons's use of a slick fashion photograph enables him to satirize life as it appears when seen through the prism of slick fashion photography, we need not depend on our own poorly honed artistic sensibilities" and Court looked instead to Koons's own words, which had been offered to substantiate his parody theory); *Bourne,* 602 F. Supp. 2d at 508 (after noting that "Second Circuit has given weight to an artist's own explanation of their creative rationale when conducting the fair use analysis," Court properly made its own assessment of the way secondary work "may reasonably be perceived" as commenting).

11

4.   The Public Benefit of Promotion of and Access to Art Outweighs the Profits
      From Defendants' Commercial Use of the Substantially Transformed Images

Cariou's disdain for Prince, his appropriative art style and the gallery that has

thoughtfully and professionally represented him for the past four years is particularly apparent in

Cariou's discussion of defendants' efforts to market the *Canal Zone* series and sell the Paintings

to an international clientele of established collectors and museums.[6] Indeed, Cariou starts with a

premise (based on snippets from case holdings without making the analysis courts use to assess

the transformative nature of the works at issue), that the Paintings are "less transformative." P.

Mem. 18. He then lists activities one would expect an international art gallery to undertake in

representing a world-renowned artist client, as if to suggest that defendants have done something

unseemly by engaging in industry-standard conduct.[7] *Id.* at 18-19 (falsely accusing defendants

of "hawking" works "hastily thrown together by Prince without much thought"). They have not.

During discovery, Gagosian turned over documents detailing the gallery's efforts to

market the Paintings, which cost Gagosian Gallery $434,730.47 in expenses in promoting the

Canal Zone series. At the request of plaintiff, Gagosian stipulated to the $10,480,000 in gross

sales generated from Paintings that were sold before defendants pulled the series during the

pendency of this lawsuit, and the $6,288,000.00 that was paid to Prince as his share of the

profits. Ex. N-O. In doing so, the Gagosian defendants readily acknowledges that the gallery is

a commercial enterprise, which they hoped would yield a return on their continued investment

and belief in Prince. LG Tr. 41. But analysis of the commercialism factor does not end here.

The Supreme Court in *Campbell* warns against the application of a *per se* rule of presumption

---

[6] Cariou's reliance on the Doeringer affidavit says more about Cariou and the weakness of his case that he
feels the need to proffer the wholly irrelevant statement of a third party concerning an unrelated event in
an effort to try to prejudice the defendants in the eyes of this Court.

[7] Though Lawrence Gagosian did not approve the sale of leftover *Canal Zone* announcement cards to
Rare Posters for a dollar a piece, those sales nonetheless fostered the promotion of and public exhibition
of the Paintings. LG Tr. 77-78.

against fair use when commercial use is present, as Cariou seems to advocate. *Campbell*, 510 U.S. at 585; *see also* P. Mem. 12-13. Instead, *Campbell* instructs that "the more transformative the new work, the less will be the significance of other factors, like commercialism, that may weigh against a finding of fair use." *Id.* at 579. Also relevant is the broader public benefit of promoting and affording access to the arts.[8] *See, e.g., Blanch*, 467 F.3d. at 254; *see also* D. Mem. 12-17. Thus, the commercial gains derived by defendants should be discounted in light of the broader public benefits of promoting and providing access to the art, and the substantially transformative nature of the Paintings.[9] *See* D. Mem. 16-17.

5. Prince's Sharply Different Creative Goals in Using the Images as Raw Materials to Create the Paintings Confirm the Transformative Use of the Images

In assessing the purpose and character prong of the first fair use factor, courts in this Circuit consider whether the purpose in using the original work is "plainly different from the original purpose for which it was created." *Bill Graham Archives* v. *Dorling Kindersley Ltd.*, 448 F.3d 605, 609 (2d Cir. 2006) cited with approval in *Blanch*, 467 F.3d at 252-53 ("The sharply different objectives that Koons had in using, and Blanch had in creating, 'Silk Sandals,' confirms the transformative nature of the use."); *Bourne Co.*, 602 F. Supp. 2d at 509 (work which was different in tone and message "could not have been more different" and thus was transformative); *see also* D. Mem. 15-16. Thus, Cariou's argument that he and Prince had "the

---

[8] Cariou cannot, on the one hand, fault defendants for having exploited the Paintings, while on the other, suggest that defendants are not entitled to the weight given to the promotion and public exhibition of the arts merely because they made the decision, in good faith and in keeping with accepted mitigation practices, to "retir[e] the unsold art to storage, where no one from the public can see it." P. Mem. 19.

[9] Because Prince's use of the Images was transformative, the Paintings are not derivative works as a matter of law. *See Castle Rock Entm't v. Carol Publ'g Group*, 150 F.3d 132, 143 (2d Cir. 1998) ("Although derivative works that are subject to the author's copyright transform an original work into a new mode of presentation, such works--*unlike works of fair use*--take expression for purposes that are not transformative."). Since the Paintings were not derivative works, the decision of Rizzoli International to include a copyright designation in the *Canal Zone* catalogue (LG Tr. 91) was perfectly appropriate.

same *aesthetic* purpose" to create beautiful art is not determinative of the first prong. P. Mem.
15 (emphasis added). Indeed, if comparable aesthetic purposes were the test, there could never
be a finding of fair use since it is hard to imagine that any creator of an original work would
purposefully set out to create something aesthetically displeasing. It follows then, that Prince's
use of the Images has not, as Cariou urges, superseded the objects of Cariou's work just because
both artists set out to create something beautiful. *See id.*

      In any event, as shown in Defendants' Memorandum, Prince did not merely repackage
the Images (and thereby supersede them); he used them as raw elements "in the creation of new
information, new aesthetics, new insights and understandings." *Blanch* at 253; *see also Lennon v.
Premise Media Corp.*, 556 F. Supp. 2d 310, 324 (S.D.N.Y. 2008) (though plaintiffs contended
that defendants' use of song "Imagine" was not transformative because it was unnecessary to use
it to further the purposes defendants articulated, court held that such use "posed no obstacle to a
finding of fair use" because "[d]etermining whether a use is transformative does not require
courts to decide whether it was strictly necessary that it be used."). As Cariou fails to even
address this determinative point in his papers, much less explain how his purpose in depicting as
realistically as possible Rastafarians in their native Jamaican environment is the same as Prince's
artistic purpose of creating a hip take on the music scene through his expression of a fantastical
post-apocalyptical world where music is the only redeeming thing to survive, the first prong
weighs decidedly in defendants' favor. *See Blanch,* 467 F.3d at 253 ("When, as here, the
copyrighted work is used a 'raw material' in the furtherance of distinct *creative or
communicative* objectives, the use is transformative.") (internal citations omitted); *see also* D.
Mem. 15-16.

B.   **Because the Copyright in the Fact-Based Images, if Any, Is Weak,**
       the Second Factor, Nature of Work, Weighs in Favor of Fair Use

As shown in Point I *supra*, the copyright protection afforded to the protectable creative

elements in the Images is non-existent, or at best, very weak. *See also* Point II(C) *infra*. Even

assuming Cariou can show that the Images, individually, or when viewed as part of the fact-

based compilation for which they were taken, are enough to meet the minimum creativity

required for copyright protection, *and* that Prince's alteration and use of those Images satisfies

the "improper appropriation" prong of the copying element of a copyright infringement claim,

the existence of some degree of creativity (*i.e.*, choice of lighting, film, camera, time of day, film

speed) is not enough, to carry the second fair use prong. As the Second Circuit in *Blanch*

instructs:

> Two types of distinctions as to the nature of the copyrighted work have emerged
> that have figured in the decisions evaluating the second factor: (1) whether the
> work is expressive or creative, such as a work of fiction, or more factual, with a
> greater leeway being allowed to a claim of fair use where the work is factual or
> informational, and (2) whether the work is published or unpublished, with the
> scope for fair use involving unpublished works being considerably narrower.

467 F.3d at 256. *See also* 4 *Nimmer on Copyright* § 13.05[A][2][a] ("the more creative the

work, the more protection it should be accorded from copying," whereas, "the more

informational or functional the … work, the broader should be the scope of the fair use

defense."). As the Images have been published, and they were, according to Cariou, intended as

part of a factual compilation that is likely to be of historical significance (PC Tr. 285-86), the

second prong weighs in favor of fair use, notwithstanding the presence of some degree of

protectable elements in the Images. *A.V. v. iParadigms,* LLC, 562 F.3d 630, 640 (4th Cir. 2009)

([I]f the disputed use of the copyright work is not related to its mode of expression but rather to

its historical facts," then the creative nature of the work is mitigated") (internal citations

omitted). But, even if it were determined that the second factor somewhat favors Cariou, it is of "limited usefulness" where, as here, the work is being used for a transformative purpose. *Blanch*, 467 F.3d at 257; *see also Graham Archives*, 448 F.3d at 612-13 ("even though [original] images are creative works . . . the second factor has limited weight in our analysis because the purpose of [the] use was to emphasize the images' historical [i.e., factual] rather than creative value."); RP Aff. ¶¶ 45, 53, 54 (Prince was looking for black and white figures to further his theme). Thus, whatever marginal creativity may be extant in the Images, it is not enough to defeat defendants' fair use defense, as Cariou urges (P. Mem. 19-20).

C.   **Not Only the Amount, But the Substantiality, of Prince's Use of the Images was Reasonable to Carry Out His Creative Purpose**

At first blush, it might be tempting to focus solely on the number, amount and large scale of the Images Prince incorporated as raw elements of his Paintings, as Cariou has done. P. Mem. 21-22. However, *Campbell* teaches that in deciding the third prong, courts are to look not only at the amount of the underlying work used, but also its substantiality – i.e., its "value." According to *Campbell*, this factor "calls for recognition that some works are closer to the core of intended copyright protection than others," citing *Feist*, 499 U.S. at 348-51 (contrasting creative works with fact-based compilations; *see also supra* at Point II(B); D. Mem. 20-23.

Though Cariou relies on *Campbell* in his analysis of the third prong (P. Mem. 21), he does not mention, much less address, the substantiality prong. Instead he focuses solely on the quantity and enlarged size of the Images taken, and in doing so, grossly overstates his case by accusing Prince (without any record cite), of "taking *entire* Photographs of Rastas and copious portions of landscapes" as if to suggest that Prince did this in each of the Paintings. P. Mem. 21 (emphasis added). As can be readily seen from the comparison of the Images and the Paintings found in the Composite Exhibit, with the exception of four of the Images, Prince used only a portion of the Images he tore from *Yes Rasta* to further his artistic message, and in this regard, the use was reasonable. *See* RP Aff. Ex. A; RP Aff. ¶¶ 26, 34, 38-39, 45-50, 53-57; *see also* P. Mem. 21 (conceding that "[F]ragmentary copying is more likely to have a transformative purpose than wholesale copying.") (citing *Davis v. Gap*, 246 F.3d 152, 175 (2d Cir. 2001)); *Campbell*, 510 U.S. at 586-89 (copy was "reasonable in relation to the purpose of copying).

As demonstrated herein and in Defendants' Memorandum, even in those four instances in which Prince used the entirety of the Image he tore from the pages of *Yes Rasta,* the amount taken was reasonable when viewed in light of the creative purpose for which it was being used. *See Graham Archives*, 448 F.3d at 613 (acknowledging that the Second Circuit and its sister circuits has never ruled that copying an entire work "*favors*" fair use, held: "At the same time, however, courts have concluded that such copying does not necessarily weigh against fair use because copying the entirety of a work is sometimes necessary to make a fair use of the image.") cited in P. Mem. 21-22; *see also* D. Mem. 20-21. Here, three of the Images that were copied in their entirety (Ex EE at pp. 1-2, 95-96, and 133-34), were landscape shots which Prince used as backdrop to carry out his tropical theme and onto which he collaged raw elements and added painterly elements to create an entirely new work. *See Graham Archives* at 613 (third factor does not weigh against fair use where images were copied in their entirety "to provide a visual context" and then combined with other raw elements and original graphics to further transformative purpose);[10] *Bourne*, 602 F. Supp. 2d at 509 ("The Second Circuit found it plain that superimposing face of Leslie Neilson on a photographed body intended to look like Demi Moore was 'transformative' of Leibowitz's original photograph.") (citations omitted).

In the Painting entitled *Graduation*, Prince scanned, enlarged, and cropped a page taken from *Yes Rasta* (Ex. EE, p. 118) in which a single Rastafarian is shown standing against a

---

[10] The absence of alterations, reconceptualized messages and transformational purposes renders Cariou's reliance on *Warner Bros. Entm't v. RDR Books*, 575 F. Supp. 2d 513, 544-48 (S.D.N.Y. 2008) misplaced.

tropical landscape that Cariou had intentionally blurred out of focus. *See* RP Aff. Ex. A, p.1.
Prince then added raw elements, such as appropriated images of a guitar and hands of a rock star,
changed the image tint to blue, and then rescanned and printed the new work directly onto
canvas. *See* RP Aff. at ¶ 32; P. Mem. 4. In this post-apocalyptic, music-themed series, the
Rastafarian in the Image was Prince's lead guitarist, which explains why the man is the focus of
Graduation and why he has been scanned, enlarged, altered and the outline of his body cut out
and applied as a raw element in other Paintings in the series. RP Aff. at ¶ 32; *see also* RP Aff.
Ex. A.

      In deciding the third factor, however, "'what is relevant is the amount and substantiality
of the copyrighted *expression* that has been used, not the *factual content* of the material in the
copyrighted works,' thus calling for 'thought not only about the quantity of the materials used,
but about their quality and importance, too.'" *Blanch v. Koons*, 396 F. Supp. 2d 476, 482
(S.D.N.Y. 2005) (citations omitted) (emphasis in original) aff'd, *Blanch,* 467 F.3d 244 (2d Cir.
2006). Thus, the quality of copyright protection of the Image which appears in *Graduation* is
very weak. *Id.*; *see also Leibowitz v. Paramount Pictures Corp.*, 137 F.3d 109, 115-16 (2d Cir.
1998) (even though entire image replicated with exacting precision, photographer "entitled to no
protection for the appearance in her photograph of the body of a nude, pregnant female."); *see
also supra* at Points I and II(B); D. Mem. 15-16, 22-23.

      The marginal importance of the Images used, coupled with Cariou's admission that the
images in *Yes Rasta* must be viewed as a whole to appreciate their distinctiveness, also weighs
against a finding that Prince took "the heart of" Cariou's compilation work consisting of fact-
based images, the factual content of which was not original to Cariou. *See, e.g., NXIVM Corp. v.
Ross Inst.*, 364 F.3d 471, 481 (2d Cir. 2006) (rejected "heart of the work" theory where plaintiff

conceded book was an assemblage, and it reflected "no objective core.") cited in P. Mem. 20-21;[11] *see also* D. Mem. Point 21.

The balance of Cariou's discussion of this factor is spent reciting holdings from cases, which he fails to apply the facts of this case except to make the general and conclusory allegation (paraphrased from one of the cases) that Prince's "unrestrained copying and enlargement" was "excessive." P. Mem. 21-22. Cariou fails to offer any evidence that Prince's copying was unrestrained. If it had been, one would expect to see a wholesale reproduction of all of the images in *Yes Rasta*, which Prince did not do. Prince also repeated many of the same Images (P. Mem.4-5; RP Aff. Ex. A) to further his creative expression of a music-based message by repeating band members throughout the series (RP Aff. ¶¶ 32, 38, 42, 45, 49, 58-61).

Cariou's allegation that Prince's "enlargement" of the Images was "excessive" not only confirms that the Images were altered, a factor weighing in favor of transformative use, but it stands in stark contrast to the argument Cariou repeatedly made elsewhere in his brief, when it suited his purposes to do so, that the Images were "unaltered." P. Mem. 4-5, 21-22; *see also* PR Aff. Ex. A. In any event, this Court need only compare the size of the pages in *Yes Rasta* (12.25 x 9.75 inches) with the size of each of the Paintings, which range from 40 x 26 ¼ inches to 100 ½ x 154 ½ inches (Ex. N at A), to confirm that *each* of the Images used as raw elements in the Paintings was enlarged, and then further altered and/or combined with other elements, and/or collaging and painterly techniques to produce an entirely new expressive meaning and message. Prince's use of the Images thus, was reasonable to carry out his artistic purpose when viewed in light of Prince's overall creative and artistic purpose for the *Canal Zone* series. *See Campbell*,

---

[11] The three cases Cariou cited for his "heart of the work" argument are inapposite because there was no alteration of the original works in those cases. *Rogers*, 960 F.2d at 311; *Harper & Row, Publrs. v. Nation Enters.*, 471 U.S. 539, 565 (1985); *Campbell v. Koons*, 91 Civ. 6055 (RO); 1993 WL 97381, at *3 (S.D.N.Y. Apr. 1, 1993).

510 U.S. at 586-87 ("[T]he extent of permissible copying varies with the purpose and character

of the use"; therefore, this inquiry requires the court to return to the first factor.); *see also*

Leibowitz, 137 F.3d at 116 (fair use found where elements were copied "to an extreme degree"

though use of digital computer enhancement and defendant took more of original that necessary

to conjure up original; will not necessarily tip third factor against fair use in light of "overriding

purpose and character").

**D.   Cariou's Claim That the *Canal Zone* Exhibition Led to a Decision to "Cancel" a
        Show Featuring *Yes Rasta* Is Neither Evidence of Market Usurpation Nor Credible**

Plaintiff has offered no evidence (nor can he) that defendants have ever offered the

Paintings as a market substitute for the Images, such that the exhibition and sale of the Paintings

has completely usurped the market for the Images, as is required to carry the fourth factor. *See*

Blanch, 467 F.3d at 258. As the Second Circuit has made clear:

> The focus here is on whether the defendants are offering a market substitute for
> the original. In considering the fourth factor, our concern is not whether the
> secondary use suppresses or even destroys the market for the original work or its
> potential derivatives, but whether the secondary use usurps the market of the
> original work. As we stated in Wright, the relevant market effect with which we
> are concerned is the market for plaintiffs' expression, and thus, it is the effect of
> the defendants' use of that expression on plaintiffs' market that matters, not the
> effect of defendants' work as a whole.

NXIVM Corp., 364 F.3d at 481-82, citing *Wright v. Warner Books, Inc.*, 953 F.2d 731, 739 (2d

Cir. 1991). As plaintiff has failed to carry his burden on this point (much less address the

applicable market usurpation test), the fourth factor weighs decidedly in favor of fair use. *See id.*;

see also D. Mem. 22; P. Mem. 22 (in arguing harm test that *Campbell* and courts in this Circuit

have rejected, Cariou admits he cannot make requisite usurpation showing: "defendants' actions

at least harmed the potential market for *Yes Rasta*") (emphasis added).

Indeed, the only evidence Cariou proffered is his suggestion that Celle, the owner of a

bookstore and gallery featuring photography, "*cancelled* Cariou's show." *See* P. Mem. 12

(emphasis added). Such a "cancellation" – even assuming it occurred (a fact which is not plausible based on the record before the court (*see infra*)) – is not evidence of market usurpation. *NXIVM Corp.* at 482 (affirming determination that Goldie Hawn's cancellation of visit with plaintiff after defendants disseminated allegedly infringing materials is not cognizable market harm under Copyright Act).

In any event, as a careful review of the transcript of the Celle deposition confirms, there was no show to be "cancelled" because Cariou had not, as of the time of the *Canal Zone* exhibition (or to this date), actually committed to engaging Celle as his agent, or do a show of *Yes Rasta.* CC Tr. 47. As Celle explained it, "I was very committed, I wanted to represent him. We agree on it but we never really pursue it, no." *Id.* at 133; *see also id.* at 133-34 (when asked, "You never got to an agreement?" Celle answered: "No. In general when I do a show with somebody – when I do a show with an artist, I do not do a show if I don't represent him, because it's very expensive to put a show together.) (When asked if Celle ever gave Cariou a contract to review or sign, Celle answered: "No, no. It didn't go so far."); *id.* at 160 (Cariou's unresponsiveness led Celle to believe he must have found someone else to represent him and so, out of timing concerns, went with another artist). Moreover, Cariou, who was not responding to her attempts to reach him, did not know until after he commenced this action, when he called Celle to enlist her help with it (CC Tr. 96), that she purportedly told him she had decided not to pursue featuring him as the first artist of her soon-to-be opened bookstore and gallery. *See id.* at 101-105; *see also* Opp. Aff. Ex. C (complaint contains nothing about "cancelled" show). In that call, Cariou also learned that Celle remains willing to represent him. CC Tr. 106.

Cariou's post-action story should thus be rejected for the further reason that it is wholly lacking in credibility and corroboration, even by the account of a witness who retained Cariou's counsel the day before her deposition, and who is a former girlfriend of Cariou's photography

21

assistant. CC Tr. 58-59. Celle's testimony also renders suspect the prescient timing of Cariou's

decision, which he purports to have made because he was "waiting for the proper opportunity"

"and proper timing" (after nine years of inertia) to exploit the images in *Yes Rasta* as he has

claimed in this case. PC Tr. 221-22; *see also* D. Mem. Fact Sections D and G. Thus, even when

viewed in the light most favorable to plaintiff, his story, which is rife with inconsistencies and

wholly lacking in credibility, must be rejected. *See Jeffreys v. City of New York,* 426 F.3d 549,

555 n. 2 (2d Cir. 2005) (summary judgment proper where plaintiff failed "to explain away these

obvious inconsistencies with any 'plausible explanation'") (internal citations omitted); *Salinger

v. Fredrik Colting*, 641 F. Supp. 2d 250, 258-60, n.3 (S.D.N.Y. 2009) (Batts, J.) (finding party's

uncorroborated position in lawsuit, which was inconsistent with party's pre-action position and

conduct, lacking in credibility).

POINT III
DEFENDANTS GAGOSIAN GALLERY AND LARRY GAGOSIAN ARE NEITHER VICARIOUS NOR CONTRIBUTORY INFRINGERS

Nowhere in Point II (or elsewhere in his opening brief) does Cariou allege or offer any

evidence that either Gagosian Gallery or Larry Gagosian had any involvement in, much less

control over, any aspect of Prince's creation of the Paintings, including his decision to use the

Images in the manner he did. In doing so, Cariou has conceded that neither of the Gagosian

defendants can be liable as a vicarious infringer under the holding of the case he cites for this

point. *See Faulkner v. Nat'l Geographic Soc.*, 211 F. Supp. 2d 450, 472-73 (S.D.N.Y. 2002)

cited in P. Mem. 25. As *Faulkner* makes clear, to establish vicarious liability, Cariou must

adduce "meaningful evidence" that Gagosian Gallery and/or Lawrence Gagosian exercised

control of Prince's creative process, or their "paths must cross on a daily basis, and the character

of this intersection must be such that the party against whom liability is sought is in a position to control the personnel and activities responsible for the direct infringement." *Faulkner* at 473 (citations omitted).

The undisputed evidence shows that Prince, who created the Paintings in his studio in the Hamptons with help from two assistants in his studio in upstate New York, worked alone. RP Tr. 174-75; RP Aff. ¶ 24. It also is undisputed that Lawrence Gagosian works mainly out of the office located on Madison Avenue in New York, and none of Gagosian Gallery's eight offices worldwide are located in the Hamptons. LG Tr. 15, 19-20. On this record, then, Cariou's vicarious liability claim should be dismissed as frivolous. *See Faulkner* at 473 ("the notion that the control must be substantial and have practical force – remains sound").

In the same way, Cariou has not, and cannot, come forward with sufficient evidence to show that Gagosian Gallery and/or Lawrence Gagosian should be contributorily liable because there is no evidence that either of them "*with knowledge of* the [allegedly] infringing activity, induce[d], cause[d] or materially contribute[d] to the infringing conduct...." *Faulkner* at 473 cited in P. Mem. 25. As there is no evidence that either of the Gagosian defendants controlled or was involved in Prince's creative process, it thus was not possible for them to even know the source from which Prince obtained the Images he used as raw elements. Moreover, while the Gagosian defendants readily acknowledge their participation in producing the *Canal Zone* catalogue and promoting the exhibition, these facts alone are not enough to sustain a contributory liability claim. Instead, Cariou must show that either of the Gagosian defendants "knew or should have known of the infringing activity *at the time of* [their] material contribution." *Id.* at 473-74.

Cariou cites no case to support his novel theory that because the Gagosian defendants knew Prince to be a known appropriation artist, that they should have also known he had appropriated the Images (allegedly) in violation of Cariou's rights as the compilation copyright holder. P. Mem. 25. Indeed, to presume such a fact would mean that any time a gallery represents an artist of a well-known genre that the gallery will, by reason of the artist's reputation, always be contributorily liable even where, as here, there is no evidence to substantiate a "knew or should have known" theory. Specifically, the record shows that although Prince has been a prolific appropriation artist of international acclaim for more than 30 years, he has never been sued, until this lawsuit. RP Tr. 25. This fact, coupled with his reputation for being an "accomplished, educated and informed artist," as Cariou readily admits in his Amended Complaint at ¶ 28 (Ex. E), provides further evidence that there was no reason for either of the Gagosian defendants to know, at the time they worked with Rizzoli International to create the *Canal Zone*, or marketed the series, or launched the exhibition that Prince had violated any right of Cariou's (a premise which defendants respectfully deny). *See Inwood Labs., Inc. v. Ives Labs., Inc.*, 456 U.S. 844, 854, n. 13 (1982) (service provider not contributorily liable merely for failing to "reasonably anticipate possibility of a third party's infringing conduct").

Plaintiff's assertion that the Gagosian defendants were put on notice of the infringement when they received the cease and desist letter, but continued with the *Canal Zone* is equally unavailing and in any event factually incorrect. Continuing to sell and market the allegedly infringing work after receiving a cease and desist letter is not infringement because the issue of fair use still needs to be determined. *See Faulker* at 474-75. In any event, defendants withdrew the Paintings from the market shortly after they received the notice, upon learning that plaintiff had filed this infringement action, even though they believed then, as they do today, that (even assuming Prince's use constitutes copyright infringement), it is nonetheless fair as a matter of law. RP Aff ¶ 28; LG Tr. 144-46.

CONCLUSION

For all of the reasons set forth herein, in Defendants' Memorandum, and in the accompanying affidavits and exhibits thereto, defendants Richard Prince, Gagosian Galley and Lawrence Gagosian respectfully request this Court to enter an order denying plaintiff's motion for summary judgment, and granting defendants summary judgment on the grounds that Prince's use did not infringe on any right of Patrick Cariou, or in the alternative, that Prince's use was fair as a matter of law.

Dated: June 14, 2010
      New York, New York

                    WITHERS BERGMAN LLP

                    By: _____/s/_____
                        Hollis Gonerka Bart (HB-8955)
                        Dara G. Hammerman (DH-1591)
                        Azmina Jasani (AJ-4161)
                        430 Park Avenue, 10th Floor
                        New York, NY 10022-3505
                        Phone: (212) 848-9800
                        Fax: (212) 848-9888
                        Attorneys for Defendants Gagosian Gallery
                        Inc. and Lawrence Gagosian

                    By: _____/s/_____
                        Steven M. Hayes (SH-2926)
                        Hanly Conroy Bierstein Sheridan
                        Fisher & Hayes LLP
                        112 Madison Avenue
                        New York, NY 10016-7416
                        (212) 784-6414
                        Attorneys for Defendant Richard Prince

CERTIFICATE OF SERVICE

The Undersigned hereby certifies that a copy of the foregoing was served upon the

following via ECF on this the 14th day of June, 2010:

Daniel J. Brooks
Schnader Harrison Segal & Lewis LLP
140 Broadway, Suite 3100
New York, New York 10005-1101
(212) 973-8000
Attorneys for plaintiff, Patrick Cariou

/s/
_____
COUNSEL FOR DEFENDANTS GAGOSIAN
GALLERY INC. AND LAWRENCE GAGOSIAN
Hollis Gonerka Bart (HB-8955)
Dara G. Hammerman (DH-1591)
Azmina Jasani (AJ-4161)
Withers Bergman LLP
430 Park Avenue, 10th Floor
New York, New York 10022
(p) 212-848-9800
(f) 212-848-9888

document number: NY23802/0005-US-870740/5

26

UNITED STATES DISTRICT COURT
SOUTHERN DISTRICT OF NEW YORK
---x
PATRICK CARIOU,   :
                                                      :
                                   Plaintiff,   :
                                                      :   08 Civ. 11327 (DAB)
               -against-   :
                                                      :
RICHARD PRINCE, GAGOSIAN GALLERY,   :
INC., LAWRENCE GAGOSIAN and RIZZOLI   :
INTERNATIONAL PUBLICATIONS, INC.,   :
                                                      :
                                   Defendants.   :
---x

**REPLY MEMORANDUM OF LAW IN SUPPORT OF
PLAINTIFF'S MOTION FOR SUMMARY JUDGMENT**

SCHNADER HARRISON SEGAL & LEWIS LLP
140 Broadway, Suite 3100
New York, New York 10005-1101
Telephone: 212-973-8000
Facsimile: 212-972-8798
Attorneys for Plaintiff Patrick Cariou

On the Brief:
Daniel J. Brooks, Esq.
Eric A. Boden, Esq.

TABLE OF CONTENTS

i

TABLE OF AUTHORITIES

CASES

STATUTES

OTHER AUTHORITIES

PRELIMINARY STATEMENT

This memorandum of law is respectfully submitted on behalf of plaintiff, Patrick

Cariou, in reply to the memorandum of law of defendants Richard Prince, Gagosian Gallery, Inc.

and Lawrence Gagosian, filed on June 14, 2010 in opposition to Cariou's motion for summary

judgment ("Def. Opp. Mem."), and in further support of Cariou's motion. Accompanying this

reply memorandum are the declaration of Daniel J. Brooks, dated June 24, 2010 ("Brooks Rep.

Dec.") and exhibits thereto, and a response to defendants' Local Rule 56.1 counter-statement.

ARGUMENT

POINT I

PRINCE'S APPROPRIATION OF CREATIVE AND PROTECTABLE ELEMENTS OF CARIOU'S VALIDLY COPYRIGHTED WORK RENDERS ALL OF THE DEFENDANTS LIABLE FOR COPYRIGHT INFRINGEMENT

Copyright infringement has two elements: "(1) ownership of a valid copyright,

and (2) copying of constituent elements of the work that are original." *Feist Publ'ns, Inc. v.*

Rural Tel. Serv. Co., 499 U.S. 340, 361 (1991). To be "original," a copyrighted work must have

been independently created by the author and must possess "at least some minimal degree of

creativity," although "the requisite level of creativity is extremely low; even a slight amount will

suffice." *Id.* at 345. "The vast majority of works make the grade quite easily, as they possess

some creative spark, 'no matter how crude, humble or obvious' it might be." *Id.* (citation

omitted). "Originality does not signify novelty; a work may be original even though it closely

resembles other works so long as the similarity is fortuitous, not the result of copying." *Id.* "No

author may copyright his ideas or the facts he narrates." *Harper & Row, Publishers, Inc. v.*

Nation Enters., 471 U.S. 539, 556 (1985). Copyright only protects the form in which facts or

ideas are expressed, and not the facts or ideas themselves. *Id.*; *see also Feist*, 499 U.S. at 350

(noting "idea/expression" and "fact/expression" dichotomies).

Despite the extremely low bar on the level of creativity needed to make a copyrighted work "original," defendants claim, implausibly, that Cariou's Photographs are so lacking in creativity and, therefore, originality, that Prince's taking of the Photographs was not the type of "improper appropriation" required in order to sustain a copyright infringement claim. A review of the cases cited by defendants exposes the frivolity of this argument.

Citing *Feist* and *Maxtone-Graham v. Burtchaell*, 803 F.2d 1253 (2d Cir. 1986), defendants claim that because "facts" are not original or copyrightable, the "fact-based images of Rastafarians in their Jamaican landscape that Cariou depicted as realistically as possible, are not protectable as a matter of law." Def. Opp. Mem. at 2. From defendants' discussion and lengthy quotation from *Feist* (*id.* at 3, 4), one would never know that the case involved the white pages of a telephone directory from which listings were extracted by the defendant when it compiled its own directory; that the issue before the Supreme Court was "whether the copyright in [plaintiff's] directory protects the names, towns, and telephone numbers copied by [defendant]"; and that plaintiff's only claim to creativity was that it had arranged the names alphabetically. *Feist*, 499 U.S. at 343-44, 363. Reiterating that "originality is not a stringent standard [and] does not require that facts be presented in an innovative or surprising way[,]" but that "some minimal degree of creativity" is required, the Court concluded that "[T]here is nothing remotely creative about arranging names alphabetically in a white pages directory. * * * It is not only unoriginal, it is practically inevitable." *Id.* at 363. *Maxtone-Graham* is equally inapposite, addressing only the fair use defense of an author who prepared an essay on abortion in which he quoted from verbatim factual interviews conducted by the plaintiff with women who discussed their experiences with abortion. *Id.* 803 F.2d at 1255-56. Notably, while the case did not even address "improper appropriation," in analyzing the second fair use factor the Court did state that the "verbatim interviews," while "'essentially reportorial in nature[,]'" nevertheless "contain[]

2

elements of creative journalistic effort. 'Creation of a nonfiction work, even a compilation of pure fact, entails originality.'" *Id.* at 1262-63 (quoting *Harper & Row*, 471 U.S. at 547). By no stretch of the imagination does either of these cases hold, or even suggest, that Cariou's "fact-based" Photographs are "not protectable as a matter of law." Def. Opp. Mem. at 2.

To the contrary, it has been widely recognized, for well over a century, that photographs of real people, places and events can be creative and protectable. *Burrow-Giles Lithographic Co. v. Sarony*, 111 U.S. 53, 60 (1884) (originality of photographic portrait of Oscar Wilde arose from the posing of the subject, selection of his clothing, background, light and shade, and by "suggesting and evoking the desired expression"); *Rogers v. Koons*, 960 F.2d 301, 307 (2d Cir.) ("Elements of originality in a photograph may include posing the subjects, lighting, angle, selection of film and camera, evoking the desired expression, and almost any other variant involved."), *cert. denied*, 506 U.S. 934 (1992); *Mannion v. Coors Brewing Co.*, 377 F. Supp. 2d 444, 450 (S.D.N.Y. 2005) ("Almost any photograph 'may claim the necessary originality to support a copyright.'") (citation omitted); *Eastern Am. Trio Prods., Inc. v. Tang Elec. Corp.*, 97 F. Supp. 2d 395, 417 (S.D.N.Y. 2000) (photographs of "common industrial items" possessed sufficient originality and creativity to be protectable; originality may be based upon factors such as the "choice of subject matter, angle of photograph, lighting, determination of the precise time when the photograph is to be taken, the kind of camera, the kind of film, the kind of lens, and the area in which the pictures are taken."); *Monster Communications, Inc. v. Turner Broad. System, Inc.*, 935 F. Supp. 490, 494 (S.D.N.Y. 1996) ("photographic images of actual people, places and events may be as creative and deserving of protection as purely fanciful creations."); *Strauss v. Hearst Corp.*, No. 85 Civ. 10017 (CSH), 1988 WL 18932, at *5 (S.D.N.Y. Feb. 19, 1988) (a photographer's "efforts to create an aesthetically attractive, technically competent photograph" of fishing gear involved "plainly creative expressions.").

3

Cariou testified that he made all of these creative decisions in taking and developing the Photographs. *See* declaration of Daniel J. Brooks, dated May 7, 2010 ("Brooks Dec."), Ex. D at 51-64, 133-34, 137-38, 143-44, 152, 169. Cariou's Photographs, far from being mere facts (like names in a phone book), or mere "reproduc[tions of] reality" (like xerox copies), are "partial, two-dimensional impression[s]" of three-dimensional reality, seen through a professional photographer's "creative, or even distorting, eye." *Sarl Louis Feraud Int'l v. Viewfinder Inc.*, 627 F. Supp. 2d 123, 128 (S.D.N.Y. 2008). As such, they are creative, "original," and protected by the Copyright Act.

In addition to arguing the irrelevant proposition that facts are not copyrightable, defendants also rely on the truism that ideas are not protectable. Defendants rely principally on *Bill Diodato Photography, LLC v. Kate Spade, LLC*, 388 F. Supp. 2d 382 (S.D.N.Y. 2005), where the defendant allegedly copied the idea depicted in plaintiff's prior photograph by commissioning an ad showing the bottom of a bathroom stall through which one could see a woman's feet, astride a toilet, in stylish, colorful shoes, with a handbag on the floor. *Id.* at 384. Had Prince borrowed Cariou's idea by going to Jamaica and, for example, photographing a Rasfarian on a donkey, rather than simply stealing that Photograph (among many others), defendants might have some basis for arguing – based upon *Diodato*, 388 F. Supp. 2d at 390, 392 – that the idea of a man on a donkey is not protectable and that "similarities inher[ing]" in or "deriv[ing]" or "naturally flow[ing] from [that] idea" (*e.g.,* the angle of the donkey's ears, the way in which a man would sit astride a donkey) are similarly not protectable. *See* Def. Opp. Mem. at 2-4. But, unlike the defendant in *Diodato*, Prince did not appropriate Cariou's ideas; he appropriated the creative expressions of those ideas, which are protectable and copyrightable. *Harper & Row*, 471 U.S. at 556. The cases relied upon by defendants involving the *scenes a faire* doctrine (Def. Opp. Mem. at 3), under which elements of an image that flow naturally and

4

necessarily from an appropriated idea are no more protectable than the idea itself, are distinguishable inasmuch as Prince appropriated Cariou's Photographs, not the underlying idea. Similarly misguided is defendants' reliance on *Diodato* for the proposition that Cariou "cannot monopolize the various poses [he] used" or the "technique" he used "to blur the background, so as to bring the subject into sharp focus." Def. Opp. Mem. at 3. While *Diodato* would foreclose Cariou from asserting that other photographers may not, in their own photographs, use poses similar to those he used in *Yes Rasta* (or may not blur the background of their own photographs), the law does preclude the improper appropriation of Cariou's actual Photographs, including their creative, protectable elements, one of which is the subjects' poses. *See, e.g., Burrow-Giles*, 111 U.S. at 60; *Rogers v. Koons*, 960 F.2d at 307.

Defendants also baldly assert – without citing any objective, scientific study – that Cariou's Photographs of Rastafarians are typical. Def. Opp. Mem. at 3. Even if this *ipse dixit* (on a subject Prince admittedly "knew nothing" about (*see* declaration of Daniel J. Brooks, dated June 11, 2010 ("Brooks Opp. Dec.") Ex. A at 156; affidavit of Richard Prince, sworn to May 13, 2010, ¶ 18)) rested on admissible evidence, it would not matter: "Originality does not signify novelty; a work may be original even though it closely resembles other works so long as the similarity is fortuitous, not the result of copying." *Feist*, 499 U.S. at 345.

The Gagosian defendants contend that they are not vicariously liable because they had no control over Prince's creation of the Paintings and are not contributorily liable because it cannot be shown that they knew or should have known of Prince's infringing activity. Def. Opp. Mem. at 22, 23. As to the first point, vicarious liability, which requires neither "an intention to infringe or knowledge of infringement" (*Shapiro, Bernstein & Co., Inc. v. H.L. Green Co., Inc.*, 316 F.2d 304, 308 (2d Cir. 1963)), flows from the Gagosian defendants' control over the advertising and exhibition of the *Canal Zone* show and the sale of the Canal Zone Catalogues

5

and Paintings, not from any control over Prince's creative process. As to the second point, as the

defendants knew (*see* Brooks Dec. Ex. C, ¶ 18; Ex. G at 17-18, Ex. H at 91-92), Prince was a

"flagrant appropriator" (Note, *Beyond Rogers v. Koons: A Fair Use Standard for Appropriation*,

93 COLUM. L. REV. 1473, 1513 (1993)), whose retrospective at the Guggenheim Museum was

named *Spiritual America*, after a photograph by Garry Gross of a prepubescent Brooke Shields

emerging nude from a bathtub, which Prince "re-photographed," paying Gross for the rights nine

years later. Brooks Rep. Dec. Ex. A at 18-20, 68-74; Exs. C, D. Moreover, after receiving

Cariou's cease and desist letter on December 11, 2008, the Gagosian defendants continued

selling the catalogue and exhibiting, bartering and selling the Paintings; while they may quibble

that the March 2009 exchange was between them and Prince and that *It's All Over*, sold in

August 2009 for $1.1 million, was obtained through that exchange, there is no avoiding their

sale, to which they stipulated, of *Inquisition* on June 8, 2009, for $800,000. *See* Cariou's

memorandum of law in opposition to defendants' motion for summary judgment, at 15.

POINT II

DEFENDANTS' USE OF CARIOU'S PHOTOGRAPHS WAS NOT FAIR

A.   First Fair Use Factor

      With one exception, all of the cases relied upon by defendants for their contention

that Prince's appropriation of Cariou's Photographs was transformative (Def. Opp. Mem. at 5, 9,

13-14) involve instances where the secondary use commented on the original (*Campbell v. Acuff-*

Rose Music, Inc., 510 U.S. 569, 580 (1994); *Bourne Co. v. Twentieth Century Fox Film Corp.*,

602 F. Supp. 2d 499, 507 (S.D.N.Y. 2009)); or was a satire "target[ing] the genre of which [the

original was] typical" (*Blanch v. Koons*, 467 F.3d 244, 254 (2d Cir. 2006)); or criticized the

original (*Lennon v. Premise Media Corp.*, 556 F. Supp. 2d 310, 323 (S.D.N.Y. 2008)); or

incorporated the originals into a biography, "a form[] of historical scholarship, criticism, and

6

comment that require[s] incorporation of original source material for optimum treatment of [its] subjects" (*Bill Graham Archives v. Dorling Kindersley Ltd.*, 448 F.3d 605, 609 (2d Cir. 2006)). Here, in sharp contrast, Prince admitted that the Photographs were not the subject of his Paintings and that he was not commenting on Cariou's Photographs or on Cariou's technique or methodology in taking those Photographs. Brooks Dec. Ex. E at 30, 281-82. Defendants leave unanswered a number of questions: If Prince may nevertheless randomly take the Photographs because he likes them, "loves" the "look" and wants to use them in order to pay homage to artists he admires and to depict a post-apocalyptic fantasy, where would the line be drawn? Is there any copyrighted image, however unrelated, that Prince could not take in order to further these purposes? Is Cariou's copyrighted work due no more respect and protection than the urinal which Duchamp famously appropriated? May copyright protection be "eviscerate[d]," as Judge Leisure put it in *United Feature Syndicate, Inc. v. Koons*, 817 F. Supp. 370, 379 (S.D.N.Y. 1993), whenever an appropriation artist comes across copyrighted images he likes?

Prince's latest improper attempt to change his deposition testimony – by claiming, in ¶ 7 of his supplemental affidavit, sworn to June 11, 2010, that he "understood," when asked if he made comments with his work, the word "comment" to mean a "political comment" – should be disregarded. *Perma Research & Development Co. v. Singer Co.*, 410 F.2d 572, 578 (2d Cir. 1969) (party opposing summary judgment may not submit affidavit contradicting his own deposition testimony). In any event, defendants' use of this new assertion to contend that Prince "effectively comments generally on aspects of society and the music scene" (Def. Opp. Mem. at 11) misses the point: to be transformative, the comment must be at least in part about the appropriated material, not society in general. *See Bourne*, 602 F. Supp. 2d at 506, 507 (finding that the defendants "were clearly attempting to comment in some way on the wishful, hopeful scene in Pinocchio with which the song is associated[]" and distinguishing

7

MCA, Inc. v. Wilson, 425 F. Supp. 443, 453 (S.D.N.Y. 1976), where the defendant's "song commented on life, and sexual mores, but not the original work.").

The only case cited by defendants not involving comment or criticism is *Reyes v. Wyeth Pharm., Inc.*, 603 F. Supp. 2d 289 (D. P.R. 2009) (Def. Opp. Mem. at 9), in which the defendants' "public service educational" ad of a woman holding plaintiff's sculpture was not commenting on the sculpture, but sought to "raise awareness concerning RA [rheumatoid arthritis] and treatment options available for people suffering from RA[,]" conveying an "implicit message" – that the woman in the ad "suffer[ed] from RA and yet, because of treatments currently available, [could] creat[e]" the sculpture – which differed from the "message involved in the sculpture itself," rendering the ad "somewhat transformative." *Id.* at 293, 296-97. The transformative purpose in *Reyes* – teaching – is one enumerated in the preamble to the fair use statute, 17 U.S.C. § 107, distinguishing *Reyes* from this case.

B.   Second Fair Use Factor

Defendants claim that Cariou's Photographs are factual, rather than works of fiction, and are, therefore, entitled to less protection. Def. Opp. Mem. at 15. Defendants fail to explain, however, how a photograph can be anything other than "factual," or why the Court should disregard the substantial authority cited in plaintiff's memorandum of law in support of his motion for summary judgment ("Pl. Mem."), at 19-20, establishing that aesthetic photographs, even of actual people, are routinely deemed to be creative and imaginative, fitting within the core of copyright protection and, even though factual or informational in nature, ordinarily making the second fair use factor weigh in favor of photographer-plaintiffs.

C.   Third Fair Use Factor

Defendants admit that Prince appropriated four of Cariou's Photographs in their entirety, but deny that Prince also took "entire Photographs of Rastas and copious portions of

8

landscapes." Def. Opp. Mem. at 16. In fact, with respect to the 22 Paintings depicted in the

Canal Zone Catalogue, Prince did appropriate entire portraits of Cariou's Rastafarians (usually

cropping out the landscape background) in 17 Paintings (Brooks Dec. Ex. N, #s 1-9, 15-22; Ex.

U) and appropriated substantial portions of landscapes in five Paintings (Brooks Dec. Ex. N, #s

1, 5, 7, 8, 14; Ex. U); *see also* Ex. O, PR00029, PR00030 (also appropriating entire Rastas).

This taking of the essence of these portraits, even without the landscapes, contrasts with what

Koons did in *Blanch*, 467 F.3d at 248, taking only a fragment, the legs and feet, from a photo

"showing a woman's legs and feet resting on a man's lap in a first-class airplane cabin that, in its

essence, 'was supposed to have an erotic sense.'" As explained previously (Pl. Mem. at 20-22),

Prince's alterations of the Photographs (*cf. Rogers v. Koons*, 960 F.2d at 305, 312 (black and

white photo altered into polychromatic painted three-dimensional wood sculpture));

enlargements which emphasize rather than minimize Cariou's work (*cf. Bill Graham Archives*,

448 F.3d at 611); and addition of other images do not change the fact that he appropriated

substantial portions of Carious' work, making the third fair use factor weigh against fair use.

D.   Fourth Fair Use Factor

Overlooking documentary proof that, on August 28, 2008, before anyone knew

about Prince's *Canal Zone* Paintings, Christiane Celle sought to represent Cariou and exhibit his

work, and that Cariou expressed interest (Brooks Dec. Ex. SS), defendants imply that Cariou and

Celle have concocted this narrative. Def. Opp. Mem. at 21-22. Defendants claim (*id.* at 21) that

Cariou never "committed" to the project with Celle, overlooking undisputed testimony that

Cariou met with Celle twice, once in New York and once in Paris, all well before Prince's *Canal*

Zone show, went through *Yes Rasta* to identify Photographs for the show, and that Cariou, in

Celle's view, "wanted to do a show." Brooks Dec. Ex. D at 227; Ex. J at 39-44. Defendants

point to the absence of a written contract between Cariou and Celle's gallery (supposedly

9

proving that there was no show to cancel) (Def. Opp. Mem. at 21), even though there also was no

written contract between Prince and Gagosian Gallery. *See* Brooks Rep. Dec. Ex. A at 90-91;

Ex. B at 23-24. Despite Celle's undisputed testimony that she cancelled Cariou's show because

it had been "done already" at the Gagosian Gallery (Brooks Dec. Ex. J at 89), thereby

"superseding the objects" of Cariou's work, defendants argue that the market for the Photographs

was not "completely usurped" (even though *Blanch*, which defendants quote for this point, never

uses the phrase "completely usurp") (*see* Def. Opp. Mem. at 20). Finally, defendants fault Cariou

for asserting harm to the "potential market" for his work (*id.*), even though the fourth fair use

factor employs the words "potential market" and despite *Campbell*'s explanation that this factor

"requires courts to consider not only the extent of market harm caused by the particular actions

of the alleged infringer, but also 'whether unrestricted and widespread conduct of the sort

engaged in by the defendant . . . would result in a substantially adverse impact on the potential

market' for the original." 510 U.S. at 590 (citation omitted).

CONCLUSION

For the foregoing reasons, Cariou's motion for summary judgment should be

granted.

Dated: New York, New York
June 24, 2010

SCHNADER HARRISON SEGAL & LEWIS LLP

By: _____
Daniel J. Brooks
Eric A. Boden
140 Broadway, Suite 3100
New York, New York 10005
(212) 973-8000
Attorneys for Plaintiff Patrick Cariou

WITHERS BERGMAN LLP
Hollis Gonerka Bart (HB-8955)
Dara G. Hammerman (DH-1591)
Azmina Jasani (AJ-4161)
430 Park Avenue, 10th Floor
New York, New York 10022
212.848.9800 (p)
212.848.9888 (f)
Attorneys for Defendants Gagosian Gallery, Inc.
and Lawrence Gagosian

HANLEY CONROY BIERSTEIN
SHERIDAN FISHER & HAYES LLP
Steven M. Hayes (SH-2926)
112 Madison Avenue
New York, NY 10016-7416
(212) 784-6414
Attorneys for Defendant Richard Prince

UNITED STATES DISTRICT COURT
SOUTHERN DISTRICT OF NEW YORK
---X
PATRICK CARIOU,
                            Plaintiff,
                   -against-
RICHARD PRINCE, GAGOSIAN GALLERY, INC.,
LAWRENCE GAGOSIAN, and RIZZOLI
INTERNATIONAL PUBLICATIONS, INC,
                           Defendants.
---X

08 CIV 11327 (DAB)

**DEFENDANTS' JOINT MEMORANDUM OF LAW IN
REPLY TO PLAINTIFF'S OPPOSITION TO DEFENDANTS'
JOINT MOTION FOR SUMMARY JUDGMENT**

TABLE OF CONTENTS

i

TABLE OF AUTHORITIES

ARGUMENT

Any consideration of the pending summary judgment motions must begin with Cariou's

56.1 Counter-Statement in which he admits that the following facts are "not disputed":

- "Drawing inspiration from his birthplace, the Panama Canal Zone, where he had visited in 2005 and the storyline of his *Eden Rock* screenplay, Prince imagined a make-believe, post-apocalyptic enclave set in a tropical location, the *Canal Zone*, in which bands and music are the only things to survive." D. 56.1 Stmt. ¶ 61.

- "Guitars, naked women and Rastas were all ingredients in the *Canal Zone* Paintings, but the guitar is the primary subject." *Id.* at ¶ 73.

- "Prince added images of guitars to his Paintings to establish groupings of men and women as contemporary musical bands in order to create a rock and roll theme throughout the paintings in the *Canal Zone* series." *Id.* at ¶ 74.

- "Through his *Canal Zone* paintings, Prince sought to pay homage to artists such as Willem de Kooning, Cezanne, Warhol and Picasso." *Id.* at ¶ 82.

- "In creating *Yes Rasta*, Cariou's intent was to create a beautiful portraiture book, to document the Rastafarian culture and the surrounding landscapes, and to capture as closely as possible the subject being photographed." *Id.* at ¶ 116.

- "Prince used the *Yes Rasta* Images and changed them from documentary photographs into elements of a fictionalized, post-apocalyptic world, which related to his screenplay pitch, and his desire to do a series of paintings in a tropical setting with an emphasis on musical groups and the importance of music, while still making strong art historical references." *Id.* at ¶ 174.

P. C-S 56.1 at ¶¶ 61, 73, 74, 82, 116.[1] Cariou also admits each fact about Prince's creative

intention, the techniques, Images and other raw elements he used, and the meanings of the titles for

each Painting.[2] These admissions, and the flawed legal theories Cariou advances, confirm that he

failed to carry his burden on summary judgment on fair use. Specifically, by admitting that Prince's

use of the Images as raw materials "changed them from documentary photographs into elements of

a fictionalized, post-apocalyptic world," Cariou concedes that the Paintings have a new expression,

---

[1] "P. C-S 56.1" refers to Plaintiff's Counter-Statement, Pursuant to Local Civil Rule 56.1, of Undisputed Material Facts, in Opposition to Defendants' Motion for Summary Judgment. "D. C-S 56.1" refers to Defendants' Rule 56.1 Statement of Uncontested Material Facts in Response to Plaintiff's Statement Pursuant to Local Rule 56.1. "P. Opp. Mem." refers to Plaintiff's Memorandum of Law in Opposition to Defendants' Joint Motion for Summary Judgment. "D. Opp. Mem" refers to Defendants' Memorandum of Law in Opposition to Plaintiffs' Motion for Summary Judgment. "Reply Aff." refers to the accompanying Affidavit of Hollis Gonerka Bart in Reply to Plaintiff's Opposition to Defendants' Joint Motion for Summary Judgment. All other capitalized terms have the meaning ascribed to them in D. Opp. Mem. at n.1.

[2] P. C-S 56.1 at ¶¶ 29-30, 46-47, 56, 58-62, 64-65, 67, 70-74, 76-77, 79-87, 183-88, 190-202, 204-07, 209-21, 223, 225-306, 308-321, 325-370, 372-403.

meaning and message, and in doing so, concedes that the Paintings are transformative. *See Blanch v. Koons*, 497 F.3d 244, 252-53 (2d Cir. 2006) ("*Blanch*"); D.Mem. 14-16; D. Opp. Mem. 5-13; *see also United States v. City of New York,* 637 F. Supp. 2d 77, 98-99 (E.D.N.Y. 2009) (where defendant's response to plaintiff's 56.1 statement conceded that certain statements were true, defendant could not create an issue of material fact in its memorandum of law by disputing those very same, already conceded facts); *accord* Local Civil Rule 56.1(c). Given Cariou's further concession that Prince had a genuine creative rationale for appropriating the Images (P. C-S 56.1 at ¶ 61), and the now undisputed transformative techniques Prince used to create the Paintings, including how the Image was altered,[3] summary judgment is warranted on this ground alone, particularly since there has been no showing of bad faith in the creation, exhibition or marketing of the Paintings.[4] On this record, plaintiff's conclusory statement that "Prince's appropriation was not transformative" (P. Opp. Mem 2) is insufficient to defeat summary judgment on the transformative prong of the first factor.[5] *See Bourne Co. v. Twentieth Century Fox Films Corp.*, 602 F. Supp. 2d 499, 503 (S.D.N.Y. 2009) (Batts, J.).

Likewise, Cariou's admissions that the Images are part of a documentary on Rastafarians in their Jamaican landscape, and that Prince used them to further his creative intent to depict a "fictionalized, post-apocalyptic world, which related to his screenplay pitch, and his desire to do a series of paintings in a tropical setting with an emphasis on musical groups and the importance of music" (P. 56.1 C-S at ¶ 174) confirms that these bodies of work were created for very different

---

[3] Cariou's unsubstantiated claim that the images were "unaltered" must be rejected given the testimony of NancyScans, which fully corroborates Prince's sworn statements on this point. Reply Aff. at Ex. A; RP 169-70.

[4] While Cariou notes that the Images were taken from *Yes Rasta*, which bears a copyright notice on the colophon page, Cariou cites to no case that holds that this fact alone is evidence of bad faith. *Cf. Blanch* at 255-6.

[5] Defendants make no comment to plaintiff's three-page discussion of purported settlements by other appropriation artists (P. Opp. Mem. 2-4), except to say that presumably the parties in those cases concluded that there was a reason to settle on terms they felt were reasonable, but the propriety of their assessments has nothing to do with whether Prince's use of the Images was transformative.

2

purposes. Thus, regardless of whether there is some degree of protectable originality in the Images (a point that is not conceded), this is of "limited usefulness" on the second factor "where the creative work of art is being used for a transformative purpose." P. Opp. Mem. 17-18 citing *Blanch* at 257;[6] *see also* PC Tr. 164, 170-71, 173, 176-79 (even plaintiff had difficulty finding his own images).

Cariou's admissions that the Paintings were the result of a two-year creative process, and that the manner Prince created each Painting are "not in dispute" (P. 56.1 C-S ¶¶ 58-9, 61) also confirm that Prince's choice of subject matter and the 25 sources from which he selected images was deliberate. As such, the fact that Prince worked quickly and would "randomly take images that fit into [his] artistic vision and message for each work" does not mean that Prince gave no thought to what or how much he was taking; rather it provides further evidence that the Images were interchangeable for his purposes and therefore, of little value or importance. Cariou's disingenuous attempt to spin his repeated admission that "you have to take the whole book as a whole" as instructions for film processing (P. Opp. Mem. 18) does not compel a different result. His unequivocal answers to later questions about "*another* example" of how *Yes Rasta* needs to be considered as a whole confirms there is only one credible interpretation of his testimony; that the images in *Yes Rasta* must be viewed as a whole to appreciate their distinctiveness. PC Tr. 61, 81; *see also id.* at 117. In any event, as Cariou wholly failed to address the substantiality prong of the third factor, this factor also weighs in defendants' favor. *See* D. Opp. Mem. 16-20; *see also Pilgrim*

---

[6] Cariou's reference to *Monster Commc'ns, Inc. v. Turner Broad. Sys., Inc.*, 935 F. Supp. 490, 494 (S.D.N.Y. 1996) is misleading. While the court acknowledges that images of people and places "may be as creative and deserving of protection as purely fanciful creations," it holds that, "there is a public interest in receiving information concerning the world in which we live." *Id.* More factual work "may strengthen somewhat the hand of a fair use defendant as compared with an alleged infringer of a fanciful work or a work presented in a medium that offers a greater variety of forms of expression." *Id.* Thus, even if this Court were to find the Images creative on some level, they are nevertheless factual and informational in nature, and largely not protectable.

Though defendants inadvertently cited to incorrect pages to evidence that the Photographs were taken in Negril, Lucille and other public places, the record supports this fact. *See* PC Tr. 38, 73-74, 119-20, 131-32, 138.

3

v. The McGraw-Hill Cos., Inc., 599 F. Supp. 2d 462, 474 (S.D.N.Y. 2009) ("[Plaintiff] effectively concedes [the argument made by defendant on summary judgment] by not addressing [it] in her opposition to summary judgment"); *Maysonet v. Thompson*, 2005 U.S. Dist. Lexis 7311, at *16-17 (S.D.N.Y. Apr. 21, 2005) (same).[7]

Cariou also failed to carry his burden on the fourth factor as he still has not addressed the market usurpation standard required for this factor, and instead continues to urge the "harm" theory that was rejected by the Second Circuit, thus explaining why he cites no case law supporting his view. *See* D. Mem. 11, 23-26; D. Opp. Mem. 22-24. As it is now undisputed that Cariou never actually committed to do a show with Clic Gallery, Cariou cannot under any theory carry the market factor. *See* P. 56.1 C-S ¶ 157 (admitting "Celle never finalized an agreement with Cariou to represent him. As Celle stated, 'I was very committed, I wanted to represent him. We agree on it but we never really pursue it.'"); *see also* CC Tr. 133-4, 160; D. Opp. Aff. Ex. C.

Plaintiff's reliance on tertiary authority and dicta in a Second Circuit decision rendered over 30 years ago, intimating the theoretical possibility of a conspiracy claim confirms there is no reason for this Court to go against the weight of measured authority in this District, which holds that there is no recognized claim for conspiracy. *See* D. Opp. at 13, n. 6. Thus, the only remaining issues before this Court are whether Prince had to, or in fact did, comment with his Paintings, and if not, whether his appropriative use nonetheless falls within Section 107's illustrative purposes; and whether Prince's statements on this point lack credibility.

A.   Prince's Transformative Use Of The Images To Further A Different Message Falls Within Section 107, Even If Prince Is Not Seen As Commenting

Cariou's suggestion that Prince must comment for his use of the Images to be transformative

---

[7] Cariou's claim that it is irrelevant that *Yes Rasta* is registered as a compilation misses the point. Defendants do not dispute that a compilation copyright gives its owner rights to the underlying work. However, the fact that a work is registered as a compilation evidences that its core expression is as a compilation. *NXIVM Corp. v. Ross Inst.*, 364 F.3d 471, 481 (2d Cir. 2006) (core of expression can not be identified apart from the compilation in its entirety).

4

(P. Opp. Mem. 5-9) is contrary to well-settled law in this Circuit. In making this argument, Cariou

improperly conflates the analysis of the sub-prongs used in this Circuit to determine the first factor.

See Leibovitz v. Paramount Pictures Corp., 137 F.3d 109, 114 (2d Cir. 1998) (Court analyzed sub-

prongs separately, holding: "Plainly, the ad adds something new and qualifies as a 'transformative'

work. Whether it 'comments' on the original is a somewhat closer question."). Indeed, the Second

Circuit has expressly declined to adopt the interpretation advanced by Cariou. *See Bill Graham*

Archives v. Dorling Kindersley Ltd., 448 F.3d 605, 609-11 (2d Cir. 2006) ("*Graham Archives*") (in

rejecting plaintiff's argument that each image should be accompanied by comment or criticism,

found plaintiff's position to be a "limited interpretation of transformative use" because "use of the

disputed images is transformative *both* when accompanied by referencing commentary *and when*

standing alone") (emphasis added); *see also Calkins v. Playboy Enters. Int'l. Inc.*, 561 F. Supp. 2d

1136, 1141-42 (E.D. Cal. 2008) (first prong weighed in favor of magazine where photograph was

used to personalize model purely to "inform and entertain" and was thus put into an entirely

different context and therefore, transformative).

In any event, even if this Court were to find that Prince was not effectively commenting

through the messages he undisputedly was conveying with his Paintings (*see* D. Opp. Mem. 9-12),

Prince's use of the Images to further his appropriative purpose falls squarely within the type of

illustrative purposes in Section 107. As the Second Circuit has observed:

> While there are no categories of presumptively fair use, courts have frequently
> afforded fair use protection to the use of copyrighted material in biographies,
> recognizing such works as forms of historic scholarship, criticism, and comment that
> *require incorporation of original source material for optimum treatment of their*
> *subjects.*

Graham Archives at 609 (emphasis added) citing *Campbell v. Acuff-Rose Music, Inc.,* 510 U.S. 569,

584 (1994). In the same way, Prince used source material, including the Images, to achieve

optimum treatment of the meaning and messages he was endeavoring to express through the

5

Paintings. As the now-undisputed record reveals, Prince used the Images of Rastafarians and

tropical landscapes to further his creative expression of Rastafarians as band members in a post-

apocalyptical society on the tropical island of St. Barts. P. 56.1 C-S ¶¶ 61, 174, 201. By taking

Images from a book documenting Rastafarians in their native landscape as realistically as possible,

Prince is assured that the authenticity of the Images is unassailable, a justification accepted by the

Second Circuit.[8] *See Blanch* at 255 (appropriation artist showed a justification for using image

where he attested that "[b]y using an existing image, I also ensure a certain authenticity or veracity

that enhances" his stated artistic purpose). As Prince explained his appropriative style at his

deposition, "I feel that I like to get as much fact into my work and reduce the amount of

speculation." RP Tr. 44-45. *See also* P. 56.1 C-S, ¶ 35 (admitting there "is no dispute" that Prince is

"not interested in what is actually there," and is instead "really interested in making art that . . .

transforms something that's already existed without getting involved in the original intent of the

image."). This is the very essence of appropriation art. *Rogers v. Koons,* 960 F.2d 301, 304 (2d

Cir. 1992) (appropriation art defined as: "when the artist finishes his work, the meaning of the

original object has been extracted and an entirely new meaning set in its place."); *see also Blanch* at

246, n.1 citing *Ames*) at 1477-80; D. Mem. 2. As the promotion of the arts is at the very core of the

Copyright Act, the Paintings, which were undisputedly intended to be a hip take on the music scene

that uses guitars and other pop culture elements and historical art references to communicate

messages through a creative expression that is plainly different than Cariou's fact-based

---

[8] Though plaintiff continues to urge that Prince could have used stock photos to achieve the same purpose (P. Opp. Mem. 9-10), the availability of substitutes is not determinative of whether a work is transformative. *Lennon v. Premise Media Corp. L.P.,* 556 F. Supp. 2d 310, 324 (2d Cir. 2008) (fact that "defendants manifestly could have proceeded without the plaintiff's images...posed no obstacle to a finding of fair use" since "[d]etermining whether a use is transformative ... does not require courts to decide whether it was strictly necessary that [the original work] be used ... as opposed to some other image"). In any event, the fact that substantially similar images are readily available on the Internet merely confirms that the Images are deserving of little if any copyright protection. D. Mem. 20-21; D. Opp. Mem. 2-3.

documentary, Prince's creation of the Paintings fits within the purposes found in Section 107. *See Blanch* at 253 (use of image as part of a "massive painting" found transformative where appropriation artist's stated objective was not to "repackage" image, "but to employ it 'in the creation of new information, new aesthetics, new insights and understandings.'") (internal citation omitted); *see also* D. Mem. 12-17; D. Opp. Mem. 15-16.

B.   There Is No Basis To Disregard Any Statement In Prince's Affidavits, Which Are Credible And Necessitated By The Deficiencies In Plaintiff's Examination Of Prince

As shown above, Cariou admitted in his 56.1 Counter-Statement that there "is no dispute" as to Prince's purpose and techniques, the messages he was trying to communicate through, or the importance titles played in conveying the transformative nature of the Paintings. In doing so, Cariou has mooted his suggestion that statements in Prince's Affidavit concerning his messages should be disregarded as incredible "*post hoc* rationalizations." *See* P. Opp. Mem. pp. 10-15. In any event, as a review of the entirety of Prince's deposition confirms, plaintiff's examination of Prince was geared largely to creating credibility issues rather than discovery of Prince's creative intentions. Reply Aff. Ex B and C (chart of Prince deposition topics and time dedicated to each). For example, though there are 29 Paintings at issue in this case, plaintiff questioned Prince about the creative rationale behind only six of them, but even as to those six Paintings, plaintiff rushed Prince through his answers, often interrupting him before he could finish. *See* RP Tr. 330-43, 346-66; *see also id.* at 341-42, 356, 358-59. Indeed, plaintiff urged Prince to use brevity in answering his questions. *Id.* at 341 ("I think you're answering the questions but then you seem to feel you need to give me more information. . . . And if you have to you have to, but I'd like to get out of here at 6:15."). Prince's attempts to explain his creative process also were met with mockery, which further chills the discovery process. *Id.* at 357-60, 364-66. On this record, then, an affidavit from Prince detailing his rationale and the techniques he used to create the Paintings was the proper way to place before the

7

Court a cogent statement demonstrating Prince's fair use of the Images. Thus, the fact that some of these sworn statements, including those relating to Prince's messages, were not adequately covered, if at all, in his deposition, affords no basis to disregard Prince's sworn statements concerning the messages he was conveying through his Paintings. Likewise, the pre-action documents do not contradict Prince's Affidavit. *See* Brooks Dec. Ex. F, T, DD, EE; Ex. M. The press release, which Prince first saw at his deposition, focuses on the techniques he used to create the Paintings. RP Tr. 294. The Frey essay reflects Frey's interpretation of Prince's pitch, but was not entirely in keeping with Prince's artistic intention for the *Canal Zone* series. RP Tr. 221-23. The three pages of the 13-page interview transcript, which dealt with the *Canal Zone* exhibition focus on Prince's discovery of the Rastafarian images and his screenplay pitch.[9] Brooks Dec. Ex T at C75-77. That pitch, which was done in outline form, provides only a summary treatment of Prince's screenplay. *Id.* In sum, these documents do not reference the messages Prince was conveying through the Paintings because they were written with a completely different focus. However, the common theme of each of these contemporaneous documents, like Prince's truthful testimony on the subject, is that the *Canal Zone* series evolved from his vision of a fantastical post-apocalyptical society consisting of survivors comprised of bands and their music. *Compare* Brooks Dec. at Ex. F, T, DD, EE; Ex. M *with* RP Tr. 207-8, 214-18. Thus, whether this vision is called a "subtext" to his pitch or a message in his Paintings (P. Opp. Mem. 11-12), the fact remains that Prince has been consistent that this post-apocalyptical society is "one of the ingredients" of the *Canal Zone* series and the storyline from which it evolved. RP Tr. 277-79; D. Mem. 4-5; *see also Collins English Dict.* (2003) ("subtext (n.) –

---

[9] The interview transcript also provides pre-action corroboration of the importance Prince placed on the titles he gave to the Paintings: "[T]he Rastas and the lesbians started starring in these pictures and were kind of like bands- there are, like, five people to a picture, and every picture has a title to it. It sort of becomes an allegory." Brooks Dec. Ex. T, C00076. Thus, Prince's inability to recall each of the titles with precision does not undermine the importance he gave to them at the time (*see* D. Opp. Mem. 20), and in any event, is largely a function of plaintiff's refusal to give him the documents that would have refreshed his recollection on this point. (RP Tr. 216-17).

an underlying theme in a piece of writing."). As such, Prince's sworn statements in his affidavit

concerning his messages about the redemptive value of music in this post-apocalyptic world and

equality between the sexes (i.e., the band members), merely amplify, and are fully consonant with,

his deposition testimony and the pre-action evidence. *Palazzo v. Corio*, 232 F. 3d 38, 43-44 (2d Cir.

2000) (use of affidavit to address issues not thoroughly or clearly explored during deposition, or to

clarify deposition testimony that was "ambiguous, confusing or simply incomplete" or to amplify or

explain prior deposition testimony was proper).[10]

The snippets of Prince's deposition testimony Cariou quotes of out context does not change

the analysis. The answer "I don't really have a message" was in response to a nonsensical question

at the end of a line of questions about Prince's appropriative technique generally, and not about the

Canal Zone series specifically. RP Tr. 45-46 (". . . Q. Is it part of your message now that your

artwork is more believable because it was taken from someone else? A. I don't really have a

message."). It is understandable that Prince would answer a question which mixes technique with

message that he has no message as to the believability of his appropriation artworks generally.

Moreover, as is evident from the transcript, and as explained in his RP Supp. Aff. ¶ 7, Prince

struggled with the words "message" and "comment" as they were used (interchangeably by counsel)

in questions posed to him at his deposition:

Q. What is your *message* or what is the meaning of this painting [*Back to the Garden*], what

---

[10] Defendants never argued that Prince "only found the copy of *Yes Rasta* after he had already written his screenplay in 2007" as Cariou claims. P. Opp. Mem. 11. To the contrary, the pages cited by plaintiff are silent as to the year of Prince discovered *Yes Rasta*. *See id.* citing D. Mem. at 4-5. Those pages do cite to the Prince Affidavit as record support for the "fluid" process by which Prince created the *Canal Zone* series starting in 2005. RP Aff. ¶ 17("At the time that I painted my de Kooning series, I was already thinking about the *Canal Zone* series, and therefore, I had also been looking for black and [white] images of figures of men that I could put next to my de Kooning women."). The statements in Prince's Affidavit, and the description of this process in defendants' memorandum, concerning the evolution of the *Canal Zone* series are thus, fully consonant with Prince's deposition testimony and pre-action evidence. *Compare* RP. Aff. ¶¶ 16-17 and D. Mem. 4-5 *with* RP Tr. 153-54, 158, 236, 239-40, 266 and Brooks Dec. Ex T [Interview]; *see also* RP Tr. 266 (when asked if *Yes Rasta* inspired his idea for the screenplay pitch, Prince truthfully answered, "No."). As such, there is no basis to strike these highly probative and credible statements from Prince's Affidavit.

9

is it that you're trying to get across?

A. As I said, I'm trying to make a kind of fantastic, absolutely hip, up to date, contemporary take on the music scene. And it's my way of dealing with this idea that I've always had, which are the three relationships that exist in the world, which are men and women, men and men, and women and women. . . .in any artwork I don't think there's any one message. *I'm not a political artist.* If you can tell me who the president of France was when Gauguin was in Tahiti I'll give you a thousand dollars. Politicians come and go, art comes and comes. . . .

Q. This has the guitar, right?

A. Yes.

Q. So is this what you were talking about, *commenting on* the music scene?

A. The guitar, again, is what I think my contribution is to the image, one of the contributions to this particular image, just like the mask was my contribution to the nurse paintings. Once I make some sort of connection. Now, if that hadn't been made, this guitar, this collage, which turns this – the original intentions of this image into something completely different, obviously, he's playing the guitar now, it looks as if he's always played the guitar, that's what my message was.

Q. Okay.

A. Is to sort of tell people, hey, this guy is playing the guitar.

Q. Understood.

A. And –

Q. I'm kind of – I don't mean to cut you off, but I'm trying to finish by 6:15.

RP Tr. 338-41 (emphasis added); *see also* RP Aff. ¶ 37. As such, Cariou's reliance on an answer lifted out of context from a line of questions Prince was prevented from answering completely affords no basis to disregard his affidavit where he has given a complete, uninterrupted description of his creative intent. However, this sequence does confirm that even plaintiff and his counsel understood Prince's message to be the same thing as his comment on the music scene, thereby confirming that to the extent a comment is required, Prince has made it through his credible messages, which are now undisputed. P. C-S ¶¶ 61, 174.

CONCLUSION

For all the reasons herein, in Defendants' Memorandum, Defendant's Opposition Memorandum, and in the affidavits and exhibits, defendants respectfully request this Court to enter an order denying plaintiff's summary judgment motion, and granting defendants summary judgment on the grounds that Prince's use of the Images did not infringe on any right of plaintiff, or alternatively, that Prince's use was fair as a matter of law.

Dated: June 24, 2010
    New York, New York

WITHERS BERGMAN LLP

By: _/s/_

    Hollis Gonerka Bart (HB-8955)
    Dara G. Hammerman (DH-1591)
    Azmina Jasani (AJ-4161)
    430 Park Avenue, 10th Floor
    New York, NY 10022-3505
    Phone: (212) 848-9800
    Fax: (212) 848-9888
    Attorneys for Defendants Gagosian Gallery Inc.
    and Lawrence Gagosian

By: _/s/_

    Steven M. Hayes (SH-2926)
    Hanly Conroy Bierstein Sheridan
    Fisher & Hayes LLP
    112 Madison Avenue
    New York, NY 10016-7416
    (212) 784-6414
    Attorneys for Defendant Richard Prince

11

CERTIFICATE OF SERVICE

The Undersigned hereby certifies that a copy of the foregoing was served upon the

following via ECF on this the 24th day of June, 2010:

Daniel J. Brooks
Schnader Harrison Segal & Lewis LLP
140 Broadway, Suite 3100
New York, New York 10005-1101
(212) 973-8000
Attorneys for plaintiff, Patrick Cariou

                                    /s/
                         _____
                         COUNSEL FOR DEFENDANTS GAGOSIAN
                         GALLERY INC. AND LAWRENCE GAGOSIAN
                         Hollis Gonerka Bart (HB-8955)
                         Dara G. Hammerman (DH-1591)
                         Azmina Jasani (AJ-4161)
                         Withers Bergman LLP
                         430 Park Avenue, 10th Floor
                         New York, New York 10022
                         (p) 212-848-9800
                         (f) 212-848-9888

document number: NY23802/0005-US-874221/5

12

UNITED STATES DISTRICT COURT
SOUTHERN DISTRICT OF NEW YORK
-----------------------------------X
PATRICK CARIOU,

      Plaintiff,

    -against-

RICHARD PRINCE, GAGOSIAN GALLERY, INC.,
LAWRENCE GAGOSIAN, and RIZZOLI
INTERNATIONAL PUBLICATIONS, INC.

      Defendants.
-----------------------------------X

08 Civ. 11327 (DAB)
MEMORANDUM & ORDER

DEBORAH A. BATTS, United States District Judge.

   This matter is now before the Court on cross-motions for
summary judgment. Defendants Richard Prince, Gagosian Gallery,
Inc., and Lawrence Gagosian seek a determination that their use
of Plaintiff's copyrighted photographs was a fair use under the
relevant section of the Copyright Act, 17 U.S.C. §§ 107(1)-(4),
and that Plaintiff's claim for conspiracy to violate his rights
under the Copyright Act is barred by law.[1] Plaintiff seeks
summary judgment in his favor on the issue of liability for
copyright infringement.

   For reasons detailed herein, the Court finds (1) that

---

  [1]Named Defendant Rizzoli International Publications, Inc.
was voluntarily dismissed from this action by stipulation of
dismissal entered by the Court on February 5, 2010.

Defendants' infringing use of Plaintiff's copyrighted photographs
was not fair use under the Copyright Act; and (2) that
Plaintiff's conspiracy claim is barred by law. Accordingly,
Defendants' Motion is GRANTED in part, and Plaintiff's Motion is
GRANTED in its entirety.

I. BACKGROUND

Familiarity with the affidavits, declarations, deposition
transcripts, and other evidence before the Court is assumed, and
the undisputed facts are set forth here only briefly.

Plaintiff Patrick Cariou ("Plaintiff" or "Cariou") is a
professional photographer. PC Tr. 45-46, 279-80.[2] Cariou spent
time with Rastafarians in Jamaica over the course of some six
years, gaining their trust and taking their portraits. PC Tr. 34-
48. In 2000, Cariou published a book of photographs which were
taken during his time in Jamaica. Brooks Decl. Ex. L. The book,
titled Yes, Rasta and released by PowerHouse Books ("Yes,
Rasta"), contained both portraits of Rastafarian individuals (and
others) in Jamaica and landscape photos taken by Cariou in

---

[2]"PC. Tr.," used herein, refers to the transcript of Patrick
Cariou's deposition testimony. "RP Tr.," "CC Tr.," "LG Tr." and
"AM Tr." refer to the deposition transcripts of Richard Prince,
Christiane Celle, Lawrence Gagosian, and Alison McDonald,
respectively. Similarly, "RP. Aff." refers to the affidavit
filed by Richard Prince.

Jamaica.[3] Id.

Cariou testified at length about the creative choices he made in determining which equipment to use in taking his photos, the staging choices he made when composing and taking individual photos, and the techniques and processes he used (and directed others to use) when developing the photos. See e.g., PC Tr. 49-66, 133-34, 137-38, 143-44, 152, 169. Cariou also testified that he was heavily involved in the layout, editing, and printing of the Yes, Rasta book. Id.; PC Tr. at 180-208. According to the colophon page included in Yes, Rasta, Cariou is the sole copyright holder in the images that appear in Yes, Rasta. Brooks Decl. Ex. L.

Defendant Richard Prince ("Prince") is a well-known "appropriation artist" who has shown at numerous museums and other institutions, including a solo show at the Guggenheim Museum in New York City. RP Aff. ¶¶ 3, 5. Defendant Gagosian Gallery, Inc. (the "Gallery") is an art dealer and gallery which represents Prince and markets the artworks he creates. LG Tr. 22-25; RP Tr. 270, 294. Defendant Lawrence Gagosian ("Gagosian"; collectively with the Gallery, the "Gagosian Defendants") is the

---

[3]The portraits and landscape photographs Cariou published in Yes, Rasta are collectively referred to herein as the "Photos," "Cariou's Photos," or the "Yes, Rasta Photos."

President, founder, and owner of the Gagosian Gallery, Inc. LG

Tr. at 16.[4]

In or about December 2007 through February 2008, Prince

showed artwork at the Eden Rock hotel in St. Barts. See RP Tr. at

187-88. Among the works shown was a collage entitled Canal Zone

(2007), which consisted of 35 photographs torn from Yes, Rasta

and attached to a wooden backer board. See RP Decl. Comp. Ex. A.

at 20-24; see also RP Tr. at 179-80. Prince painted over some

portions of the 35 photographs, and used only portions of some of

the photos, while others were used in their entirety or nearly

so. See generally RP Decl. Comp. Ex. A at 20-24. Though Canal

Zone (2007) was not sold, Prince sold other artworks at that show

through Gagosian. RP Tr. 187-88, 197-98. Portions of Canal Zone

(2007) were reproduced in a magazine article about Prince's Canal

Zone show at the Gagosian Gallery. RP Tr. at 198-201. Prince

intended that Canal Zone (2007) serve as an introduction to the

characters he intended to use in a screenplay and in a planned

series of artworks, also to be entitled Canal Zone. RP Aff. ¶ 48.

Prince ultimately completed 29 paintings in his contemplated

Canal Zone series, 28 of which included images taken from Yes,

---

[4]Gagosian testified that he "may have given" "a small piece"
of the Gallery to his sister. LG Tr. at 17.

Rasta.[5] See RP Decl. Comp. Ex. A. Some of the paintings, like

"Graduation (2008)" and "Canal Zone (2008)," consist almost

entirely of images taken from Yes, Rasta, albeit collaged,

enlarged, cropped, tinted, and/or over-painted, while others,

like "Ile de France (2008)" use portions of Yes, Rasta Photos as

collage elements and also include appropriated photos from other

sources and more substantial original painting.[6] See RP Decl.

Comp. Ex. A (comparing Prince paintings with Cariou Photos used

therein); compare Brooks Decl. Ex. M (Canal Zone catalog) with

Brooks Decl. Ex. L (Yes, Rasta book). In total, Prince admits

using at least 41 Photos from Yes, Rasta as elements of Canal

Zone Paintings. RP Decl. ¶ 24.

The Gallery showed 22 of the 29 Canal Zone paintings at one

of its Manhattan locations from November 8, 2008 to December 20,

2008. Brooks Decl. Ex. M at 1; LG Tr. at 25, 50; RP Aff. at Ex.

A. The Gallery also published and sold an exhibition catalog

from that show, similarly entitled Canal Zone, which contained

---

[5]The allegedly infringing works in the Canal Zone series, together with Canal Zone (2007), are referred to collectively herein as the "Paintings," "Prince's Paintings," or the "Canal Zone Paintings."

[6]In reaching its determination herein, the Court has examined fully the exhibits and reproductions provided by the Parties and has compared the 29 Canal Zone paintings with the Yes, Rasta Photos. The Court sees no need to describe each work in great detail.

reproductions of many of the Canal Zone Paintings (including some Paintings which were not shown at the Gallery) and photographs of Yes, Rasta Photos in Prince's studio. See Brooks Decl. Ex. M (Canal Zone exhibition catalog). The Gagosian employee who was the Managing Editor of the catalog testified that she never inquired as to the source of the Rastafarian photographs contained therein. AC Tr. at 42.

Other than by private sale to individuals Cariou knew and liked, the Photos have never been sold or licensed for use other than in the Yes, Rasta book. PC Tr. 86-94. However, Cariou testified that he was negotiating with gallery owner Christiane Celle ("Celle"), who planned to show and sell prints of the Yes, Rasta Photos at her Manhattan gallery, prior to the Canal Zone show's opening. PC Tr. at 96-98; see CC Tr. 39-40, 42-44. Cariou also testified that he intended in the future to issue artists' editions of the Photos, which would be offered for sale to collectors. PC Tr. 92-94; 97-98.

Celle originally planned to exhibit between 30 and 40 of the Photos at her gallery, with multiple prints of each to be sold at prices ranging from $3,000.00 to $20,000.00, depending on size. CC Tr. at 40-42, 46, 66-68, 127-28, 153-55. She also planned to have Yes, Rasta reprinted for a book signing to be held during the show at her gallery. CC Tr. at 87-88, 155-56. However, when

6

Celle became aware of the Canal Zone exhibition at the Gagosian Gallery, she cancelled the show she and Cariou had discussed. PC Tr. at 98; CC Tr. 63-64, 71. Celle testified that she decided to cancel the show because she did not want to seem to be capitalizing on Prince's success and notoriety, CC Tr. at 89, 105-06, and because she did not want to exhibit work which had been "done already" at another gallery, CC Tr. 89, 91, 105.

II. DISCUSSION

A. Summary Judgment

A district court should grant summary judgment when there is "no genuine issue as to any material fact," and the moving party is entitled to judgment as a matter of law. Fed. R. Civ. P. 56(c); see also Hermes Int'l v. Lederer de Paris Fifth Ave., Inc., 219 F.3d 104, 107 (2d Cir. 2000). Genuine issues of material fact cannot be created by mere conclusory allegations; summary judgment is appropriate only when, "after drawing all reasonable inferences in favor of a non-movant, no reasonable trier of fact could find in favor of that party." Heublein v. United States, 996 F.2d 1455, 1461 (2d Cir. 1993) (citing Matsushita Elec. Industr. Co. v. Zenith Radio Corp., 475 U.S. 574, 587-88 (1986)).

In assessing when summary judgment should be granted, "there

7

must be more than a 'scintilla of evidence' in the non-movant's favor; there must be evidence upon which a fact-finder could reasonably find for the non-movant." Id. (citing Anderson v. Liberty Lobby, Inc., 477 U.S. 242, 252 (1986)). While a court must always "resolv[e] ambiguities and draw [ ] reasonable inferences against the moving party," Knight v. U.S. Fire Ins. Co., 804 F.2d 9, 11 (2d Cir. 1986) (citing Anderson, 477 U.S. at 252), the non-movant may not rely upon "mere speculation or conjecture as to the true nature of the facts to overcome a motion for summary judgment." Id. at 12. Instead, when the moving party has documented particular facts in the record, "the opposing party must set forth specific facts showing that there is a genuine issue for trial." Williams v. Smith, 781 F.2d 319, 323 (2d Cir. 1986)(quotation omitted). Establishing such facts requires going beyond the allegations of the pleadings, as the moment has arrived "to put up or shut up." Weinstock v. Columbia Univ., 224 F.3d 33, 41 (2d Cir. 2000) (citation omitted). Unsupported allegations in the pleadings thus cannot create a material issue of fact. Id.

A court faced with cross-motions for summary judgment need not "grant judgment as a matter of law for one side or the other," but "'must evaluate each party's motion on its own merits, taking care in each instance to draw all reasonable

8

inferences against the party whose motion is under consideration.'" Heublein, Inc. v. United States, 996 F.2d 1455, 1461 (2d Cir. 1993) (quoting Schwabenbauer v. Bd. of Educ. of Olean, 667 F.2d 305, 313-14 (2d Cir. 1981)).

To prevail on a copyright infringement claim, two elements must be proven: (1) ownership of a valid copyright, and (2) copying of constituent elements of the work that are original. See Harper & Row, 471 U.S. at 548; Feist Publ'ns., Inc. v. Rural Tel. Serv. Co., Inc., 499 US at 348, 363 (1991) (holding that alphabetical arrangement of names in telephone directory was not protected by copyright, since alphabetical arrangement "is not only unoriginal, it is practically inevitable."). To be "original," a copyrighted work must have been independently created by the author and must possess "at least some minimal degree of creativity," although "the requisite level of creativity is extremely low; even a slight amount will suffice." Id. at 345. "The vast majority of works make the grade quite easily, as they possess some creative spark, 'no matter how crude, humble or obvious' it might be." Id. (citation omitted).

"[T]he applicability of [the fair use defense to copyright infringement] presents mixed questions of law and fact," Arista Records, LLC v. Doe 3, 604 F.3d 110 (2d Cir. 2010) (citing Harper

9

& Row Pubs., Inc. v. Nation Enters., 471 U.S. 539, 560 (1985)),
but may nevertheless be determined on a motion for summary
judgment where the record contains facts sufficient to evaluate
each of the statutory factors, Harper & Row at 560.

B. Copyright in the Photos

   Cariou's ownership of a valid copyright in the Photos is
undisputed. However, Defendants assert that Cariou's Photos are
mere compilations of facts concerning Rastafarians and the
Jamaican landscape, arranged with minimum creativity in a manner
typical of their genre, and that the Photos are therefore not
protectable as a matter of law, despite Plaintiff's extensive
testimony about the creative choices he made in taking,
processing, developing, and selecting them.[7]

   Unfortunately for Defendants, it has been a matter of
settled law for well over one hundred years that creative
photographs are worthy of copyright protection even when they
depict real people and natural environments. See, e.g.,
Burrow-Giles Lithographic Co. v. Sarony, 111 U.S. 53, 60 (1884)

---

   [7]Defendant's arguments concerning whether ideas can be
protected by copyright are irrelevant to this case: Plaintiff
seeks recourse for Prince's use of his original creative works,
not for any use of or infringement on the ideas they portray.

10

(photographic portrait of Oscar Wilde was original creative work, since photographer posed the subject, selected his clothing, background, light and shade, and "suggest[ed] and evok[ed] the desired expression"); Rogers v. Koons, 960 F.2d 301, 307 (2d Cir. 1992) ("Elements of originality in a photograph may include posing the subjects, lighting, angle, selection of film and camera, evoking the desired expression, and almost any other variant involved."), cert. denied, 506 U.S. 934 (1992); Mannion v. Coors Brewing Co., 377 F. Supp. 2d 444,450 (S.D.N.Y. 2005) ("Almost any photograph 'may claim the necessary originality to support a copyright.'") (citation omitted); Eastern Am. Trio Prods., Inc. v. Tang Elec. Corp., 97 F. Supp. 2d 395, 417 (S.D.N.Y. 2000) (photographs of "common industrial items" were protectable); Monster Comm.'s, Inc. v. Turner Broad. Sys. Inc., 935 F. Supp. 490, 494 (S.D.N.Y. 1996) ("photographic images of actual people, places and events may be as creative and deserving of protection as purely fanciful creations").

Accordingly, Cariou's Photos are worthy of copyright protection.

C. Fair Use

From the infancy of copyright protection, some opportunity

11

for fair use of copyrighted materials has been thought necessary
to fulfill copyright's very purpose, "[t]o promote the Progress
of Science and useful Arts. . . ." Campbell v. Acuff-Rose Music,
Inc., 510 U.S. 569, 575 (1994) (quoting U.S. Const., Art. I, § 8,
cl. 8). At the Constitutional level, while the "Copyright Clause
and the First Amendment [are] intuitively in conflict, [they]
were drafted to work together to prevent censorship" such that
"the balance between the First Amendment and copyright is
preserved, in part, by the idea/expression dichotomy and the
doctrine of fair use." Suntrust Bank, 268 F.3d at 1263 (citing
Eldred v. Reno, 239 F.3d 372, 375 (D.C. Cir. 2001) (quoting
Harper & Row, 471 U.S. at 560)).

   "Copyright law thus must address the inevitable tension
between the property rights it establishes in creative works,
which must be protected up to a point, and the ability of
authors, artists, and the rest of us to express them- or
ourselves by reference to the works of others, which must be
protected up to a point. The fair-use doctrine mediates between
the two sets of interests, determining where each set of
interests ceases to control." Blanch v. Koons, 467 F.3d 244, 250
(2d Cir. 2006); see also Warner Bros. Entertainment Inc., v. RDR
Books, 575 F.Supp.2d 513,540 (S.D.N.Y. 2008) ("At stake in this
case are the incentive to create original works which copyright

12

protection fosters and the freedom to produce secondary works which monopoly protection of copyright stifles—both interests benefit the public.") (quoting Pierre N. Leval, Toward a Fair Use Standard, 103 Harv. L. Rev. 1105, 1109 (1990) (hereinafter "Leval") (noting that although "the monopoly created by copyright ... rewards the individual author in order to benefit the public[,]" on the other hand "the monopoly protection of intellectual property that impeded referential analysis and the development of new ideas out of old would strangle the creative process.")

The doctrine of Fair Use was codified in Section 107 of the 1976 Copyright Act. Section 107 calls for a four-factor test:

Limitations on exclusive rights: Fair use:

Notwithstanding the provisions of sections 106 and 106A, the fair use of a copyrighted work, including such use by reproduction in copies or phonorecords or by any other means specified by that section, for purposes such as criticism, comment, news reporting, teaching (including multiple copies for classroom use), scholarship, or research, is not an infringement of copyright. In determining whether the use made of a work in any particular case is a fair use the factors to be considered shall include-

(1) the purpose and character of the use, including whether such use is of a commercial nature or is for nonprofit educational purposes;
(2) the nature of the copyrighted work;

(3) the amount and substantiality of the portion used in relation to the copyrighted work as a whole; and

(4) the effect of the use upon the potential market for or value of the copyrighted work.

17 U.S.C. § 107.

In applying the fair use doctrine, "[t]he task is not to be simplified with bright-line rules, for the statute, like the doctrine it recognizes, calls for case-by-case analysis." Campbell, 510 U.S. at 577-78. In conducting that analysis, "all [of the four factors] are to be explored, and the results weighed together in light of the purposes of copyright." Id.

D. Applying the Four-Factor Analysis

1. The Purpose and Character of Prince's Use of the Photos

i. Transformative Use

"The central purpose of the inquiry into the first factor is to determine, in Justice Story's words, whether the new work merely supersede[s] the objects of the original creation or instead adds something new, with a further purpose or different character, altering the first with new expression, meaning, or message; it asks, in other words, whether and to what extent the new work is 'transformative.'" Salinger v. Colting, No. 09 Civ. 5095 (DAB), 641 F.Supp.2d 250, 256 (rev'd on other grounds 607

14

F.3d 68 (2d Cir. 2010); Campbell, 510 U.S. at 579 (internal

quotations and citations omitted). Although a transformative use

is not strictly required for the Defendant to establish the

defense of fair use, "the goal of copyright, to promote science

and the arts, is generally furthered by the creation of

transformative works. Such works thus lie at the heart of the

fair use doctrine's guarantee of breathing space within the

confines of copyright, and the more transformative the new work,

the less will be the significance of other factors, like

commercialism, that may weigh against a finding of fair use." Id.

(citing Sony Corp. of America v. Universal City Studios, Inc.,

464 U.S. 417, 478-80 (U.S. 1984) (Blackmun, J., dissenting).

The inquiry into the first factor of the fair use test,

"'the purpose and character of the use,' may be guided by

the examples given in the preamble to § 107, looking to whether

the use is for criticism, or comment, or news reporting, and the

like." Campbell, 510 U.S. at 578-79 (citing 17 U.S.C. § 107)

(identifying parody as a use akin to the illustrative uses

identified in the preamble).

As the Second Circuit clearly noted in Castle Rock, the fact

that a work "recast[s], transform[s], or adapt[s] an original

work into a new mode of presentation," thus making it a

15

"derivative work" under 17 U.S.C. § 101, does not make the work "transformative" in the sense of the first fair use factor. Castle Rock, 150 F.3d at 143. Nevertheless, Defendants invite this Court to find that use of copyrighted materials as raw materials in creating "appropriation art" which does not comment on the copyrighted original is a fair use akin to those identified in the preamble to § 107.

The cases Defendants cite for the proposition that use of copyrighted materials as "raw ingredients" in the creation of new works is per se fair use do not support their position, and the Court is aware of no precedent holding that such use is fair absent transformative comment on the original. To the contrary, the illustrative fair uses listed in the preamble to § 107 — "criticism, comment, news reporting, teaching [...], scholarship, [and] research" — all have at their core a focus on the original works or their historical context, and all of the precedent this Court can identify imposes a requirement that the new work in some way comment on, relate to the historical context of, or critically refer back to the original works. See, e.g., Campbell, 510 U.S. at 579 (transformative use is use that "alter[s] the first with new expression, meaning, or message"); Bourne v. Twentieth Century Fox Film Corp., 602 F.Supp.2d 499 (S.D.N.Y. Mar. 15, 2009)(Batts, J.) (parody song which commented both on

16

the copyrighted original and on famous person associated with original was transformative); Blanch v. Koons, 467 F.3d at 252-53 (use of copyrighted fashion advertisement as "raw material" was transformative because artist used it to comment on the role such advertisements play in our culture and on the attitudes the original and other advertisements like it promote); Liebowitz v. Paramount Pictures Corp., 137 F.3d 109, 114 (2d Cir. 1998) (superimposition of Leslie Nielsen's face on photo of body intended to resemble pregnant Demi Moore commented on original photo of Moore by holding its pretentiousness up to ridicule). C.f. Rogers v. Koons, 960 F.2d 301, 310 (2d Cir. 1992), cert. denied, 506 U.S. 934 (1992) (sculpture drawn from copyrighted photograph was not fair use because while the sculpture was a "satirical critique of our materialistic society, it is difficult to discern any parody of [or comment on] the photograph . . . itself.")

"If an infringement of copyrightable expression could be justified as fair use solely on the basis of the infringer's claim to a higher or different artistic use . . . there would be no practicable boundary to the fair use defense." Rogers v. Koons, 960 F.2d at 310. The Court therefore declines Defendants' invitation to find that appropriation art is per se fair use, regardless of whether or not the new artwork in any way comments

17

on the original works appropriated. Accordingly, Prince's
Paintings are transformative only to the extent that they comment
on the Photos; to the extent they merely recast, transform, or
adapt the Photos, Prince's Paintings are instead infringing
derivative works. See Castle Rock, 150 F.3d at 143.

Prince testified that he has no interest in the original
meaning of the photographs he uses. See e.g., RP Tr. at 338.
Prince testified that he doesn't "really have a message" he
attempts to communicate when making art. RP Tr. at 45-46. In
creating the Paintings, Prince did not intend to comment on any
aspects of the original works or on the broader culture. See
e.g., RP Tr. at 357-60; 362-64. Prince's intent in creating the
Canal Zone paintings was to pay homage or tribute to other
painters, including Picasso, Cezanne, Warhol, and de Kooning, see
RP Tr. at 164-67, 300-01, and to create beautiful artworks which
related to musical themes and to a post-apocalyptic screenplay he
was writing which featured a reggae band, see, e.g., RP Tr. 7,
30, 207-08, 218, 232, 251-52. Prince intended to emphasize
themes of equality of the sexes; highlight "the three
relationships in the world, which are men and women, men and men,
and women and women"; and portray a contemporary take on the
music scene. RP Tr. 338-39. With regard to the paintings in
which Prince collaged guitars onto portraits of Rastafarian men

18

which were taken from <u>Yes, Rasta</u>, Prince testified that his message related to the fact that the men had become guitar players. <u>See</u>, <u>e.g.</u>, RP Tr. at 340 ("[H]e's playing the guitar now, it looks like he's playing the guitar, it looks as if he's always played the guitar, that's what my message was."); <u>see</u> <u>also</u> RP Tr. 166-68, 279.

Prince also testified that his purpose in appropriating other people's originals for use in his artwork is that doing so helps him "get as much fact into [his] work and reduce[] the amount of speculation." RP Tr. at 44. That is, he chooses the photographs he appropriates for what he perceives to be their truth — suggesting that his purpose in using Cariou's Rastafarian portraits was the same as Cariou's original purpose in taking them: a desire to communicate to the viewer core truths about Rastafarians and their culture. <u>See</u> <u>Bill Graham Archives v.</u> <u>Dorling Kindersley Ltd.</u>, 448 F.3d 605, 609 (2d Cir. 2006) (considering, in weighing transformativeness, whether the new purpose in using an original work was "plainly different from the original purpose for which it was created.")

On the facts before the Court, it is apparent that Prince did not intend to comment on Cariou, on Cariou's Photos, or on aspects of popular culture closely associated with Cariou or the

19

Photos when he appropriated the Photos, and Price's own testimony
shows that his intent was not transformative within the meaning
of Section 107, though Prince intended his overall work to be
creative and new.

As this Court and others in this jurisdiction have found,
where a work is not "consistently transformative," and "lacks
restraint in using [Plaintiff's] original expression for its
inherent . . . aesthetic value," the "transformative character of
[that work] is diminished." Salinger v. Colting, No. 09 Civ. 5095
(DAB), 641 F.Supp.2d 250, 262 (rev'd on other grounds 607 F.3d 68
(2d Cir. 2010)); Warner Bros. Enter. Inc. v. RDR Books 575
F.Supp.2d 513, 544 (S.D.N.Y. 2008) (citing Bill Graham Archives
v. Dorling Kindersley Ltd., 448 F.3d 605 (2d Cir. 2006). See
Suntrust Bank, 268 F.3d at 1280 (Marcus, J., concurring) (finding
that issue of transformative character cuts "decisively in
[Defendant's] favor" where the ratio of "the borrowed and the new
elements" is "very low, and the incongruity between them wide").

Accordingly, while there may be some minimal transformative
element intended in Prince's use of the Photos, the overall
transformativeness varies from work to work depending on the
amount of copying. In the works most heavily drawn from Cariou's
Photos, such as those in which Prince uses entire photographs or

20

unaltered portraits taken from Yes, Rasta, there is vanishingly

little, if any, transformative element; in those where Cariou's

Photos play a comparatively minor role, Defendant has a stronger

argument that his work is transformative of Cariou's original

Photos.[8] Overall, because the transformative content of Prince's

paintings is minimal at best, and because that element is not

consistent throughout the 28 paintings in which Prince used the

Photos, the "transformative use" prong of the first § 107 factor

weighs heavily against a finding of fair use.

ii. Commerciality

The second prong of the first factor of the § 107 test asks

whether the otherwise infringing work "serves a commercial

purpose or nonprofit educational purpose." Suntrust Bank, 268

F.3d at 1269 (citing § 107(1)). The less transformative a work,

the more importance should be attached to "the extent of its

---

[8]Many of the Paintings which have the strongest claim to
transformative use are also those in which the amount and
substantiality of the Photos used is least reasonable: those
which feature, as their central elements, strikingly original
Rastafarian portraits taken from Yes, Rasta Photos. See
discussion of third Section 107 factor, infra. For that reason,
even the most transformative Paintings have only a weak claim to
fair use, since the four § 107 factors must be "weighed together
in light of the purposes of copyright." Campbell, 510 U.S. at
577-78.

commerciality" in determining whether the first factor favors a
finding of fair use. Campbell, 510 U.S. at 580-81 (if "the
commentary has no critical bearing on the substance or style of
the original composition . . . the claim to fairness in borrowing
from another's work diminishes accordingly (if it does not
vanish), and other factors, like the extent of its commerciality
loom larger."); see American Geophysical Union v. Texaco Inc., 60
F.3d 913, 922 (2d Cir. 1995) ("The greater the private economic
rewards reaped by the secondary user (to the exclusion of broader
public benefits), the more likely the first factor will favor the
copyright holder and the less likely the use will be considered
fair.") "[C]ourts are more willing to find a secondary use fair
when it produces a value that benefits the broader public
interest." Blanch v. Koons, 467 F.3d 244, 253-54.
"Notwithstanding the fact that artists are sometimes paid and
museums sometimes earn money, the public exhibition of art is
widely . . . considered to have value that benefits the wider
public interest." Id. (citations and internal quotations
omitted).

The Canal Zone show at the Gagosian Gallery was advertised
in seven different newspapers, five of which included
reproductions of Cariou's Photos as altered by Prince. AM Tr. at
42-50; LG Tr. at 36. The Gagosian Defendants sent some 7,500

22

invitation cards, featuring a reproduction of a Prince work
containing a Cariou Photo, to clients of the Gallery, LG Tr. at
35, AM Tr. at 29-33, and sold the leftover invitations to a
poster company, AM Tr. at 55-59. As a result of these and other
marketing efforts, Gagosian Gallery sold eight of the Canal Zone
Paintings for a total of $10,480,000.00, 60% of which went to
Prince and 40% of which went to Gagosian Gallery. Brooks Dec.
Ex. P ¶ 2 and Ex. A; LG Tr. at 48. Seven other Canal Zone
Paintings were exchanged for art with an estimated value between
$6,000,000.00 and $8,000,000.00. Brooks Dec. Ex P ¶ 3; LG Tr. at
136-37, 149-50. Gagosian Gallery sold $6,784.00 worth of Canal
Zone exhibition catalogs. Brooks Dec. Ex. P ¶ 4. The facts
before the Court do not establish whether any of the Paintings
have ever been made available for public viewing other than when
they were offered for sale at the Gallery.

This Court recognizes the inherent public interest and
cultural value of public exhibition of art and of an overall
increase in public access to artwork. However, the facts before
the Court show that Defendants' use and exploitation of the
Photos was also substantially commercial, especially where the
Gagosian Defendants are concerned. Accordingly, given the
overall low transformative content of Prince's Paintings, the
commerciality prong of the first § 107 factor weighs against a
finding of fair use.

23

iii. Bad Faith

The first § 107 factor requires the Court to consider "the propriety of a defendant's conduct," which is an integral part of the Court's analysis of the character of the use. NXIVM Corp. v. Ross Inst., 364 F.3d 471, 478 (2d Cir. 2004) (citations omitted). Though not in itself determinative, "it has been considered relevant within this subfactor that a defendant could have acquired the copyrighted [material] legitimately." Id.

Here, Prince testified that he does not have a different standard or weigh different considerations when appropriating works with a disclosed author than he does when using materials that are in the public domain; to Prince, the question of whether an image is appropriate for his use is "just a question of whether [he] like[s] the image." RP Tr. at 100. Prince's employee contacted the publisher of Yes, Rasta to purchase additional copies of the book, but apparently neither Prince nor his employee ever asked the publisher about licensing or otherwise sought permission to use Yes, Rasta or the Photos contained therein legitimately. RP Tr. 236-41, 183. Nor did Prince attempt to contact Cariou by email and inquire about usage rights to the Photos, even though Yes, Rasta clearly identified Cariou as the sole copyright holder and even though Cariou's publicly-accessible website includes an email address at which he

24

may be reached. <u>See</u> PC Tr. 238-40, 254, 260. Under these circumstances, Prince's bad faith is evident. Moreover, since the record establishes that the Gagosian Defendants were aware that Prince is an habitual user of other artists' copyrighted work, without permission, and because the record is equally clear that the Gagosian Defendants neither inquired into whether Prince had obtained permission to use the Photos contained in the Canal Zone Paintings nor ceased their commercial exploitation of the Paintings after receiving Cariou's cease-and-desist notice, the bad faith of the Gagosian Defendants is equally clear.

Because Prince's use was at most only minimally transformative of Cariou's Photos, because the use was substantially though not exclusively commercial, and because Prince and the Gagosian Defendants acted in bad faith, the first factor in the fair use analysis weighs heavily in favor of Plaintiff.

2. The Nature of the Copyrighted Work

"The more the copyrighted matter is at the center of the protected concerns of the copyright law, the more the other factors, including justification, must favor the secondary user

25

in order to earn a fair use finding." Leval at 1122. "The statutory articulation of this factor derives from Justice Story's mention ... of the 'value of the materials used.' Justice Story's word choice is more communicative than our statute's 'nature of,' as it suggests that some protected matter is more 'valued' under copyright that others. This should not be seen as an invitation to judges to pass on [artistic] quality, but rather to consider whether the protected [work] is of the creative or instructive type that the copyright laws value and seek to foster." Id. at 1117. A key distinction that has emerged "in the decisions evaluating the second factor [is] whether the work is expressive or creative, such as a work of fiction, or more factual, with a greater leeway being allowed to a claim of fair use where the work is factual or informational." 2 Abrams, The Law of Copyright, § 15:52 (2006).

Here, the Court finds that Cariou's Photos are highly original and creative artistic works and that they constitute "creative expression for public dissemination" and thus "fall[] within the core of the copyright's protective purposes." Campbell, 510 U.S. at 586. Consequently, this factor weighs against a finding of fair use.

3. The Amount and Substantiality of the Portion Used

The "amount and substantiality of the portion of the
copyrighted work used [] must be examined in context [and] the
inquiry must focus on whether the extent of [the] copying is
consistent with or more than necessary to further the purpose and
character of the use." Castle Rock, 150 F.3d at 144 (quoting
Campbell, 510 U.S. at 586-87) (internal quotations omitted). The
Court must examine not only "the quantity of the materials used,
but their quality and importance too." Warner Bros. Enter., Inc.,
575 F.Supp. at 546 (quoting Campbell 510 U.S. at 587).

"[W]hatever the use, generally it may not constitute a fair
use if the entire work is reproduced." Weissmann v. Freeman, 868
F.2d 1313, 1325 (2d Cir. 1989) (citing 3 Nimmer on Copyright §
13.05[A] at 13-80). Moreover, the amount and substantiality
factor weighs in favor of the copyright holder "where the portion
used was essentially the heart of the copyrighted work." Wright
v. Warner Books, Inc., 953 F.2d 731, 738 (2d Cir. 1991) (quoting
Harper & Row, 471 U.S. at 565) (internal quotations omitted).

"As the statutory language indicates, a taking may not be
excused merely because it is insubstantial with respect to the
infringing work." Harper & Row v. Nation Enters., 471 U.S. at 565
(citation omitted) (emphasis in original) (quoting Judge Learned

27

Hand, who "cogently remarked, 'no plagiarist can excuse the wrong by showing how much of his work he did not pirate.'")

In a number of his Paintings, Prince appropriated entire Photos, and in the majority of his Paintings, Prince appropriated the central figures depicted in portraits taken by Cariou and published in Yes, Rasta. Those central figures are of overwhelming quality and importance to Cariou's Photos, going to the very heart of his work. Accordingly, the amount of Prince's taking was substantially greater than necessary, given the slight transformative value of his secondary use, and the third factor weighs heavily against a finding of fair use.

4. The Effect of the Use Upon the Potential Market for or Value of the Copyrighted Work

The fourth fair use factor requires courts "to consider not only the extent of market harm caused by the particular actions of the alleged infringer, but also whether unrestricted and widespread conduct of the sort engaged in by the defendant would result in a substantially adverse impact on the potential market for the original." Campbell, 510 U.S. at 590 (internal quotations omitted). The inquiry "must take account not only of harm to the original but also of harm to the market for derivative works." Id. Harm to the market for derivatives weighs against a finding

28

of fair use "because the licensing of derivatives is an important economic incentive to the creation of originals." Id. at 593. "Potential derivative uses include only those that creators of original works would in general develop or license others to develop." Warner Bros. Enter., Inc., 575 F.Supp. at 549 (quoting Campbell, 510 U.S. at 592) (internal quotation marks omitted). See also id. at 550-51 (finding that where Defendant's derivative work "is only marginally transformative, [it] is likely to supplant the market for [Plaintiff's derivative work]") (citing Campbell, 510 U.S. at 591).

Defendants' protestations that Cariou has not marketed his Photos more aggressively (or, indeed, as aggressively as Prince has marketed his Paintings) are unavailing. As the Second Circuit has previously emphasized, the "potential market" for the copyrighted work and its derivatives must be examined, even if the "author has disavowed any intention to publish them during his lifetime," given that an author "has the right to change his mind" and is "entitled to protect his opportunity to sell his [works]." J.D. Salinger v. Random House, Inc., 811 F.2d 90, 99 (2d Cir. 1987) (emphasis omitted); see Castle Rock, 150 F.3d at 145-46 (finding the fourth factor to favor Plaintiff even where Plaintiff "has evidenced little if any interest in exploiting this market for derivative works" because copyright law must

29

"respect that creative and economic choice"). The fact that
Plaintiff has not marketed his work more aggressively is
therefore irrelevant.

Here, it is undisputed that a gallery owner discontinued
plans to show the Yes, Rasta Photos, and to offer them for sale
to collectors, because she did not want to appear to be
capitalizing on Prince's Paintings and did not want to show work
which had been "done already" at the nearby Gagosian Gallery. CC
Tr. 89, 91, 105. It is therefore clear that the market for
Cariou's Photos was usurped by Defendants. Moreover, licensing
original works for secondary use by other artists is the kind of
derivative use "that creators of original works would in general
develop," Warner Bros. Enter., Inc., 575 F.Supp. at 549, and
widespread unlicensed use in new artworks would destroy the
market for such licenses, see Campbell, 510 U.S. at 590.
Accordingly, the Court finds that Prince has unfairly damaged
both the actual and potential markets for Cariou's original work
and the potential market for derivative use licenses for Cariou's
original work.

Because Defendants' secondary use has unfairly damaged the
original market for the Photos and, if widespread, would likely
destroy an identifiable derivative market for the Photos, the
fourth § 107 factor weighs against a finding of fair use.

30

5. Aggregate Analysis

The Court has considered the four factors set forth in §
107, and found that none favors a finding of fair use. Moreover,
"the monopoly created by copyright" does not unduly "impede[]
referential analysis [or] the development of new ideas out of
old" when copyright law is enforced under circumstances like
those presented here. Leval at 1109. Accordingly, the purposes
of copyright are best served by extending protection to Cariou's
Photos.

Having conducted a case-specific analysis of the four
factors laid out in 17 U.S.C. § 107 in light of the purposes of
copyright, the Court finds that Defendants are not entitled to
the defense of fair use.

E. Liability of the Gagosian Defendants

Copyright infringement has two elements: "(1) ownership of a
valid copyright, and (2) copying of constituent elements of the
work which are original." Feist, 499 U.S. at 361.

Here, it is uncontroverted that the Gagosian Defendants
copied original constituent elements of Cariou's copyrighted
Photos when they published the Canal Zone exhibition catalog,
created and distributed invitation cards featuring reproductions

31

of Cariou's Photos, and otherwise distributed reproductions of Cariou's work as appropriated by Prince. Moreover, by exhibiting and selling Prince's unauthorized works, the Gagosian Defendants infringed Cariou's exclusive rights, as copyright owner of the Photos, to reproduce, prepare derivative works based upon, distribute, sell, and display the Photographs. See Copyright Act, 17 U.S.C. § 106(1), (2), (3), and (5). The Court therefore finds the Gagosian Defendants directly liable for copyright infringement.

The Gagosian Defendants are also liable as vicarious and contributory infringers.

"The concept of vicarious copyright infringement was developed in the Second Circuit as an outgrowth of the agency principles of *respondiat superior*." Faulkner v. Nat'l Geo. Soc., 211 F.Supp.2d 450, 472 (S.D.N.Y. 2002)(citations omitted). "Vicarious liability extends beyond an employer/employee relationship to cases in which a defendant has the right and ability to supervise the infringing activity and also has a direct financial interest in such activities. Benefit and control are the signposts of vicarious liability." Id. (citations omitted).

Here, the record establishes that Gagosian was "handling

32

everything" to do with the marketing of the Canal Zone Paintings beginning at the time Price first showed Canal Zone (2007), which Prince thought of as a "preview" of the characters he would use in the Canal Zone Paintings, in December, 2007. See, e.g., RP Tr. at 185-87 (describing Gagosian's role in the Eden Rock show and describing Gagosian's home as an "off-off-off Broadway" location where previously unseen paintings could be shown and sold). The Court therefore finds that the Gagosian Defendants had the right and ability to supervise Price's work, or at the very least the right and ability (and perhaps even responsibility) to ensure that Prince obtained licenses to use the Photos before they made Prince's Paintings available for sale. The financial benefit of the infringing use to the Gagosian Defendants is self-evident. Accordingly, the Gagosian Defendants are liable as vicarious infringers.

"One who, with knowledge of the infringing activity, induces, causes, or materially contributes to the infringing conduct of another, may be held liable as a contributory infringer." Faulkner, 211 F.Supp.2d at 473 (citations and quotations omitted) In other words, "the standard for contributory infringement has two prongs, the 'knowledge' prong and the 'material contribution' prong." Id. "Knowledge of the infringing activity may be actual or constructive . . . In other

33

words, this prong is satisfied if the defendant knew or should have known of the infringing activity at the time of its material contribution." Id. at 474 (citations and quotations omitted). "Advertising or otherwise promoting an infringing product or service may be sufficient to satisfy the material contribution prong." Id. at 473-74.

Here, the Gagosian Defendants were well aware of (and capitalized on) Prince's reputation as an appropriation artist who rejects the constricts of copyright law, but they never inquired into the propriety of Prince's use of the Photos. The Court concludes that the Gagosian Defendants knew or should have known of the infringement at the time that they reproduced, advertised, marketed, and otherwise promoted the Paintings. Accordingly, the Court finds that the Gagosian Defendants are liable as contributory infringers.

Because Plaintiff has established a prima facie case of copyright infringement as against all Defendants, and because the defense of fair use does not apply, Plaintiff's Motion for Summary Judgment on the issue of liability is GRANTED in its entirety.

34

F. Plaintiff's Claim for Conspiracy Under the Copyright Act

Defendants argue that Plaintiff's fifth claim for relief, which charges conspiracy to violate his rights under the Copyright Act, must be dismissed as failing to state a claim on which relief may be granted.

No Party has called the Court's attention to any Second Circuit or Supreme Court authority which provides that a cause of action for conspiracy to violate the Copyright Act may lie under New York or Federal law. Nor is conspiracy proscribed by the Copyright Act itself. See generally Copyright Act, 17 U.S.C. § 501 et seq.; Calloway v. Marvel Entertainment Group, No. 82 Civ. 8697 (RWS), 1983 WL 1152, at *5 (S.D.N.Y. 1983).

In the absence of contrary authority, the Court finds Judge Sweet's reasoning in Irwin v. ZDF Enterprises GmbH, No. 04 CIV. 8027 (RWS), 2006 WL 374960 (S.D.N.Y. February 16, 2006) persuasive. In Irwin, Judge Sweet considered whether the Copyright Act foreclosed a common law conspiracy claim based on copyright infringement and determined that "[b]ecause copyright law already recognizes the concepts of contributory infringement and vicarious copyright infringement . . . which extend joint and several liability to those who participate in the copyright infringement . . . [a] civil conspiracy claim does not add

35

substantively to the underlying federal copyright claim . . ."
Irwin at *4 (citations and quotations omitted).

The Court therefore finds that Plaintiff's Fifth Cause of
Action must be dismissed.

III. CONCLUSION

For reasons stated herein, the Court GRANTS Plaintiff's
Motion for Summary Judgment on the issues of copyright
infringement, fair use, and liability. The Court DENIES
Defendants' Motion for Summary Judgment except as pertains to
Plaintiff's Fifth Cause of Action, for conspiracy, which is
DISMISSED.

It is further ORDERED:

That, pursuant to 17 U.S.C. § 502, Defendants, their
directors, officers, agents, servants, employees, and attorneys,
and all persons in active concert or participation with them, are
hereby enjoined and restrained permanently from infringing the
copyright in the Photographs, or any other of Plaintiff's works,
in any manner, and from reproducing, adapting, displaying,

36

publishing, advertising, promoting, selling, offering for sale, marketing, distributing, or otherwise disposing of the Photographs or any copies of the Photographs, or any other of Plaintiff's works, and from participating or assisting in or authorizing such conduct in any way.

That Defendants shall within ten days of the date of this Order deliver up for impounding, destruction, or other disposition, as Plaintiff determines, all infringing copies of the Photographs, including the Paintings and unsold copies of the Canal Zone exhibition book, in their possession, custody, or control and all transparencies, plates, masters, tapes, film negatives, discs, and other articles for making such infringing copies.

That Defendants shall notify in writing any current or future owners of the Paintings of whom they are or become aware that the Paintings infringe the copyright in the Photographs, that the Paintings were not lawfully made under the Copyright Act of 1976, and that the Paintings cannot lawfully be displayed under 17 U.S.C. § 109(c).

That the Parties shall appear before this Court on May 6,

37

2011 at 11:00am for a status conference regarding damages, profits, and Plaintiff's costs and reasonable attorney's fees.

SO ORDERED.

Dated: New York, New York

          March 18, 2011

                                   Deborah A. Batts
                                   Deborah A. Batts
                                   United States District Judge